INGRID BERGMAN
My Story

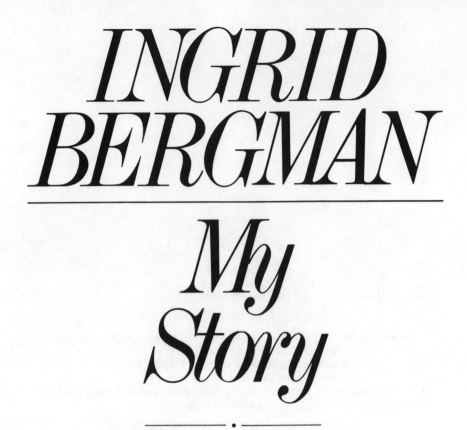

INGRID BERGMAN

My Story

By Ingrid Bergman and Alan Burgess

DELACORTE PRESS/NEW YORK

Published by
Delacorte Press
1 Dag Hammarskjold Plaza
New York, N.Y. 10017

Manufactured in the United States of America

First printing

Designed by Giorgetta Bell McRee

Library of Congress Cataloging in Publication Data

Bergman, Ingrid, 1915–
Ingrid Bergman, my story.

Filmography: p. 494
1. Bergman, Ingrid, 1915– 2. Actors—Sweden
—Biography. I. Burgess, Alan, joint author.
PN2778.B43A34 1980 791.43′028′0924 [B] 80–15420

ISBN 0–440–03299–7

Author's Note

After I hung up the phone, having said no to writing my memoirs as I had for the last twenty years, my son Roberto gave me a look of great concern. "Mother," he said, "do you realize that when you are dead many people will throw themselves on your life story taking information from gossip columns, rumors, and interviews. We, your children, can never defend you because we don't know the truth. I wish you'd put it down."

That gave me a lot to think about. Therefore, my dear children—Pia, Roberto, Isabella, and Ingrid—here is the truth.

Acknowledgments

For their generous help and cooperation in the collection of material for this book, we are deeply indebted to: Pia, Roberto (Robin), Isabella, Isotta Ingrid, Lars Schmidt, Irene Selznick, Kay Brown, Ruth Roberts, Liana Ferri, Ann Todd, David Lean, Britt Engstrom, Warren Thomas, Marti Stevens, Marcella and Fiorella Mariani, Franco Rossellini, Federico Fellini, Ercole Graziadei, Sergio Amedei, Robert Anderson, Helen Tubbs, George Cukor, Alfred Hitchcock, Mike Frankovitch, Lord Bernstein, Joe Steele, Griffith James, Liv Ullmann, Ingmar Bergman, Goran and Marianne von Essen, Cornell Capa, Danny M. Selznick, Mrs. Simon B. Buckner, J. Fred Coots, Irwin Shaw, Mrs. Frederick Guest, Shelley Wanger, Sally Burchell, Mrs. Erich Remarque, and Mary Hemingway. We are also immensely grateful to our editor, Jeanne F. Bernkopf, for her unremitting assistance.

Prologue

S he came out into the cool air of Hollywood's La Cienega
Boulevard, and she felt dazed. She looked at the glowing neon,
the headlights of the passing traffic, and taking Petter's arm
she urged him toward the playbill outside the movie theater, saying,
"Petter, we must get this director's name straight. If there is such a
man who can put *this* on the screen, he must be an absolutely
heavenly human being!"

Her eyes quickly scanned the poster and caught one end-credit:
"Music by Rossellini." "God Almighty," she exclaimed, "he's even
written the music!"

Rarely can anyone look back and identify the exact moment of no
return, the precise moment of utter and fundamental change. Yet
because of one film, *Open City,* Ingrid Bergman's life changed.
Roberto Rossellini's life changed. Dr. Petter Lindstrom's life
changed. And children were given life.

As she says:

———— • ————

The realism and simplicity of *Open City* was heart-shocking. No
one looked like an actor and no one talked like an actor. There was
darkness and shadows, and sometimes you couldn't hear, and
sometimes you couldn't even see it. But that's the way it is in life
. . . you can't always see and hear, but you know that something

almost beyond understanding is going on. It was as if they'd removed the walls from the houses and rooms, and you could see inside them. And it was more than that. It was as if you were *there,* involved in what was going on, and you wept and bled for them. . . .

———————— • ————————

On that spring evening in 1948 when Ingrid Bergman, accompanied by her husband, Dr. Petter Lindstrom, walked into that small theater, she was the most popular and successful actress in the world, and would certainly have given any actress a very close race for the title of the most popular film star ever. It took exactly eighty-nine minutes, the running time of *Open City,* to start the tremors that would shatter that popularity and send Ingrid down the slippery slope of public adulation toward what was to become an epic scandal of the twentieth century.

Ten minutes after she took her seat and the lights dimmed, her radiant face looked a little puzzled. Sixty minutes and the tiny worry-line in the middle of her forehead had grown a little deeper. Seventy minutes and she was moved to tears. And as the screen darkened she became aware that she had just been through one of the most emotional experiences of her entire career.

That career, which had started back in her native Sweden in 1934, was now, fourteen years later, at its peak. She had been Number One at the box office for the past three years; she had won more magazine popularity contests than she could remember; a recent nationwide poll by *Daily Variety* surveying two hundred professionals—all with twenty-five or more years in the business—placed Greta Garbo as the best actress of all time in "the era of silent movies," but awarded Ingrid Bergman top place in the "era of sound," above both Spencer Tracy and Greta Garbo. The Hollywood gag current at that period ran: "Do you know, last night I actually saw a film *without* Ingrid Bergman in it."

To the movie barons who commanded and ordered the lives of thousands in that sun-drenched slab of California, she was worth a large percentage of Fort Knox's gold reserves, which certainly had attached a sort of "divinity" to her person.

Indeed, three years earlier, Ingrid had come rather close to that dangerous state of grace when, costarring with Bing Crosby in *The*

Bells of St. Mary's, she had played Sister Benedict, the nun who believed that prayer solved all problems. It was a state of divinity unappreciated by many angry Catholic mamas who upbraided Ingrid for a performance which influenced their impressionable young daughters to enter the closed confines of a convent.

Ingrid realized that there was nothing she could do about that. It was not the sort of mistake she made when she wrongly identified the "music by Rossellini" on the playbill.

———————— • ————————

I didn't realize until later this was *Renzo* Rossellini, Roberto's younger brother. We went home and I raved to everyone about what a marvelous film it was and what a genius Roberto Rossellini must be. I wanted to know more about him but nobody knew anything at all. In 1948, foreign films didn't rate in Hollywood. They were all right for immigrants in little art theaters: they could speak the language—they didn't have to read subtitles. But certainly such films didn't make money. So gradually I began to believe that maybe this man makes one good movie, and then you don't hear of him anymore. Sad, but that's the way it is.

Then a few months later I was in New York doing a radio show because I always tried to get out of Hollywood when I'd finished a picture. When you didn't work the only thing people ever said was, "Are you working?" "How was your last picture?" "Was it Box Office?" "How much money did it make?" So I went to New York and usually did something on radio which paid for the hotel and trip, and I had a chance to see the theater which I loved. And I was walking on Broadway and suddenly—suddenly—I saw that name Rossellini outside a cinema again: some tiny cinema on Broadway. A film called *Paisan.* I went in alone, and I sat there once more riveted to my seat.

So he *had made* another great movie! And nobody had ever heard of him! I looked down the theater. It was almost empty. What was going on? This man had made two great films and he was playing to empty houses. I think it was at that moment the idea came to me. Maybe if this man had somebody who was a *name* playing for him, then maybe people would come and see his pictures. Of course he had Anna Magnani in *Open City* and she was a great actress, and I guessed a big name in Europe, but she wasn't then a big name in America. And this immense feeling grew inside me that movies like this simply *must* be seen by millions, not only by the Italians but by millions all over the world. So, I thought, I am going to write him a letter.

Then, as I walked back to the hotel I began to get uneasy; I mean, how could I write a letter to someone I'd never met? I was supposed to be a film star. But did that matter? No, of course it didn't.

I was so excited, and that very same evening I had dinner with Irene Selznick—Irene was the wife of David Selznick, my first Hollywood producer, and one of my very best friends—and she knew me very well. I said, "Irene, I've seen this second movie of this man called Rossellini, and it's absolutely marvelous. I want to write to him. I've had ten years of doing the same kind of beautiful, romantic movies. Now I want to do something realistic, I want to do something like *Paisan.*"

Irene looked at me as if I'd gone crazy. "But you can't," she said. "You just can't."

"Why can't I?"

Irene didn't answer. She has this habit of looking at you very long and thoughtfully before she gets round to what she's going to say. So I just waited.

"He'll misunderstand it. It will sound very peculiar. You can't just say, "Listen I want to come to Italy. . . ." Then she looked at my face, stopped, and started again.

"Wait a minute. Maybe *you* can. Maybe you're the only one who can write the sort of letter which will *not* be misunderstood."

So I wrote the letter which I hoped was a bit funny, not too eager. I said I could speak very good Swedish and English, my French was just beginning, and in Italian I only knew "Ti amo," and that was because I played an Italian girl in Erich Maria Remarque's *Arch of Triumph,* who spoke only English until, on her deathbed, she whispered to Charles Boyer, "Ti amo." I thought it was a light-hearted letter and when I showed it to Petter back in Hollywood, he thought it was all right too.

Dear Mr. Rossellini,

I saw your films *Open City* and *Paisan,* and enjoyed them very much. If you need a Swedish actress who speaks English very well, who has not forgotten her German, who is not very understandable in French, and who, in

Italian knows only "ti amo" I am ready to come and make
a film with you.

Ingrid Bergman

I took it back to Hollywood with me because I had no address for
Roberto Rossellini and didn't know anyone who would have the
address, so the letter just lay around. Then one day a few weeks
later I was walking along a street in Hollywood and a man stopped
and asked me for my autograph. As I was writing it, he said, "I'm
Italian you know."

"Are you?" I said. "Then do you know someone called Roberto
Rossellini?"

"Of course, yes, he's our great film director."

"Have you any idea how I could find him in Italy. Where he
works?"

"Of course. Minerva Films, Roma, Italy, that'll find him for
sure."

I went home, picked up the letter, changed the date, put Minerva
Films, Rome, Italy, on the envelope, and posted it.

That letter had the most peculiar journey of any letter in history.
Minerva Films was a studio where Roberto often worked. But he'd
had a great row with them; there were lawsuits going on. Roberto
enjoyed nothing more than a lawsuit. Every morning he picked up
the telephone and thought: Now who can I have a fight with? So
they were fighting like mad and Roberto was definitely not on
talking terms with them. On top of that, the night my letter arrived
Minerva Films burnt down. Big blaze. Nothing left but ashes.

That's where the touch of the poet comes in, because when
they're clearing up they scrape round in the debris and find my
letter. Singed but intact. And the Minerva Film people open it, and
read what it says. They find it very funny: Ingrid Bergman of
Hollywood writing to Roberto Rossellini saying, "I want to come
and make a movie for you, and ti amo."

So they ring up Roberto and say, "Minerva Films here, Mr.
Rossellini . . ."

And Roberto says, "I'm not talking to you" and slams down the
phone. So they ring him again, and this time they say very quickly,
"Look, we have a very funny letter for you . . ."

"I don't want it." Bang! The phone goes down again.

They ring the third time.

"It's from Ingrid Bergman addressed to . . ." Bang! Roberto's pretty quick on the phone. It is a very persistent secretary for she rings for the fourth time, and now even Roberto realizes that he'll have to make some short statement to choke them off.

"Mr. Rossellini . . . the letter . . ."

"I don't want it. Throw it away. Stop ringing me up." Bang!

If they'd given up then, I doubt very much if I'd ever have met Mr. Rossellini. But they sent the letter round to him by hand and Roberto, who did not understand one word of English, was forced to take a look at it. Maybe the American stamps or the Hollywood postmark impressed him because he called in Liana Ferri, who in those days did most of his translation work for him, and he said, "What's this say?"

When Liana finished translating the letter, Roberto still had the same blank look on his face.

"Well?" asked Liana.

"Well, *who* is this Ingrid Bergman?"

I suppose you should know at this point that, as one of Italy's top directors, Roberto had a few odd mannerisms: he didn't like actors at all; he didn't really care much for films either; and he rarely, if ever, went to the cinema.

So Liana began to try to explain who I was. No he'd never seen me. Never heard of me.

Liana went on trying: *"Intermezzo . . .* that was the picture which made her famous . . . with Leslie Howard, the English actor? . . ."

"Ah," Roberto did one of those great big Italian gestures which looks as if he's trying to embrace the Colosseum.

"Wait a minute . . . not with Leslie Howard . . . the Swedish version, that's what I saw . . . yes . . . just before the war ended. . . . I was up north in this small town . . . there was a bombing raid on . . . no one knew if it was the Americans, or the Germans, or both of them who were bombing us . . . but no one liked it as the bombs were exploding everywhere. I ran into the nearest place to shelter. A cinema . . . what better place to lose one's life than in a comfortable seat in a cinema. And they were showing this film. *Intermezzo,* yes. I saw it through three times, not because I liked the girl or the picture . . . but because it was a very long bombing raid. That was her was it . . . the blond girl?"

"Yes," Liana said patiently, "that was her, the blond girl. Better send a cable."

————————— • —————————

The cable arrived on May 8, 1948, at 1220 Benedict Canyon Drive, Beverly Hills, the home of Dr. Petter Lindstrom and Miss Ingrid Bergman.

I JUST RECEIVED WITH GREAT EMOTION YOUR LETTER WHICH HAPPENS TO ARRIVE ON THE ANNIVERSARY OF MY BIRTHDAY AS THE MOST PRECIOUS GIFT. IT IS ABSO-LUTELY TRUE THAT I DREAMED TO MAKE A FILM WITH YOU AND FROM THIS MOMENT I WILL DO EVERYTHING POSSIBLE. I WILL WRITE YOU A LONG LETTER TO SUBMIT TO YOU MY IDEAS. WITH MY ADMIRATION PLEASE AC-CEPT THE EXPRESSION OF MY GRATITUDE TOGETHER WITH MY BEST REGARDS. ROBERTO ROSSELLINI, HOTEL EXCELSIOR, ROME.

Ingrid was excited. Petter was noncommittal. And Roberto was already approaching various bankers in Rome to raise the money for the epic film he was to start—with the world's Box Office Number One. His letter arrived shortly afterwards:

Dear Mrs. Bergman,
I have waited a long time before writing, because I wanted to make sure what I was going to propose to you. But first of all I must say that my way of working is extremely personal. I do not prepare a scenario, which, I think terribly limits the scope of work. Of course I start out with very precise ideas and a mixture of dialogues and intentions which, as things go on, I select and improve. Having said so much, I must indeed make you aware of the extraordinary excitement which the mere prospect of having the possibility to work with you, procures me.
Some time ago . . . I think it was at the end of February last, I was traveling by car along the Sabine (a region north of Rome). Near the source of the Farfa an unusual scene called my attention. In a field surrounded by a tall barbed-wire fence, several women were turning round just like mild lambs in a pasture. I drew near and understood they were foreign women: Yugoslavs, Polish, Rumanians,

Greek, Germans, Latvians, Lithuanians, Hungarians. Driven away from their native countries by the war, they had wandered over half Europe, known the horror of concentration camps, compulsory work and night plunder. They had been the easy prey of the soldiers of twenty different nations. Now parked up by the police, they lived in this camp awaiting their return home.

A guard ordered me to go away. One must not speak to these undesirable women. At the further end of the field, behind the barbed wires, far away from the others, a woman was looking at me, alone, fair, all dressed in black. Heeding not the calls of the guards, I drew nearer. She only knew a few words of Italian and as she pronounced them, the very effort gave a rosy tint to her cheeks. She was from Latvia. In her clear eyes, one could read a mute intense despair. I put my hand through the barbed wires and she seized my arm, just like a shipwrecked person would clutch at a floating board. The guard drew near, quite menacing. I got back to my car.

The remembrance of this woman haunted me. I succeeded in obtaining authorization to visit the camp. She was no longer there. The Commander told me she had run away. The other women told me she had gone away with a soldier. They would have married and, with him, she could have remained in Italy. He was from the Lipari Islands.

Shall we go together and look for her? Shall we together visualize her life in the little village near Stromboli, where the soldier took her? Very probably, you do not know the Lipari Islands: in fact very few Italians know them. They earned a sad fame during fascism, because it is there that the enemies of the Fascist Government were confined. There are seven volcanoes in the Tyrrhenian Sea, north of Sicily. One of them, the Stromboli, is continually active. At the foot of the volcano, in a bay, springs up the little village. A few white houses, all cracked by the earthquakes. The inhabitants make a living out of fishing and the little they can pluck up from the barren land.

I tried to imagine the life of the Latvian girl, so tall, so fair, in this island of fire and ashes, amidst the fishermen, small and swarthy, amongst the women with the glowing eyes, pale and deformed by childbirth, with no means to communicate with these people of Phoenician habits, who speak a rough dialect, all mixed up with Greek words, and with no means either to communicate with him, with the man she got hold of at the camp of Farfa. Having looked into each other's eyes, they had found out their souls. She, in these glowing, intelligent, swift eyes of his, had discovered a tormented, simple, strong, tender man.

She followed this man, being certain that she had found an uncommon creature, a savior, a refuge and a protection after so many years of anguish and beastly life, and she would have had the joy to remain in Italy, this mild and green land where both man and nature are to a human scale.

But instead she is stranded in this savage island, all shaken up by the vomiting volcano, and where the earth is so dark and the sea looks like mud saturated with sulphur. And the man lives beside her and loves her with a kind of savage fury, is just like an animal not knowing how to struggle for life and accepting placidly to live in deepest misery.

Even the God that the people worship seems different from hers. How could the austere Lutheran God she used to pray to, when a child, in the frigid churches of her native country, possibly stand comparison with these numerous saints of various hues.

The woman tries to rebel and tear herself away from the obsession. But on all sides, the sea bars the way and there is no possible escape. Frantic with despair, unable to withstand it any longer, she yet entertains an ultimate hope of a miracle that will save her—not realizing that a profound change is already operating within herself.

Suddenly the woman understands the value of the eternal truth which rules human lives; she understands the mighty power of he who possesses nothing, this extraordinary strength which procures complete freedom. In reality she becomes another St. Francis. An intense feeling of joy springs out from her heart, an immense joy of living.

I do not know if in this letter, I have been able to express the fullness of my meaning. I know it is difficult to give concrete meaning to ideas and sensations which can only receive life through imagination.

To relate, I must see: Cinema relates with the camera, but I am certain, I feel, that with you near me, I could give life to a human creature who, following hard and bitter experiences, finds peace at last and complete freedom from all selfishness. That being the only true happiness which has ever been conceded to mankind, making life more simple and nearer to creation.

Could you possibly come to Europe? I could invite you for a trip to Italy and we could go over this thing at leisure? Would you like me to go in for this film? When? What do you think of it? Excuse me for all these questions but I could go on questioning you forever.

Pray believe in my enthusiasm.

Your Roberto Rossellini.

A trip to Italy? A film in a completely different setting. It made good sense to Ingrid. In the twenties, thirties and forties, commercial air travel was almost nonexistent; radio circuits were weak; journeys by ship took ages; life-saving drugs which obviated health hazards had not been invented. But the moving talking picture was everywhere. In jungles, deserts, outbacks, South Sea islands, mountain fortresses, frozen outposts, wherever the human race gathered in large or small groups—and its influence can never, adequately, be assessed.

The American movies meant stars. And one of the brightest stars was Ingrid Bergman. But she had never thought of her responsibilities in that light. She had never seriously considered the notion that with world fame came corresponding penalties; that *real* privacy was no longer possible. Her life belonged to the millions of fans who adored her. And because she breathed conviction and purity into every role she played, she "belonged" more than anyone else. She said, "As a matter of fact when the big scandal broke loose I thought I would have to give up acting—to save the world from disaster I mean—for it seemed that I had corrupted everybody in the world."

Ingrid, innocent that she was, had thought she had the inalienable right to decide what she did with her private life. It was an assumption that was to bring her, in the next few years, almost intolerable unhappiness.

Chapter 1

There was a sense of urgency about the young girl in the tweed skirt, beige-colored sweater she had knitted herself, and common-sense walking shoes who hurried toward the bright open quayside of Stockholm's Strandvägen. Approaching eighteen, she was now beginning to fill out a bit. A year or so earlier, her Aunt Hulda's suggestion that she should wear three pairs of woolen stockings to pad out her calves had not added to her assurance; in her own words, she had been "the thinnest child ever."

She lacked security. She was terribly shy. She was frightened of people, and of the world generally. And at that moment she was extremely apprehensive. This was, without doubt, the most important morning of her life. If she muffed this opportunity, the world ended. She could forget her daydreams of vast audiences applauding as she made her tenth curtsy at the conclusion of a monumental opening night.

She had made her promise to Uncle Otto. If this attempt failed, she might become a salesperson or somebody's secretary, but those dreams of theatrical fame would stop. Uncle Otto was convinced that actresses were little different from prostitutes! "You can't tell me, young lady. I've seen those love scenes they do on the stage and in those films; you can't tell me they don't go on doing the same thing —*afterwards*!"

She wouldn't even attempt to argue with him. She knew that he was trying to fill in for her father, to see that she had a good education and was brought up properly. Her compulsive involvement with play-acting, the restless urge to go on the stage, distressed him enormously. As a staunch, if not punctilious Lutheran, he felt it was his duty to save her from a life of shame; as her guardian he owed that to her father's memory. But he knew that she was stubborn and determined; he knew that to dismiss this passionate dream of hers out of hand, not to give her even the opportunity, would leave her heartbroken and would not be fair. Therefore he had given her one chance.

"All right," he had said. "You shall have the fees you need for the extra tuition. You can try for the Royal Dramatic School. Take the examinations—do whatever auditions you have to do. But if you fail, that's the end of it. Understand that. No more of this actress nonsense. And I want your promise, because I know you will keep that promise. Do you accept this?"

Accept it? She had leapt at it. Without professional training, for which she needed money—her own money it was true, left in trust to Uncle Otto by her father—her chances would be diminished. And as for failing, that was inconceivable. Beyond her comprehension. God could not have influenced her for all these years if he intended her to fail. Certainly she knew that there were seventy-five applicants this year and that only very few would be selected.

But if the judges had to choose only *one,* then she *had* to be that one. Otherwise life would be insupportable.

She paused in front of the massive, pale gray facade of the theater. Beyond stretched the waterfront, backed by the symmetrical curve of seven-story apartment buildings, shops and offices, surmounted by the domes of copper cupolas, tarnished to a pale sea-green by the salty winds blown in from the northern seas. She breathed in deeply. She belonged to this city of lakes and ferryboats and glittering water. She had been born no more than a hundred yards from this theater, in the apartment above her father's photographic shop along there on the Strandvägen.

She regarded the broad stone steps. Four impressive lamps, their bulbs round and opalescent as immense onions, dominated the entrance. On either side of the doors stood gilded statues of male and female figures, representing the Muses, including her beloved Thalia, Ingrid's goddess of the theater. She went around to the stage door and crossed to the office where the porter peered at the list of applicants to be auditioned that morning.

"Miss Bergman? You're number sixteen which means you've got quite a while to wait before they're ready for you."

She went outside again, crossed the road to the small park against the quayside, stared straight in the eye of the giant, bearded, bronze head of John Ericsson, Swedish engineer and inventor of the first armored battleship, mentally rehearsed her opening line, made one or two tentative leaps to prepare for her magnificent entrance, wandered around a bit, looked at the passing seagulls, and returned to the theater still fifteen minutes before her time was due.

Some weeks previously she had delivered to the Royal Dramatic Theater her big brown envelope which contained the three pieces she had chosen for her audition. The jury would select the two she was to perform. She was aware that she could be failed at either the first or second test. If she failed, the porter would give her back the big brown envelope, and that would be the end of her. But if she passed, she would get a smaller white envelope which would tell her the date of her next audition, and which of her audition pieces the jury wished to hear.

Ingrid had discussed her choice of material with Gabriel Alw, her drama teacher. "The first audition must be the most important," she said. "Practically everybody else will be doing heavy dramatic pieces, Camille or Lady Macbeth, wailing and weeping all over the stage. I think the jury will be so bored having to watch a procession of young girls breaking their hearts. Can't we make the jury laugh?"

Gabriel had agreed with her diagnosis. "Good idea. And I know a play by a Hungarian which would be just right. A peasant girl, pretty and gay, is teasing this bold country boy who's trying to flirt with her. She's even bolder than he is. She leaps across this small stream toward him. Stands there, hands on her hips, laughing at him. How's that for an entrance? You make a flying jump out of the wings onto the stage, and you stand there, legs apart, hands on hips, as if to say, "Here I am. Look at me! Are you paying attention!"

———————— • ————————

So this was the play I work on. I wait in the wings and then I'm called. You do the audition on the stage, all by yourself. Any other dialogue is thrown at you from the wings, in my case, by the boy who was playing the country lad, who also acted as prompter if I dried up. So here I go. A run and a leap into the air, and there I am in the middle of the stage with that big gay laugh that's supposed to stop them dead in their tracks. I pause, and get out my first line. Then I take a quick glance down over the footlights at the jury. And I can't believe it! They are paying not the slightest attention to me. In fact the jury members in the front row are chatting to the others in the second row. I dry up in absolute horror. I simply can't remember the next line. The boy throws the cue at me. I get that out. But now the jury are talking in loud voices and gesticulating. I go blank with despair. At least they could hear me out, let me finish. I can't concentrate, can't remember anything. I hiss to the boy, "What's my next line?" But before he can say it, I hear the voice of the chairman of the jury: "Stop it, stop it. That's enough. Thank you, thank you miss . . . next please, next please."

I walk off stage. I don't see anybody or hear anything. I walk out through the foyer. I walk out into the street. And I'm thinking—Now I have to go home and face Uncle Otto. Now I have to tell him that I'm thrown off the stage after about thirty seconds. I have to say, "They didn't listen to me. They didn't even think I was worth listening to." Now I can't think of becoming an actress ever again. So life isn't worth living. I walk straight across to the quayside. And I know there's only one thing to do. Throw myself into the water and commit suicide.

———————— • ————————

She stood near the little kiosk where the ferry tickets to Djurgården and Skansen were sold. There was no one about; a few seagulls screaming in the distance, two or three floating on the surface. Far away across the water the graceful golden tower of the Nordiska Museum. The water was dark and shining. She took a step closer and peered at it. It *was* dark and shining . . . and *dirty*. She would be covered with dirt when they pulled her out. Not like Ophelia floating beneath the crystal-clear, lily-fragrant stream in Shakespeare's Arden Arcadia. She'd have to swallow that stuff. Ugh! That was no good.

Temporarily, suicide was set aside. But still in despair she turned on her heel and began the uphill walk through the shops and main streets up to the apartment block where she lived. The long slender legs had no animation now. In the apartment her two girl cousins were waiting for her. They were the last people she wanted to see.

Oh, for the comfort of her room where she could throw herself on the bed and weep and weep and weep and weep. . . . If only Mama or Papa were alive and could comfort her. Why did they have to die so soon? And now Britt and Margit just wouldn't leave her alone. "What's taken you so long?" "Yes, where've you been?" Stupid questions. How could she tell these two horrible, grinning girls that by now, if the water hadn't been so dirty, she'd be a romantic corpse floating out to sea?

"Lars Seligman has been on the phone. . . ." Lars? What could he want? They were close friends, he also trying to pass his auditions. "He said he'd been down to the office to collect his white envelope. . . . And he asked what sort of envelope you'd got. . . . And *they said you got a white envelope too. . . .*"

A white envelope? She'd got a white envelope? Could they be telling the truth? There was no time for discussion. She turned and ran. She raced down the stairs, she ran into the street. It was downhill all the way, but she would swear her feet never touched the ground until she reached the theater. She arrived at the office as if blown in by a storm wind. "What sort of envelope have I got? Please tell me what sort of envelope I've got?" The porter smiled: "A white one, Miss Bergman . . . we wondered where you'd been. Here it is. Good luck. . . ."

She tore it open. "Your next audition will be. . . ." She couldn't read the date, but she read that they would like her to audition with the piece she had chosen from Rostand's *L'Aiglon.* She floated out in the sweet summer air. Oh, how wonderful life was, oh, how lucky she was to have Britt, and Uncle Otto, and Aunt Hulda, and wasn't Stockholm the most beautiful city in the whole wide world, and that dark and shining water stretching away to some distant enchanted horizon was the most glorious thing she had ever seen.

———————— • ————————

I was so happy to be accepted that I didn't bother to ask why they'd been so brusque and inattentive when I leapt onto the stage. It was not until many years later in Italy that I got the answer. I was in Rome and there was Alf Sjöberg who was one of the jury at that audition. And it all came back to me, and I said, "Tell me, please tell me, why at that first audition did you all treat me so badly? I could have committed suicide, you treated me so nastily, and disliked me so much." Alf stared at me as if I'd gone mad. "Disliked you so much! Dear girl, you're crazy! The minute you leapt out of the wings onto the stage, and stood there laughing at us, we turned round and said to each other, 'Well, we don't have to listen to her, she's in! Look at that security. Look at that stage presence. Look at that impertinence.' You jumped out onto the stage like a tigress. You weren't afraid of us. 'No need to waste another second, we've got dozens more to look at. Next please.' So what are you talking about. You might never make as good an entrance in your life again."

———————— • ————————

From Rostand's *L'Aiglon* she had chosen the part of a crazy boy. The third selection she had offered was a sequence from Strindberg's *The Dream*. It seemed important to demonstrate to the jury her ability at comedy, madness, and tragedy. The jury agreed with her supposition. In the autumn of 1933 Ingrid Bergman became a drama student at the Royal Dramatic School in Stockholm.

Uncle Otto with his impeccable fairness congratulated her on her success, and never again raised his voice in protest against the hazards of her profession. Indeed he thoroughly enjoyed the Swedish films she made. He had been concerned about her choice of a career he felt would bring her only unhappiness, but he was man enough to admit that he was thoroughly mistaken. Sadly, he did not live to see her greatest successes.

There is little doubt that the death of her mother, when Ingrid was three years old, and of her father when she was thirteen, had a great effect on her. Her father, Justus Bergman, was her only real pillar of strength through those first twelve years of her life. His was a joyous and an all-embracing love.

———————— • ————————

I was so proud of him, even though sometimes he wasn't all that proud of me. You see, as a little girl, I was always being something else; a bird, or a lamppost, a policeman, a postman, a flowerpot. I remember the day I decided to be a small dog. I was quite disconcerted when my father refused absolutely to put a leash around my neck and take me for a walk. Did him no good though. I still trotted at his heels woofing at all the passers-by and cocking my leg up against every tree we passed. I don't think he was really very happy about this performance. But of course it all came out of being a lonely child.

I used to dress up . . . and my father helped me to put funny hats on, a pipe in my mouth, glasses, that sort of thing—he was terribly interested in the art of photography and he photographed me as I was having fun in his big shoes and all that. And I stood in front of the mirror and played everything from big bears to old ladies and young princes: I played all the parts, and I made them all up because I started this earlier than I could read. Then my father said I should sing, it would be so much more beautiful if I sang the words. I should be an opera singer. So I got singing lessons when I was about eight years old. And I sang and I sang, and my father wanted me to play the piano; actually Papa forced me to play the piano, because I didn't like it very much.

In fact I kept telling him he was not educating me correctly. I should be looked after properly like all the other kids. For example, I wanted to be like everyone else at school and have my weekly pocket money, one krona. But when I said, "Can I have my pocket money, Papa?" he'd stick his hand in his pocket, fish out a handful of money, and hold it out to me. "There, take as much as you want. Here, take it." And I'd say, "No, no, no, that's too much, too much. You mustn't do that, you mustn't spoil me. I should just have one krona a week."

"Oh, don't be silly, money's just there to be spent. Take it."

"No Papa, I won't. Here, look I'll take two kronor. Put the rest away. You must learn to look after money." So I had to educate him, about educating me.

It was the same thing about school. Papa thought education after a certain level was a waste of time—that you should always do the thing you loved to do. When I was between ten and eleven, he'd laugh.

"What d'you want to go to school for? You can do your sums now and you can write. Now you're wasting time. Much better you go straight into the opera. You're having singing lessons and you're practicing music. That's life. That's the real stuff of life. Being an artist. Being creative. Much more important than sitting in school and learning about history and geography. I know people at the opera. Let's give up school. . . ."

He loved painting and art, music and singing so much he was

certain his daughter loved it too, and would be a great opera star. He'd have been a little disappointed if I'd done what he wanted, because my singing never amounted to anything. But I was too young to be a Bohemian like him. I'd say, "It's not right to talk like that, Papa. I have to learn my lessons. I can't give up school until I'm older." Oh, I had a lot of trouble with my father.

I knew even then, from all my schoolfriends, that this was the way you did things in Sweden. If you intended to settle down and get married—and every girl in the school was indoctrinated with that idea—you started school at seven, and studied for eleven years, and then you got a diploma. After that you'd make up your mind whether you wanted to try for the university. I didn't want to do that. I wanted to do the normal period of schooling and then get into the Royal Dramatic School. But Papa would look at me with that wicked glint in his eye and say, "You could start in the opera? It'd be much more fun. What about starting in the opera?"

Now I look back, I realize how impossible he must have been, but how lovable. I loved him very much. So very much. And my mother did too.

You see, when I became engaged to Petter I decided I'd better clear out all the jumble I had left in the basement of the apartment house where I had lived with my Aunt Ellen, my father's sister. She died in my arms when I was thirteen and a half and I was so shocked I left the house and never returned, and all the stuff was jumbled down in the basement storeroom. But now Petter and I were setting up house, so we got the key and went down to see if there were bits and pieces, furniture and utensils we might use. It was quite eerie. Everything had just been pushed away the day after she died, things from the kitchen, furniture, bed linen, all just piled into this basement room.

But I found one important thing; a box all neatly tied up, and in it the letters my mother had written to my father from Germany when they were engaged. Unofficially engaged, because my mother's parents were totally against it. My mother came to Sweden from Hamburg one summer. Every day she used to walk through these woods, and in the woods my father was painting. And during those daily meetings they fell in love.

I took that box of letters to bed with me that night and read them until the early hours. It was the first time I had got to know my mother as a woman in love with my father, and I cried and cried as I read about all the difficulties they had. Her family didn't think he was good enough for their daughter. He was an artist. He didn't have a steady job. They were rich and he was poor. My mother's two other sisters, Aunt Mutti and Aunt Lulu, had married well. It was unthinkable that Friedel, my mother, should marry an *artist* and a Swede at that; that was very much beneath her. But not to my mother it wasn't.

All this I got in the letters. She talked about her engagement ring: how she wore it on a string round her neck in the daytime, and only put it on her finger when she went to bed at night; how her mother came into the room when she was asleep and saw the ring and woke her and wanted an explanation and made a terrible scene. And how my mother said, "I want to marry this man and no one else, even if I have to wait all my life. And I'm never going to marry anybody else, never!"

Such a heartbreaking story of love lay in those letters. How concerned she was about him. And how she lectured him. If he really meant what he said about getting married, he *had* to get a job. He couldn't go on and on and just *paint!* That was not a serious job. I mean you can sell a painting, but how often do you actually do that? So he had to get a job and get one pretty quickly. And of course sometimes she was a bit jealous of him. He had written to her saying that he was painting a model. And my mother, I suppose, like me, was always reforming him, and she was certain that it must be a nude model. So she wrote to him saying, "Now Justus you must never ask me to pose 'like that'!" So sweet. She did pose for him. But always with her clothes on.

I could put myself so easily in her place, because I was at the same age, and I was just about to marry Petter, though without any of the difficulties she had encountered. She had to wait seven long years before she could marry my father, and by that time he had set up his photographic shop on Strandvägen in a good part of town and was doing quite well. He did film developing. They did hand-painted photographs in those days; and he sold frames and cameras. And he still painted portraits, so he managed to put together so good a business that her parents eventually gave their consent.

Their worlds were so different. My father was a bohemian, an artist, very easygoing, and my mother was the complete bourgeois. But they were very happy together. My mother had three children. The first died at birth and the other a week after birth, and I arrived seven years after that. I don't remember my mother at all. My father filmed me sitting on her lap when I was one, and then again when I was two, and at three he photographed me putting flowers on her grave.

Papa was mad about moving pictures as well as stills. Who knows, if he'd lived he might have gone into Swedish movies. Certainly he experimented with moving pictures and naturally photographed my mother with his movie camera. When I was in Hollywood, David Selznick had this old film processed and developed for me, and I was able to play it back and see my mother *moving* for the first time in my life.

It was Aunt Ellen who replaced my mother. She was one of fourteen children, seven boys and seven girls, and Ellen was the only girl who was not married. My father's parents kept one daughter at home to look after them when they were old; when they died, she moved around among her brothers and sisters and looked after their problems. So when my mother died, Aunt Ellen came to us. I was three years old and really loved her and I called her Mama. She was always a bit upset about this, especially in the shops where they knew her as *Miss* Bergman.

Aunt Ellen was short and plumpish and had a heart condition, and didn't go out of the house very much at all. Although she was extremely kind and thoughtful, she never approved of the antics of my father and me when it came to acting. Like Uncle Otto, she was a strong Lutheran and she thought acting was sinful. She used to say, "That's the devil sitting on your back." I couldn't understand that, and I used to answer, "The devil isn't sitting on my back. I've looked and I can't see any devil."

Every year my father used to take me to Germany to visit my German grandparents and my two aunts. Father used to deliver me and stay for a while, and then leave me in their care and go off to England or some part of Europe. And that used to be terrible—terrible! When my father left I used to go into the toilet and cry. And my grandmother would see I was away a long time, and she'd call, "What are you doing? What are you doing?" And I would try and stop sobbing because I knew she would hear me. She was furious that I was sobbing because I had to stay with her. The truth was I was afraid of them, and I was never very happy there. I remember my grandfather as a very strong and determined man. They were terribly strict and they had brought up their children in the same hard way. The trouble was I so loved my father, I was so used to him, and he was just like a big brother.

I suppose I received the normal sort of Germanic discipline for children in those days; that's probably why I'm so orderly today. My grandmother once woke me up in the middle of the night because I'd thrown a dress over a chair and not folded it away. She made me get out of bed (I was about ten years old), and fold up my dress and underwear, and put it neatly on the chair. Then she pointed at my shoes, and I said, "But I *have* put them by my chair, Grandmama, and they are tidy."

"Yes, my child, but they're not neat. They should lie together with both toes level and pointing the same way."

Those are things that stay with you and influence you all through your life, so now I'm absolutely obsessed with orderliness. I can't live in a house where there is disorder; I become absolutely ill. In Italy I used to go into Robin's room and clean it up when he was at school, and he'd come home and say, "Look Mama, I can find my things in my *own disorder;* I can't find them in your *order.*" And he won that fight. He couldn't keep me out of his room because there was no lock on the door. But he simply unscrewed the door handle and took it to school with him, and that defeated me. Anyway, he's much tidier now.

But I loved staying with my young and pretty Aunt Mutti. She'd married a very rich Frenchman who had coffee plantations in Haiti. They had a big house with a garden and servants and a private boat on the Alster Lake; they were really well-off. Most of the time he spent in the Caribbean, and at first she went over there with him, but she didn't like the island heat, and the black people with their dancing and music frightened her. So more and more they became separated. He took their sons out to Haiti with him, and she didn't like that very much either. What broke up the marriage finally, I think, was when her eldest son died of a tropical disease. They never got divorced, but the marriage just petered out.

When I was young I loved her. She always wanted a little daughter. That is why I called her Aunt Mutti—which in German means mother—instead of her real name, Elsa. As her sister's only child she made such a fuss over me. Mind you, there were certain things I didn't like about her. I thought she was too strict with her servants. I remember saying to myself, "If ever I get any money and can afford to have a house like this, I shan't treat the servants the way Aunt Mutti does." I also remember I didn't like to go into shops with her very much, because she would see a piece of material she liked—"Yes, that piece up there on the top shelf?"—and the poor girl would have to go on dragging down length after length until half the shop was on the counter and then Aunt Mutti would look discontented and say, "No, no. Not quite right. Thank you very much, I'll come back some other time." And I could see what the salesgirl was saying in her mind: "Please, please don't ever come back again!"

Such things do stay with you. Nowadays I hardly ever go into a shop without buying something, sometimes things I don't need— because they've taken so much of their time to be nice and show me things, and I don't want them to feel I've been ungrateful. . . . Nevertheless, I loved staying with Aunt Mutti.

But Grandmama, that was different. I remember, I was sitting in the garden one summer by myself, being ladylike, orderly, and, I expect, trying to think nice thoughts. Father had been gone for a long time, and suddenly I heard that whistle—he had a little catchy whistle which he used to find me in crowds, to tell me where he was—and I heard it behind me. And I couldn't believe it. I didn't turn round to see if it was really him because I thought I was hearing things. Then he whistled again, and I turned and there he was. And I just flew. Such security. Such warmth. Papa was back. Life was suddenly all right again.

You see it was my father's enthusiasm over my play-acting that turned me into an actress. I must have been about eleven when he took me to the theater for the first time; I'd been to several operas with him but I didn't really think much about those.

But that first play. My eyes popped out.

Grownup people on that stage doing things which I did at home, all by myself, just for fun. And they were getting paid for it! They were making their living doing it! I just couldn't understand how these actors could behave like me, invent a world of make-believe, and call it work! And I turned to my father at the first intermission, and they probably heard me all over the theater I was so excited, as I said, "Papa, Papa, that's what I'm going to do."

And that feeling has never altered to this day. I get up at six o'clock and I go to the studios and it's a work of love, and I'm so happy. I go to the theater, and I sit in my dressing room and put on the make-up and the costumes, and I keep saying, "And I get paid for it too!"

My father's death, of course, was a terrible blow to me, even though I didn't really understand it. You see at twelve years I didn't realize that he had cancer or what cancer was, and he tried to break it to me gently. He showed me this X ray of his stomach and said, "You see, this is a cancer growing here, and darling, pretty soon I won't be able to get any food down into my stomach, so you see that's serious."

I remember looking down at the X-ray plate and thinking I must cheer him up and saying, "But look, there's lots of room down this way. The food can get in this way, of course it can."

He got very thin, and I heard afterwards how he went to his best friend—I knew him as Uncle Gunnar—who kept a flower shop, and he said, "I don't want Ingrid at her age to see her father dying so slowly, and God knows how long it will take me. I'm going to Germany. I've heard in Bavaria there's a miracle doctor who can do marvelous things, so I'll go down and see him. Maybe he will cure me. If not, I'll come back in a box."

So he went off to Bavaria with Greta, a girl he was very much in love with. She was in her early twenties, and he was in his middle fifties. He'd first brought her into the house as my governess, and then he'd fallen in love with her. But Aunt Ellen and Aunt Hulda, severe and strictly religious, disapproved entirely. How could he fall in love again when he'd been married to this wonderful woman who was my mother? And look how young this girl Greta was. They didn't seem to understand that my mother had been dead for ten years and that he needed love, and mine wasn't enough and Greta's was. In the summer before he got sick, we used to go to the little house by the lake which belonged to Aunt Ellen and go swimming, and it was such fun to be with her.

I loved Greta. She was so beautiful. My father painted her many times.

I think he felt guilty because of the age difference, and finally Aunt Ellen and the family more or less chased her away.

When my aunts and uncles spoke badly about her in my presence I tried to defend her. And they'd say, "Do you know where your father is? He's not at home with you, is he?" And I'd answer "No, he isn't, but it doesn't make any difference. I am very busy with all my homework. I know he'll be along later." Then sometimes they'd say, "You *do* know where he is. He is with *her!*" And I could have killed them for daring to criticize my father, and I would say, "I don't mind! I am glad he is with Greta! I'm glad!"

Then he went off to Bavaria with Greta and everyone was shocked but me. She stayed there with him to help him die, and I loved her for it.

The miracle doctor couldn't do anything to help. My father painted a little, and years afterwards Greta gave me the last thing he ever did, a painting of the view from his window where they lived. Then he came home, so thin it was dreadful. But as a child you can never believe that your father is going to die. Then in his last days my Aunt Mutti came up from Hamburg, and said to the other relatives, "Greta has the right to come in and be by his side in these last hours of his life. So please allow it."

She came back and we sat on either side of his bed, just the two of us. I remember my father turned his head to look at Greta, and then he turned his head to look at me, and I smiled at him. And that was the end.

Greta moved almost entirely out of my life although when I was fifteen she did one very important thing for me: She got me my first job in a film. But then I didn't see her until many many years later when she was married and had her own children.

The death of my father was of course a shattering experience, and then, only six months later, Aunt Ellen died. She woke me up calling in the night and I went into her bedroom. Her breathing was very labored, and she gasped, "I feel really ill. Will you call Uncle Otto?"

Her face was dark, and that breathing!

I rushed to the phone and my cousin Bill answered and said he'd come at once. They lived just around the corner.

I went back and said, "Cousin Bill's on his way." My aunt whispered, "Read the Bible to me. Read the Bible."

So I opened it and I began to read, and I read and read without knowing what I was saying, while I could see her gradually getting worse and worse. At last she said, "I'm going to die. I'm going to die. Oh, why don't they come, why don't they come?"

She was quite black in the face and suddenly she gasped, "Key —key."

And I understood immediately what she meant. Our apartment was high up, and instead of running down the stairs to open the door, we'd throw the key down so visitors could let themselves in. And I'd forgotten in the panic. I'd completely forgotten. Bill must be waiting outside. I rushed to the window. There he was; he'd been calling but I hadn't heard. Strangely enough, as he stood there, two nursing sisters had walked by, and he'd pleaded with them and said, "Would you please wait here because someone's sick up in that apartment, and I'll rush home and telephone and ask them to throw down the key." But at that moment I'd opened the window and had just thrown it down. I ran back to my aunt. She could hardly breathe now, and her face was black. I took her in my arms and held her, and then the nurses came in and pulled me away. But it was too late, and they couldn't have done anything anyway. Bill put a coat around my shoulders and said, "Come on, come on home with me."

Coming so soon after my father's death six months earlier, it was a terrible shock, and I think, inside, I really took a long time to get over it.

Uncle Otto and Aunt Hulda did everything they could. They were a hard-working, middle-class Swedish family, and I started a new life in that house with my five cousins.

There was open country not far from our apartment and my youngest cousin Britt and I used to play there. She was younger than I, and we were inseparable friends because the other cousins were so much older; there was five years between Britt and the next. I remember every night we used to go for a walk, just the two of us, and in the winter it was dark at four o'clock, but in those days no one bothered about two little girls alone in the street at night —there was no danger. And in the summer, during our school holidays, there was the little summer house which Aunt Ellen had left to me in her will, about an hour's boat ride from Stockholm.

Often Britt and I would stay there alone all week, and the boys and Aunt Hulda would join us on the weekends. It was a fresh-water lake called Mälaren, and we swam and sunbathed.

As I grew older, I realized that it was Aunt Hulda who was the strong one in that family; she sacrificed herself for those five children and for me. I remember I had a very nice room with my mother's piano and my father's desk and some of his paintings in it. Britt and her sister shared another room; the boys slept in other rooms, but Aunt Hulda slept out in the corridor in a collapsible bed which she pushed up every morning. It was a most uncomfortable corridor with no windows. Aunt Hulda was the first one up in the morning—to do the shopping, and prepare the food, and get us children off to school. I don't quite know how they worked out the money; they ran a shop which made frames, and then of course my father's business was still going on, and I think Aunt Hulda was in charge of the whole thing. I've never seen a woman who could count quicker—quick as a computer she was—but above all she insisted that all of her children, and that included me, got a good education.

"I don't care if my children hate me for what I do," she would say, "but you're all going to get an education."

She sent Britt and me to the Lyceum School, the most expensive girls school in Stockholm. All the boys had successful careers; one an army colonel, another a professor, and the third a dentist, but no one in the family was very artistic. No one had time to be artistic; they worked too hard. I still went on with my play-acting in my room.

All through those years when my father was dying and afterwards, I was encouraged by his best friend, Gunnar Spangberg, who kept the florist shop where actors and actresses often bought flowers. Practically every Sunday he used to invite his friends along for Sunday supper, and being a wonderfully wise man, as well as a lovable one, he'd ask me along as well. Then he'd ask me to do a little turn, perhaps read a poem . . . and of course very soon I didn't stop at poetry. You couldn't keep me away from drama. Every Sunday evening I performed. I changed my voice and acted all the parts, gesticulated like mad, a one-girl show in fact. His friends were all in their fifties and sixties (to me they were all terribly old) but I was their floorshow every Sunday after supper, and sometimes I could make them laugh or cry. They seemed to like it: Could I do that scene again? Would I be sure to come back next Sunday, they'd loved it so much. . . . I had a whole repertoire of stories and scenes I'd made up, and they were so lovely—they applauded everything I did.

It was Uncle Gunnar who gave me the *Book:* a thick, leather-bound volume about four inches square. It had a metal lock and key and my name embossed on the cover. It was such an exciting gift for a fourteen-year-old girl. I decided I would reveal to the *Book* my innermost thoughts about acting, and that very first entry established how serious I was going to be:

> Dear Book. Ever since I was a child I loved the theater but I never thought that maybe I could become an actress. It was in the fall of 1929 that I realized that I wanted to give myself absolutely to the theater. Uncle Gunnar said I

should be an actress; there was no question about it. He told me to learn more poems, and it was then I decided to the Muses I must go, to Thalia, one of the goddesses of the theater.

I dreamed how one day I would stand at the Oscar Theater and the public would sit there and see this new Sarah Bernhardt. I never talked to anyone very much about my plans. I kept them to myself. I know I dreamed that perhaps one day I might be able to play against Gösta Ekman, who was my ideal.

Papa wanted me to go in for opera because he liked music so much. But I don't think there is so much difference between opera and theater. I am sure he would not have forbidden me to venture along the thorny road to the heaven of stars.

The contrast between my acting exhibitions and my normal behavior was so different that it was unbelievable. I was the shyest human being ever invented. I couldn't come into a room without bumping into the furniture and then blushing. If people asked me what my name was, I'd blush bright scarlet. At school, I knew the answers to many of the questions but I'd never answer them because as soon as I was on my feet I'd go a deep crimson and start to stammer. That's why it seemed so silly to Uncle Otto and my cousins that I wanted to be an actress.

They said, "How can you? You're so awkward."

Since those days I've discovered that many actors and actresses are like this—extremely shy people. When they're acting, they're not themselves; they're somebody else; the *other* people they're pretending to be are responsible for the words coming out of their mouths.

I suppose it was like that the first time I ever gave a public performance. It was at school. Christmas time. Our form mistress had forgotten they'd put a stage up for the seniors' play, in the gymnasium, so we couldn't do our exercises. So she said, "Now you've got this next hour free. Just sit quietly and I'll come back and then we'll go off to the next lesson."

The teacher left us and I looked at the stage. My first real stage and something happened to me. I flew up onto it. Standing there I'd never felt so happy in my life. The week before I'd seen a play called *The Green Elevator*. I told the other girls about it and asked if they would like me to play it for them. "Yes," they chorused, "yes." I asked some of them to take part. I think they all thought I'd gone mad.

It was one of those bedroom farces. There were seven characters, and I remembered exactly what they did, as well as some of the dialogue. It was about a husband with a hangover, and his involvement with his wife and girlfriend. So there I am, the shyest pupil in the class, directing all the rest of the cast, our classmates roaring with laughter.

They made so much noise that my teacher came running back, saying, "Whatever's going on? You're making so much noise that you're disturbing the class next door." I think she nearly collapsed when they said, "Ingrid Bergman's acting a play for us."

Anyway she wasn't having any nonsense like that. There was half an hour to go, so she shooed us all outside, told us to go to the park, and come back when the time was up. But the girls all wanted to know how the play ended. So I stood on a park bench and went on acting. As a matter of fact, a few members of the public, wondering what was going on, stopped to listen too! So naturally, I never forgot my first *stage* performance.

It was now that I met Greta again. She was studying music and singing and, since she was so beautiful, she often earned money as a film extra; she would be photographed lounging about at a railway station, sitting at a dinner party, walking across a hotel lobby. I was fascinated. And I pleaded with her, "Please let me come with you one day so that I can see how a movie is made."

She did better than that. She actually got me taken on for a day's work. I arrived at the studio and found about a dozen other young girls, most of them quite a bit older than me. They put make-up on us, and about ten o'clock they told us to line up in the studio and said they were ready to shoot. The director told us we all had to look frozen and hungry and miserable. Then the camera went past us a couple of times and he said, "That's it. Thanks very much, girls. You can go now."

Go! At ten fifteen in the morning? I'd only just arrived! They couldn't get rid of me that easily. It was far too exciting. Besides, my face was all plastered over with this thick yellow make-up and I was smart enough to know that if I kept it on everyone would think I was waiting to appear in a scene. So there I was, the girl with the yellow face, marching from set to set, absolutely enthralled.

Then suddenly it was six o'clock and everybody was going home. Naturally I was the last one to leave, and naturally, I wasn't taking off my magic yellow face for anybody. But as I got to the front door, there stood one rather puzzled man.

"Where've you been all day? I've been waiting here with your money. We looked everywhere for you."

I said, "I like it here: there was so much to see."

I suppose he understood film-struck kids for he quieted down and said, "Here's your money" and off he went. And I looked at the money. Ten kronor. Ten whole kronor for having enjoyed one of the very best days in my life. I was fifteen years old and it was the first money I had ever earned.

———————— • ————————

At school, Ingrid's shyness was so intense that occasionally it became a nervous affliction, an allergy for which her doctor could find no explanation. Her fingers swelled up and she couldn't bend them. Her lips and eyelids swelled too.

She could actually feel the swellings begin to form. No one knew why they came or how to cure them. She was sent to a hospital where she was given some sort of mild ray treatment, and eventually the swellings disappeared of their own accord.

Drama school ended all her illnesses, and most of her inhibitions.

Chapter 2

Drama school was marvelous. I was so happy. I changed for the better from one day to the next. I became a terribly happy person, outgoing, relaxed, because I was doing exactly what I wanted to do. And it was so very easy for me. I had no difficulty in understanding what they meant when they explained how to handle your voice or move across a stage. We had ballet lessons, fencing lessons, lessons on the history of the theater, voice projection, posture—and we played scenes. There was nothing very exciting about the school itself, just a couple of large rooms on one of the upper floors, and a big table where everyone carved their names: a lot of famous names, then and afterwards. Greta Garbo, Signe Hasso, Mai Zetterling, Viveca Lindfors. I felt I belonged to *something* at last. I was accepted. I remember arriving at that little stage door at the side of the Royal Dramatic Theatre and just standing there, so happy, thinking, I belong! This is my home. I can go in there and they will say "Hallo Ingrid" and I am part of this. I was so proud. More than that, all students could go and see all the performances for *nothing.* Not from the stalls of course, but the top gallery. We could go to the theater *every* night, and see these marvelous actors and actresses. We were not allowed in during rehearsals, but we got in just the same. The ushers had the key to the top balcony but we were just as clever with a hairpin. Of course, the directors down there knew what was going on—they'd done the same thing in their time—and occasionally they'd shout up, "Is there anyone up there?" when we giggled too loudly at a laugh line. And we would freeze again.

Oh, it was so exciting sitting up there in the darkness, under the chandeliers, the gilt and the gold, with that flow of wonderful theatrical creation going on down there on that brightly lit stage.

It was not until after my eighteenth birthday that I went out on my first real date. In Sweden in the early thirties, most of the teenagers—fourteen, fifteen, and sixteen-year-olds—went to dances, walked around hand in hand, and fell madly in love for about twenty-four hours at a time. I'd had a few of these infatuations by the time I was fifteen. Then I made an awful discovery. I was not popular at all with boys. I was too tall for them, or I was too gawky; I was too serious, I blushed, and I couldn't keep a conversation going. I was a terrible failure. There was only one thing to do. I pretended I disliked boys. I said, "I hate men." It had a nice finality to it, and it made me a bit more impressive: a man-hater, I hated all men.

But the girls weren't very much impressed with me either. So I slipped away into my lonely play-acting, and my obsession with the theater.

Then one day I was asked by one of my cousins to make up a foursome with a handsome young dentist called Petter Lindstrom. I was told he was very old. Over twenty-five. But very good looking, charming, and besides he actually owned a car!

But I said, "I can't go, why ask me? I've nothing to wear. And the Grand Hotel ... I've never been there in my life ... I have never been out in a foursome. . . . And a big restaurant where you dance and have supper? Oh, I don't think so . . . oh, no, no! . . ."

Really I suppose inside I was terribly excited. It didn't need much to talk me into it. Off we went to the Grand Hotel, where Petter was going to meet us. We three sat down in the restaurant facing the revolving doors. Ten minutes, twenty minutes—no Petter. And the excuses, "Well, he's very busy, he's a dentist you know, but don't worry, he'll be along. He had these patients, and *they* might be late, and he can't leave them in the middle of the session can he? Don't worry, he'll be here." Then about half an hour later, I saw this young man walk through the door, and I knew at once it was Petter Lindstrom. I said, "That's him, isn't it?"

"Oh yes, that's him. Hallo Petter. . . ."

"Sorry I'm a bit late."

"No bother. Now this is Ingrid. Ingrid . . . Petter Lindstrom."

He sat down beside me, and the first thing he said to me was, "I like your hair."

I had it all brushed back from my forehead and held in a little knot at the back like a schoolteacher.

And the next thing he said was, "What a deep voice you have . . . what a beautiful voice."

So I thought, that's not bad, he likes my voice, and he likes my hair, and I felt a lot better.

Then we danced, and we had a very nice evening, and they took me home. A few days later they called me up and said that Petter wanted the four of us to go out again. I was very impressed with him.

At eighteen anybody over twenty-five is so sophisticated, and I was going out with *a man of the world,* with his own *car.* Then we started to meet regularly. He called me up and invited me to lunch. Looking back, I'd say it was a slow friendship, which gradually turned into love.

Certainly I got plenty of encouragement from Uncle Otto and Aunt Hulda; they loved Petter, he was established, he had a good job; in fact everybody loved Petter. He was a good sportsman, he was very bright. Certainly I began to depend on him.

I began to ask him questions, rely upon his judgment. He was very busy, but we began to meet every Saturday for lunch, and then every Sunday we'd go out into the country; all through that winter we went on long walks or cross-country skiing.

I think it took a long time for Petter to realize that he was in love with me. I don't think that falling in love with an actress was in his plans at all. He was very interested in the theater, many of his friends were artists. We went to the theater and movies, but I don't think that marrying an actress was part of his future. We just liked each other, liked going out together. . . . He fell in love almost without realizing what was happening.

———— • ————

What sort of man was this Petter Lindstrom who was to be such a large influence in the life of Ingrid Bergman? He was tall, with light-brown hair. And handsome. Very handsome. A good middle-weight boxer, an outstanding skier, and a marvelous dancer. He loved physical gestures, challenging in locked-arm contests of strength. He laughed a lot, sometimes played the buffoon, possessed a great sense of fun. And he loved Ingrid. In those early years they got along very well indeed.

After three months Ingrid's other love affair—with the Royal Dramatic School—was put under considerable strain by an incident that left her bewildered and very unhappy.

Swinging down the corridor one day she passed, without knowing it, Alf Sjöberg, who had been one of the audition judges, the same man she would quiz many years later in Italy. He was just going into rehearsal with a new play. He turned and stared after her. Five minutes later he was in the office of Olof Molander, Director of the Royal Dramatic Theatre.

"Olof, that new girl, the blond one, she suits the part in my play to perfection."

"Alf, don't be absurd. She only joined in September. She's an absolute beginner. You'll have to take one of the girls who has been here the necessary two years."

"But I want *her.* She's got the right look, the right innocence. You can't run a theater like the civil service. There must be exceptions to every rule that was ever made. Blame it on me. Say it's all my fault. . . ."

Olof Molander hesitated, then said: "All right, have it your own way. But there'll be trouble."

Ingrid simply could not believe her luck. Just three months and she was going to leave the schoolroom and start in rehearsals with big stars like Inga Tidblad and Lars Hanson. It was like moving through the gates of heaven: she'd been playing scenes with boys and girls the same age as herself, and suddenly . . .

—————— • ——————

I mean, I arrived during the first three days of reading, and everyone was still walking around with their scripts, but I was walking around with a script too, and this was the *real* thing. My heart was just bursting with excitement at working with *them*! I'd got what they call in Swedish "a bloodied tooth": I had tasted acting with real professional actors. The timing, the inflections, the discipline . . . Oh, I'm sure I was awful, but the thrill . . . it was glorious. And it lasted just three days. I was so excited I could hardly breathe and Alf Sjöberg said he was very pleased with me—but then the crunch. The other students—the girls who had done their full time at the school, and now were used to take over the smaller parts for the next two years—were livid. They were spitting with rage. I was so hated, they actually attacked me physically: I was kicked, while one girl began hitting me over the head.

And the accusations they made, about the things I must have done to get the part. Uncle Otto would have had a heart attack if he'd heard. The row was almost a riot, and Olof Molander just had to give in. He saw Alf Sjöberg and said: "I'm sorry, but she's got to come out of your cast. Either she leaves the cast or there'll be a house revolution. The older students simply won't accept that a girl who's only been here three months gets a big part in a play, the sort of part many of them have been waiting nearly five years to achieve."

So back I went to square one, still hated by the older girls. I was bitterly disappointed, naturally, but at that age you're pretty resilient and bounce back. Though of course, one rather important item had not escaped my attention. You study for three years in the Royal Dramatic School. Then, if they think you're suitable material, they engage you on a two-year contract where you probably get little walk-on parts. "Tea is served." "The cab is waiting . . ." And that's five years of your life. That's what the others were griping about. And I could understand their feelings. It might happen to me too. So maybe I didn't have all those years to spare either.

Summer came. The term was over. The school closed for three months. Now practically all my fellow students rushed off on a very cheap package tour to study Russian theater, and I really should have gone too. But I had fallen in love with Petter Lindstrom. I didn't want to stay away from him.

So I stayed behind. But I was not working and Petter was. So what could I do all day? I had to do something. I went to see Uncle Gunnar, because with that florist shop of his he had all sorts of contacts with the film world. Maybe I could go out to the Swedish Films studios and get a small job as an extra like I did when I was fifteen. But I just couldn't go to the studios and expect them to say: "Come in, we'd love to see you." I needed an introduction.

I knew an actress named Karin Swanstrom came into his shop from time to time. She was a fine comedy actress, but now she was the artistic director of Swedish Films. Maybe if Uncle Gunnar could give her an extra bunch of roses, I'd be able to go out and ask her advice. Anyway, I asked him.

The next time I saw him he gave me a big smile and a wink and said: "The things I do for you. I told Karin you were my little girl;

I'd known you since you were born; your father was my best friend, and you're now an orphan. Karin was so moved that you can catch a tram out to Swedish Films tomorrow and she'll see you."

Greta, who had got me that first job, had played in films regularly, and she wasn't even an actress. No, the theater and Sarah Bernhardt and Eleanora Duse, those were the real landmarks in life.

When Karin Swanstrom asked, "Now my dear girl, what can you do?" I took a deep breath and said: "I can read poetry. Would you like to see my performance?"

"Yes, I'd love to see it."

So off I went. I was perfectly at home. I'd been doing this since I was six. Reading poetry from well-known Swedish poets! I could dramatize this sort of thing.

Karin watched me emoting all over the room, and she didn't look ill, so that wasn't too bad a start. "All right," she said, "in the next few days I'll arrange for you to have a film test." Then she stopped and said, "No, wait a minute, I'll see if I can arrange it now." She rang a number, and said, "Ah, Gustav . . . I see you have a bit of a gap tomorrow. I wonder if you could be a dear and do a test for me? Yes, it's a young girl, a pupil at the Royal Dramatic School, and she's trying to get a job in the summer break. Maybe we could find her a job in a movie somewhere? You're a bit busy, Gustav? I know you are, but this would be a very great favor. . . ."

———— • ————

Gustav Molander, the brother of the Royal Dramatic School director, was a famous Swedish movie-maker. He was far from enthusiastic about testing an unknown, but Karin knew how to handle him. She got him to agree to a screen test the next morning at ten o'clock.

As usual, Ingrid gave herself plenty of time to reach the studio, and that morning she began a routine which she continued all through her career in Swedish films. The tram route to the studio passed the small graveyard where both her parents were buried. She got off the tram and walked to the small bench under the birch tree near their graves. She sat down, bowed her head, and said a little prayer to her father, asking for help.

Ingrid has never been totally reassured by the idea of God. She has always had difficulty in reconciling the failure of God, surely dedicated to protecting the weak, the innocent, and the oppressed, to use

His omnipotent power to diminish or end the brutal injustices in the world. But if she could not pray easily to God, she could to her father.

She found that whenever she went to the graveside her conversations were always with her father. Her mother had died before Ingrid was old enough to confide in her. But she could tell her father: "I have a really difficult scene today, Papa. Make me calm. Give me confidence."

When she arrived before Gustav Molander for the test, she was excited rather than nervous, and determined to learn all she could.

————————— • —————————

They asked whether I was nervous. No. Why, should I be? It's a film test? I know, but you haven't frightened me yet. What do you want me to do? Turn left, turn right, laugh . . . that's easy. Say something. Do you want me to do it again? Can I see what you've done? Is it allowed? Tomorrow? Can I come tomorrow? Thank you very much."

What scared me was not the test itself but the next day when I saw what I'd done. That was a big shock. You know what you look like in a mirror. You've seen photos of yourself. But when you see yourself on the movie screen for the first time, that's a very different image. You see yourself as other people see you. And it doesn't fit in at all with your own conception. You see your teeth from another angle . . . are those my teeth? You see your nose . . . Oh, my God, is that my nose? It isn't like that, is it? You see all these things in a mirror—you've grown used to living with them and you invent excuses for them. And suddenly they're all here, and they're all different from what you thought. They belong to a stranger. I was plump, and I didn't like that nose. And why was I spinning around like that, laughing and talking too much? I just didn't like myself. Oh dear, I knew at once, they wouldn't want to put me in a movie.

————————— • —————————

Gustav Molander, balding, plumpish, kindly, and civilized, was reassuring. All the coolness, disinterest, and slightly offended dignity of the day before had vanished. He was a man of acute perception, and he recognized a rare and original talent when he saw one. He could have watched the rushes of a thousand girls that day: girls more beautiful than Ingrid, better trained than Ingrid, but not one in a thousand, not one in a million, would have achieved the necessary miracle. The miracle was that peculiar transmutation from the live girl performing in front of a camera into the flickering image on a silver screen, a transmutation identified by words of spectacular banality, but total accuracy as "star quality." Miss Ingrid Bergman had star quality.

So he was both extremely impressed and slightly amused that Ingrid's initial reaction seemed to be one of deep depression.

"I didn't look very good, did I?" she said pessimistically. "I think if I did some more I could be better later."

It was a phrase which became her trademark in Swedish Films. After practically every scene she would say, "I think I'll be better later." So inevitably, the film crews hailed her appearance with, "Here comes Betterlater."

Gustav was more reassuring: "It was very good. Remember it's the first time you've been photographed. The lights weren't quite right."

"But I didn't look very good?" Ingrid said doubtfully.

"You looked *very* good," Gustav contradicted. "You have personality. It came across very well. You have great possibilities."

Karin Swanstrom raised a practical issue. "The thing now," she said, "is what do we do with you?"

"There's Edvin's *The Count of the Monk's Bridge,*" suggested Gustav.

"That's right. We haven't finished casting that . . . the maid has quite a nice little part."

"And my own film is starting shortly," continued Gustav. He did not add that he already had the young Miss Bergman firmly in his mind as his next leading lady.

Karin smiled at Ingrid. "So I'll have to start preparing a contract for you."

"All right," Ingrid said, "but remember I've got to go back to school for the autumn term." Still, she was not worried. At eighteen, in the midsummer of 1934, autumn was a lifetime away.

When Ingrid arrived at the Swedish Films studios a week or so later to appear in Edvin Adolphson's *The Count of the Monk's Bridge,* she had time for only one exploratory rehearsal before everyone broke for lunch. Returning to the studio an hour later, she discovered that small pots of flowers had appeared as if by magic on both sides of the path back to the set. She bent forward to read the little note hanging from one of them. It read: "*Där du går, där blommar jorden.* Where you go, there blooms the earth."

It is doubtful if in all the future years of extravagant praise, Ingrid ever received a gesture more appropriate or lyrical than that little note from Gustav Molander. It was, from him, a deeply felt gesture toward a girl in whom he divined the seeds of greatness.

The Count of the Monk's Bridge was a comedy, its plot almost a travelogue, recording a day in the life of a group of young bohemians attempting to get around the strict drinking laws current in Stockholm in 1933. Ingrid as Elsa, a maid in a seedy hotel, is pursued by leading roisterer Edvin Adolphson, who also directed the film. Plump and round-faced, she appears in her first scene struggling into a black-and-red striped dress in time to rush to the window and shout a greeting down to Edvin in the street. It was scarcely a motion picture debut to immortalize her in the history of the cinema.

In her *Book* she wrote of her first director:

> Edvin says very little except to tell me that I should go very far because of my impudence and audacity. I am completely impossible, he says, because I am always criticizing what he does, and I am constantly putting my foot in it. I think he means the scene with Tollie Zellman.

———— • ————

I was supposed to come into the fish shop and stand in line at the counter. Selling the fish was one of Sweden's greatest comediennes, a very fine actress, Tollie Zellman. She was wrapping the fish up in newspaper for the customer who was just ahead of me. I looked at her wrapping the fish and then I went around the counter and I said, "Look here, that isn't the way you wrap a fish. I'll show you how. You wrap a fish like this. I've seen how they do it at the market. Put it there and turn the paper over like this, then turn in that edge and roll it over like that. See?" So I smiled at her and went back to my place in the line. And there was rather a long silence and then Tollie Zellman said in a very loud voice, "And who's this?" Then I realized I'd just acted instinctively and it really wasn't my place to instruct her and I started to blush. Edvin laughed a bit nervously, I think, and said, "Well, she's a young girl who's just started."

"Oh," said Tollie, "she starts well, doesn't she?"

Nevertheless, at the end of the film Edvin Adolphson and I were very good friends despite all my interference.

————————— • —————————

After that first film all the producers and administrators at Swedish Films knew they had seen a young woman of immense potential.

Gustav, Karin Swanstrom, Edvin, and Ivar Johansson all pressed her to reconsider her future. Why stay at drama school when so many golden opportunities awaited her with Swedish Films? This was a shortcut to success, unavailable at drama school. Her own inclination was to follow their advice. After all, the academy had demonstrated conclusively that seniority was far more important than acting ability.

In the *Book,* she wrote:

> I am offered a contract which promises me seventy-five kronor [seven dollars fifty cents] every day with a five thousand kronor [five hundred dollar] guarantee the first year, the second year six thousand kronor, the third year seven thousand five hundred kronor. Two thousand kronor every year to take private lessons. They would give me all the clothes I used in each film, and they would get me an engagement in the theater if they could. How can you refuse such a contract? But I do not want to give up my theatrical career.

In August, Ingrid requested an interview with the Royal Dramatic Theatre director. It was painful.

"You're telling me you want to leave and work in *moving pictures?*" Olof Molander's tone was icy.

Ingrid was prepared for his deprecating attitude. "You may be right about movies, Mr. Molander—I know they're not important. But to me it's a short cut. I can do a couple of movie parts and get myself a little reputation, and then come back to the school to continue my education, and perhaps get small parts like the one I had with Mr. Sjöberg."

Olof Molander was unimpressed by her argument: "Now listen to me, Miss Bergman." His voice was dictatorial, his sympathy nonexistent. "You have talent. I will admit that, but if you go to the movies now, you will destroy that talent. If you stay with us you will become a good actress, possibly even a great actress. You will not make a success of movies or any other acting requirement, because you have no training, as yet, for any sort of professional performance. You will not be able to handle your posture, your voice, or your emotions. You know nothing about life. All this you will be taught in the next two years here!"

Contemptuously he swept away all her attempts at compromise. And he upset her deeply. She had come contritely to explain her dilemma, and he treated her like a stupid schoolgirl.

"I'm sorry," Ingrid answered doggedly, "but I've made up my mind."

There was a short pause, then the emotional thunderstorm. And Olof Molander made the elementary mistake of trying to bully her. *"You've* made up your *mind?* Young woman, you will *not* leave this theatrical school! You are only a student. I forbid you to go! Understand that. I forbid you to leave!"

The pause was quite lengthy, as the once blushing, uncertain, and inhibited Ingrid took her first step toward some degree of independence.

"I don't see how you can forbid me," she said quietly. "We have no contract between us. You accepted me. The lessons are free. I don't pay anything, and I don't get paid. If I don't want to come back to school in September you can't put me in prison for it. And now you've made up my mind for me. I am leaving."

Gustav Molander, a far less blustery man than his brother, raised an eyebrow when Ingrid reported what the theater director had said, but he made no comment.

But Olof had created a serious doubt in Ingrid's own mind. She felt he was right about her lack of training. She *did* need all those dramatic lessons she was going to miss. But Swedish Films' contractual offer of two thousand kronor every year for private lessons clinched the deal for her.

———— • ————

So I took all those extra lessons, dancing and movement and voice production. One lovely actress who taught me, Anna Norrie, was in her seventies. I remember especially one piece of her advice. "Ingrid," she said, "if you do a gesture on the stage don't do anything *little*, little turns, little shrugs, little movements. If you do a gesture, make it a big gesture. Never be afraid of gestures, sweep out your arms. Do it from the point of the shoulder here. Big gestures. Always big gestures. Naturally it's different for movies."

And of course you pick up things watching yourself on the screen; I was tall, and like most tall young girls I was a bit ashamed of my height. I saw myself on the screen beginning to creep through scenes like a hunchback. So I took corrective exercises to straighten up and stand tall. I learned intonations, how to breathe . . . voice inflections . . . how not to press that word, that word is unimportant, throw it away. I never stopped learning. I'm still learning today. I love learning. You learn acting from life, and that goes on round you all the time.

> Dear Book: Now I jump right into the second film, *Ocean Breakers*. I have been up north to Söderhamn, and out to the tiny fishing island of Prästgrund, where always there is the smell of rotting fish, but I loved every second. Now I am back, I am healthy, strong, and brown and five kilos fatter than when I left.
>
> It was wonderful. I was a prima donna on the island two hours out to sea. For the very first time people asked for my autograph. Ivar Johansson is the world's funniest and best director. I was sometimes ugly like a witch, but Ivar says that is right for a fishergirl. They all praise me, and I must keep my head with all these compliments. I only wish I had been really good in every scene. In the rehearsals I think it is good, but then there is a take and somehow it is not the same. One thing that made me happy was that Sten Lindgren, the actor who plays my clergyman lover, believes our love scenes are so passionate that possibly they will not get past the censor.

———— • ————

Ocean Breakers was a lusty melodrama, full of the sins of the flesh and the retribution it brings. The local minister, taken by passion, seduces the young fishergirl played by Ingrid. Overwhelmed with his terrible burden of guilt, he flees into the storm where a bolt of retributive lightning strikes him down. In the Swedish film world of 1933, Lutheran ministers who strayed from the path of virtue were inevitably doomed by the end of reel three. Barely alive, and with all memory obliterated, he is carried away to a distant hospital. Poor,

pregnant, and misunderstood, Ingrid bears the baby, and the igno-
miny. But she keeps silent about the true identity of the father. The
minister, eventually recovered, returns to the village. The shock of
realizing what Ingrid has been forced to endure restores his memory
and plagues his conscience. At once he repents, confesses his sin from
the pulpit to the assembled villagers, thunders his determination to
atone. He will become a farmer. He will make an honest woman of
Ingrid and marry her. It was a redemption which did not seem too
awful to contemplate—considering that he now had pretty fishergirl
Ingrid to keep him warm in bed—and sent the audiences away
happy, and even envious, from the theater.

Dear Book: It is November 1934. We go from one film to
another. I never stop. Role after role. I am not pleased
with this. I thought I had filmed enough for a while. But
no, they want me to be Astrid in *Swedenhielms.* I said,
"You should not overdo things. You are milking me too
much. Not three in a row." What made me change my
mind was when they told me that Gösta Ekman was going
to play the lead. To be in the same film as Gösta. That is
marvelous.

Several days in advance I was completely destroyed by
my nervousness that at last I was going to meet the man
that I looked up to as a god on this earth. We met and I
liked him immediately. He is one of God's great artists,
and I am delirious that I have been chosen to take one of
the crumbs that has fallen from his table.

First he said I was terribly sweet, but I'm sure he says
that to everyone. It was as if I had known him all my life;
as if he was my father, he inspired me in a very mystical
way. He gave me little tips and I was in heaven. My
happiness cannot be described when he said later, "You
are really very talented. I like you very much. You help
me to play because your face and expressions reflect every
word I say. That is very rare nowadays."

When they wanted him to do a close-up without me he
refused, saying, "I must look at her because she inspires
me." He also said that if I wanted to do a play in the
theater I should let him know because I could become a
great actress. That he also probably says to everyone, but

dear Book, I am so happy. Dear good God, let him remember and like me in the future. I sit and stare at him
when he plays, so full of admiration. I wonder if he feels
how my eyes follow him like a dog's. I adore him more
than ever.

19 January 1935. My first opening night—*The Count of
the Monk's Bridge.* I have difficulties to think clearly and
I mostly sit and just stare. My only thought is that I hope
God has not forgotten me. I feel insecure and secure at the
same time. I am unsure about all the publicity there has
been. I hope that the public will think I can live up to it.
What would Mama and Papa have said if they could see
me here in my loneliness. I long to be able to creep into
someone's arms to find protection and comfort and love.
Tomorrow I shall write after the opening.

What did I expect of the critics—praise? That they
would praise me to the skies; the greatest film actress they
had ever seen? They say, "Ingrid Bergman doesn't give
any strong impression." And: "A somewhat overweight
copy of that promising young actress Birgit Tengroth."
And: "Hefty but quite sure of herself." One said: "A
beautiful and statuesque girl."
For the first time: failure.

Had she known that the red-and-black striped dress in which she
made her first film appearance is today preserved in the costume
department of the Swedish Film Industry alongside an equally
treasured gray silk evening gown worn by Greta Garbo on her first
movie appearance in 1924, perhaps she might have been less depressed.
At that time she was very upset about her comparison with Birgit
Tengroth, and the opinions which suggested one Birgit was enough.
Later in tears she asked her beloved Gösta Ekman what she should
do. Gösta, with infinite experience, said gently, "Ingrid, as an actress
if they talk about you and write about you, that is good. It is only
when they *don't* talk about you and write about you that you should
worry."
It was only when *Swedenhielms,* with Gösta Ekman, was released,

her first film directed by Gustav Molander, that the critics really took notice. The *Svenska Dagbladet* declared: "Swedish film production has for the first time in many years reached not only international standards but high international standards."

———— • ————

I found working with Gustav wonderful. He had this marvelous facility for light comedy but there was always a serious thread underneath, something which gave it a basic reality in the same way that Chaplin's comedy had a basic reality of documentary fact. Gustav especially taught me how to underplay, to be absolutely sincere and natural. "Never try and be cute," he said. "Always be yourself, and always learn your lines." On the set he gave me a great sense of security. He was never rushing off to telephone or attending to a dozen other details like some directors I've known; he was always concentrating on *you.*

———— • ————

The next picture she made was *Walpurgis Night.* Gustav Edgren directed it. Ingrid, as a secretary falling in love with her boss, went through a series of emotional climaxes which made the Swedish press give it critical approval and label it "an adult movie." Then with the comedy, *On the Sunny Side,* she was back under Gustav Molander's tutelage.

By 1936, after no more than eighteen months in the profession, Ingrid Bergman was being acclaimed by the Swedish press: "Ingrid Bergman's great breakthrough . . ." "Ingrid Bergman is blindingly beautiful and acts with strong inspiration. . . ." "She handles every line with perfection. . . ." "Ingrid Bergman has matured as an actress and as a woman. One simply must give up before her beauty and talent. . . ."

Even America's *Variety,* viewing the Swedish film with subtitles, had now begun to take notice: "This picture should be a best seller in the Swedish neighborhoods. One of the better characterizations is that of Ingrid Bergman. She is pretty, and capable of rating a Hollywood berth."

One of the most important pictures she made with Gustav Molander was *A Woman's Face* in which she played the tragic part of a young girl with a hideously disfigured cheek.

This girl had been burned in a fire and one side of her face was completely distorted. I adored the story and pleaded with Swedish Films to let me do it. "No," they said, "we can't. Your audience won't accept it—a beautiful girl with a disfigured face. No, definitely not. Besides, we have this marvelous movie called *Only One Night* which we want you to do next."

I thought *Only One Night* was a piece of junk, so I bargained with them. "Look, I'll only do your film if you let me do the girl with the distorted face." So we compromised. I did their film and then we started on *A Woman's Face*. Petter helped me. He did something quite brilliant, inventing a sort of brace which fitted inside my mouth and pushed out my cheek. Then, with glue, we pulled the eye down on the other side—it wasn't possible to get the right effect with ordinary make-up—and then, oh, did I look a fright. Of course you only saw me looking like Frankenstein in the beginning of the film; then I have plastic surgery and become as beautiful as you can get. . . ."

"The technicalities of the distorted face were fine," said Gustav Molander, "but I couldn't get the story right. The right ending just wouldn't come. Anna Holm, embittered by her hideous face, is deeply involved with a blackmailer. Plastic surgery repairs her face so we have the original Ingrid back again and she looks lovely, but the blackmailer manages to keep his grip upon her and insists in involving her in a plan to murder a young boy and steal his fortune. To save the boy Anna shoots the blackmailer dead. Now how—in those days when films needed if not happy endings then at least repentance—did we solve that problem and leave Anna Holm facing a happy future? I suspended shooting for two days to try and work out a solution. I didn't succeed. So I asked Ingrid her opinion. She thought about it for a couple of minutes, then without hesitation, she gave me her answer. And it was the right answer. It was Anna Holm's answer for she had *become* Anna Holm. "I shall go on trial for murder," said Ingrid, "and that's the end of the film. What happens next, whether I receive clemency or not, we leave to the audience to guess."

(*A Woman's Face* was remade in 1941 by Metro-Goldwyn-Mayer and starred Joan Crawford in the role played by Ingrid. But Hollywood's code of ethics made it clear that Joan, utterly repentant, would be free, and smiling happily, as she headed toward that distant horizon known as "The End.")

Chapter 3

When Petter Lindstrom and Ingrid Bergman were married at Stöde Lutheran church on July 10, 1937, it was the happy union of a lovely twenty-one-year-old girl and a handsome young man of thirty.

———————— • ————————

When I think about it, I suppose I only had about a year of freedom, on my own, in my whole life. I was twenty-one, and earning a reasonable salary in Swedish films, and I had a little flat in the center of Stockholm. A very smart modern block of flats with little red sun-awnings over the window, and I was so house-proud. I was also very much in love with Petter. I remember, oh so well, that present he gave me for my twenty-first birthday. I opened the box and inside, wrapped in tissue paper, was this most beautiful silver fox fur. A real fox with black fur touched with silver, and when you put it around your neck the mouth clipped on to the tail. They were the very smartest thing in the thirties. I had never seen anything more lovely in my life. I flew to the telephone to thank him. There was one of those loose rugs on the polished floor and over I went, twisting my ankle. I crawled the rest of the way and dialed Petter, and I was trying to say it's marvelous but nearly crying with pain at the same time.

He came racing around and I'd broken my ankle and had to go

to the hospital. But I insisted on taking my fox fur with me, made him put it back in the box and wrap it up carefully. There was nothing more precious in my whole life. They set the ankle and put me in a bed and the fox fur was under the bed. I don't really know what the doctor thought, but when he came in I was sitting up in bed in my nightgown with the fox fur around my neck.

————— • —————

Eleven days before their wedding, Ingrid wrote:

> My golden one, my everything on earth, my wonderful only love. If you could only be here in the dressing room and I could sit on your lap, how fine that would be, because it is so devilishly dull without you. It is going to be five hours before I can see you, and eleven days before we marry. That is terribly long. How can I bear it? If I could only kiss you and really kiss you again. You will never leave me, will you? I shall never leave you.
>
> I want to be with you always, always, always. Oh, soon there will be only eleven days before the marriage. Now I have to go to the photographers, but I'm thinking about you all the time. How fine you are, and how nice you are compared with other men. How crazy I am about you. I think I'm going to burst. In five hours and eleven days, I'll come . . . I'll come. . . .

They had become engaged the year before:

————— • —————

We decided to get engaged in July—the seventh day of the seventh month. It was my mother's lucky number so I guessed it must be mine too. And we drove down to Hamburg to celebrate the engagement party with my Aunt Mutti. I remember I was very pleased with my design of the engagement rings. Real platinum. Very romantic. Outside the ring, two lines were engraved all round, always close together, but swinging up and down to show the "ups" and "downs" you expect of marriage, but never breaking.

I remember we took a special trip to the little church in Hamburg where my mother and father had been married, and ex- changed our rings there.

In those old-fashioned days in Sweden in the thirties, you got engaged for a year to see if you really suited each other. And I wanted to get married on the seventh day of the seventh month with a seven at the end of the year as well. But the Swedish picture I was working on, a comedy called *Dollar,* directed by Gustav, overran so we had to move the date to the tenth.

There was only one little bit of trouble at our wedding. Petter was very much against any kind of publicity. He wanted a nice, quiet, private ceremony.

Imagine his irritation when he found someone hiding in the bushes in Papa Lindstrom's own front garden all ready to snap pictures and write an article. Someone hauled her out and Petter was being very stern when Papa Lindstrom came out and said, "Petter, my boy, you musn't talk like that to a young lady on your wedding day—I mean, good manners. Now, young lady, will you please come in and have a cup of coffee with us."

So in came Bang—her real name was Barbro Alving, but she's always written under the name of Bang—and I discovered it was her very first writing assignment, and my very first wedding, so we had something in common. We chatted away and became good friends, and we've been good friends ever since.

Petter and I had set up house first of all in a small apartment in Stockholm, and our friend Mollie Faustman gave us a small black cat which proceeded to scratch the place to pieces. We lived very happily together. We had a maid and I didn't do much cooking because I've never been either attracted to it or any good at it. I realized years later in Hollywood that I had to take some interest when my daughter came in saying, "Mummy, I've got to learn how to boil an egg. How do you boil an egg?" And as I wasn't very clear about it, I decided it was about time that at least I bought a cookbook. But housework I was very good at. The scrubbing and cleaning of a house or apartment from top to bottom has always satisfied my Scandinavian soul. One of my friends always says, "How you've wasted all these years being an actress when you could have been the best charwoman in the business."

Petter and I went about our careers as if we were going to live "happily ever after." He had a very successful dental practice, and was studying for his doctor's degree—he'd completed three years of it by the time war broke out—and I was a successful young actress. We had lots of mutual friends: in the literary world, Bang and Mollie Faustman, a journalist and painter, Einar Nerman who even then was a very famous cartoonist, many friends in films and the theater. We both worked very hard, we were deeply in love and in the natural course of events I became pregnant. Not that I intended something as normal as the "natural course of events" to stop me making films.

Of course I knew that having made a little success in my own country, Swedish pictures were not the beginning and end of acting. In fact there was no way I was going to remain in Sweden. The world was too big and wide and inviting. There was a place called Hollywood with all those talented directors, and big budgets and big movies. But I also knew that my experience and my English were not good enough for that yet. And in the thirties there were all those marvelous French movies and wonderful actors; however, my French wasn't so good either. But German was my second language. And after Petter and I were married, I did get an offer from UFA in Berlin.

It was in this period too that I learned something new about Petter: his real concern for me. I was in Berlin for the UFA screen test. I was feeling very lonely and very lost in the hotel when I went down to the reception, and there, down in the lobby, not quite hiding behind a newspaper, was Petter! I was so happy. He had come down to take care of me. He said, "I suddenly realized how lonely you'd be on your own, and how nervous, because you don't know how to handle people. So I thought I'd better be around just in case. But don't tell anybody I'm here, because I know these film people. They don't want husbands around. But I am here if you need me. You've got to act like a young actress confident enough to stand on her own two feet. That's what they expect you to be."

So Petter stayed in a third-rate hotel across the street, and I stayed in this luxury hotel at the film's expense. He realized even then that a husband might be an obstacle in a movie actress's career.

Of course you can look at it from the other viewpoint and say that he *should* have let me go; that he should have taught me to be on my own. Because, in fact, he so tied me down by being helpful that for the rest of my life I've been helpless without a man to tell me what to do. Except when I'm doing my own work, that is. When I'm on stage, or in front of that camera, nobody can tell me anything except the director because I know instinctively what to do, and, I think, how to do it. But in my private life, if anyone asks "Do you want this room or that room?" I don't care. Or, "Would you like fish or meat?" I don't know. It's not important to me. You choose for me.

Men make women helpless by deciding and telling them what to do. Men in my life taught me to be dependent, beginning with my father, and after that Uncle Otto, who didn't want me to become an actress, and then Petter, even before our engagement—not that it was Petter's fault. I was the one who asked him for advice and help in those early days.

The UFA contract was for three pictures. The first was called *Die Vier Gesellen (The Four Companions)*. It told the story of four girls who form an advertising agency, and all the trouble they get into with men. It wasn't a big budget film, but it was a new challenge. Could I perform in German? Could I make sense in that language when I was supposed to be shaken by passion, emotion, tears, anger? It was all very well to chatter away in German round a dinner table, but to play dramatically in that language and make an impact? That I had to find out for myself.

Of course, as soon as I began to work in Germany in 1938, I couldn't miss what was happening there. The picture was directed by Karl Fröhlich, and he was a very worried man. I saw very quickly that if you were *anybody* at all in films, you had to be a member of the Nazi Party. As soon as I got into the studio in Berlin I felt the atmosphere. You get an "atmosphere" in every studio: America, Britain, Italy, France, Germany, Sweden. Naturally the difference between an American studio and one in Italy, for example, is the difference between hamburger and spaghetti, but they are both good. Usually there's a good atmosphere because people collect together and enjoy making a movie.

In Berlin, in that year of 1938, the "atmosphere" not only in the film studios, but everywhere else, was frightening.

Karl Fröhlich took me to one of those great Nazi rallies in Berlin to impress me, I suppose. An enormous stadium, floodlights, bands, steel-helmeted storm troopers, Hitler marching in, and dozens of little girls running up all carrying bunches of flowers . . . you still see it all on old newsreels on television. And there's Hitler beaming and kissing them. Then the *Sieg Heil* with their arms stretched out in the Nazi salute. I just looked round in amazement. And Karl Fröhlich almost had a fit. He whispered in sheer terror, "My God you're not doing the Heil Hitler salute!" And I retorted, "Why should I? You're all doing it so well without me."

"You're crazy! You must do it. We're being watched."

"Who's watching us? They're all watching Hitler."

"I'm being watched. Everybody knows who I am. I can't get into trouble because of you. We're under all sorts of pressures. You've got to be very careful how and when you talk. We do *not* make jokes here. It's all very serious. . . ."

I never did raise my arm in a Nazi salute, and later in the privacy of his office I protested, "But I'm a Swedish actress only here for a few weeks."

"That won't help you if it comes to a showdown. You're half-German. These people are ruthless and dangerous. They've got spies and "ears" everywhere. And another thing. If you get an invitation from Dr. Josef Goebbels to tea—and you're pretty certain to get one—you just say "Yes." You don't argue or have a headache. You go! He likes young actresses, and there's no question of discussion. You go!"

"But why should I? I'm not interested in Dr. Goebbels and his tea. I don't know what I could talk to him about. I mean he's—what is he? Minister for Propaganda or something—and I'm just an actress."

Karl Fröhlich got very nervous. It was almost unbelievable to see a man in his position behaving like this. He was really frightened. "If you refuse to go and have tea with him, I shall get into terrible trouble. I really mean that. Don't you understand?"

"No I don't. But I'll see about it when it happens."

I asked other people at the studio what the fuss was all about having to go and take tea with Dr. Goebbels, and they said, "Well he's just very fond of young actresses, and he's not accustomed to anyone saying no."

But I never had to make a decision. I never got an invitation. I wasn't his type. So poor Karl Fröhlich got nervous all for nothing.

That sort of pressure went on all the time in Germany in 1938. I remember my nice dialogue teacher. She was very anti-Hitler. There were certain days—when Hitler was driving by or they declared a Nazi festival—when everybody had to hang the Nazi flag out of the window. She didn't buy a flag. The Nazis came into her flat and said, "Why haven't you hung out your flag?" "I haven't got one," she said. "Then buy one!" they insisted. She said, "I earn very little money by giving German lessons, and I've got a son to take care of...." They said, "That's no excuse. Next time you hang out the flag."

She took no notice. Didn't buy a flag. Came the next flag day, she didn't hang out her flag. The same day all her windows were smashed by stones. She put the glass back, and still didn't buy a flag. Another flag day, no flag; windows smashed again. And now she found out that her little boy was getting beaten up every time he went to school, and she had no answer to that. So she went and bought her flag, repaired her windows, and hung out her flag every time after that. They'd defeated her.

My leading man, Hans Sohnker, also took me to one side and said, "Now listen, Ingrid, listen carefully to me. Do you think we like this situation any more than you do? But what are we to do? Where do we start? People are disappearing all the time. We protest, and we risk not only our own lives, but those of our family and friends. We know the Jews are in a terrible position, but so is anyone else who dares to oppose them. People are sent to these camps. We've no information about them. People whisper, 'Where? What camps? What are we talking about?' But we don't dare to question what they're doing . . . All Germany is scared to death. . . ."

So I wasn't at all sorry to leave Germany. And Karl Fröhlich was very sweet about it, knowing that by this time I was very pregnant and about to burst every dress at the seams, so he hurried the last scenes along.

———————— • ————————

In his small car Petter picked up Ingrid in Berlin and off they sailed through that last summer of peace in a Europe soon to be submerged by the war. It was a memorable summer holiday. First to Paris, where Ingrid visited the actual shop where Charlotte Corday had bought the two-franc knife with which she had stabbed her victim, and then down to Monte Carlo. Young and happy and gay, they swirled around the floor of the Casino at the *thé-dansant,* and as they nibbled their patisserie between the fox-trots and the waltzes, they met two pleasant, middle-aged Swedes. Their fellow countrymen were very complimentary. What a lovely pair they made. How did they manage to dance like that . . . to keep so athletic and slender?

That made Ingrid's holiday. She still laughs at the memory today. "Slender! And there I was—eight months pregnant!"

It was true she was going to be very busy producing a baby, but with her glowing health and strength she would be up and around and rehearsing her dialogue while she fed the baby. And she still had two more contracts with Nazi-dominated UFA.

Back in Sweden, Petter went to the offices of Ingrid's agent, Helmer Enwall, and told him that the UFA contract had to be pushed into a back drawer and if possible cancelled. Under no circumstances were contracts with Nazi Germany to be sought or exchanged. And would Helmer *please* do his utmost to find her an engagement in either England or America—anywhere in fact, outside the doomed geography of central Europe.

———————— • ————————

It was *acting* I had to find. A few offers had already come from Hollywood, but they were just contract offers from Fox and Paramount and RKO and others. Those Hollywood studios had agents all over Europe snapping up anyone who stood out a bit from the others. But they weren't offered *roles* and directors, they were offered *contracts:* which meant the actor or actress was tied down by contract for seven years; shot off to Hollywood, where they might be stuffed into any old film or any old part that the movie bosses thought fit for them. They might spend the entire seven years playing bit-parts as housemaids or butlers. So I said "no" to all of them.

Meanwhile, I was busy getting ready to have my baby. Having a baby seemed to me the most natural thing about being married. It never occurred to me that I shouldn't have a child, or that it would interfere with my career. I was so surprised when I arrived in America that everybody should be shocked that I had had a baby. "A child! You've ruined your figure! You've ruined your image as a beautiful young movie star! And please, *please* don't have any photographs taken with your child, and please don't bring it up in conversation that you're a mother!" In those days the movie stars of Hollywood adopted children if they wanted them; they just didn't have their own.

When I first went across to America I always thought it a bit strange because Petter wanted me to go so much. He was very generous and insistent about the whole thing. If he had said, "I don't want you to go," I certainly wouldn't have gone, because I could never make up my mind in those days without him. I just didn't have an opinion. Or if he'd said, "Stay here. If war breaks out you may be needed as a nurse or something," I would have stayed. Or if he'd said, "We're married, we should stay together, you don't really want to go to Hollywood do you?" I certainly wouldn't have gone. But he said the opposite. He *wanted* me to go to Hollywood to film *Intermezzo—* yes, he'd manage with Pia, and his mother would look after her for the months I would be away.

———————— • ————————

The exact progression of incidents which finally led to Ingrid's first journey to Hollywood is difficult to chart, and certainly many people had a hand in the process. And no matter how much Helmer Enwall was able to help behind the scenes, undoubtedly the main springboard which jetted Ingrid toward success was *Intermezzo.*

Intermezzo was her sixth Swedish film, based upon an idea by Gustav Molander, who collaborated on the script, and also directed. It was made in 1936. It was the picture which in due course turned Ingrid from an actress into a world-famous star. Ingrid played the role of a lovely, lonely, and talented piano teacher who falls in love with the world-famous and happily married violinist, Gösta Ekman.

Dear, dear Book. This is June 19, 1936. My admiration for Gösta is pretty well unbearable. Gustav Molander is often so sick of him and that I can understand, but for me he is still God Almighty himself. Now *Intermezzo* is finished. Gösta says I am a big star, and Gustav is very very happy with me, and sent flowers and a note which said, "You lift and clean and beautify my movie."

I got an enormous bouquet. Forty carnations—I counted them—because they thought I had done so well. That last evening when the last scenes were shot, Gösta said he was going to miss me very much. He was very happy that we hadn't got tired of each other; at least he was not tired of me. We said good-bye. I kissed him and gave him a big hug. I write this in detail because I am so full of him. I will remember everything he said to me. I don't want to work with other people, only with him. I know he is married and twenty years older than me. I know he has a son exactly my own age, born in August too. Once I thought, If only I could marry his son, that would be heaven.

I have sent him a monkey—not a real one—as a gift. If only he could understand how much I like him. I hope the monkey tells it for me. Dear God, I thank you for your goodness in allowing me to know this wonderful man.

The movie reveals how they drift into a passionate but hopeless love affair, which, after intense heart-searching and unhappiness, is finally resolved when Gösta returns to his wife and children. Rinsed in a wash of soft violin chords and romantic pianoforte, the lovers are slightly dented by the experience but facing the future with firm chin and misty, optimistic eyes.

It was the old eternal-triangle story, but nevertheless it touched an answering chord in the breasts of millions of viewers who had either suffered, or would have liked to have suffered, the same agonies.

Interviewed many years later, Gustav Molander said, yes, it would be easy for him to take the credit for discovering Ingrid Bergman. Yes, he'd made her first film test. Yes, he'd encouraged her to stay in pictures. Yes, he'd got the idea and written and directed *Intermezzo*.

"She always moved with wonderful grace and self-control," he said. "She spoke her lines beautifully and her radiant beauty struck me the first time I saw her. She appreciated compliments, accepted them shyly, but they never altered the three totally original characteristics of her work: truth, naturalness, and fantasy. I created *Intermezzo* for her, but I was not responsible for its success. Ingrid herself made it successful through her performance.

"The truth is, nobody discovered her. Nobody launched her. She discovered herself."

Dear Book. 12 January 1938. Gösta Ekman is dead. How is it possible that I shall never see him again, never talk to him again? That man who has meant so much to me in my work—my beloved Gösta. He has been sick since the New Year. Every day I have followed the newspaper reports, and hoped and prayed that he would recover.

Now he has gone. It feels so empty. It is as if my beloved Thalia had disappeared. I can find no words for my grief. Dear God, give him peace and help us poor people who must live without him.

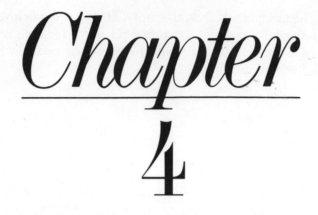

Chapter 4

When the Swedish version of *Intermezzo,* with subtitles, arrived in New York and Hollywood, the Los Angeles *Daily News* made the bold announcement that not only was it the best picture ever sent by Sweden to the United States, but as good if not better than anything Hollywood now had on the entertainment market: "Miss Bergman not only has beauty, a quality common enough in Hollywood, but she is endowed with an emotional intensity which is extremely rare. This combination makes her a person who could easily develop into a great actress: even a star. Hollywood producers ought to form a pool to bring her out to this country, if only to keep her out of Swedish pictures which are getting altogether too good."

Whether or not David Selznick ever read the review or had it brought to his attention is difficult to ascertain, but certainly around this time he was dispatching a directive to Katherine Brown, the story editor and talent spotter who ran his New York office, to intensify her search for good foreign films which Selznick International could remake for the American market.

Kay Brown worked at 230 Park Avenue. Among the employees in that building was a young Swedish elevator boy, whose immigrant parents had raved one night about a new Swedish picture *Intermezzo* and a new young star Ingrid Bergman. Knowing that Miss Brown was professionally interested in such things, he dutifully reported his parents' conversation to her when she entered his elevator the next morning. Perhaps Kay Brown was influenced by this information; she did see a screening of the film and wrote to David Selznick.

"I reported on *Intermezzo* to David as story material," she said, "but I did not go overboard about it. But I went *madly* overboard about the girl. I thought she was the beginning and end of all things wonderful. So I sent the film out to David. In those early days we were such a small and friendly organization, and with our coast-to-coast teletype communication we could insult each other with love and affection. David said to his friends in Hollywood, 'You know that crazy dame I've got in New York? I send her out to discover possible remakes of foreign films, and she goes crazy about one of the girls in a movie, and passes up one of the best screen stories in the world.'

"I never did think it one of the best screen stories in the world, but I was sent to London, where an agency held the screen rights, to buy them, but not to get Ingrid. I bought the rights without much trouble, and since I was there with Jock Whitney—the Chairman of the Board of Selznick International—who'd also seen *Intermezzo* and, naturally enough, had also fallen in love with Ingrid Bergman —we thought we might at least try and get in touch with her. So there we were in Claridge's Hotel with a pocketful of small change trying to get through to Sweden. Finally I did get through to Petter Lindstrom, and he said very politely, 'Miss Bergman is busy at the moment and cannot talk to you,' which was reasonable enough because—although we didn't know it at the time—Ingrid was busy having her baby. So both Jock and I went back to New York. There were no quick plane trips like these days. Five days each way over a wild Atlantic Ocean in mid-November. And no sooner was I back in my flat than I got a wire from David: Return to Sweden and get Ingrid Bergman. David had changed his mind.

"He also wired: 'In connection with terms for her, I might point out that she was not even starred in Sweden since the title of *Intermezzo* stars Gösta Stevens and Gustav Molander. A cold shudder has just run through me on the realization that maybe we are dealing with the wrong girl. Maybe the girl we are after is Gösta Stevens. You had better check on this. . . .'

"I did check on this and found that the 'girl,' Gösta Stevens, was in fact the *man* who collaborated with director Gustav Molander on the screenplay, and neither had starred in the picture. So I go back to London, and through our contact get a lawyer, and we fly to Stockholm through the most horrible snowstorm, and of course those little planes weren't pressurized in those days, and it was very very cold, and my ears won't stand it. My face and neck swell up, and I'm sitting in my hotel room and I'm so sick I'm just ready to die. Then there's a knock at my door and I go to open it and there are those two lovely people, Petter and Ingrid. Ingrid has on a dark beaver coat and hat and, with that beautiful high coloring she has, she looks absolutely divine. She's carrying a small bouquet of yellow and blue flowers—the Swedish colors—and she's so sweet and shy, as she says 'Welcome to Sweden.' Then they announce that they can't have dinner with me, because they have to go off to relatives; but two nights later when we know each other better, they admit they really had no place to go, but were just scared to death at the thought of meeting me, and feeling the way I did, and the way I looked, I wasn't surprised.

"Next day I go out to her home and meet Helmer Enwall, the agent, and a lawyer, and we start to talk about the contract. Ingrid doesn't say a word, but sits in the chair and smiles and goes on knitting clothes for the new baby. I wrangle about the contract, and the lawyer just sits around waiting to write down what we decide. The third day we go on wrangling about the contract, but we are getting to like each other better now. So we sign a one-picture contract with the right of an option to do another picture if everything works out.

"Selznick wanted the usual seven-year contract, but he'd never met Petter Lindstrom and that was no go with Petter; he was just going to see how things worked out.

"Toward the end of that visit I looked around and I thought, Oh, God, I'm taking this sweet and innocent girl away. This is her home, maybe it's not going to work, leaving her husband and baby like this. . . . You can't conceive that childlike air of innocence which surrounded her. I can remember having terrible qualms about what I was doing to this wonderful young couple, and you know you feel a personal responsibility if you're a half-decent citizen, if you do a thing like that. . . ."

———————— • ————————

I remember Kay told me that the producer was David Selznick who'd made *The Prisoner of Zenda, A Star Is Born, A Tale of Two Cities, Rebecca,* and *Gone With the Wind,* and that they were hoping to get Willie Wyler, one of the most distinguished directors in Hollywood, and that Leslie Howard was playing the lead opposite me. And I remember when I was with her alone, she said, "You know you've got a lovely home and a lovely baby. You're happy here. If I were you I would think it over very carefully." I thought it was so nice of her giving me that advice. And I said, "Well if there are people as nice as you in America and in Hollywood, then I'm sure I shall like it, so I shall go, and take the risk."

———— • ————

Certainly if David Selznick had known Kay Brown was offering his potential clients such advice he would have dropped her off the top of the Empire State Building.

Small and slender, with a shrewd head, a keen sense of humor, and a warm heart, Kay Brown became Ingrid's firm friend from that moment on, and when Ingrid arrived in New York on the *Queen Mary* on May 6, 1939, she was there to meet her.

———— • ————

Kay took care of me, installed me in the Chatham Hotel, showed me the city, and suggested that I stay for a couple of weeks to brush up my English, or rather brush up my American, because as soon as I arrived I realized I'd made one terrible mistake. In Stockholm I'd taken lessons from a language teacher from *England.* Now I was a Swede with an *English* accent, and I almost died when I arrived in New York and didn't understand *one word* the Americans were saying. So I said to Kay, "I've got to do something drastic about this. Every night I'm going to the theater, and I'm going to sit through three acts listening to *every* word they speak, so that I learn fast."

"Good idea," says Kay. So I ask in the hotel lobby about plays and they tell me that something called *Tobacco Road* has been running for ages, and it's a great success. Of course what they don't tell me is that it's set in the deep South, in hillbilly country, and I sit there and I don't understand *one word* of the dialect in which they're speaking.

I breathe deeply and next morning I go down to the hotel lobby again, and tell them that *Tobacco Road* wasn't quite right for me so this time can they recommend something more *American*? Why surely they can. What can be more American than Raymond Massey in a play called *Abraham Lincoln*? American from start to finish. So I go off for a second time and nearly have another seizure, because I can't understand a word of this play either. It's played in mid-nineteenth century dialect, nothing like the American language I've heard in the movies, and at this rate I'm going to arrive in Hollywood speaking in sign language.

I panicked quite a bit and rushed off to tell Kay Brown all about it. She laughed her head off, but she did choose a few plays for me after that, and I began to understand the words, but even Kay was quite worried about my accent and my general lack of English.

———————— • ————————

During her two weeks in New York the indefatigable Ingrid filled every day seeing films and plays, and one morning took a bus out to the World's Fair where she started systematically in one corner at nine and walked through every hall examining every exhibit, ending her tour at eleven at night.

By this time, Kay Brown had received a memo from David Selznick on the procedure to be adopted with Ingrid:

> I had a talk with Mr. Whitney today on the subject of changing Miss Bergman's name and asked him to discuss it further with you. Since talking with him a few other thoughts occurred to me in connection with the subject.
>
> I think you ought to check with a couple of foreign departments as to the value of her present name abroad. Of course there is nothing whatsoever to prevent our using her own name abroad and the new name every place else —or at least it doesn't seem to me that there is anything against this, but this point might be checked too. . . .
>
> If we change her name for only part of the world, then I think we can forget the idea of simply changing the spelling of it, because I don't think Ingrid Berjman is a particularly good name either. Ingrid Berriman is a lot better but certainly this is no name you would go out of the way to tack on to a personality either.
>
> Ingrid Lindstrom is also, I think, hard to remember. Perhaps the best thing to do would be to wait until she gets here, in accordance with the first paragraph of your letter. I don't think we ought to go into any big publicity campaign in advance of her appearance for us for several reasons including the possibility of resentment against us

as a company for importing another foreigner after the agitation concerning Vivien Leigh; and also because building up on foreign importations has reached a point where the American public resents the players when they do appear. I think it a lot better to let them sneak in, more or less in the manner of Hedy Lamarr, who was discovered by the public through her appearance in *Algiers* rather than through any advance publicity build-up. I think that the best thing to do would be to import her quietly into the studio, go about our business of making the picture with only such publicity attendant upon her casting as would be the case with any unimportant leading woman, and then feed an important and favorable public reception of her when the picture is finished.

With this policy in mind, I think we should avoid interviews with her at the boat and should let her arrive in Los Angeles very quietly, which will give us the opportunity to discuss a change of name with her after she arrives at the studio. . . .

———————— • ————————

Kay and I caught the train across America to Los Angeles, and there was no David Selznick on the platform to meet me. In my foolishness I thought he would be waiting there to meet me with open arms; I mean, I've come all the way from Sweden and now this long journey across America, and no Mr. Selznick, only some publicity man who puts us in a limousine, and we're driven out to Hollywood to the Selznick home. Apparently I am to stay there for a day or two. That was an odd thing for them to do, because the Selznicks didn't usually have actors and actresses, just arrived, stay in their home. But maybe Irene Selznick felt sorry for this poor unprotected naïve little girl from Sweden who couldn't cope and couldn't speak English very well, and who might get lost in the Beverly Hills Hotel.

Kay and I walk across the lawn where Irene Selznick is sitting. She's listening to the radio and there's a horse race in progress, and I say, "How do you do," in my best English, and Irene gives a loud, "Ssssshh," because she's listening to the race. So I sit down and think, I've come halfway round the world to listen to a horse race, and get shushed when I open my mouth.

Kay and I sit very quietly while Irene hears if her horse has won, then she turns around and says, "How do you do," and "Would you like something to eat?" and she is very nice. Then Kay leaves and I begin my plaintive, "Where is Mr. Selznick?"

"He's at the studio. Now come along, I'll show you the guest room."

I carry my one suitcase up the stairs, and Irene says, "Are your trunks coming later?"

Now, as I've explained, my English, at the moment, isn't very good, and I have my dictionary with me all the time. Trunks? What is that. I look up trunk and I decide it cannot have anything to do with elephants or with trees, and it must be this bit to do with luggage. I reply, "I have no trunks, this is my luggage."

"But you're coming to stay for three months?"

"Yes."

"Do you think you have enough clothes with you?"

"But what do I need clothes for? I'm going to be in the studio all day and I'm going to work. I have my costumes for the movie, and we work six days a week, and for Sunday I have a bathing suit and a pair of slacks. So what do I need clothes for?"

"Well, I'm giving a party for you tomorrow night where I'm going to introduce you to all our friends in Hollywood. Do you have an evening dress?"

"Oh, yes. In my last picture I wore a very nice evening dress and after the film I bought it from the film company secondhand. I have it in my suitcase."

"Good, and you have your make-up box?"

"Make-up box? What is that?" I go back to the dictionary, and I can't find make-up box, but at last I understand.

"I don't have a make-up box because I do not use make-up."

"You mean you have nothing on your face?"

"No."

"Oh," said Irene. "Welcome to Hollywood."

"Thank you. Is Mr. Selznick coming home soon?"

"Mr. Selznick often works late at the studio. He's very busy at the moment making a film called *Gone With the Wind*. He'll be along later." Then Irene says, "I have a dinner engagement at the Beachcomber tonight with Grace Moore, Miriam Hopkins, and Richard Barthelmess. You'd better come along with me."

Now that sounded very exciting: all those famous names, real movie stars, even though I was still worrying at the back of my mind, why Mr. Selznick didn't come home for dinner.

We arrived at the Beachcomber, and I'd never been in a place before which was so dark, and I'd never seen such rum drinks before . . . and we drank them out of *pineapples* and *coconuts*! Then as I peered through the darkness, it seemed to get a bit lighter, and my God, there was Grace Moore sitting *with us.* Then Richard Barthelmess arrived and Irene introduced me to everyone as the new actress from Sweden. I sat next to Irene so that she could help me with my English and we started talking about acting, and it came up that I'm tall. I said, "I'm very tall," and Richard Barthelmess said, "You don't look very tall to me." I said, "Not sitting down I don't, but my legs are very long." When we were ready to leave, Richard Barthelmess stood up first, and as I started to get up, he said again, "You don't look very tall to me, no you're not *all* that tall." And I said, "I haven't finished yet, wait till I straighten up, I'm still bent." Then I came right up and I was a full head taller than he, and I realized that they were all very short. I also realized that this was going to be a shock to everybody—that I was so tall.

After dinner we went back to Miriam Hopkins's house. She had a lot more people waiting there for a movie in her private projection room. I'd never heard of such a thing before. Down from the ceiling came the screen, and the projection room was behind a painting. We all sat round on cushions on the floor and watched the movie. And I kept saying to Irene, "Where is Mr. Selznick, isn't he going to have any dinner at all?" And Irene would reply, "Oh, he'll be along soon, don't worry." Then I became so interested in the movie I forgot all about Mr. Selznick, until I felt a hand on my shoulder, and heard a man's voice saying: "Mr. Selznick has arrived and he's in the kitchen eating, and he'd like to see you."

I got up, and I thought, Finally, I'm going to meet my boss. I walked out to the kitchen and I suppose it must have been about one o'clock in the morning, and there was this man lying *on* the table . . . well it looked to me as if he was lying half across it, and he was shoveling food into his mouth. As I came in the door he glanced across at me, and said, "God! Take your shoes off."

Of course already I was feeling self-conscious about my height, so I said, "It won't help, I'm wearing very flat-heeled shoes."

He made a sort of groan, and I thought, Here we go again. I'm going to be some sort of freak. I said, "Do you mind if I sit down?" And he said, "Of course not. How was your trip?"

And then, after a pause—"Of course you realize your name's impossible."

"Is it? Why?"

"Well the first name to start with. We can't pronounce it. You'd be called Ein-grid, and Bergman is impossible too. Far too German. There's obviously trouble with Germany coming up, and we don't want anybody to think we've hired a German actress. Of course there's your married name, Lindstrom, that's very close to Lind-bergh—Charles Lindbergh, the great flier. He's a great favorite in this country at the moment; his nickname is Lindy, maybe you could take that name?"

I was very cold to that. I said, "I don't want anybody else's nickname. In fact I don't want to change my name at all. My name is Ingrid Bergman, that's the name I was born with, and that's what I'm going to be called in America, and people will just have to learn how to pronounce it. If I change it and they don't like me in America, how foolish I shall look going home to Sweden with a new name."

Mr. Selznick thought about that, and ate some more food, and said, "Well, we'll discuss that in the morning. Now what about make-up, because your eyebrows are too thick, and your teeth are no good, and there are lots of other things. . . . I'll take you to the make-up department in the morning and we'll see what they can do. . . ."

Now it was my turn to think. I said, "I think you've made a big mistake, Mr. Selznick. You shouldn't have bought the pig in the sack. I thought you saw me in the movie *Intermezzo,* and liked me, and sent Kay Brown across to Sweden to get me. Now you've seen me, you want to change everything. So I'd rather not do the movie. We'll say no more about it. No trouble of any kind. We'll just forget it. I'll take the next train and go back home."

I don't really know why I took such a strong line. After all, I was only twenty-three years old, and I was used to doing what men told me to do, and I don't know where I got the courage to say, "no," to everything he said.

The minute he began to talk about publicity, I said, "No, I don't want to do that. It's not my way of doing things."

So we just sat there staring at each other.

He had stopped eating now.

Chapter 5

David Selznick was six feet tall with dark glossy hair, a face and figure which tended to sag in congenial places as he fought a constant and losing battle against a weight problem, bright inquisitive blue eyes behind thick glasses, and an intense charm illustrated by his proposal of marriage to his beloved Irene, daughter of movie magnate Louis B. Mayer, in a letter which deserves to be preserved in any compendium of true love letters. After discussing various film matters, he added, seemingly as an afterthought,

> I've been thinking of you and decided to marry you if you'll have me. I'm middle-aged to be sure; I have a hammer toe and I run into things; I'm ex-arrogant, and once I wanted to be a big shot; I snore loudly, drink exuberantly, cuddle (i.e. snuggle) expansively, work excessively, play enthusiastically, and my future is drawing to a close, but I'm tall and Jewish and I do love you. David-in-quest-of-his-Mate.

From 1926 onward he worked his way up through Metro-Goldwyn-Mayer, RKO, and Paramount. In 1936 he formed his own independent film company, Selznick International, and joined the select coterie of successful movie moguls. By that time he probably knew as much about the industry as anybody else on earth, and with boundless energy and enthusiasm made certain that everyone around him was also aware of it. He rewrote scripts, lectured producers, instructed directors, nagged actors, interfered endlessly with every department under his control to a degree which drove many people to the edge of a nervous breakdown—as if to justify his oft-quoted maxims: "Great films are made in their every detail according to the vision of one man, not in buying part of what he has done. . . ." And . . . "nothing matters but the final picture." His application was endless, his attention to detail phenomenal, and he had that rare talent of all gifted impresarios of extracting from creative people their maximum contribution. He was, undoubtedly, lightly brushed with genius. Indeed, as he stared owlishly at the big blond Swedish girl who was probably the first woman in movie history to say "No-o-o" in three different cadences to *everything* he said, he was then in the process of making almost simultaneously Daphne Du Maurier's *Rebecca,* which became an immense hit, and *Gone With the Wind* which, few dispute, was the best film ever produced in Hollywood.

Now at the height of his fame, David Selznick followed the old Hollywood tradition of not only finding stars but of "making" them. To import a famous New York or London stage actor, a leading player in his or her world, did not necessarily guarantee success. But it *was* possible, by following hunches, manipulating, exaggerating, and even inventing facial changes, mannerisms, and physical attributes, to manufacture a star.

Only a few years before Ingrid's arrival in Hollywood, electrolysis removed an inch of hairline from the forehead of a pretty young girl of Spanish descent, thus giving her an extraordinary beauty which, allied with her natural ability, and backed by skillful exploitation, produced Rita Hayworth. No doubt such thoughts had duly registered in David Selznick's subconscious as he stared ruminatingly across the kitchen at the rounded and happy features of Ingrid Bergman. But short of sawing her off at the knees, there seemed little he could do to improve her. Then suddenly he was struck by an apocalyptic vision: a simple idea but as vital to David Selznick's scheme as the gravitationally inspired apple which dropped on Newton's head.

———————— • ————————

Suddenly he became very quiet. He looked at me very hard, and he said, "I've got an idea that's so simple and yet no one in Hollywood has ever tried it before. Nothing about you is going to be touched. Nothing altered. You remain yourself. You are going to be the first "natural" actress. Tomorrow morning I'm taking you to the make-up department myself, and we're going to work this all out."

Next morning I was sitting in the make-up chair and this highly qualified make-up man was looking at me and uttering "Ums" and "Ahs" . . . "These eyebrows have got to be plucked, and there're some wrinkles here that need attention, and we'll need caps on these teeth because they're a bit uneven and stand out a trifle." And a lot of important publicity men were standing around looking serious, and thinking up all sorts of new gimmicks. And after the make-up man had said all this, and the publicity men had said their piece, David Selznick went mad. He yelled: "Understand this, you are not going to take one eyebrow or one hair away. You are not going to do *anything*. If you alter anything at all I'll kill you. We're testing her tomorrow and we're testing her just like that, just like she is. Her name's going to be her *real* name, because no one in Hollywood's history has ever used their real name before. And above all, there are going to be no interviews . . . no *interviews*. And no pictures! She's under wraps. You understand?"

They understood, and I was glad David had said what he did, because I'd spent a lot of time at that kitchen table last night saying, "I don't want to be sold like they've sold so many other actresses from Europe. . . . Here's the greatest star that Poland or France or Bulgaria has ever produced. They're marvelous at this and marvelous at that. And six months later they've disappeared. No one ever hears of them again. They just couldn't live up to the publicity, and they're killed stone dead before they start. Why don't we just make a movie? Let the movie come out, and then if people decide they like me, you can do the publicity and I'll give interviews. But let me try and creep into the affection of the American public, not crash in like a brass band." And he thought about that and said, "Yes, okay. I like that . . . yes, I like that."

Next day we did the test. I've seen it, because after David Selznick's death many years later, they made a movie about him and his work, and they asked me to take part in it and talk about him, and there was the test: "Ingrid Bergman—No Make-up—Take 1." Bang goes the clapper board, and there I am so red in the face it's unbelievable, because I blushed at everything they said to me, or if they flattered me. So that, plus the heat of the lamps, and the excitement of working in Hollywood, meant that even the simplest dialogue made me blush. In those days they were filming in black and white and they were just forced to put a cover over me so I wouldn't look dark, like a live lobster.

That same night the Selznicks had a party and I was the guest of honor. I sat on a couch all by myself in my secondhand dress, which I thought was very smart with its pink top and all sorts of colors mixed up in the skirt, big balloon sleeves, and a belt. I sat there looking at all these people as they came in: Clark Gable, Joan Bennett, Cary Grant, Gary Cooper. I didn't need anyone to talk to, I was just stupefied with happiness, just looking. And now and then Irene Selznick passed by, and I'd ask, "Who's that over there?" And she'd say, "It's so-and-so, he's a famous director." Then one group stood near my couch and I was introduced to Ann Sheridan, who was apparently the "Oomph" girl. I didn't know what "oomph" meant but I thought I had better find out and so at the first available moment I slipped up to my room and opened the dictionary. But I couldn't find "oomph" with one "o" or two "o's" so I guess I never knew what "oomph" meant. And then I realized that there was a man sitting on the couch next to me, and he was being very nice and sympathetic, but I couldn't really understand what he was being sympathetic about. He said, "Don't let this get you down. We all came to Hollywood for the first time, and it was hard for all of us. . . ."

I said, "Get me down? I'm so happy I can't believe it. All these famous people, and I can sit here and see them all in real life. Look, Norma Shearer, Claudette Colbert, and look who's coming in now . . . Ronald Colman! I just can't believe I'm here!"

Of course he'd heard the conversation going on at the bar and I hadn't, and I wouldn't know about it for several years to come, so he went on trying to cheer me up. "Well, they don't talk to you now," he said, "but they will later on. We've all gone through this. And just to start you off, next Sunday I'm giving a party, and won't you come and join us? A pool party, we eat around the pool . . . just bring your bathing suit."

I thought that was wonderful, he actually had a swimming pool. And I said, "I'd love to come and I'd better know your name?" "I'm Ernst Lubitsch," he said. So that was very nice, because I knew he was a famous director.

One thing did slightly concern me, and I asked Irene about it. "But where's Leslie Howard?" I said, and she almost dropped down dead. "Oh, my God, we forgot to invite him." And I said, "But he's my leading man and the one person I wanted to meet and you haven't invited him!" "Oh, don't worry," said Irene, "you'll meet him on the set soon enough."

Of course I did meet Leslie Howard, and I thought he was a wonderful person, but I never got to know him very well. He had this English reserve, and he was never the type of person who went out to have a drink or who frequented parties. He was very much by himself. I never met his wife. His wife was in Hollywood and they had a house, but he was always with his secretary. She was a lovely young woman and apparently he was very much in love with her. And she was killed in an air raid in London, and he died in an air crash shortly afterwards, so only tragedy was lying ahead for Leslie Howard.

But if I'd known what was going on with all the loud talkers around the bar, I'd have fallen through the floor too. The general topic of conversation was that David Selznick had just bought himself a nice big healthy Swedish cow. If David thought that this girl had even the remotest potential of becoming a second Garbo, then here was a thousand dollars to prove he didn't know what he was talking about . . . that sort of thing. Actress? Look at the size of her! Yes, she could play a Swedish masseuse, or maybe a cook or a Swedish laundress. But I'll lay you another thousand she'll never even rate in a "B" picture.

David Selznick got so mad he almost exploded. All these idiots doubting *his* judgment. . . . Right, he'd take that bet, and the other bet, and any bet of any size they'd like to lay. And he'd raise them twice the amount of any bet they made. The bet was that within one year, that girl Ingrid Bergman sitting on the couch would be a star celebrity. And if they didn't accept their *own* appraisal of that fact he'd pay up.

I wasn't a star in under a year but I guess they'd forgotten the bets by that time, and anyway I sat there, smiling happily at everybody, and enjoying myself enormously, not understanding a great deal of what was going on. I left Irene Selznick's house a week later and I went into a house David Selznick had rented for me. I had a young woman who took care of me; drove the car, cooked the food, took me to the studio, and brought me home again. On the next Sunday I told this girl I was invited to Ernst Lubitsch's party and was taking my bathing suit and we were all going to eat around the pool, and would she drive me there? We found the address and off we went. When we arrived, the place was packed with cars, so

I got out and she tried to park in the drive. I walked into this wonderful hall where people were having such fun talking, drinking, and laughing, and then through to the living room where other people were having fun, talking, laughing, drinking. And I asked one of the waiters, "Where is Mr. Lubitsch?" "Oh," he said, "I think he's probably by the pool in the garden."

I walked through the den, then through the library, and into the drawing room. Finally, after going through a lot of rooms I got out into the garden. Everybody was swimming, and jumping into the pool, and laughing and drinking, all having so much fun. I continued to walk around until I saw another waiter. "Is Mr. Lubitsch here?" I asked. "Well he was here, maybe he's back in the house now," he said. I walked around the garden and there they were playing tennis. Then I went back into the house and I walked through all the rooms—through the bedrooms where girls were powdering their noses—and came back into the big hall again. No Mr. Lubitsch anywhere. I went out into the drive where my young woman had just managed to get the car parked, and I said, "We're going home."

I never found Mr. Lubitsch.

The first Monday in the studio I was introduced to Ruth Roberts. And David Selznick said, "Now this is your language coach. And this is the woman you're going to live with, eat with, and sleep with; you're going to stay with her day and night, because you're going to get your accent and dialogue from her."

I thought, Oh God, what a bore! But I hadn't been with Ruth for more than a few hours when I realized how wrong I was. Ruth was Swedish too, but she didn't reveal that until much later. And it was strange that within those first few weeks I'd met the women who were to become three of the main pillars of my life: Kay Brown, Irene Selznick, and Ruth Roberts.

I adored Kay from the time she came to Sweden, and after all the discussion about the contract and whether I should or shouldn't take it up. And Irene took one look at me and I suppose from that first moment of the single suitcase and my secondhand evening dress, she knew she had one of the world's leading innocents on her hands. She decided she had better instruct me on the wicked ways of Hollywood and how to duck or side-step.

"I think you should stay here a few days with us," she had said. So we sat up every night and she trained me for what I could expect in Hollywood; for she had seen so many actresses just go under, "You'll meet all these famous producers," she went on, "at least that's how they'll describe themselves, even though they've never been inside a studio in their lives. You'll find they've got the finest role on earth just waiting for you, and they'll go on, 'Now what about some publicity shots on the beach to start with.' "

You weren't naked in those days; it was thought a bit shocking even if you were photographed in a low-cut bathing suit. I was instructed in all these things; being offered this great role over dinner, and what about a nightcap in his flat afterwards. As it turned out I was fortunate, and I got the parts without any of this. But Irene was very wise and very helpful. She knew what she was talking about. I recognized it all as it was coming toward me, and said, "no."

You see I was not very beautiful when I was young, and I didn't belong to that group of actresses who were sexy, who had "it." I wasn't a sweater girl or a bathing belle. All the interviews referred to me as "the girl next door." And I suppose that meant natural, and down-to-earth, which of course is quite normal nowadays, but in the late thirties in Hollywood not at all the vogue.

I liked Irene immensely, and David too when I got to know him. He was especially enchanting when he'd had a few drinks, and you were at his home and he was entertaining friends. He'd never stop talking and it was such interesting talk. He was so full of ideas. And he'd never let you leave. If you said, "I'm tired, I think it's about time I went," he'd rush to the door, hold his arms out wide to prevent you getting out, and say, "You're not going home. I won't let you. I've just had this marvelous new idea for you." So you'd stay and listen and it usually was a marvelous idea which left you pretty excited.

Next morning you'd say, "That was a pretty good idea you had last night, David. Now what are we going to do about it?" And he'd look at you through his big glasses and say, "What idea? I don't remember any idea."

That first morning I arrived on the set and I was sitting in the trailer with Ruth Roberts going over the dialogue for the opening shot, when I heard what seemed to be a big argument going on outside. I looked through the door and there was David Selznick with Willie Wyler who was supposed to be directing the film. They were indeed having a big argument. They hadn't even called me for the first scene yet, so I said to Ruth, "Now look at these two, what is the matter with them? . . ." Then I saw Willie Wyler going past our door like a tornado, and there was a great slam as he went through some other door. I peeped out and said to David Selznick, "What happened?"

"Oh," he said cheerfully, "you've just lost your director."

My very first morning on a Hollywood film set and I've lost my director because David's had a big row with him!

Of course when I got to know David Selznick better I realized that this was typical of his behavior. He had to do everything himself. He interfered with everybody. That was David.

———————— • ————————

David Selznick was soon intrigued by Ingrid. Especially on the set. At last he had found someone who matched his own conception of what every actor or actress should be prepared to do for art. His memo to his publicity director reveals his admiration:

June 22nd 1939

Dear Mr. Herbert,

I think there is a publicity angle on Ingrid Bergman which could be wisely built up and which could be used with her for years.

Miss Bergman is the most completely conscientious actress with whom I have ever worked, in that she thinks of absolutely nothing but her work before and during the time she is doing a picture, and makes no engagements of any kind and no plans that for one minute distract her from her picture work. She practically never leaves the studio, and even suggested that her dressing room be equipped so that she could live there during the picture. She never for a minute suggests quitting at six o'clock or anything of the kind, and, on the contrary, is very unhappy if the company does not work until midnight, claiming that she does her best work in the evenings after a long day's work.

More to the point of my first paragraph, she is simply frantic about spending any of the company's money. She was terribly upset about a dress being thrown out because the test proved it was not becoming to her, and suggested that perhaps a new collar could be built for it to make it more attractive, or that it could be dyed, or that something else could be done with it so that the money wouldn't be wasted.

She was amazed about having a stand-in and said that despite the fact that she was starred in ten pictures in Sweden she has never had a stand-in and did all the standing-in for lights, etc., herself.

Because of having four stars in *Gone With the Wind*, our star dressing room suites were all occupied and we had to assign her a smaller suite. She went into ecstasies over it and she said she had never had such a suite in her life.

When I found it necessary to switch cameramen, taking a staff man (Harry Stradling) off *Intermezzo* and putting him on *Rebecca*, tears came into her eyes and she wanted to know whether it would hurt his standing, because after all he was a very good cameraman and it didn't matter if she was photographed a little worse—she would rather have this than hurt him.

All of this is completely unaffected and completely unique, and I should think it would make a grand angle of approach to her publicity, spreading these stories all around, and adding to them as they occur, so that her natural sweetness and consideration and conscientiousness become something of a legend. Certainly there could be nothing more popular, and nothing could win for her the affection of fans more than this, particularly in view of the growing nonsense that stars are forcing us to put up with, and more pertinently because of the general public conception, which is largely true, that foreign stars are a goddam nuisance with their demands, and their temperaments.

This is the first approach to her on publicity that I would be willing to spring now without waiting for the picture's release. It is completely in keeping with her fresh and pure personality and appearance which caused me to sign her, so that the publicity would be completely consistent, and would be the opposite of the comparison with Garbo, Dietrich, and other exotic numbers with whom she cannot compete, any more, in my opinion, they can compete with her.

Ingrid's new director was Gregory Ratoff, a Russian whose bull-like yells during shooting were rumored to have frightened actors and actresses into nervous breakdowns. But those who knew him better declared that all he was doing was working as hard as he could to bring out their best performances. On a set during a take he insisted on absolute silence. Before each scene he would yell: "Bot kaviet," "Be quiet."

Once he had just issued his warning, when he was overtaken by a fit of coughing. He tried to choke an apology to his cameraman, coughed even more, dropped his script, and knocked over a stool. "Pipple," he roared at the studio when he could talk, "ve needink kaviet durink rehearsal—vould you also be keeping *me* kaviet, pliz."

That first morning on the set he approached Ingrid, smiled, and glanced at the script. "Repeat after me, pliz . . ." and in his Russian accent gave her the line. True to her fine ear, Ingrid repeated the words in the same excruciating accent. Language teacher Ruth Roberts clutched at the nearest technician for support. As soon as Gregory's back was turned she scuttled to Ingrid's side: "Ingrid, Ingrid, please, *please . . . never* repeat what he says. Use the accent we have rehearsed!" Ingrid obeyed without hesitation. But getting the accent right was sometimes difficult.

———————— • ————————

I worked with Ruth for weeks on end, and one day there was a word which I just could not get. I said, "Why am I not saying it exactly as you are saying it?" Ruth said, "Now listen to the word carefully as I give it to you again." But still I couldn't get it. So I said sadly, "If only you could give me one Swedish word. If only you could say a Swedish word which is like it so that I would know how to put my mouth, then I'm sure I could get it out." Ruth looked at me very hard and then she said a word in Swedish which is very difficult to pronounce, and she pronounced it *perfectly*. And my eyes opened and I said, "You speak Swedish?"

"I am Swedish."

"Then why—"

"Because, Ingrid dear, if I'd told you earlier you'd have been jabbering away in Swedish, and my job is to get your English right."

———————— • ————————

Later, interviewed about what she felt about her director, and perhaps aware that her own English was roughly in the same category as Gregory's, she murmured charmingly, "He is only outside a barking man. Inside he is sincere and earnest. I owe him very much."

Gregory bore David Selznick's constant interruptions, suggestions, retakes, and interference with Slavic fortitude. A letter to Ingrid, written some two years later, said a great deal about their relationship:

> My Sweetest Swedish Baby,
> Your husband may not like the way I address you. You are my sweet angel and when I think of you and how we worked together in your first two pictures [he was also to direct her in *Adam Had Four Sons*] I can say that these are the sweetest memories of all my career as a director.
> . . .

———————— • ————————

When I came to the Selznick studios that first day and saw what American film studios were really like, I almost fainted. I couldn't believe these huge studios and all the people, cameramen, electricians, grips, carpenters, arc lights. And what were they all doing? In Sweden the film crew and technicians added up to about maybe fifteen; in America there were sixty to a hundred. Of course I learned they were all specialists. Everyone was doing his particular job, and with all the unions they certainly had a lot of people working, but it was also very noisy and there was always a lot of waiting: the man who was supposed to move that table one inch wasn't on the set—so where was he?—and no one was allowed to move the table that one inch until he was found and came. But then I got used to it and it was wonderful because you could get whatever you wanted. If you wanted pink elephants tomorrow, you got pink elephants. If you wanted flies that would buzz in front of your face, they fetched the fly man and there they were buzzing around. It was a dream place to work as an actress. Everything you could get, and in Sweden they had never heard of such things. In Sweden you filmed winter scenes in winter and summer scenes in summer.

And then of course there was that first scene in *Intermezzo.* My very first Hollywood film entrance and David Selznick saying,

"This is your first impact upon the American audience and it's got to be sensational—sensational!"

I looked at the script and I saw I come in through the door, take off my hat and coat, hang them in the hall, and move to the doorway. And I look through and what do I see? I see this world-famous violinist and he's playing the violin, and playing the piano is his lovely small daughter. Now how do you hang up your coat, stand in the doorway, look through at this pretty domestic scene, and make it sensational?

"Now," said David for the tenth time, "I've got to have the impact of a new face that has arrived on the American screen so that the audience will be suddenly aware and go 'Ahhh.' " I said, "But how do I do that? With what means? I'm just looking at a man and his daughter playing the violin and the piano?"

"I don't know. Let's do it." So we did it. "Let's do it again." We did it again. We did it again ten times. He looked at it in the rushes. "I think it can be better. Do it again. Maybe something happens." I mean, I knew David Selznick did everything to perfection, re-writes and rewrites, retakes and retakes, but we shot that scene I don't know how many times, if I say thirty I don't think I exaggerate. And would you believe it, we'd *finished* the movie and we were *still* doing retakes of that first scene. It was my very last day and my very last hour. In 1939 you took a train across America from Los Angeles, and then you caught the boat from New York. And so there was a car waiting to take me to the train. "No. Hold it. One more retake." "But David I've got to pick up my luggage from the house." "We'll send for it. Get Miss Bergman's luggage. Send a car. You'll catch the train, don't worry."

I had to race out of that studio, still wearing the clothes I wore on the set; shouting good-bye to the crew, and throw myself into the car to catch the train by seconds . . . that's David Selznick for you.

———————— • ————————

David Selznick got the opening effect he wanted, but it was thanks to a technical fault overlooked, despite thirty takes in the can. Graham Greene, then film critic of the *Spectator,* wrote in January 1940:

"The film is most worth seeing for the new star Miss Ingrid Bergman who is as natural as her name. What star before has made her entrance with a *highlight gleaming on her nose-tip?* The gleam is typical of a performance which doesn't give the effect of acting at all but of living—without make-up. Mr. Howard with his studied inflexions can't help seeming a little false besides the awkward truth of the young actress, and I am afraid we shall regretfully remember this first picture after the grooming and training have done to her what they did to Anna Sten."

Mr. Greene was completely right about the new star, and completely wrong about her being spoiled by grooming and training. Ever afterwards *she was her own woman.* To this day she will argue about the word "technique" and what it means when applied to acting. For her, acting comes from the heart, from instinctive reflexes, from built-in understanding, sympathy, identification, and belief.

She looked so young that most bars wouldn't serve her: at twenty-three she looked sixteen. But she had one major pleasure. She had discovered the great American ice cream parlor:

———————— • ————————

They never had any of that kind of ice cream in Sweden. They didn't even have ice cream parlors, and certainly not hot fudge sundaes and banana splits. I'd never seen such things. So the first time I tasted them I lost my head, and I ate and ate and ate. But I couldn't order more than two ice creams in one drugstore: it was too embarrassing to ask for a third, so I used to go to another drugstore and order two more ice creams there. I knew I'd put on so much weight, but I told myself, "I'd better eat more and more and more, and then I'll be sick and get rid of it." The trouble was I was so strong and healthy that I never did get sick, I only got fat. I couldn't pass Schrafft's in New York—they didn't have Schrafft's in Hollywood in those days—without going in to have some hot fudge sundaes. But the strange thing is that when I came to Italy where they had maybe the world's best ice cream, I lost my sweet tooth because of all the spaghetti. By the time I'd had a big plate of spaghetti, and then had meat, or fish, and the salad and the fruit, I could not get around to the ice cream any more. I was terribly worried that I would get fat on spaghetti, but maybe all the troubles and anguish I went through in Italy kept me thin; the spaghetti didn't touch me. I got thinner and thinner. . . .

On August 5, 1939, aboard the "Super Chief," she wrote to Ruth Roberts:

> The train is rattling on at breathtaking speed, taking me farther and farther away from Hollywood. I arrived at the very last moment; I didn't even have time to find my carriage but had to board the train when it was already moving. At that last moment a little boy came rushing up with a present from Selznick. After that I sat almost paralyzed, looking out of the window, thinking of everything that had happened and of the fact that I was actually on my way home. What a marvelous time I have had in Hollywood! So many nice people—I'm bringing their voices with me in my trunk on the recording you gave me. Oh Ruth, what a gift! I can't tell you how happy I am! Could you please send me the name of the soundman again? I didn't sleep much last night, although I was so tired. I had too much to think about. If you return to the studio, please give them my love. Yet again, thank you for your friendship and for our nice evenings together. Is my Swedish hard to understand? I'm just being lazy. If you say a word about not approving, I shall send you a very elegant, well-spelled English letter.

She did not know whether she would ever see Ruth again, or America, or Hollywood. But she had loved all of it and she hoped that they would want her back: that David Selznick would take up his option for a second picture. His cable reached her on the *Queen Mary* in mid-Atlantic:

> Dear Ingrid. You are a very lovely person and you warm all our lives. Have a marvelous time but come back soon. Your Boss.

In mid-Atlantic, she wrote in her *Book* about David Selznick:

> From the first minute, I liked him and every day my admiration and my affection grew. He knew his metier so well; he was artistic and stubborn and worked himself to

the bone. Sometimes we worked until five o'clock in the morning. I would come to him with all my problems. He left important meetings to come out and discuss with me a pair of shoes. Hundreds of times he saved me from the publicity department. I trusted him when we saw the rushes and he told me what he thought. His judgment was very hard but it was just. To work for him is often terribly demanding and very hard on the nerves. But always there is the feeling that you have somebody to help with understanding, encouragement, and wisdom, and that is beyond price. When I left, he asked me to sign an enormous photograph, and I wrote: *For David, I have no words, Ingrid.* Which is true.

I'd been away for more than three months. Petter was very pleased to see me. I couldn't say the same thing about Pia. She took one look at me and yelled her head off. She wanted no part of her mother, but she got used to me after a while. We took up our marriage where we had left off, Petter working hard as a dentist and training to be a doctor, and I back in Swedish Films again.

Just before I left for Hollywood we'd moved into this lovely yellow house by the sea in Djurgården Park near Stockholm, but before we even had time to settle down came the war which changed all our lives. I remember I was just sewing up the hems of the new curtains for the living room when I heard over the radio that Germany had invaded Poland, and that Britain and France had declared war on Germany.

This was a big shock because I'd been so often in Germany visiting my aunts and grandparents. I knew the Nazis were evil but I did not think they would involve us all in another European war. I'd been so excited coming back from Hollywood and picking up all the old threads again and then going straight into my next Swedish film, *A Night in June*, that I just hadn't seen the war coming. Now there it was, right next door to us. I wrote to Ruth in the fall of 1939.

I am in my old Swedish dressing room again waiting for my next scene. It is so easy to play in my own language I think I am dreaming. And no trouble with my clothes.

I have bought everything myself and it has all been okayed without a lot of tests, and no trouble with my figure and I'm eating everything I want. But still I was very happy with Selznick, very very happy. And perhaps I will be back soon. I am so glad our picture turned out to be a success as I have heard and read, and again I want to thank you because without your help I should have doubted the success very much. But I am afraid of the trip back during this war. This dreadful war! We still don't feel very much of it up here in Sweden, but many people think we will get involved this time. Here are the stills I promised you in my last letter. Hope you will enjoy them. I have moved into an old, unmodern house, but very charming it is. With affection and love, Ingrid.

It was not long after I sent that letter to Ruth that I got a telegram from David Selznick telling me to put myself on the list for departure. To take my child and my husband and go immediately, before it got impossible to move. He did not know what I was going to do, but he wanted me in America to be on the safe side. So after only four months back in Sweden, Petter decided that I should go with Pia, for he was terribly worried that we should both come to harm. He did not intend to leave Sweden: he was a man of military age, and a medical man at that, and he had served some time in the army already. He would not try to escape or evade his responsibilities. But he insisted we had to go.

Of course it wasn't easy. All the French and British ports were closed to civilian traffic, and boats were being sunk by submarines. But Petter took us on a train down across Europe together with a young Swedish girl to help look after Pia. Everything was blacked out. We passed through Berlin and that was blacked out, with people scurrying around in the darkness like ghosts, and everyone frightened.

So down across Germany and Austria and the north of Italy to Genoa. The Italian liners were still crossing the Atlantic to New York. We spent the night there: December 31, 1940. We stayed in a hotel and I think it was the saddest New Year's Eve ever. Pia was a year old. She was sleeping upstairs with the young Swedish girl. Petter and I sat downstairs in the dining room where they were having their New Year's Eve dance.

Everybody was dancing and screaming, aware that the war was

right outside their door, and trying to shut that out because who knew what would happen before the next New Year? And we danced and we were very sad, and we too tried to pretend that we didn't know there was a blackout and bombers flying in the night . . . but we did know. And I thought, I'm leaving the next morning with Pia, and maybe I'll never see Petter again. I was leaving with his child and he might get involved with the war and not survive . . . oh, those were terrible moments.

I remember standing on the deck of the *Rex*, this huge Italian liner with the horns blowing, people cheering and shouting, and a band playing. There was something desperately sad about it all —as if our lives were suddenly being torn apart. Petter was running along the dockside waving to us while I held up Pia and waved her hand to him. It seemed that maybe we should never see each other again, and my tears were falling all over Pia.

On the boat I receive another telegram from David Selznick saying that when I arrive in New York I must tell the press that I am going to do *Joan of Arc;* that's why I'm coming over—the next picture is going to be *Joan of Arc.* And I am so pleased, so pleased. I've always wanted to play *Joan of Arc,* I don't know where the desire came from, but ever since I can remember I have wanted to play Joan. There is a little chapel on the boat, and I go down there, on my knees and say, "Thank you, God. Now Joan and I will finally make it. And Joan, I just hope I can do your story justice." Then I get off the boat in New York and the Selznick publicity man meets me, and he whispers, "Don't talk too much about *Joan of Arc*— yes?" And I say, "What do you mean?"

"Well, we're not going to make it, not just yet anyway, but we'll tell you about that later. You just smile and say there's a movie coming up and you're going out to California."

———————— • ————————

And Ingrid smiled—because she was back in America and back in New York, and she loved New York.

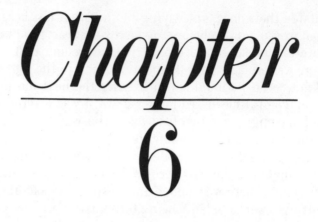

Chapter
6

Intuitively perceiving that young Ingrid Bergman was an actress outside the usual pattern, the New York press warmly welcomed her back to their city.

"Picture the sweetheart of a Viking," wrote Bosley Crowther of *The New York Times,* "freshly scrubbed with Ivory soap, eating peaches and cream from a Dresden china bowl on the first warm day of spring atop a sea-scarred cliff, and you have a fair impression of Ingrid Bergman. She calmly walked off the boat with Pia (that's the tot) slung under her arm and while lunching with this reporter she said as a matter of course that next day was the nurse's day off, so she would have to stay in the hotel with Pia. The English language is a little problem which Miss Bergman has not yet quite overcome. Naturally she is working hard on it. During luncheon conversation she hesitated whether to use 'eldest' or 'oldest.' When told that either was correct she popped a despairing smile and inquired, 'But why must you have two?' "

———————— • ————————

They didn't want me in California. They had nothing out there for me for the time being, and David Selznick was busy with the war, so they thought it was better for me to stay in New York. In New York for two or three months there were things to do. I could go to the theater. I could take Pia to the zoo. And then Kay, who knew

I was going mad for lack of work, was rung up by a producer, Vinton Freedley. He had a part which I might like in a play called *Liliom*. Burgess Meredith was going to play the lead. He didn't say what part I was to play, just sent round the script. I hadn't much stage experience at that time: I'd played at the Comedy Theater in Stockholm for a two-week run between movies and got fairly good notices, and in 1937 a group of us Swedish actors and actresses rented the Oscars Theater and put on a comedy by the Hungarian dramatist Bus-Fekete. We filled the theater for two months, but I'd never acted in English on the stage, and I said to Kay, "What about that?"

She said: "We'll get a teacher, it's not going to be overnight." I read the play and I was a bit surprised. I read the second lead which was that of Marie, a young girl, a funny girl, a fat and laughing girl —the friend of Liliom's girlfriend Julie. I called Vinton Freedley back, "I think you've made a mistake. I'm not jolly enough, and I'm not fat and round enough yet for the part . . . I'm a different type. . . ."

He said, "Fat and jolly? What are you talking about? Julie isn't fat and jolly." I nearly dropped the phone. "Julie! You want me to play Julie, the lead . . . all those words?"

He said, "Yes, of course. . . ." "Well, you'll have to send the play round again," I said, "because I didn't read for that part. But you know my English is poor? . . ."

"You can learn. You can get a teacher."

I accepted, and I got a new teacher, Miss Rooney, because Ruth Roberts was busy in California.

———— • ————

She wrote to Ruth Roberts:

> Great things happen here. Don't you think *Liliom* is too good to be true. Kay is wonderful, and yesterday over the phone, David, poor man, didn't know how to fight against us two strong women and gave in. He said "Yes" and now I am going to do it!! I am so happy, Ruth. I love the play and it is wonderful to be on the stage again. But of course I am frightened too, but perhaps I forget that in my joy. I am not forgetting Joan but of course I am thinking and dreaming more about Julie. I hope that David will prepare

Joan right away now and not think any longer of another picture first.

The opening night is May 24th. And if the public come we are going to play 6–8 weeks, so not before end of May will I be back in Hollywood.

———— • ————

Both Jock Whitney and Kay were a little worried about my voice, so one day they came to the theater a little ahead of time, and sat up in the top balcony and called "Okay. Into your lines!" and so I did. And they said, "Yes, that's fine, we can hear you plainly . . . that's very good."

Then Vinton Freedley arrived and he was a bit puzzled as to what was going on, and asked, "Why are you doing this?"

And I said, "Because I've played so little on the professional stage . . . a couple of months that's all. . . ."

"What are you talking about? You've done *Mary Queen of Scots,* you've done *Mädchen in Uniform* . . . you've done. . . ."

"No, I haven't, that was Signe Hasso. . . ."

I knew exactly how he'd made the mistake. Signe had arrived in America about six months after me. She had stayed on, received a lot of publicity, and had appeared in several plays in Sweden. So now there was about a lifetime of dead silence and then Vinton said, "Oh, my God, I've got the wrong girl." He turned to Kay, furious. Kay said, "Well how were we supposed to know who you wanted? You asked for Ingrid. Signe is working out in California, and you asked for Ingrid. . . ."

"Oh my God!" said Vinton. "Oh my God! And it's too late to change now."

So there I was with a big New York opening coming up, and I'm the wrong girl, and my English is really not very good.

———— • ————

Liliom was a fantasy written in 1908 by the Hungarian dramatist Ferenc Molnár. This was its fifth revival. It was the story, later made into the musical *Carousel,* of a swaggering, unregenerate fairground-barker, chased by all the girls and loved by Julie, a simple serving-maid.

Just to add to our confusion, Ferenc Molnár, who is now a man in his seventies, arrives. He has seen most of the revivals and I don't think he is absolutely overjoyed to see either Ingrid Bergman or Burgess Meredith in the roles of Liliom and Julie. He has a long look at me, noting that I am a lot taller than Burgess, and then he has a long look at Burgess and says, "He's playing Liliom?" Yes? Then he turns back to me, "Why don't you play Liliom?"

That was a great help.

But of course we could fix the height thing fairly easily. Every time Burgess came close to me I sat down, or he bent over . . . It's the sort of thing you do in films when the heights are wrong, sit down, lie down, lean over something.

An hour or so before the curtain is due to rise, I hear music coming from Burgess Meredith's dressing room. I dash in and there is Burgess sitting hunched up in a chair surrounded by gypsy violinists all playing away like mad to inspire him.

I go out and face my first American theater audience. Vinton Freedley is not sure whether or not he's got the great American disaster on his hands, and I wasn't sure either. I knew I had so much to learn of the language. Acting in your own tongue is one thing; you recognize every little mistake you make and cover it. But I could make a terrible mistake in English and not know that I'd done it.

Then of course there was stage fright. Cameras are one thing— no trouble, but that audience out there sitting in the stalls and balconies waiting for me, they petrify me. Would my mouth even open, let alone utter a single word?

I get my cue. I am on the stage. I open my mouth. Words come out. We are on the way.

Later in life she would reflect upon her strange ability to face her big occasions in films and theaters with comparative calm. Always there would be stage fright, but experience taught her that it was no more than that, that once she was "out there" confidence would return. She might forget a line of dialogue, fluff her lines—she did that very often at the beginning of a run—but she knew that the audience would understand and be charitable, and she would not be thrown off balance no matter what happened. Always embedded in her soul was the determination that she was going to be—not just a *good* actress, or an *adequate* actress—but a *great* actress. No conceit about this. She was going to reach that pinnacle or die in the attempt. Mediocrity was not good enough.

If hard work would insure that goal, then twenty-four hours a day for three hundred and sixty-five days a year was the price she would gladly pay. Insecure as she was in real life, as soon as the imitation life on stage, or in front of the camera began, she was relaxed, self-assured, confident, and determined.

The first good news they received when the final curtain came down was that Ferenc Molnár announced that he was absolutely delighted with Miss Bergman's performance. And on the whole the reviews were good. Walter Winchell headed his column: "Burgess Meredith's *Liliom* is splendid," and said that "Ingrid's poise, restraint, and magnetism reaches out over the bulbs to touch you. . . ." The *Daily News* critic called Ingrid "the warmest and most satisfying of the Julies and the least peasant-like in type."

Another critic said: "Mr. Meredith and Miss Bergman can make you cry as easily as not. The two of them in the second act provide some of the loveliest moments brought to the theater by any play of this century."

———— • ————

Burgess Meredith was kind and warm and outgoing.

Irene had warned me in Hollywood: "If a man is going to be nice to you, it's because he wants something from you. . . . Don't believe he takes you out to dinner just for your company. You never get anything for free, not even dinner. . . ." But Burgess was not *after* me, he was *looking* after me. Of course he was a little taken with me, I would hope he was; and he sang a little song for me, "If I cannot *win* you with so much *gin-in* you, good-bye little girl, good-bye." But he didn't say good-bye.

Burgess was sweet to everyone. Everyone was a chum. He made me understand and love the American character from the very beginning. He was the one who showed me the enormous friendliness they have; that they laugh at *themselves.* That is very difficult for the Swedes, the Italians, and the French to do. The Americans laugh because the joke is against *them.* And they have nothing

Papa Justus Bergman and his wife, Friedel, shortly before Ingrid was born.

Justus Bergman and Ingrid, aged three, hold his photograph of Mama, who had recently died.

Ingrid at age five.

Young Ingrid was always a willing subject for her father's photography.

Ingrid, with her grandmother on the way to the Hamburg Zoo.

Self-portrait: In Justus Bergman's photography shop was a self-operating passport cubicle. She loved to use it.

Papa: the strongest influence in her young life.

The seventeen-year-old bathing beauty—a publicity chore she refused in Hollywood.

Her very first appearance in a Swedish film, *The Count of the Monk's Bridge.* The dress is now in the museum of the Swedish Film Industry.
(SWEDISH FILM INDUSTRY)

A film session in the courtyard below the window of *The Count of the Monk's Bridge.*
(SWEDISH FILM INDUSTRY)

Ingrid and her leading man, Sten Lindgren, in *Ocean Breakers*. (SWEDISH FILM INDUSTRY)

In *On the Sunny Side*. (SWEDISH FILM INDUSTRY)

With Gösta Ekman in *Intermezzo*. (SWEDISH FILM INDUSTRY)

Ingrid and Petter,
the year they became engaged.

The wedding:
July 10, 1937.

In *A Woman's Face*. Petter helped her achieve the realistic effect.
(SWEDISH FILM INDUSTRY)

With Edvin Adolphson
in *Only One Night*.
(SWEDISH FILM INDUSTRY)

The young mother.
Ingrid with Pia.

Pia and
Petter Lindstrom.

As she looked in 1939 on her arrival
in New York for her first American
film, *Intermezzo*. (UNITED PRESS
INTERNATIONAL PHOTO)

With Ruth Roberts, her first
language teacher and soon her
close friend.

With Leslie Howard in *Intermezzo*. (SELZNICK PROPERTIES)

On the set of *Intermezzo*. (SELZNICK PROPERTIES)

With Burgess Meredith in *Liliom*. (VANDAMM STUDIO)

With Warner Baxter in *Adam Had Four Sons*. (COLUMBIA PICTURES CORPORATION)

With George Sanders in *Rage in Heaven.* (M-G-M)

With Robert Montgomery in *Rage in Heaven.* (M-G-M PHOTO BY CLARENCE BULL)

As the barmaid in
Dr. Jekyll and Mr. Hyde.
(M-G-M)

With Spencer Tracy in
Dr. Jekyll and Mr. Hyde.
(M-G-M)

Clowning on the set. Victor Fleming takes over the role of Mr. Hyde and prepares to stun Spencer Tracy. (M-G-M)

A birthday present from Spencer Tracy:
the cactus from Mr. Hyde, flowers from Dr. Jekyll.

against success; it's great that you are a success. That's very unlike the Swedes, who are jealous of success, angry that you're earning more money, angry because he's got a better part than mine. In America, success is something to be proud of, not ashamed of. "Good for you," they say. That laughter and that wonderful lack of envy I learned about for the first time, and I shall always remember because of Burgess Meredith.

———— • ————

To Ruth she wrote:

I'm glad you get some rest after your picture. It would be heaven if we could start a picture together in a month. But no. Nothing happens. David and Kay are still looking, and now I don't care because a week from today Petter leaves Sweden to take the *Washington* from Italy 1st of June. It is unbelievable that the time has come when he soon will be here with his child and wife. If only Italy stays out of the war and nothing else happens at the last minute. He sounds very hopeful himself on the telephone. Our play closed last Saturday and I was sorry to leave. It is always dreadful with closings. Remember *Intermezzo?* I cried.

I thought at first to go direct out to you and place the nurse and Pia at the Garden of Allah in a nice bungalow, and go back to New York when Petter arrives. But it will be too expensive, so now I take them outside New York to the country, and wait for Petter there. The money I save now I am going to spend in taking a wonderful room in 34th floor overlooking Central Park. I want to see his face when he sees that wonderful town down below, the town with 8 million people, the town I never get tired of.

———— • ————

But that didn't work out at all the way I wanted. I picked him up at the airport and took him to the hotel, and he didn't like being so high up in the sky and having to look down. He said, "How dirty everything is in New York, how dirty" . . . and of course it *is* pretty dirty in New York. And he walked about in his stocking feet and said, "Look the carpets are filthy and my socks are filthy" . . . and I kept saying, "Look out of the window. Look at this beautiful town, this is the most exciting town in the world." But Petter couldn't get to like it, and soon he had to go back to Sweden to clear things up so that he could rejoin us in America. So that was not a success.

———————— • ————————

From Windmill Cottage, Amagansett, on August 20, 1940, she wrote to Ruth:

> I feel very lonesome since Petter left and Long Island bores me no end. I have decided to leave for New York next week. If by the 15th September I still haven't got a stage play I will come right out to you. I'm still negotiating. Dan O'Shea, David Selznick's representative in New York, says he is able to get me another picture soon but I don't believe in that anymore, I don't want to get disappointed again. Did you, by the way, read in the paper that I didn't do anything because I had a feud with David Selznick and he had given Joan of Arc to Joan Fontaine instead. Sensitive as I am nowadays, that little surprise did not increase my good humor. As far as I know it's not true but you know very little these days.

On September 2, she wrote from the Hotel Volney in New York:

> Now we are back here, thank God, after having been in suitcases all summer. I feel so happy to have all my things unpacked on clean shelves. Now I will try to find a school and brush up my English and take some exercise and lose this five extra pounds I have gained in despair. (I gain because I feel sorry for myself so I must give her a little ice cream). And perhaps soon I will be nice and be able to go around with people again.
>
> Kay says David will not do *Joan* for a very long time. He has turned down all Kay's suggestions. Dear God if I could only make *Joan* come to life instead of this disgusting idleness and ice cream eating. Don't think I am dying to play on the stage again. I would just as soon make a movie. I am one of the few actresses who really thinks

movies are wonderful (and absolutely with no eye to money). A good part on the screen is just as good—that's my idea. But work, please, work.

——————— • ———————

I went to Hollywood with Pia, while the Swedish nursemaid decided she would sooner go back to Sweden. As soon as I got there I realized that David and the studio had completely changed their minds about *Joan of Arc.* "There's no love story in it . . . and now the English and the French are allies and fighting against the Nazis, so that would be bad propaganda for them, and anyway it's a boring story, the whole thing." But I think that now I am in Hollywood David has to do something about me or else I will camp on his front porch. So he loans me out to Columbia Pictures to do another picture with Gregory Ratoff directing. It was taken from a novel called *Legacy* and called *Adam Had Four Sons.* I'm the new governess who arrives to look after Warner Baxter's young sons. His wife dies shortly afterwards, the stock market crash of 1907 wipes him out, so they're broke and I'm sent back to France. Ten years later at the end of the First World War Adam has made a fortune again so he sends for me, the boys come home from the war, Adam at last realizes he's in love with me, and it all ends happily ever after.

In my *Book* I wrote:

> October–December 1940. At last something my teeth could bite into but it was not such a good apple. We had a script to work with but the dialogue was made up minute by minute as we went along, and they had no idea how to end the picture. Ruth Roberts was an enormous help, and great affection for the crazy Gregory Ratoff, so it all left a very pleasant souvenir.

It wasn't a very good picture. But as long as a part makes sense, and the character is a human being, I will try because I can't do artificial people on the screen. Nothing done with such a character can make it real to audiences.

——————— • ———————

The critics liked what she did with the part.

"Somehow," said Mary Ellen Leary in the *San Francisco News,* "you believe in her."

"Anybody," said Kay Brown, "who could get away with a stinker like *Adam Had Four Sons* must have a great future ahead of her."

One aspect of the film pleased Ingrid as she viewed the first rushes: "It is very good. I *myself* can understand myself when I talk."

She finished *Adam Had Four Sons* at three in the morning, and started work on *Rage in Heaven* with Robert Montgomery and George Sanders seven hours later. David Selznick had obviously seen the light: If he wished to please the lady, he had to find her work. And so he lent her to Metro-Goldwyn-Mayer.

But not only had he found her work, he had also found her trouble.

———————— • ————————

Robert Montgomery came into my dressing room the first day. I knew that he had starred in Metro's *Night Must Fall* as a psychopath some time before and had been a great success, and I suppose Metro was trying to repeat the success with him playing a similar role. But Bob had other ideas. He was very nice about it, but he was not going to act he said. I didn't understand what he meant. He was an actor and he wasn't going to act?

"I'm very sorry to do this to you, but I'm forced to do this movie, so I intend to just say the lines but not act."

"But how does that work?"

"I don't know how it works, I don't care. I'm not going to do what they tell me to do. I'll listen but I shan't take any notice, I'll just say the lines blah-blah-blah but I shan't act."

Then he explained. He was under contract to Metro-Goldwyn-Mayer, a seven-year contract that most actors had in those days, and he got paid every month, and they stipulated how many movies and what sort of movies they were. Now Robert was very popular, a superb comedian and much in demand, so as soon as he finished one movie he was pushed into another. It was a conveyor-belt system and he was exhausted. He had pleaded with them: "No more movies . . . I'm dead tired. I just can't go right into another movie. I want to be with my family. I want to have a month off, go somewhere with the kids." But they had told him, "Nothing doing." So he was here in *Rage in Heaven.* "If I refuse they'll suspend me without pay. I've got a wife, children, a big house, a swimming pool, I need the money . . . But I'm going to make my protest."

He said the same thing to George Sanders, who nodded his head and looked wise, but I don't think he understood anymore than I did. Until we started to film. Then we understood. The director would explain what he wanted to Bob, and Bob would look up at the sky as if he wasn't hearing a word, and the director would say, "Now Bob, have you understood what I'm talking about?" and Bob would answer, "Now are we going to shoot this scene? Right, let's get going." And he'd go straight into this blah-blah-blah act of his, no inflections, nothing, same speed, same pace.

The first director lasted two weeks. Then the second one came in and Robert Montgomery went on the same way, his face just an impassive mask. So the second director quit and that's when they brought in Mr. W. S. Van Dyke II. . . .

———— • ————

W. S. ("Woody") Van Dyke II was a Hollywood veteran, a no-frills, no-nonsense, film in-the-can-or-else man who knew his trade backwards. When the graying, crew-cut, breeches-wearing director arrived on the Metro set, in Ingrid's eyes all he needed was a whip and revolver.

———— • ————

I understood Mr. Van Dyke was considered very hard. He was a military man who walked around in breeches and knee boots and shouted and screamed. He really was very difficult and I didn't like him at all. It made very little difference to Bob who went on saying his lines blah-blah-blah, but I tried to do mine as well as I could. As Bob was supposed to be a hidden manic-depressive who had escaped from a French mental hospital, it was probably easier for him. George Sanders was fed up with the whole thing and most of the time he slept. He would come out from his dressing room yawning, do his little bit, and go back to sleep again. He couldn't care less about it; just another bad movie.

I couldn't work at all happily under such circumstances because it was just a question of "Get it in the can," "Let's get this picture off the ground," "Let's get moving." So I went to David Selznick and said, "You always told me that you'd help me if I had difficulties. Now would you please ask them to change the director again or please take me out of the picture altogether. I can't work with this man. He should be commanding soldiers not actors; he's got no idea how to handle human beings with feelings. . . ."

"Oh," David said. "Well, I can't really interfere with another studio's directors. Van Dyke has a big name, he's very experienced. It's only a movie after all and in a couple of weeks you'll be through with the whole thing. It'll be better next time, I've got lots of ideas for you after that, you'll see."

Well I knew David had rented me out and taken a lot of money, and I didn't want to walk out on it—I've never walked out on a picture in my life and I don't suppose I ever shall—but I thought at least I can tell the director what I think of him. So next time he came into my dressing room, I said, "Why didn't you stay with the army, the way you go on marching and yelling? You don't know anything about people's feelings. You certainly can't direct a woman. You are certainly not interested in anything but 'Finish the picture,' no matter what sort of picture it is. You don't give us any possibility of acting; you don't give us any advice on that at all. Why don't you put on roller skates so you can go quicker from one place to another?"

He was very surprised, flabbergasted in fact. He said, "Well, my girl, if you think you are going to talk to your director like that, I'll tell you what. You are going to be fired."

"That will be great. That's all I want. That is what I was hoping when I went to see Mr. Selznick. But he won't take me off the picture. So will you be so kind as to fire me straight away."

He was quiet and he went away, and a little later he came back to my dressing room. "Am I really so hard, really so brusque with people, and so unpleasant?"

"Yes, you are. I've never worked with anybody that is so unpleasant."

"Oh! All right, I don't know how, but I will try and change. You know, you are very good in this part."

"I'm trying to do my best, but I'm very unhappy."

So it ended on that note. The picture was put together, released, and Bob Montgomery got the most glorious reviews because he gave such an original performance. You see, he was a light comedian, the rage of Hollywood, everybody adored him, and here was Bob being out of character, this absolutely flat performance as a psychopath, and people thought it was great. They didn't think he had it in him. So it turned out very well. For him.

—————— • ——————

The critics had nothing good to say for the plot or the direction. Howard Barnes in the *Herald Tribune* opened his column with: *"Rage in Heaven* has all the disagreeable aspects of a lunatic theme without any of its melodramatic excitement, but Ingrid Bergman creates something of a mood of terror single-handed. If our screen keeps overlooking her great talent much longer it will be a really black mark against it."

Hollywood columnist Louella Parsons said: "Ingrid Bergman is a fine actress. I wonder why Metro-Goldwyn-Mayer bother about Garbo's idiosyncrasies when there is a Swedish actress of her ability and commonsense available." Louella Parsons was plainly unaware that Ingrid had long admired the peerless and beautiful Garbo, and had no intention or ambition to take over or even compete with her.

—————— • ——————

She was the most beautiful woman, and I think all her performances were absolutely wonderful.

But Garbo did not want to meet me; maybe she thought I was there to compete with her. When I first arrived in Hollywood, Petter said that as a little gesture I should send her some flowers, and I did. I got a telegram back saying that she would like to see me when I was free. She asked for my phone number.

I was there for three months and I sent the flowers the very first week I arrived, but the telegram came only a few days before I left.

I remember telling George Cukor about this some time later, because George and Greta were great friends, and saying how sad I was that we'd never met and how kind she was to have sent the telegram but of course by that time I was leaving. George laughed and said, "But of course Greta wouldn't have sent the telegram unless she were certain you were leaving."

I also *saw* Greta when I arrived on the Metro lot to make my second Hollywood film, *Adam Had Four Sons.* My dressing room was in the Feature Player's Building although my rating was that of a star because the Star Building was full. You were a star if your name was above the title, a feature player if below. Naturally Greta was in the Star Building.

Outside in the parking lot stood two huge black limousines, one to take Greta to her set—because the sets were often as far as a mile away—and the other to take me to mine. I immediately said, "I don't need a car. I love to walk."

It was Ruth who finally corrected me by saying, "Stop it! If you walk, the chauffeur loses his job and he has a wife and children at home—so take the car!"

Of course the first morning, Garbo and I both being Swedes, and so punctual, came out of our dressing rooms at exactly nine o'clock, and there we were getting into our cars no more than a few feet away from each other. But she didn't take the slightest notice of me, so I decided I'd better not smile and say, good morning, either, and I realized I must be embarrassing her. After that I used to sit at my window and see her go off, and then I'd run down and get into my car.

The next time we *almost* met was when Einar Nerman, the Swedish cartoonist whom I'd known for years, was in Hollywood, and he'd known Garbo for years too. He said he was going to arrange for him and his wife and Garbo and me to have lunch together. A little later he reported back rather sadly that Garbo said she wasn't ready to meet me yet. That stunned me a bit . . . wasn't ready to meet me. I didn't know what that meant. Then, some time later I was in Einar's home and he said, "Now don't you go yet. Garbo's arriving here to meet me in a few minutes. Stay. You must meet her. You're so alike. You're going to have such a good time together." But I said, "Einar, I can't do that. I know she doesn't want to meet me. It would be too embarrassing for words." So I left.

Then many years later I was in Barbados with my husband, Lars Schmidt, at a big luncheon party, and in walked a group of people and in the middle was Greta Garbo. So now what did I do? Would we have another cool meeting?

I went down into the big garden where some people were talking. Lars and other Swedish friends were chatting to her and she must have asked if I was there, because I saw that she looked toward me, and then she came down into the garden and sat down beside me. I didn't know what to say I was so nervous. But she opened the conversation, "I understand you're in love with Barbados, and you're going to buy a piece of land here?" And I said, "Yes we just love the beach farther up from here, and we've plans for a little house."

"Oh, I wouldn't do that because here they steal everything."

"But it's not going to be a luxury house, just a small place with rough wooden furniture, no antiques or anything like that, and we may only use it for a couple of months a year, and then rent it for the rest of the time. . . ."

"But, they'll steal your clothes."

"Clothes? But all I have with me in Barbados is a bathing suit, a pair of shorts, and a pair of long pants. They're welcome to those if they really want them. . . ."

She said nothing, then stood up and walked away. And that was the end of our meetings. Maybe that explains her attitude to life; she's afraid *they're* going to steal it all away.

I suppose one of the saddest and most ironical things about our meeting there on the Metro lot the first time was that I was just starting my career in Hollywood, and without knowing it she was ending hers.

She was doing a picture called *Two-Faced Woman,* and it was a failure, and Greta Garbo was so depressed or upset that she never made another picture. Can you imagine that? She was only thirty-five years old and a most beautiful and talented actress and she never worked again from that day on. Can you imagine all those years, and you get up in the morning and what do you do? If you have children and grandchildren that's a different thing. But to be so lonely. . . .

———————— • ————————

David Selznick, realizing perhaps he had evaded his constantly repeated pledge that only the best was good enough for Ingrid Bergman, now began to look a little harder. And eventually he told her she was to star with Spencer Tracy, a favorite actor of hers, in a remake of Robert Louis Stevenson's classic horror story *Dr. Jekyll and Mr. Hyde.*

Selznick, however, had even more good news for her. After she finished *Dr. Jekyll and Mr. Hyde,* she would star in Eugene O'Neill's *Anna Christie* at the new Selznick Summer Theater season at Santa Barbara. There was a third bright star hovering over her personal skyline: *Life* magazine reported that Ernest Hemingway had made his own selection of actors and actresses he thought ideal for the movie to be made of his best-selling novel of the Spanish Civil War, *For Whom the Bell Tolls,* and he had chosen Ingrid Bergman as Maria, the young girl raped by the Fascists who found refuge in the mountains with a guerrilla band. He had seen her long ago in *Intermezzo* and thought her perfect for the part.

Ingrid was overwhelmed. Yes, she was going to adore *Dr. Jekyll and Mr. Hyde;* she loved the idea of O'Neill's *Anna Christie.* But this! She could not believe her good luck. She had never considered herself for the part. Maria was Spanish and therefore should surely be dark and Latin. But if the author thought her suitable then she was ready, willing, overjoyed, and madly impatient to begin.

David Selznick's phone rang with Swedish persistency: "Yes, Ingrid, of course I saw *Life* Magazine. You're absolutely right for the part, yes. But it does belong to Paramount Pictures. Yes, of course I've got influence with them. Yes, of course I'll ring them . . . but now listen to me, sweetheart, you've got to do *Dr. Jekyll and Mr. Hyde,* then you've got to rehearse *Anna Christie.* . . . Yes, yes, all right, I promise I'll do everything I can. Yes, Ernest Hemingway selecting you personally *must* make a great difference. Yes, you'll get the part. If my word goes for anything, you'll get the part. Now, sweetheart, go away and learn your lines for *Dr. Jekyll,* there's a good girl. It's a very nice part. . . ."

David Selznick had Ingrid playing the sweeter-than-light part of Dr. Jekyll's fiancée, and Lana Turner the role of Ivy, the tarty barmaid with her eyes fixed firmly and sexually on the handsome doctor. David had no idea Ingrid had other plans, or that she had already been in touch with the brilliant director, Victor Fleming, about it.

———— • ————

Naturally, as always, I'd been given the part of the sweet fiancée because now I had played three parts almost the same. In *Intermezzo* I played the nice piano teacher. In *Adam* the nice housekeeper, in *Rage in Heaven* I was a nice refugee. Now they gave me the part of another sweet girl in *Dr. Jekyll and Mr. Hyde,* and I really was fed up having to play it again. I went to Mr. Fleming and I said, "Couldn't we switch, and let Lana Turner play the fiancée, and I play the little tart in the bar, the naughty little Ivy?"

He laughed. "That's impossible. How can you with your looks? It's not to be believed."

"What do you know? You look at me and you look at the three pictures I've done and you know it's the same part I'm playing, but I *am* an *actress!*"

He grinned and said, "I don't believe you can play it; I mean a barmaid, a tart . . . it's Lana Turner's part."

"Will you let me do a test?"

"But David Selznick will *never* let you do a test. You've made three big pictures. A test means you're not sure that you can do it, which means you're not a *star*, and Mr. Selznick is not taking that sort of chance with one of *his* stars."

"Can we make a test without telling him?"

Fleming looked surprised: "You mean you'd really do that?"

"Of course I would. I'm dying to play *that* part. Come on, let's run a test."

In great secrecy Victor got a cameraman and a crew one night and I did the test. A lot of people afterwards asked me why. To begin with I loved this girl, this barmaid Ivy. I thought about her all the time. I thought how she would react, how she would behave. Besides, I simply had to get different parts; I could not remain typed as a Hollywood peaches-and-cream girl.

The test impressed Victor Fleming, and he rang up David Selznick and said, "David, I'm going to switch the parts. Ingrid is going to play Ivy."

David screamed, "But she just can't play that sort of role." You see David believed the Hollywood legend: the elevator boy always plays the elevator boy, the drunk's a drunk, the nurse always a nurse. In Hollywood you got yourself one role and played it forever. That's what the audience wants to see, they said, the same old performance, the familiar face.

And Victor said, "Yes she can. I've done a test. You want to see it? I'll send it over." And he did.

And David pulled a face and said, "Well . . . okay."

———— • ————

It was now clear that the war in Europe was going to be long and bitter with no future there for a young Swedish actress. So Petter and Ingrid decided that *both* their futures lay in the United States. Since Sweden seemed safe from invasion, Petter prepared to leave. He managed to book a clipper flight from Lisbon to New York but at the last minute all travel on the plane was restricted to United States citizens. Eventually he found a berth on a Portuguese freighter and chugged slowly across the Atlantic, arriving in New York six weeks later. He reached Hollywood in time for Christmas, 1940.

———————— • ————————

Now it's 1941 and Petter is over in America for good and we go to Sun Valley early in the year for a short holiday, and the telephone rings and it is David saying that Hemingway is staying in San Francisco with his wife and they're just going off to China. David has arranged for me to meet Hemingway. If I can get there. Is it possible? Possible? I am already on my way. So Petter and I race off by car and train and we meet Ernest Hemingway and his wife, Martha Gellhorn, at a restaurant in San Francisco. I've been on the snow slopes for a week so I've got a very brown face and my nose is peeling from sunburn, and he has a good long look at me before he smiles and says, "Well, I guess I didn't need to be worried."

He asks me how are my ears? He means how do they look, because Maria's hair is very short, so that the ears must not be too ugly. But I think he means, "How do you hear?" and I say "Oh, thank you, I hear very well."

I say, "It's very strange that you want me because I'm Nordic. I never thought you'd choose me for a Spanish girl?" And he says, "I've seen Spaniards just like you. They're tall and blond, many of them. You'll get the part, don't worry."

But I was worried because I knew that Paramount had the final say in the matter, not the author, and that already they were considering other girls. So Ernest Hemingway left for China and that was that.

———————— • ————————

After his holiday, Petter took up residence at Rochester, New York, to complete the two-year course which would entitle him to his American M.D. degree. On the other side of America, Ingrid rented a small apartment in Beverly Hills with a black maid called Mabel, and two-and-a-half-year-old Pia who was learning English faster than her mother. Ingrid owned what she described as "a battered rat-colored coupe which no one bothered to look inside"— she had given up chauffeur-driven black limousines as a matter of principle. The senior parking attendant on the Metro lot always remembers the evening when she found some other car had entwined its bumper with hers and she was working them up and down trying to separate them. By the time the attendant arrived to help she had succeeded, and beamed triumphantly upon him. "First film star I'd ever met in my life who didn't mind getting her hands dirty" was his comment.

A lady reporter dropping into the apartment found Ingrid holding up a spoon to little Pia, saying hopefully "Sked?" as the two-and-a-half-year-old corrected her with a firm "Spoon." Ingrid then picked up a toy cow from Pia's animal farmyard and said, "Pia, this is a rooster," but after scrutinizing the beast more closely corrected her description, "No, this is a cow." Then turning to the reporter, she said regretfully, "I have trouble keeping up so that she will not learn from me the wrong words. Think how confusing if she grew up to believe a thing which gives milk is a rooster, while a thing which marries a hen is a cow?"

But the best moment for Ingrid, the memory she still cherishes, came when she left the house at six each morning. "I'd drive down over the rise from Beverly Hills, and there below in the early morning light I could see the Warner Bros. studios, and I'd think to myself how happy and lucky I am. I can't believe it. All my dreams have come true."

———— • ————

Dr. Jekyll was the first part I played in American films in which I completely changed my character.

Spencer Tracy wasn't really very happy—not because of me, we got on well—but because he didn't like doing these two characterizations: the sane doctor and the monster Mr. Hyde. He wanted to play himself, his own personality, which of course was the warm and marvelous personality that had made him a great movie star. He hated playing this double-natured character, showing the hideous reality of the brutal and evil man living within Dr. Jekyll.

Of course that's just what I wanted to do . . . I wanted to be different, to try my hand at everything, to play every part in the world.

Spencer didn't like some of the scenes, especially the one where he had to race up the stairs carrying me off to the bedroom for his immoral purposes. Victor Fleming demonstrated. Big and strong, he picked me up and ran up the stairs as if I weighed nothing.

Spencer wailed, "What about my hernia?" So they rigged up a sling which supported me so they could hoist me upward while Spencer hung on and raced up behind me looking as if he were carrying me.

But it wasn't that easy. First they hauled me up so fast that Spencer just couldn't keep up, and Victor Fleming said, "Take her up at a natural pace. Let's try again." It was most difficult. Up and down, up and down, for the whole rehearsal time. Then, on the twentieth attempt, the rope broke. I dropped down into Spencer's arms. He couldn't hold me, and we went rolling head over heels to the bottom of the stairs. How either of us was not injured I'll never know. It was just a miracle. But there we were at the bottom helpless with laughter, roaring with laughter, while Victor came racing up, all sympathy and concern, but really so relieved that both his stars were not hurt and could continue to work.

Victor Fleming was marvelous. Although I'd known many fine directors in Sweden, this man added another dimension to what I'd known before. As soon as he came close to me I could tell by his eyes what he wanted me to do, and this has happened with very few directors in my career; I could tell if he was satisfied, in doubt, or delighted. He got performances out of me which very often I didn't think I was capable of. That scene when he wanted a frightened distraught hysterical girl, faced by the terrifying Mr. Hyde—I just couldn't do it. So eventually he took me by the shoulder with one hand, spun me around, and struck me backwards and forwards across the face—hard—it hurt. I could feel the tears of what?— surprise, shame—running down my cheeks. I was shattered by his action. I stood there weeping, while he strode back to the camera and shouted "Action!" Even the camera crew were struck dumb, as I wept my way through the scene. But he'd got the performance he wanted. By the time the film was over I was deeply in love with Victor Fleming. But, he wasn't in love with me. I was just part of another picture he'd directed.

———————— • ————————

She wrote in her *Book:*

January–March 1941. You can't get everything on a plat- ter, you have to pay for everything. I paid with *Rage in Heaven* for *Dr. Jekyll and Mr. Hyde.* I would have paid anything for this picture. Shall I ever be happier in my work? Will I ever get a better part than the little girl Ivy Petersen, a better director than Victor Fleming, a more wonderful leading man than Spencer Tracy, and a better cameraman than Joe Rothenberg? I have never been happier. Never have I given myself so completely. For the first time I have broken out from the cage which encloses me, and opened a shutter to the outside world. I have touched things which I hoped were there but I have never dared to show. I am so happy for this picture. It is as if I were flying. I feel no chains. I can fly higher and higher because the bars of my cage are broken.

Chapter
7

On Friday morning, August 1, 1941, the Santa Barbara *News* went into ecstasies about its "all-star" opening night. "The dream audience of any film producer came to life Wednesday night at Lobero Theatre when David O. Selznick opened his summer theatrical season with Ingrid Bergman in Eugene O'Neill's classic *Anna Christie*. Pretty blond Lana Turner was there on the arm of singer Tony Martin. Sophisticated George Raft came alone. Samuel Goldwyn of Metro-Goldwyn-Mayer led a parade of producers; Alfred Hitchcock and Rouben Mamoulian, famous directors were there. So was Robert Benchley with his famous smile, tall brunette Kay Francis, charming Olivia De Havilland, handsome Alan Marshal, sparkling Geraldine Fitzgerald and Richard Barthelmess."

Ingrid wrote to Jock Whitney: "People were turned away every night even after the orchestra pit and every corner were filled with extra chairs. The autograph hunters not only stormed every window and door, they even tried the roof. I felt like a real star!"

But her initial impact on the audience was amusing:

———— • ————

Before I make my first entrance as Anna Christie the audience has heard the father explain what a lovely daughter he has, and this wonderful daughter is now coming to see him, and then the audience sees what's coming in—the obvious whore.

So I come in and call out to the barman, "Gimme a whiskey and make it a double!"

And the audience collapsed—laughing. They expected, I suppose, for me to say, "Give me a glass of milk."

Oh well, we got over that.

———— • ————

The lasting love affair of the American press with Ingrid Bergman, which was to rise to a high peak of idolatry and then explode with dramatic symbolism on the volcanic island of Stromboli, was beginning to gain momentum. On August 31, 1941, New York's *PM* stated: "Miss Bergman is every reporter's dream of the most wonderful girl in the world, a female who uses no make-up and still looks beautiful; who retains a capacity to blush; who hasn't even a personal press agent; who stands in line at the box office when she wants to go to a movie, who, in short, behaves like a human being. And when in addition to her other virtues the lady has talent, they've really got something. It was with some amazement therefore that it was learned that professionally speaking at least, Miss Bergman has broken out in a rash of loose womanhood. Her most recent movie assignment was the barmaid in MGM's *Dr. Jekyll and Mr. Hyde.* And this week she will grace the Maplewood Theatre as Eugene O'Neill's *Anna Christie.* Miss Bergman when called upon to explain this sudden transformation calmly said it was her own idea. 'My husband tells me it is better to be good in a bad picture, than for me to be bad in a good one,' she says, 'but I do want the picture to be good all round.' "

Reports from all over America confirmed the view that this new young Swedish girl was original. One San Francisco paper said: "Not since the Northern Lights played on the Equator has anything happened to Hollywood like Ingrid Bergman. As unspoiled as a fresh Swedish snowball, as naïve as a country lass approaching her first smorgasbord, this twenty-four-year-old, apple-cheeked Stockholm matron is in the unique position of being a Hollywood star without having the slightest conception of what the Hollywood furor is all about . . ."

David Selznick called her: The Palmolive Garbo. Thornton Delaharty said, "Lunching with Ingrid is like sitting down to an hour or so of conversation with an intelligent orchid."

The critics were also enthusiastic about *Dr. Jekyll and Mr. Hyde.*

Howard Barnes in the *New York Herald Tribune:* "With the great Spencer Tracy in the central role, the ineffable Ingrid Bergman heading the supporting cast and Victor Fleming taking every advantage of prodigal production in his direction, it is a stunning presentation."

The years 1940 and 1941 had been the most exciting and spectacular in Ingrid's career so far. She had appeared successfully on Broadway in *Liliom,* had enjoyed her summer season in *Anna Christie,* starred in three Hollywood pictures, including the one she still thinks of today as the watershed in her personal career, *Dr. Jekyll and Mr. Hyde,* the movie in which she had been allowed to step outside the elegant cocoon that Hollywood and David Selznick were manufacturing for her. And she was working to prepare herself for the role of Maria in Hemingway's story in the hope that it would indeed be hers.

In the fall of 1941 the press reported that Ingrid was going off to Rochester to rejoin her husband and child and "take a rest," an unlikely performance by her. They rented a pleasant house and Ingrid wrote immediately to Ruth Roberts:

> Dear Ruthie . . . Here I am, believe it or not, a good wife and mother. It is really funny if you take it seriously, and try to be very good. I scrubbed and scrubbed the first days. I don't know what my Petter would have done without a Swedish woman in the house . . . which is really sweet, and if the furniture was less than 1888 it would be a dream house. The garden is not worth much, but enough for Pia to play in, and Rochester is so pretty and I am really happy here. I know Petter likes Rochester better than any other place so far, but he doesn't like to be so far away from Hollywood, and I can understand that. In all our married life through 1938, 1939, 1940, 1941 we have been together only for about twelve months . . . and now perhaps with me having to run backwards and forwards to Hollywood it will be the same thing all over again. . . .

She was also worried about her appetite. After all at any moment she might be called to test for *For Whom the Bell Tolls:*

> Oh, Ruth, I should be so hungry-looking and hipless for Maria's trousers. What shall I do? I have been eating like

a fool through my vacation, and even Petter told me to go ahead after *Anna Christie* because I needed it he thought. And now I am almost as heavy as I was when I left Hollywood in the spring. Of course I thought when I left New York a couple of days ago I should start to diet again, but then I came home and had wonderful apples, knackbröd, and goat cheese and I do think I am insane. I can go on and on as if I have a barrel to fill. I think I have tried everything to stop eating. I try to think of the part of Veronica in *Keys of the Kingdom* which David promises; a nun could not eat like that. God would leave her forever. Well, it doesn't help. Then I think about *For Whom the Bell Tolls . . .* and Maria . . . but that doesn't help either . . .

Petter went off to the hospital every day, the maid, Mabel, took Pia out for walks and helped with the chores, and Ingrid kidded herself that being a housewife wasn't all that bad.

Their initial mistake was that with a built-in desire to be neighborly and conform they had listed themselves in the telephone directory. When the Rochester papers reported with civic pride that "Ingrid Bergman Becomes Housewife Here," the telephone bell started ringing and the requests were never-ending: "My daughter is a very pretty girl and I'm sure she would make a great film star . . . could you arrange a test?" "Miss Bergman, I've just written this film script? . . ." "Miss Bergman, I have a friend who is very interested in movies? . . ." "Miss Bergman, we're having a little get-together?" "Miss Bergman, may I pop around and get your autograph? . . ." "Is that Miss Bergman? . . . gosh!" Sightseers stood in line to press the doorbell and see what luck brought to the door. Usually it was a very irate Mabel. It stopped being even flatteringly funny when on two occasions fans or thieves climbed into their bedroom and stole trinkets and various pieces of Ingrid's underwear.

The police couldn't help, the fire brigade couldn't help. Changing to an unlisted telephone number did eventually help, but in those first traumatic days there was only one way of escape—New York, and as she was already contracted to do a radio show there with Spencer Tracy this provided the quickest solution. Eventually Rochester accepted the fact they had a pretty hermit dwelling among them and left her alone. And by that time Ingrid realized that she had invented for herself a sort of living death. For as far as she was concerned, unless she was working in a movie or in a play she was wasting time. Seeing movies and plays was a substitute, but nothing could replace "the creative opiate"—her desperate and constant desire to act!

On December 6 she wrote again to Ruth:

> My radio show was a fiasco. Kay even went so far as to say I shouldn't do any more radio, it might hurt my other work. . . . Spencer Tracy read his part as though he was appearing at gun point. . . . I asked David frankly for an honest opinion, and his was, "You lose very much over the radio, you weren't bad, but I like you better on the screen." Petter said it was all right . . . in fact he even used the word "good."
>
> Did you know Signe opened here in New York and Petter and I went to the first night. The three of us went out after the show and talked until two o'clock. . . . Petter and I both thought there were various small points which she could put right. We discussed them before we met Signe and Petter thought that I should tell her! I said, "She'll be furious. She'll never speak to me for the rest of her life. And she's my *friend.* " "If you won't," said Petter, "then I shall tell her. There is nobody else to." So he started on Signe like he starts on me . . . this and that, and this and that. . . . I could have slid under the table; instead, I twisted like a porker roasting on a spit. I know he is fair and it is good for you but I could slap him in the face afterwards for telling me the truth. Signe was unbelievable. She was so thankful and asked me not to interfere, and *shut* up. Can you imagine? I just groaned. On and on he went. I was just trying to imagine what I would have said if *her* husband had talked to me as Petter did to her.
>
> Oh boy, have I gone through the same routine with Petter. "One of your legs is dragging . . . the furrow between your eyes is deeper. . . . Now watch out, keep your fingers still while you're talking, straighten your back, and why do you cock your head to the left all the time; why not try cocking it to the right for a change. . . ."
>
> I think he is wonderful. Nobody in the world would tell me things like that. I have told him that even if I stop loving him I can't live without him. I got more than I

deserved in my tough piece of male, but dear God how I love him, and how I like you my Ruth because you understand my eccentricities.

I am going to Schrafft's. Perhaps I may have an ice cream because it is Sunday, but I don't know. Last time I had one Petter saw the extra pound I had put on right away and said he was very surprised where it had come from after all the exercise I had taken . . . and there were still five pounds more that I must get off.

She had one desperate pang of mother guilt when she returned from her short stay in New York:

Pia is lovely. Unbelievable how good she is. First evening I was home she sat up in bed and looked at me, "Is it true, Mama, you are here tomorrow too!" Oh dear! I got qualms!

In a later letter Ingrid wrote,

Now I am knitting Pia's doll, sweaters and skirts. She is an extraordinary child. I told her that for Christmas we were going to give away all the toys she didn't like or she thought other children would like. But she should collect them and choose which ones herself because they were hers and I would have nothing to say. And Ruth, I nearly cried. I saw her for an hour go very carefully through all her things. I was scared she would be either too stingy or too generous, not knowing good from bad things. But she was much better than I would have been. She was so sweet. Very good things she gave away saying, "I don't think I play very much with that." But an old dolly, very, very dirty, she kept, and before I could check myself I cried out, "Are you really going to keep that dirty old thing?" She looked at me with her big eyes and said, "Yes, she is dirty but she really was a very good girl." And her mother was quiet. All this from a three-year-old!

I still have no hope for a production in February. Nothing is done, nothing is bought. Kay is going to take Dan O'Shea's place during his vacation, maybe she can achieve a miracle. Only my reading and knitting save me.

January 12:

I have plenty to do as usual, and having a home, husband and child ought to be enough for any woman's life. I mean, that's what we are meant for isn't it? But still I think every day is a lost day. As if only half of me is alive. The other half is pressed down in a bag and suffocated. What shall I do? If only I saw some light in the offing.

January 27:

I plan my day as if in school. Letters and papers in the morning take so long. Walk in the park with Pia so long. Lunch. Answer letters. Play the piano. Paste my clippings. Coffee. English lesson. Dinner. Read. Sleep. It seems an awful lot. We have snow up to our waist. Pia is happy. Sometimes naughty but all children are. Petter has an examination today. He reads half the night and I sit there beside him and read too. I love it. Then we have a snack at one or two and then I'm sleepy all next day.

Ernest Hemingway and Gary Cooper had been friends ever since Gary first played the part of the young soldier in *A Farewell to Arms.* For Hemingway, Cooper was the only one to play the part of Robert Jordan, the idealistic American college professor who fell in love with Maria. It took various deals before Paramount could get Cooper from MGM, but it was arranged. But when it came to Maria a different sort of reality influenced Paramount's thinking. They had under contract a very beautiful actress and famous ballerina, Vera Zorina. They knew that Hemingway wanted Ingrid Bergman, but they had accommodated him over Gary Cooper; they didn't really have to cough up another hundred and fifty thousand for a second star when Vera was waiting and willing.

Sam Wood had wanted Ingrid, but as an old professional he saw the sense in Paramount's choice. Besides, Vera Zorina had class. She was talented and beautiful. No one in America had heard of Vivien Leigh before David Selznick cast her as Scarlett O'Hara. Vera might become as big a star as Leigh.

The letter she wrote to Selznick in answer to his telegram expressed her sadness:

I am grateful to know exactly how the situation is. I'm sorry I lost it, not only because it would have been an interesting part, but because to win it would have been a feather in our hat, and I know you wanted that. Of course I think the reasons Wood gives are a trifle ridiculous. My height for example—if you think how I have faked it with men like Burgess, Spencer Tracy and Warner Baxter. With so much practice in walking with bent knees I surely could look a wee little maid beside Cooper, but I guess he put it nicely. I surely appreciate your wisdom in handling the case. With your wisdom and my intuition we should go far. Your last line in the wire makes me feel very good "To get down to considering Ingrid's future without this complication." Yes, I do hope to play in your yard instead of going over to unreliable neighbors and if I could only forget the old Swedish proverb: "While the grass is growing the cow is dying" I'm sure everything would be fine.

On February 21 to Ruth:

I am so fed up with Rochester and Main Street I am ready to cry. I have moments when I am all right and love a small town and married life. But for four days I have been sitting in a corner without talking much to Pia or Petter. He is home so little he does not notice my moods as much as the rest of the crew. I haven't been to the park with Pia, and Mabel is pretty mad she has to go twice a day. Petter is mad I don't exercise half an hour every day and get slim. I don't care about anything . . . My English teacher is still here every day and I know now 466 words more. I have your lists with 500 so very soon I have consummated 1000 in 6 months. . . .

And she couldn't stop herself writing to Selznick:

I'm down now, deep down. When I came to New York this time I felt sure that you had made a definite decision to start a picture in February. It seems however that you still have not made up your mind regarding scripts. I came over to make pictures with *you,* and since your cable of January 1940 regarding *Joan of Arc,* I have experienced a series of postponements and changes in your plans. Month after month I have been told by you, by Dan or by Kay, that you at last were going to start a production again. I cannot stand being idle. In these days more than ever I feel one has to work, one must *accomplish* something. I feel very sad.

February 27:

Oh my darling Ruth, I don't like to hate people, I don't like my head to dance around in scarlet fury, but that is what it is doing and I can't stop it. I am beginning to hate David and Co. What shall I do? I think they treat me worse and worse. I should maybe not tell you this, but I am a woman. You know our old favorite *Gaslight* or *Angel Street,* as it is called here on the New York stage. David is able to buy it for an enormous sum (as they say). But he is willing to buy it IF, IF, IF. . . . They want my whole contract changed!!!! The terms are unbelievable. It is absolute prison. Even a trip home to Sweden would be pure charity from their side. And seven years!!!! I think they have lost all decency, and they know they can press me now because I am so down I'm almost willing to scrub floors in David's office.

You know the idiotic rush from their side. From one day to the other this must be decided. Everything right away but if you ask for something you can be very happy indeed if you get an answer at all and how you have to wait!!!! Kay was going to come up and settle it with signatures before today, because today was the contract about the purchase of *Angel Street.* If I objected they would cancel.

To my utter delight we said NO! NO! NO! Not even a conference was necessary. We would never sign those terms. I wanted to say it much ruder but Petter is always so damn polite. I wanted to say, "To hell with you" but I guess Petter's way is better.

If I am going to sit here for another year or maybe two, I am prepared. I shall have lots of sweaters knitted, and books read. But I am never going to sell myself. I never thought I should be able to say these things about David whom I liked so very very much. But times change.

On March 22, 1942 she wrote to Ruth:

> Darling, darling, it is all set. I am so excited, I am spilling ink all over my bed. We have signed with an agent, Charles Feldman, who promised to handle me himself, anyway until he goes into the army. Petter and I certainly feel relieved to be able to leave all the contracts to somebody else. New York looks fine and after my first outburst meeting Kay and using all the indecent words in my vocabulary—she didn't spare hers either—we are now not talking about Selznick Productions and getting along wonderfully. I shouted so at least sixty floors could hear me that I hoped and prayed that David didn't take up the option for next year.
>
> I have one radio interview Tuesday on the Book of the Month Club, and one American Cavalcade Monday 30th when I play Jenny Lind. If it wasn't radio I'd be thrilled but at least I'm very happy to have something to do.
> . . .

It was the most frustrating period of Ingrid's life. The end of August 1941, had found her triumphant and sought after. The spring of 1942 found her depressed and unhappy, certain she would end her days as the best looking housewife in Rochester. Kay Brown had been to Hollywood and reported that Ingrid was not forgotten, but had slipped out of the top five. But Ingrid didn't care about her league position. She wanted work. She read scripts, novels, manuscripts, short stories, in Swedish, English, and German.

Ingrid could not be patient. As she put it, God Almighty, where did patience get you? She would be playing grandmothers before she had played a quarter of the roles of her own age group. They were making hundreds of movies in Hollywood each year—movies to help the war effort, movies to hearten people, to amuse them, to make them cry. Wasn't there a single part for her? All this talk about her being a "marvelous property" that could be ruined by a bad picture.

Ingrid blew out tongues of Swedish fire. She was not a "property." She needed sustenance. The rumors and counter-rumors were endless. "David wants you in *Keys of the Kingdom* starting in the fall of 1941 . . . not a lead but a very good part . . . no, not 1941, maybe spring of next year, . . . oh, sorry, but there are delays." "What about a film based on Mary Webb's *Precious Bane*?" "But the heroine has a hare-lip? Do you mean to tell me you're considering a lead played by Ingrid Bergman with a hare-lip?" "Yes." "And Ingrid's agreed?" "Yes." "Absolutely impossible." "Well, maybe we could write around that lip, give her a *nice* disfigurement?" "What's that, the hare-lip is pivotal to the whole story? Sorry, David will never hear of that." "Well, what will he hear of? St. Joan?" "Oh dear, Ingrid, please don't mention that, it's entirely the wrong time. Now there's Hal Wallis at Warners, he's had this idea sculling around for months now. A North African story, and he thinks you'd be absolutely great. Script? I don't think he's got a script yet. Cast? Well, I don't think they've got round to casting yet. But they're talking of Bogart. Yes, Bogie. Great actor."

On April 21, 1942, she received the news she had waited for for nearly a year:

> Oh, Ruth, I have often wondered how I would take the day I received news that definitely I have another film because I knew it had to come sometime. Well, now I know. I was warm and cold at the same time. Then I got such chills I thought I must go to bed and of course a terrific headache into the bargain. I didn't really think I would take it like that. I tried to get drunk for celebration at dinner, but I could not. I tried to cry. I tried to laugh, but I could do nothing. I went to bed three times and went down again because Petter couldn't sleep either with me kicking around in bed. But now it is morning and I am calmed down. The picture is called *Casablanca* and I really don't know what it's all about . . .

In May 1942, she was back driving her rat-colored coupe down Sunset Boulevard.

———————— • ————————

In *Casablanca* I fell right back to where I'd come from. David O. Selznick liked it because at last I was going to wear lovely gowns and clothes and look pretty. Oh, it was so difficult in Hollywood to play against what Hollywood made you. As I have said, they type-cast everyone. All the actors—Gary Cooper, James Stewart, Cary Grant, Humphrey Bogart—they were always playing themselves. But I came from Sweden where acting meant the certainty of change. You played old people, young people, nasty people, good people, but you rarely played what *you* looked like or what you were. You got inside somebody else's skin.

Now Michael Curtiz, the Hungarian director of *Casablanca* and a very experienced and talented director, picked up the same old theme: "Ingrid, you're so wrong, that's not what they do in America. America is type-casting. The audience wants it at the box office. They pay their money to see Gary Cooper being Gary Cooper, not the hunchback of Notre Dame. So you are going to ruin your career by trying to change and do different things. From now on you should simply be Ingrid Bergman; do the same thing, play the same sort of role all the time, and you develop this one attractive side that the audience will love."

I said, "No, I'm not going to do that. I'm going to change. I'm going to change as much as I can."

I liked Michael Curtiz. He was a good director but *Casablanca* started off disastrously and it was not his fault at all. From the very start Hal Wallis, the producer, was arguing with the scriptwriters, the Epstein brothers, and every lunchtime Mike Curtiz argued with Hal Wallis. There had to be all sorts of changes in the script. So every day we were shooting off the cuff: every day they were handing out the dialogue and we were trying to make some sense of it. No one knew where the picture was going and no one knew how it was going to end, which didn't help any of us with our characterizations. Every morning we said, "Well, who are we? What are we doing here?" And Michael Curtiz would say, "We're not quite sure, but let's get through this scene today and we'll let you know tomorrow."

It was ridiculous. Just awful. Michael Curtiz didn't know what he was doing because he didn't know the story either. Humphrey Bogart was mad because he didn't know what was going on, so he retired to his trailer.

And all the time I wanted to know who I was supposed to be in love with, Paul Henreid or Humphrey Bogart?

"We don't know yet—just play it well . . . in-between."

I didn't dare to look at Humphrey Bogart with love because then I had to look at Paul Henreid with something that was not love.

They were going to shoot two endings because they couldn't work out whether I should fly off by airplane with my husband or stay with Humphrey Bogart. So the first ending we shot was that I say good-bye to Humphrey Bogart and fly off with Paul Henreid. Then if you remember, Claude Rains and Bogie walk off into the fog, saying that famous phrase, "Louis, I think this is the beginning of a beautiful friendship." And everybody said, "Hold it! That's it! We don't have to shoot the other ending. That's just perfect, a wonderful closing line."

But they hadn't known it was the closing line until they heard it. And they certainly didn't know it was going to turn out to be a classic and win an Oscar.

They were a wonderful group of actors, but because of the difficulties of the script we'd all been a bit on edge and I'd hardly got to know Humphrey Bogart at all. Oh, I'd kissed him, but I didn't know him.

He was polite naturally, but I always felt there was a distance; he was behind a wall. I was intimidated by him. *The Maltese Falcon* was playing in Hollywood at the time and I used to go and see it quite often during the shooting of *Casablanca,* because I felt I got to know him a little better through that picture.

———— • ————

Perhaps the essential reason why *Casablanca* is now a classic, a cult, and a legend is that it was concerned with *our* war! Rarely, if ever, have an actor and actress had the opportunity to work so dramatically, if unknowingly, on our emotions, when defeat seemed a possibility and victory far away. *Casablanca* had a major impact on the Allied war effort.

Yet when she completed her work on it, if someone had informed her that with this picture she had entered the movie legends of the twentieth century, she would certainly have uttered one of her most vowel-stretching, "No-o-o's."

While Ingrid was still working on *Casablanca* she began to hear the rumors filtering down from the mountains that all was not well with *For Whom the Bell Tolls.* The first "rushes" had reached Paramount and reporters, sensing big news from the bogus Spanish battlefront, were treated to many alibis, one perhaps the most original in the history of cinema: "Light was apparently draining off Vera's face when she was photographed from above."

The truth of the matter was much simpler.

———————— • ————————

The real trouble was that Vera was a ballerina. Yet she had to run around those mountains like a little wild animal. And Vera was afraid of damaging her legs. They were to her what my face was to me. If an onrushing train came against me, I would protect my face. Vera would protect her legs. So when they saw the first rushes of the film taken in the mountains this came through quite clearly; and they decided that Vera was unsuitable. They took her off *For Whom the Bell Tolls,* and gave her another picture.

As soon as I finished *Casablanca,* I was to go home to Rochester —to Petter and Pia!

Then the news came through from the Selznick office. Paramount wanted to test me. No, not an acting test, they knew all about that—but how would I look with my hair cut off? And would I have my hair cut off? I said I was willing to have my head cut off for the part of Maria. I made the test on the day after we finished *Casablanca.* They didn't cut off my hair, they just back-combed it and pinned it up.

Sam Wood was going to arrive on Sunday, see the test, and immediately ring me to say what he thought. I'll never forget that Sunday. The phone was a yard away from me and I was sitting all day waiting for it to ring. I couldn't eat, I couldn't drink. I looked at the telephone as if it were a snake waiting to strike. It rang! I snatched it up! It was Petter ringing from Rochester. "What's the news? Have you heard anything yet?" I told him I would ring him back the instant I had any news. I put the phone down. I went on looking at it. I was still looking at it at midnight. No phone call from Sam Wood. I could draw only the obvious conclusions. He hadn't liked the test. He would have called if he liked it. It would be difficult to ring up and start making excuses.

The next day I was at the Warner studios making the stills for *Casablanca* when someone said, "You're wanted on the phone, Ingrid." I went across and put my ear against the receiver. It was David; his big deep voice said, "Ingrid, you are Maria!"

———————— • ————————

As Ingrid turned away from that phone call from David Selznick, she glowed incandescently. Warner Bros. executives said, yes, of course she could leave at once and travel up to the mountains.

She was driven the four hundred and fifty miles to the Sierra Nevada mountains, whirled through Roaring Camp and Poker Flat, where the California Gold Rush had been immortalized in Bret Harte's short stories, and jolted up narrow roads into the high peaks and vast canyons adjacent to Yosemite National Park. The winter before, Sam Wood had nearly frozen to death here filming battle scenes and shots of pack animals and exhausted men trudging along icy trails. And he was not likely to forget December 7, 1941, when with just three more days to wrap up the scenes of planes bombing the mock guerrilla camp, news flashed through on the radio that a real bombing had taken place at Pearl Harbor, that the United States was now at war, and that all aircraft were grounded.

Ingrid's car shot through the small town of Sonora, crossed the Sonora Pass, and reached the cabins specially built on the location. Ingrid got out and looked around a little bewilderedly.

———— • ————

Then I see this beautiful man coming down the mountainside toward me. He looked at me, and I looked at him, and I blushed naturally. Then he said, "Hallo Maria?" and I blushed again, and Gary Cooper said, "We'd better find Sam Wood." We found Sam Wood, and they both took me to the cabin which I was going to share with Ruth Roberts. Sam showed me the rubber soldier who stood outside at the door—they were using these dummies on the battlefield as dead soldiers. This one had a sign around his neck: "Welcome Maria." Then a little later I was outside with my script and Gary came up. He hadn't got a script, but he leaned up against a wagon and looked down at me—there were not so many people in Hollywood who looked down on me—and then he said, "Well, shall we work a bit on the dialogue between us?"

I said, "Yes, I have Ruth Roberts coming here very soon and we'll be working together on it."

Then he went into the dialogue, and I thought he was still talking to me, because he didn't change his voice. He didn't become an actor who acted, he was exactly the same. So I kept saying, "Excuse me, what did you say? I can't understand what you're talking about?" And he said a little reprovingly, "I'm reading the dialogue, that's the dialogue." So I blushed again and said, "Oh, that's the dialogue."

You see you worked with him and you had a feeling of doing so little. He didn't *do* anything. He had no expression in his face or his eyes saying these things. He just chuckled away, and talked quietly and I thought, this is not going to be any good at all. This is not going to work. Then we shot the scene and I still said to myself, he doesn't do anything. Then I saw the rushes, and there he was. . . . The personality of this man was so enormous, so overpowering—and that expression in his eyes and his face, it was so delicate and so underplayed. You just didn't notice it until you saw it on the screen. I thought he was marvelous; the most underplaying and most natural actor I ever worked with.

I so loved that Maria. When I first thought I'd got the part I'd worked on it relentlessly. I studied everything that Hemingway had written about the girl. I shut myself up for days just studying being that girl. I thought: a woman in love forgets herself, her own interests. All she is thinking of is the man she loves. What she means to him. How she can make him happy. She simply lives to fit his needs.

I sat and laughed on the set. Looking at Gary Cooper, it was so wonderful. It was unbelievable that I was there working with him.

I remember one of the reporters told me that Gary had said, "She is one of the easiest actresses to do a scene with. I don't feel I am just standing there while she is wondering if her make-up is right. Or her hair right. She has absolutely no thought of it. She lifts the scene. That's because she is so completely natural."

Oh, that pleased me very much. There was something very fine, very good in his nature, or it wouldn't have come through on the screen with such reality—such sincerity. It was Ruth who said to me, "Really Ingrid, you must stop looking at him like that. You sit there just looking! I know you are supposed to be in love with him in the picture, but not too much in love with him!"

It was a marvelous part, an enormous beautiful part. And the short hair became all the rage in America. All the women wanted the Maria cut. I suppose it had something to do with the war and the difficulties over hairdressing, but they all made a terrible mistake. They didn't know I had a hairdresser who followed me around like a shadow and rolled my hair up every minute of the day. I was rolled up in little bobby pins—we didn't have such things as hairspray in those days—and then it was combed out before I shot each scene. But of course the poor women who had their heads done in the Maria cut in the morning found that after two hours it fell down again and they looked like little rats.

We had such a lot of fun up there in the Sierra Nevada mountains in that summer of 1942. Yes, the war was on, and we hadn't forgotten it because so many among our band of Russian, Polish, French, Greek, and Yugoslav actors had suffered because of it. I was also worried about Sweden. What would happen if my country should be overrun by the Nazis? I hoped that the people of America would not turn against my people. Sweden, like Switzerland, was surrounded, cut off, made helpless by the enemy. There was very little she could do. If the tragic moment of attack should come, I hoped the people of America would not forget this.

We were so far away from the world in those mountains. It was a refuge. Ruth and I shared one cabin and all the others had cabins too, and one night Katina Paxinou, that marvelous Greek actress who had escaped from Greece when the Nazis invaded, would cook the meal, and the next night Ruth would cook, and so on. It was so primitive and romantic up there among the stars and the high peaks before the winter snows cut off the whole region.

The climate was incredible. We chilled in the morning, sweated in the afternoon sun, and froze at night. I loved my wardrobe: an old pair of man's trousers tied around my waist with a piece of string, and an old shirt. The only way I changed my costume was when I rolled up the sleeves or let them down. We were up there a long time, most of the summer and into the autumn, nine or ten weeks in all.

Then of course there was that poor horse. In the closing scene in the picture, the guerrillas have to race to safety across an open gully, under enemy fire. Gary Cooper races across last of all, his horse stumbles, falls on Gary, and breaks his leg. Well, there weren't many horses in Hollywood who could do this without really breaking your leg. But they had sent up a special horse who could do the trick. Trouble was he was brown, and all through the film Gary had been riding a dapple-gray horse. So our make-up men painted the brown horse dapple gray. But the horse didn't care for his new color at all. He was so dejected that he refused to act. For twenty-four hours he just stood there hanging his head looking sorry for himself. Then at last he did his trick, and as soon as they washed the paint off he was all right again. All the cast understood his feelings.

While we were up there in the mountains, Sam Wood read Edna Ferber's *Saratoga Trunk,* and then he gave it to me to read, and then I gave it to Gary. We liked it. We'd had so much fun on *For Whom the Bell Tolls* and got on so well, why shouldn't we make another film together?

———————— • ————————

Casablanca and *For Whom the Bell Tolls* were made "back to back" as they say in the film industry, but they were released and reviewed with a nine-month interval between them. *Casablanca* was successful from the first showing. Practically every review was a rave notice. It was a smash hit. It has been a smash hit ever since.

When the first reviews of *For Whom the Bell Tolls* began to appear, David Selznick sent Ingrid a telegram:

> Dearest client: There is nothing any of them are saying that I have not been saying for years so I hope you can imagine my pleasure and pride. As a matter of fact they are still not keeping pace with my predictions. On Sunday night I advised twenty-five people that before the year is up you will be finally recognised as the greatest actress of all time. Now if that doesn't swell your pretty Swedish head nothing ever will. But then I have been trying in vain to do that for years.
>
> Swede Lover.

But in spite of David's telegram, the reviews were mixed. While the *New York Herald Tribune* was proclaiming, "The screen has met the challenge of fine literature triumphantly," Kate Cameron in the *Daily News* found that, "There is so much that is beautiful, stirring, and profoundly interesting . . . that it grieves me to report the picture has been drawn out to an inordinate length, making it a wearisome rather than an inspiring experience in the theater."

And while Bosley Crowther's opinion in *The New York Times* was that: "Ernest Hemingway's wonderful novel of the Spanish Civil War has been brought to the screen in all its richness of color and character," Herb Sterne in *Screen* decided, "the guts of the original have been decorously disemboweled and hidden with the result that the drama, both political and sexual, bears little relationship to the brutal realities of the world in which we live . . ."

Time magazine summed it up: "Whoever else may have fumbled at the rope or muffled the clapper, the 27-year-old Swedish actress hit the bell such a valiant clang that there has been nothing like it since her great compatriot Greta Garbo enchanted half the world."

————— • —————

Ernest Hemingway had written a very big book, and it wasn't possible to put into the picture all that he'd written. But what did *not* emerge clearly was the political side of it because they were so afraid in Hollywood not to please everybody all the time. So they didn't take sides. They didn't try to suggest who was right and who was wrong. But naturally Hemingway had very strong opinions about what side *he* was on. So when he came back from China and I met him again, I said hopefully, "Did you see the movie?"

"Yes," he said, "five times."

That delighted me, "Ah," I said. "Five times! You liked it that much!"

"No, I did not. I went in to see it. After I'd seen the first five minutes I couldn't stand it any longer so I walked out. They'd cut all my best scenes and there was no point to it. Later I went back again because I thought I must see the whole *movie,* and I saw a bit more, and again I walked out. It took me five visits to see that movie. That's how much I liked it!"

————— • —————

In her *Book* Ingrid made her own assessment:

> It was my first movie in color. We worked twelve weeks in the mountains and later twelve weeks in the studios, Paramount spending three million dollars on their biggest film. I enjoyed it all so much, particularly Gary Cooper. What was wrong was that my happiness showed on the screen. I was far too happy to honestly portray Maria's tragic figure.

She made very few more entries in her *Book.* By the end of 1943 she was too busy. The last dozen pages were left blank.

Chapter

8

With her hopes pinned on the fact that she, Gary Cooper, and Sam Wood were soon going to work together on *Saratoga Trunk,* she wrote to Ruth:

Here is some news that'll make you breathe faster. After my wire to David he telephoned. He disliked the script of *Saratoga* but he liked the book, so the script would have to be improved. But he just didn't understand how the Warner people could see me in that Vivien Leigh part as Cleo Dulaine. He was going to save them from disaster by not letting me do it! I had no driving power! I could not look wicked! I simply could not get those lines in my mouth!

Well, I kicked and kicked. He asked me to consider what it would do to my reputation to play Cleo after Maria. He would call the next day. In the meantime he was going to talk to Wood (who is signed). He called the next day, thinking that I had got my senses back. But no. I started to tell him what a coward he was, that surely I never could, and never would, even try to play the part like Vivien. And wasn't it going to be fun and interesting to watch me to find out what I was going to do? If he couldn't figure out a way for me to say those lines well, I had! Was he not interested? I was not going to surprise only him, but the whole nation if they were against me in this part.

Of course Sam knew I wasn't Vivien, but if those who put their money in it were going to gamble, why not David? I don't know how much more willing he is now to let me do it. If I was down there and could talk and walk and emphasize with hands and feet what I mean, I could persuade him. I am always lousy on the phone. Anyway he had spoken to Wood. And Sam Wood said I was so good I could do anything! He wanted me very much. David would not make up a story like that, so it must be true. Isn't he nice, dear, dear, little Sammie?

David was flabbergasted. "Everybody must be crazy," he said. "You are Swedish, they don't care. You don't look French, they don't care. You can't act it, they don't care."

He is going to decide in a few days. What can I do but sit and wait. Hal Wallis called from N.Y. today. He was worried, thought maybe I had lost interest after D's talk to me. I told him what had happened and he was very, very happy. Said he spoke to Gary yesterday, who he almost had in the bag (the thought!). I bet Gary is waiting to hear what happens to the script and me first. David by the way did not for a moment think Gary would do such a small part. They try to fool me and in the end Flynn will be the hero. I am sitting on needles. I'll try to see David's side, if I lose it. And I can always say, it would be worse to be forced to do something you hated.

Love Ingrid.

Rochester, Tuesday morning when everybody was asleep:

Dear Ruth,

Oh dear, I just can't sleep. I go to bed later than anybody else, and now I am down here to write you. It is still and dark and my thoughts are wild and very bright. David called me last night. He had spoken with Sam and said, "Listen, I'm half-sold on the story. Sam has promised to do everything to make the girl fit you," and he laughed when he said, "Sam is absolutely insane when it comes to you. He is fighting for his life to get you." Ruth, it must be that rabbit stew we all ate that very last day in the mountains. But if David is half-sold I think I can sell the rest. Sam is coming to New York Sunday morning and wants to see me. David says I am not to say "Yes" right away, until I get the changes I want. If Sam agrees to my suggestions David will give up. Of course Sam will agree. . . .

January 31, 1943:

. . . I am definitely leaving Rochester Sunday night to do that Office of War Information documentary in Minnesota, *Swedes in America.*

Later:

Oh Ruth! Wonderful! Dan called just now and said Gary had signed. I have it. You have it. I don't know what to write except MINE MINE MINE, *Saratoga Trunk* is MINE! Well now I feel really good. Well now I don't feel so good because Petter got mad when he saw me writing to you again. There are so many things I must do before I leave he says. I know he is right so I leave you for my duty. Much love and I am happy we got it. Remember we read the story in the mountains so long ago. . . .

February 4. . . . Thursday morning 1943:

Darling, this is the most wonderful trip you can ever imagine. I am crazy about the Swedes. I have stayed at a farm with a family of Swedish descent, the Swensons. He is 73 and has six huge sons and they are so nice. I didn't think this kind of people existed in America . . . though I love Americans too.

I have left Pia and Mabel on the farm. You should see those farmer's sons. If it wasn't for Petter and Gary Cooper I think I should like to be a farmer's wife. Maybe Pia. . . . Well, never mind.

I live like a queen at Minnesota's largest hotel. It looks more Chinese than Nordic though. Joe Steele, Selznick's new publicity man, met me at the station and he is a tall, good-looking man. . . . I really feel as if I've come home here. People must also think that I belong to them. I visited an old people's home and spoke to an old lady who came to America in 1865. She remembered her Swedish just as well as I do. She asked me my name and I said Ingrid, and she told me all sorts of stories of how this country looked when she first arrived. I am so happy about the other picture, Ruth. There is a steady song in my heart which sings: SAARAAATOOOOGA TRUUNK! Lots of skoals. I'll see you very soon, Ingrid.

Joe Steele, David Selznick's new publicity director, met Ingrid on the platform of Minnesota Station at the start of the Office of War Information-sponsored film, meant to illustrate how Swedish emigrants had successfully assimilated into American society, to show that the United States was essentially a United Nations facing the enemy. Joe was a dignified, old-fashioned American, with little of the brashness usually associated with Hollywood publicity men. Assigned to look after Ingrid, he was not certain what to expect. The first thing that astonished him was her size: Five feet nine inches of sturdy peasant structure. The second was that she was accompanied by a pleasant black maid and a pretty, blond, four-year-old as talkative and composed as her mother. A long experience with movie stars had left Joe Steele quite unprepared for one as original as Ingrid. Her capacity to put up with discomfort and bitter cold and to use seven-foot snowdrifts as playgrounds in which to laugh and romp with little Pia amazed him. Her working hours astonished him. She performed all the publicity chores he asked of her with charm and tact, and real tears ran down her cheeks when she met gracious geriatric Swedish ladies in an old folks home. More than anything else her absolute lack of film-star importance bewildered him. Film stars just did not behave the way she did when they were marooned on a cold and foodless train with a two-thousand-mile journey ahead of them. Ingrid took advantage of the first halt to sprint off to buy sandwiches while Joe set off to find a bottle. Returning laden to the platform, they raced for the already moving train and collapsed panting into their compartment.

Writing one of his first publicity articles for a movie magazine, Joe said, "Sometimes I think she is the most beautiful woman I have ever seen. If what I have told you is not beauty, then my forty years and more have been meaningless and I have learned nothing." A deep friendship and lasting association formed between him and Ingrid which was to last for many years to come.

———— • ————

Going off on bond tours all over America to raise money for the war effort, and going to Alaska to help entertain the troops was, I suppose, part of my escape-kit during those years.

It was Petter who said, "You should be doing something to help the war effort, because we've been very lucky that Sweden is not involved, and we've been out of the war." I agreed. Petter was working at a hospital, but I was only making films. So I went off on the bond tours around America, reading poetry, telling stories, and making speeches. Petter didn't think that was enough, though, and again I agreed.

I thought I should entertain the soldiers somehow or other, but of course that was much more difficult because I was an actress not a cabaret star or an entertainer. I volunteered and got signed up by the USO and they said, "Would you go to Alaska because no one ever wants to go there? They all want to go to the South Pacific." Well, I thought, the South Pacific would be full of insects and snakes, and I didn't like either of those things, so I said sure, I'll go to Alaska. But I didn't know what to perform. Ruth said, "We'll dramatize an O. Henry story and I'll make you a Swedish dress and you can do a folk dance." And of course Pia who was about six was a great help: "Mummy, you're *so good* at telling stories," she said, "just make up some stories like you do for me, and you can sing and you can dance." "But I can't sing and dance, Pia darling," I said. "Yes, Mummy you can. You do it for me so you can do it for them. And I'll tell you what, I'll give you some of my toys and you can give them to the soldiers to play with . . ."

So that's how I started my act. I said my little girl had sent me along to give them a few toys to play with . . . and that made them laugh.

There were three other girls, one actor, Neil Hamilton, and the program was really not particularly good. But the boys in Alaska didn't get much entertainment so they were happy. Neil Hamilton was good at magic, one girl danced, another sang, and the third one played the accordian, but the main thing was that we were *girls.*

———— • ————

Ingrid's letter to Ruth was dated December 28, 1943, and headed, "Somewhere buried in snow in Alaska":

Because I am an early riser you have a chance to hear from me while the rest of the girls get ready. We are now right out in the wilderness and just as I thought it would look, a wilderness of snow. We make sometimes two stops a day. Fly in the morning, go down and give a show in the early afternoon, talk and sign autographs and pose for their cameras, then go to another place for the evening and give two shows. My voice is getting hoarse and I guess I have to add a dance number in case . . .

The first three days we spent in Anchorage. That was the biggest place. We were together with the boys all the time between shows and after. You won't believe it when I tell you that I and a boy from Palladium, Hollywood, danced the jitterbug in the middle of the Service Club with 500 boys around looking. Then I danced Swedish folk dances with a Norwegian boy. They have a wonderful time and say that we are the first ones to mix with them and not the generals. I told the big shots right away that I came to entertain enlisted men and they understood. We went to two hospitals too.

There simply is no time for your private life. I sit and sign those 5000 pictures during breakfast (the other meals are always with different boys in different mess-halls). One man said, "To see a woman like you makes you want to live again."

The boys are sometimes frozen inside and out. I used to go down and sit with them if we came a little before time for the show for they are actually frightened. It takes a lot of talking before they show up. And they're so thankful for, anything you do. It is pathetic. It seems unreal to be here. When we get up in the mornings it is all black and we trudge through the snow to our plane and fly over this wild white world.

December 29. We are right at this moment playing for I couldn't tell how many boys in a hangar. We sit in an ambulance and the stage is a truck. It is cold and I have an awful sniffle and I feel pretty down. We are going so fast from place to place. I guess we just have to stop and rest for a day. Of course it is fun, but you do have limits, and in this hangar it is so noisy. The boys are standing around us and it's a very bad acoustic. I was ready to cry

the first show we had here: it was so noisy I couldn't keep
my lines straight. We live pretty well but it is so stifling
hot inside that you faint. Impossible to keep breathing
with the cold outside.

———————— • ————————

We danced with the soldiers, and we ate with them and visited the
hospitals, and then I caught a cold because the huts were so hot
I was going out of my mind. I used to open the door and go out into
the snow saying, "I'll die with this heat," and I almost did because
I got pneumonia. I was in the hospital on New Year's Eve with the
boys, but not in the way I intended.

We flew in five little planes, just the pilot and one person behind;
five tiny people and there were no roads, all snow. You'd say,
"What's that down there? . . ." and there it was . . . just one little
collection of huts and about two hundred boys sitting with nothing
to do. They hadn't seen anybody for months. They hadn't even got
a war to fight, not a bullet went off in Alaska . . . and when they
saw these five little planes coming in, they were so happy.

———————— • ————————

Ingrid always has had a happy knack of making friends. On the
Alaskan journey the abiding friend she made was a regular Army
man who happened to be the commanding officer of the region:
Lieutenant General Simon Bolivar Buckner. Buck's foghorn voice,
iron constitution, booming laugh, and many eccentricities were welcome landmarks in a landscape totally devoid of identity. What was
a sub-zero temperature to a trained soldier? To show his contempt
for such inconveniences, Buck was always to be seen striding through
the snow without an overcoat, working on his firm belief that a man
never caught cold if he permitted wet clothes to dry on his body.

The skin of a huge bear hung on his office wall; it was unmarked
by any sign of a bullet hole. G.I. personnel in the outer office would
explain that when the bear appeared, the General had just hollered,
and the bear had died of fright.

Ingrid and Buck got on very well, and after she returned to Hollywood, the Army man who happened to be a general and the pretty
Swedish girl who happened to be a film star, like so many other
soldiers and pretty girls during that world conflict, became pen-pals.

———— • ————

I always remember how Buck used to come out onto the stage after the show and compliment us all, and add, "And how lucky we are to have Miss Bergman with us here tonight." Then he'd point to the three stars on his shoulder and say, "You're looking at these stars, aren't you? Three stars. Same as a good brandy. And they stand for the very same thing. Very old."

———— • ————

On February 1, 1944, Buck wrote:

I have just gotten all the reports from posts that you have visited, and you would be greatly gratified to note the highly eulogistic character of all of them. We have never had a show in Alaska that was more enthusiastically received, and the remarks concerning the graciousness of your own demeanor and thoughtful consideration of our soldiers would, I feel certain, please you very much. You may regard yourself as the feminine counterpart of Joe E. Brown: although you must admit he has certain points of superiority, especially in the cavernous confrontation of his mouth.

She wrote back:

How about a one-girl show? Not only have I got my voice back since returning and am strengthening it by singing lessons, but I am also dancing daily—folk dances, hula-hula, or whatever you might like? Furthermore, I am persistently playing my piano to the neighbors' despair. If you give me the chance to act a little and sign some autographs, we might have a new show for the boys.

Letter followed letter, and on July 3, 1944, he wrote her how he had been hunting with the Eskimos along the edge of the ice-pack, and that now—official secrecy prevented him from breaking the news of his address—he was swimming and diving underwater in bright blue seas, and coral lagoons. Why didn't she try a Pacific tour for a change? He was keeping fit by climbing mountains, pitching on the softball team, and hunting mountain goats.

She wrote back saying that she didn't like insects or snakes but she'd think about it.

On May 2, 1945, he wrote:

> Dear Ingrid, when I returned to my tent this evening, muddy and wet from watching the fighting on the front, I found your very welcome letter awaiting me with its cheering news. . . . We have been fighting now for more than a month on this picturesque and beautiful island with a good climate and quaint and interesting villages and customs. The natives resemble the Japs in most ways but have differences in culture and tradition that come to them from Chinese influence. Up until today we have killed 28,000 Japs but we are up against the most powerful defenses yet faced in the Pacific and have to proceed carefully and methodically so as to keep our losses down. I hope that the next big fight will take me to Tokyo . . . and I hope that the war will end in time to see you on Broadway as Joan of Arc. . . .

He never wrote again. He did not see her in Joan of Arc. Her next letter remained unopened in his tent. He could not reveal to her that his picturesque and beautiful island, with its quaint customs and interesting villages was Okinawa, where for seventy-nine days the Japanese and American forces clashed in some of the bitterest and most bloody battles of the Pacific campaign. In the middle of June, his Tenth Army forces, reinforced by elements of the Second Marine Division, went into all-out attack to clear the island and open the way for assault on the Japanese mainland itself. On June 18, directing the battle from his observation post, two shells made a direct hit. Ingrid's good friend, a gallant American officer, was killed instantly when a fragment of shrapnel pierced his heart.

Ingrid had been a pen-friend, nothing more. They had shared a few drinks and a lot of laughter; the warm compassion of friendship. She could find only one grain of comfort. Buck was a professional soldier. He knew the dangers of his trade. Wherever Buck had gone, he would face the men who had gone with him, and good commander that he was, hoot with laughter as he informed them, that he, like them, had taken the same chances, and proved that generals, after all, do die in battle.

The war went on and Hollywood went on. Ingrid began filming *Saratoga Trunk* with Gary Cooper. As Cleo Dulaine she swept through the film in a high-coiffeured black wig, satin petticoats, tightly laced bodice, flowing bustles, and bright lipstick. A far different woman from the crop-headed little mountain goat, Maria, of *For Whom the Bell Tolls.* Ingrid was absolutely delighted when her agent Charles Feldman passed her in the canteen without a second look: she had fooled him.

———— • ————

I played this nasty woman, very egotistical, spoiled, shouting and screaming, and affected in every way. People said before we started filming, "absolutely wrong for you." I couldn't care less because it was exactly what I wanted to do. I was a New Orleans bitch and that was completely new.

———— • ————

The critics approved thoroughly.

As soon as she finished *Saratoga Trunk,* Ingrid went back to Rochester to close the house and pack up. Petter was moving to California to spend his last year of internship at a San Francisco hospital, not much more than four hundred miles up the coast.

In April she wrote to Ruth:

> I am so glad to leave Rochester. We are having farewell party after farewell party and I cooked. I had a Swedish dinner yesterday for six people . . . spareribs, herrings of all kinds, they loved it. I did too. Tuesday we have eleven people from the hospital, and I am going to repeat the same dinner.
>
> David sent me the synopsis of *Valley of Decision.* My, what a woman's part. It is just what he would like me to do. Just like *Adam Had Four Sons.* The woman is a courageous, strong, sincere, GOOD BORE! She is so good all the time it makes you ill. Those governesses who bring beauty

and order to upset households, and who are unhappily in love, and who sacrifice and give up everything to help others. . . . Where is my gun!

With Feldman to jog David Selznick's reluctant arm, offers were coming. This time it was to costar with Charles Boyer in *Gaslight*, the screen adaptation of *Angel Street*, which had intrigued her when she saw it on the New York stage. There were, however, difficulties to be overcome!

———————— • ————————

First David Selznick starts his dealing, and after a little while he calls me up and says, "Sorry, but you're not going to do the picture."

"Not do the picture! And Charles Boyer as my leading man!" I nearly died. "What's gone wrong?"

"Charles Boyer wants first billing."

"So what! Let him have first billing."

"Absolutely not. You're a big star now. I've worked very hard to make you a big star. You get first billing."

"But the only difference is that Charles Boyer's name is on the left-hand side of the screen and mine will be on the right?"

"That's right. And we're not having it."

"But both the names are the same size and both are above the title of the movie. I couldn't care less which side I'm on. I don't care if I'm above the title or below it. I want to work with Charles Boyer."

"Nothing doing. Not on your life. This is a matter of prestige. If you're not top billing, we'd sooner not do the picture."

"*We'd* sooner not do the picture. *I'm* dying to do the picture."

We almost lost that movie—at least *I* almost lost that movie— because Charles Boyer was very mad and he was not going to give in because he'd been a big star far longer than I had. So I had to cry, I had to sob, I had to plead before David very, very grudgingly, gave way.

The next difficulty came with the first scene we shot. I have always pleaded with my directors: "Please, *please* don't start the film with a *love scene."* Practically every film is shot out of sequence, depending on where the locations are, or what sets have to be struck first. They burnt down the whole set of Atlanta and filmed it before they'd even finished casting *Gone With the Wind.* And I always seemed to land with a passionate love embrace before I'd been introduced to my leading man. I remember long after this, in a film called *Aimez-vous Brahms?*—it was called *Goodbye Again* in America because they said the audience would ask, "Who is Brahms?"—I took Anthony Perkins into my dressing room—he was supposed to be my young lover—and I said, "For heavens sake, kiss me!" Anthony did a double take, then he laughed and said, "Why? What for?" I said, "Because we've got to do it later in the film, and I don't know you, I'm hardly acquainted with you, and I'm shy and I blush. Much better we do our first rehearsal in my dressing room, so that I shan't start dreading the moment when we have to do it in front of a hundred technicians." He grinned, and understood, and said, "Okay," then kissed me, and said, "That hurt? No? Good." He was very sweet, and it was easier for me after that. I knew him. We were friends. You see, although the camera has no terrors at all for me, I'm very bad at this sort of intimacy on the screen, especially when the men are practically strangers.

And with Charles Boyer, it was absurd! Our opening shot, out of sequence as always, was when I arrived at a railway station in Italy. I leapt out of the carriage and raced across to where Charles was standing in the middle of the platform waiting to catch me in his arms, passionately embrace me, and kiss me. No woman in her right mind would object to being kissed by Charles Boyer, but I had to do all the running because there he was, all alone in the middle of the platform perched up on a ridiculous little box since I was quite a few inches taller than he. So I had to rush up and be careful not to kick the box, and go into my act. It was easier for us to die of laughter than to look like lovers.

But I thought Charles Boyer was the most intelligent actor I ever worked with, and one of the very nicest. He was widely read, and well educated, and so *different.* He opened the French Library on La Cienega Boulevard, and formed a French society there. He had that wonderful voice and accent, and those eyes—those beautiful velvet eyes. . . . In *Gaslight* he played the man who marries me and then tries to drive me insane, because he's really after my old aunt's jewels hidden in our rickety house.

Charles was married to Pat Pattesson, an English actress who gave up her career when she married Charles. For at least ten years they had been trying for a baby; then a few months before *Gaslight,*

Pat had become pregnant. So during the filming Charles was always rushing to the telephone to call home to see if anything was happening. And I'll never forget. The phone rang, Charles rushed off, and back he came with tears streaming down his face. He had a son! Champagne—everybody had to have champagne! More champagne and Charles's tears falling into every glass. There was no more shooting that day. You'd think no one in the world had ever had a son before.

We were all so happy for him, and he and Pat just adored that boy—little Michael—just adored him. I remember four years later when we were playing in *Arch of Triumph* together, he brought the little boy to see us on the set. He was so beautiful, just like his father, with the same velvet eyes, and Charles was so proud of him.

After *Arch of Triumph* it was years before we met again—not until the sixties. I was living in France, and I met Charles, but he was only the shadow of the man he'd been. I had heard part of the tragic story. Michael had grown into an athletic young man who, like his father, was sensitive and vulnerable. So what should Charles give Michael on his twenty-first birthday? Why, what every young man yearns for! The key to an apartment of his very own.

Young Michael fell in love with a girl; and what really happened I don't suppose anyone will ever know. The girl was at the apartment with Michael, and another boy she was supposed to love was also there. I'm told there was some sort of quarrel or argument. Michael produced a revolver and, whether he was showing off with Russian roulette or whatever it was, Michael put the revolver to his head, pulled the trigger and blew his brains out.

Neither Charles nor Pat ever recovered. They left Hollywood and tried living in Geneva, and then when Pat became ill they came back to Arizona for her health. She died there of a brain tumor in 1978, and so both those people precious to Charles had gone. I suppose life was unsupportable. He refused to talk to anyone or see anyone, and three days later he took an overdose.

He was such a peerless actor. I remember he was in Jean Paul Sartre's play *Red Gloves* in New York. I was in the theater and there were two women sitting behind me and as soon as he came on they started, "Good God. Is *that* Charles Boyer! So small! And that stomach! And he's nearly bald." And after a few seconds of this I turned around and said, "Just wait. Just wait until he starts to act." And they waited. And he acted. He acted like he always did with such magic, he held the audience in his hand. And the two ladies didn't say anything else. Only applauded very loudly at the end. And didn't look at me as they went out.

————— • —————

It was mainly Ingrid's earnings which bought the house at 1220 Benedict Canyon Drive. It was set on a hillside amid the green and elegant acres of Beverly Hills. The ranch-style house of stone and pine reminded them of a ski lodge. Its chief characteristic was a huge living room, with a wide stone fireplace, from which all other rooms radiated. In the next five years they added a swimming pool and a sauna.

It was home and they tried to settle down. But with Petter spending long hours and often nights now as a resident in neurosurgery at a Los Angeles hospital, and Ingrid working in the studios or off on bond tours, no one could say they were living together as a normal married couple.

————— • —————

Before we settled in Benedict Canyon, my movie friends were always laughing and saying, "So you have such a happy marriage? But you never live together. He's always somewhere, and you're always somewhere else—apart! Wait till you live together in the same house. Then let's ask you how your marriage is."

We had our first housewarming party, and that was my first big surprise. I made my list of all the people I wanted to come. Then I went to Irene Selznick for her advice. All the people I liked were on the list: Ruth Roberts, Irene and David Selznick, the cameraman of this picture, the writer of that script, these actors. . . . Irene looked at it and said, "This is impossible. Quite impossible. You can't mix producers with this little writer and you can't mix stars with this unknown actor." "But it's just a party," I said, "just our first housewarming party." "But you can't mix a feature player, a cameraman, and Miss Roberts, a language teacher, with the head of Columbia Studios for example. No one will enjoy themselves. It simply isn't possible."

That was my first lesson. So I had to make a completely new list, just the top people. If I wanted the other people I could have another party but the two groups couldn't mix. That was a great shock. I learned it all depended upon which group you were in. When you were in "that" group, you somehow couldn't get out of it. If you belonged to the people at the top—the Selznicks, the Goetzes, the Mayers, Cohns, and Warners—you stayed at that level. But thank goodness, there was the Hitchcock group: Hitch and Alma mixed a lot with actors they liked, and didn't care if they were stars or not. And Jean and Dido Renoir, my other dear friends, knew a wide range of people. So in the end I found myself belonging to three groups.

The first group held these enormous parties in rented restaurants, or in their homes, with huge buffets round the swimming pools, and butlers, and servants, the best of the best. Take Sam Spiegel's New Year's Eve party, for example. If you were invited to Sam Spiegel's party you knew you were somebody. And one New Year's Eve, I managed to talk Petter into going. I said, "It would be nice one New Year's Eve at least seeing what it's all about."

I couldn't believe my first New Year's in America because in Sweden it was such an important day. A family day. You stayed at home. You waited for midnight; you talked about the past and what the future might bring; and then of course you made various resolutions like, "I'll stop smoking," things like that. And then, on the stroke of midnight, all the church bells broke out all over the country, and on the radio one very famous actor, Anders de Wahl, would read Tennyson's "Ring Out Wild Bells." It was broadcast all over Stockholm from loudspeakers. You could hear it in every street in the city—you didn't even have to listen to the radio.

Quite different from America with all the yelling and screaming and drinking, where sometimes you miss midnight bells altogether because there's so much noise, and by that time half the party has passed out anyway. Petter and I stayed together at home until midnight, and we talked about the past and the future, and then we went off in our car to Sam Spiegel's party. I was looking forward to seeing all these lovely people, all the beautiful people who were at the party, because in those days I loved to go out, I loved to meet them. But we couldn't even get near the house; the cars were solid like a parking lot. I said, "Let's walk up there." But we couldn't get near the house even by walking; it was jammed with people all the way into the garden. We went home.

All through those Hollywood years I simply gave little informal parties with Swedish food, that sort of thing; I didn't even try to compete. The parties I really adored were with Jean Renoir, gathered in his Provençal-type kitchen with its big, scrubbed, wooden table, opening all sorts of California wine and comparing it with French, and the friendship, warmth and wonderful talk we enjoyed there. It was the same with Hitch, though he would never invite more than eight people at a time. "More than eight is an insult to my friends," he would say.

I found it difficult to fit into some Hollywood fashions. I never wanted a mink coat, and when I came to Hollywood and David Selznick saw that I didn't have one, he was absolutely flabbergasted; he couldn't believe it. Everybody had a mink coat! The fact that the climate makes a mink coat completely unnecessary has nothing to do with it. When you came to a party, it was the fashion to throw your coat into the ladies' bedroom. The bed was piled high with mink; it groaned under mink coats.

So when I was in New York one time, David telephoned Dan O'Shea to take me out and buy a mink coat. He didn't buy it; I had to pay for it myself. And I remember coming back to Hollywood and going to the next party, and as I threw my coat on top of all the other minks I felt disgusted. My mink wasn't half as nice as all the other minks; I still hadn't made it, my mink was too cheap because I just wouldn't buy *the* most expensive. So I sold it, and that was the end of that short story.

David was very very sad again because he thought I hadn't attained the real status of a movie star in America. The following Christmas he kindly gave me a Persian lamb fur coat which I liked much better, so that at least I owned a fur coat and didn't disgrace him.

The same thing was repeated in Rome ten years later. Roberto Rossellini said in a shocked voice, "Don't you have a mink coat?" And I said, "No." He said, "But *every* woman has a mink coat. How come you didn't buy a mink coat? I mean *everybody* in America has a mink coat." And I said, "Well that's the reason I didn't want one. Everybody has a mink coat." So what does he do?—the following Christmas he gives me a mink coat. *That* mink coat I wore because it *wasn't* that usual in Italy. Not *everyone* had a mink coat. And because Roberto had given it to me. That mink coat I still have. It's doing its first really useful job. I've sewn it inside a raincoat. A warm, useful, mink-lined raincoat. Maybe eventually one of my daughters will like it.

It's the same with jewelry. I've never been excited by that. It never thrilled me to have a diamond bracelet; I rarely wear diamond earrings or necklaces. My favorite piece of jewelry is a long gold-plated chain and locket. I've worn the plating off several times, so I take it back and have it regilded. They always say, "It's ridiculous replating this old thing." And I say, "It's for sentimental reasons, thank you very much."

Another Hollywood thing I hated was the power of those two women, Louella Parsons and Hedda Hopper, the gossip columnists. Their power shocked me, and I thought it very wrong that the film industry had allowed them to build up to such an extent that they could ruin people's careers and lives.

There was a celebration for Louella Parsons, I think it was her birthday. We were asked to pay twenty-five dollars for a dinner to honor her. She sent out the invitations, and I threw mine in the wastepaper basket. Then I got a second one. I threw that away too. Then my producer, Walter Wanger—I was making *Joan of Arc* at the time—said, "Ingrid, I understand you haven't answered Louella's invitation," and I said, "No, I don't want to go. If I don't reply she'll know I'm not coming." "Oh," he said, "you can't just throw it away like that. The picture's coming out soon. She'll try and damage the picture, because she will keep track of the people who don't come." I said, "I am not going to pay twenty-five dollars to have the non-pleasure of sitting with a lot of people in a big hall to celebrate Louella Parsons." He said, "Well, I'll pay. I'll pay." I insisted, "It's not the money. I can afford twenty-five dollars. I just don't want to go." And then he said, "Well, you must say you're sick and send her flowers." I answered, "I will not. It says here on the invitation, coming or not coming? And I'm not coming." Well he sent flowers from me, and said I was sick or something like that, to save his movie. To that extent they were afraid.

Once I was present when Hedda Hopper got furious with Gene Tierney. It was at a Sonja Henie party. Sonja was in the top bracket so her parties were among the best in Hollywood: a marquee by the swimming pool, orchestras playing, expensive gifts for everyone, lots of games with very valuable prizes, everything so elegant, food specially flown from Norway. There I sat with Gene Tierney, and she was pregnant although to look at her you'd never know it. Up came Hedda Hopper. She was furious. "What's this I hear. You're expecting a baby and you haven't told me a word about it?" Gene Tierney looked puzzled. "Well, Hedda, I didn't really know myself until recently, and there were some things I didn't really think I had to call you about." Hedda wasn't at all amused. "Wait till your next picture comes out," she snapped. "Don't think you can expect anything good about it from me."

You couldn't sit with Louella Parsons or Hedda Hopper for two minutes without their rushing away to the telephone to report some remark you'd made.

I suppose it was in Benedict Canyon that our married life began to crack a bit at the seams; perhaps it had something to do with the fact that now we were *really* living together.

In private life, compared with life when I was acting, I was, as I have said, always hesitant, a little afraid. Petter decided everything for me. He told me what to do and what to say, and I leaned on him for everything. He meant well. He took burdens off my shoulders so I could concentrate on my dialogue and go to bed early so I would look beautiful in the morning. But it meant there were so many things in life I didn't know about; I was just frightened of them. Often, in the interviews I gave, he told me I didn't say the right thing. I was talking too much, he said, and couldn't I learn from Garbo? Garbo never said anything. I tried to tell him that I didn't have Garbo's qualities. I liked to talk to people and I liked to explain. I thought that by explaining, people would understand me. But of course experience taught me that was silly.

And sometimes when Petter and I came back from a party, he would say: "You shouldn't talk so much. You have a very intelligent face, so let people think you are intelligent, because when you start to chatter it's just a lot of nonsense." So when he was present I tried very hard not to say too much because I knew he might be irritated with me when we got back home.

Petter was afraid that I would become "Hollywood"—that I would believe I was a big star when he wanted me to believe I was just an ordinary actress. But that is all I believed anyway—I was an ordinary actress trying to improve. He kept his praise very low, because as he said, so many other people were praising me that he had to keep the balance, so it wouldn't go to my head. "Not bad" was as much as I could really expect from Petter. "Good" was something close to magnificent.

To protect me, and he was quite sincere about this, as Irene had been also, he would often say, "You have to be very careful with all these handsome ladies' men around. They're all pretending to fall in love with you. They want to date you. But you must bear in mind what's behind it. Publicity. *Their* publicity: to get into the gossip columns so that people will talk about them. So be very careful."

I said to him: "You mean to tell me that you're the only man in the world who has ever fallen in love with me for my own sake, and not because I'm a famous actress?"

"Yes, I believe so," said Petter, which made me very sad. I believed him for quite a long time.

Yet he was convinced I was having affairs with all my leading men. They were very handsome leading men. Some I was very attracted to, and I think they were attracted to me. But there were certainly no love affairs. As Ruth wisely said, "She's just enough in love with him to make the love scenes look real." Who wouldn't be in love with Cary Grant, Gary Cooper, Spencer Tracy? Half the women in the world were anyway. But only very seldom did I meet them outside the studio. Cary Grant, I went out with only once when I was in New York and we met Howard Hughes. Gary Cooper and his wife we did become friendly with, and they came to our house and we went to theirs, but that was probably because Pia and their daughter Maria were friends, the same age, and going to the same school.

Sometimes Petter used to irritate me. When I was in the middle of telling him something that had happened at the studio, something I thought was very interesting, he would say, "Don't wrinkle your forehead." I would answer, "All right, all right," and continue the story. Then after another couple of sentences, he would say, "You're still wrinkling your forehead." And, "Sit up straight."

I'd try to take out the wrinkles and sit up straight, but I had the uneasy feeling he didn't listen to the story, he was so concerned about the way I was wrinkling or sitting or twisting my fingers. And I used to say to him, "You'll be right by my bedside when I die, telling me not to wrinkle my forehead."

Of course what he said has helped me an awful lot through the years. I do sit up straight, and I do stand straight on the stage; I'm not afraid of being tall. Petter did me a lot of good by nagging me, but in those days it irritated me beyond measure.

And occasionally there were the arguments about my diet. Petter wanted me very slender and thin. He always complained that he couldn't understand with all the diets I was on, how come I didn't lose weight? What he didn't know was that though at the table I ate just the right things—a little salad, juice—I had a jar of cookies in my bedroom, and right after dinner I'd go and eat them all up. And in the middle of the night I'd go down to the icebox and eat everything that was edible just to fill in after my slenderizing dinner. I remember once Petter just couldn't understand how come I couldn't lose more weight. "Oh yes," I said, "I'm losing all the time." But he went and got the scale and put it down in front of me and made me get on it. Forced me to. And there, it was clear, I had gained. I was so hurt that he showed me up and forced me on that scale. I was so humiliated. So I suppose it was just a slow accumulation of all these small things over those five years we lived in Hollywood.

Being so often apart caused a lot of the trouble. Most of my friends were in the film business, actors or producers, so at the few parties we went to it was my circle of friends we saw. Often, people I knew quite well would ask, "Who's that with you? Who's he?" And I'd say, "That's my husband. He's a doctor." But though Petter had nothing in common with my movie friends, he was soon much in demand with all the wives who sat around at those parties while their husbands talked shop or discussed parts with the beautiful movie queens. The wives were terribly pleased with Petter because he danced with them, and he was an excellent dancer. Sometimes, though, he would dance by me and say in Swedish, so no one could understand, "That's the fourth martini you've had." But I suppose many husbands and wives say little things like that to each other from time to time.

I was often surrounded at those parties by producers and directors who wanted me to work in their pictures, or to talk about their pictures. I'd try to say as little as possible because I knew Petter was looking and thought I was saying too much.

In the articles they wrote about him they always mentioned that he loved to run. In Sweden, Petter was the original jogger. But he wasn't content just to run. He'd take a rucksack and fill it with stones, or heavy bricks, so there was much more weight to carry, and better exercise. And the interviews made fun of him.

These days, of course, with the jogging craze, it would have been accepted as normal and healthy. But you must remember what Hollywood was like in those days. If you didn't conform, they looked at you very suspiciously.

I did love our house. We'd chosen it together and we'd added the swimming pool and the sauna bath. We had our daughter, and we had a dog, and I had my little car. Still, somehow, it was never enough. I was always eager to get away . . . go to New York, go away on a bond tour, anything to escape, I suppose. Ruth showed me a letter I'd written to her just before I came home once. . . . "Goodbye freedom," I'd said.

Petter felt that money had to be earned by hard work. Once you'd got it, you didn't waste it or part with it easily. I understood that philosophy. I never wasted money. We brought up Pia to know that money wasn't that easy to get. Pia wanted a bicycle. I wanted to buy her a bicycle. Petter said, "Of course she must have a bicycle but not just because she asks for it; she should wait and she should dream about the bicycle, really long for it. Then when she gets it, she'll appreciate it." Pia and I talked about the bicycle, we looked at it, we discussed the color of the bicycle, and we were saving up to buy it. And this went on and on. And led to a funny incident.

One morning, while driving out to do some shopping, I went across one of those white lines at a road junction where you were supposed to halt. I sailed straight through and naturally there was a police car waiting for me. I stopped and the policeman strolled across and he recognized me and said, "Ah-ah, Miss Bergman. I'm surprised at you doing this. You should have stopped at that intersection." And I said, "I'm sorry, officer." He took his book out, and said, "Well, I'm afraid this is going to cost you five dollars, Miss Bergman. . . ." Pia heard this, and her eyes opened wide, and she began to sob. "Boo-hoo, poor mother, what are we going to do? This is terrible, my mother doesn't have five dollars. And what is Papa going to say . . . boo-hoo-hoo . . . my mother doesn't have five dollars. . . ." I knew then we'd certainly indoctrinated Pia with the real value of money. The policeman leaned on the side of the car and looked me straight in the eye. "Miss Bergman," he said softly, "Miss Bergman, you mean to tell me you don't have five dollars!" He was really very sweet about it.

Certainly money was one of the things which did come between Petter and me. One friend of mine said long afterwards that Petter was sure that I was getting too fat and that no one would want me as an actress; therefore my acting career would end, and that sort of money would stop. He invested our money in retirement insurance for our old age; rarely did I break out and spend any. But I did on one occasion in New York with the studio publicist, Joe Steele.

Joe felt that I was too tied down, that I wasn't free to do anything. "Are we going to do this interview?" he'd ask. "Wait a minute, I'll call Petter," I'd reply. And he'd snap, "Why don't you decide for yourself?" He wanted me to be independent from Petter in such matters, and Petter didn't like that. On this occasion we had to go to some function or other, and I said, "I don't have anything to wear." Joe said, "Why don't you?" I replied, "I can't afford new clothes." Joe nearly had a fit. "Can't afford them? You're making so much money it's unbelievable. Yet, every time you're invited to a cocktail party or a lunch or theater, you say you have nothing to wear. So all right, let's go out and buy you some clothes. Now!" To me this seemed almost immoral. I don't think it had ever occurred to me that I could go out and buy clothes that I didn't *need.* Joe took me to Bergdorf Goodman, and Saks, and all those lovely New York shops and I was so nervous, you have no idea. But I bought the clothes. That evening I got together my courage and called Petter. I asked him to please send the money to pay for this whole new wardrobe. He wasn't happy about that. "What d'you need all those new clothes for?" he said.

Mainly I kept quiet because I didn't think it would do any good if I argued. But I always remember what to me was one of the breaking points. Petter was quite angry one day because he thought I'd let him down. He had asked that I never mention him in an interview, never have an interview at home, never have any photographs taken of our home, and never let anyone photograph Pia. And I respected all those wishes; many people didn't even know I was married and had a child. But once I allowed a picture to be taken of me at home in a big chair. It was just a head shot. I thought that instead of having all the trouble of going to a studio or a hotel room, I could allow that; nobody in the world would know that the background was my home; besides, no background was going to be seen anyway. But when the photograph was published, Petter recognized the chair and then he was really angry. I said, "All right, I made a mistake again. But everybody makes mistakes, you make mistakes, I make mistakes. . . ." And he said, *"I . . . I* make mistakes?" I replied, "Well yes, don't you make mistakes?" He said, "No. Why should I? I think carefully before I do something. I weigh it. I ponder over it, and then I decide."

I said to myself, "Here is going to be a divorce. I cannot live with a person who believes that he doesn't make mistakes." (Petter has since denied that he ever made that statement.)

I thought, I'll pull myself together and move out for some peace, go where I won't be frightened. It was crazy to be married to the only person I was afraid of. I was never afraid of the people I worked with; there wasn't a producer, director, or a leading man or anybody that I was afraid of. I had a good time; I could kid them, and they would laugh back. But then I would face going home to Petter.

I asked if Petter would mind if we had a divorce. He was so surprised he couldn't believe it and asked, "Why should we get a divorce? We haven't had a fight, we've never had a quarrel." I said, "No we haven't because it's no use my starting a fight or a quarrel with you. That would be absolutely useless because there isn't any such thing as my ever having a discussion with you. You're never going to see my side. So I won't argue with you. I'll go away."

But I didn't go away. I thought it was ridiculous to pack up and start a big fight about our child, and sit alone in one house while he sat alone in another.

I think I was just waiting for someone to come along and help me out of that marriage because I didn't have the strength to go. That was over three years before I met Roberto Rossellini.

———————— • ————————

Ingrid's career was still spiraling upward during the middle forties, and her insistence upon changing her roles as dramatically as possible, despite the constant warnings of David Selznick and Michael Curtiz, was paying off—never more so than in *The Bells of St. Mary's:*

———————— • ————————

Leo McCarey, who had all the charm and blarney of an Irish ancestry, and was a fine director, had already had a great success with Bing Crosby as the priest, Father O'Malley, in *Going My Way.* Then he got the idea of doing a sequel, and instead of a vinegary old Barry Fitzgerald playing opposite Bing, he'd have a rather sweet nun—me! Actually, Leo built the character of this nun on a real person. She was also a nun, but a very sporty, laughing girl, who liked boxing and tennis, who adored children and caring for them, and built for herself a life full of love and faith. Leo never forgot this nun in her long skirts and habit, racing all over a tennis court banging the ball. We didn't do the tennis scene in the picture: we stuck to boxing instead.

Leo went to see David Selznick and said he wanted me to play

Sister Benedict. David just refused. "Absolutely not," he said. "If you have made a success and you try to milk it by doing a sequel, it's inevitably compared to the first and is a failure. I'm not having Ingrid in a failure."

So a rather depressed Leo McCarey rang me up, and appeared on my front doorstep with his script under his arm. He sat down in the living room and outlined the story. I thought it was wonderful. I said, "Give me the script, I'd love to read it." I read the script. I called him back and said, "I adore it. I'd love to do it."

"Well," he said, "you'll have to help me with David because he's dead against it."

I went to see Selznick. The same old dialogue took place: It wasn't good enough. It was a sequel. Why waste my talents . . . etc., etc. "But it *is* good enough," I said, "I know it's good enough. And I want to play it."

David looked me straight in the eye, the very serious, great film producer, and asked the dynamic question: "What are you going to do while Bing Crosby is singing?"

"I'm going to look at him," I said. "That's all. I don't have to do anything but look at him."

"Look at him? You're a great actress and you're just going to look at him?"

"I shall register radiance, adoration, perhaps perplexity."

But of course David argued very well. Finally I was in despair, and David, naturally, seeing he'd won now, thought he would shift the responsibility for my not getting the picture to Leo McCarey.

"If you're so keen, I'll talk to McCarey about terms."

In other words he'd ask so much they couldn't possibly afford to have me. So he started off by doubling my normal rental fee.

And Leo said quietly, "Okay, yes."

Then David—who rented Selznick International studio space from RKO—said, "And I shall want a year's studio space—free."

"Okay, yes," said Leo.

"And I shall want the rights to *A Bill of Divorcement,*" said David.

That was an RKO film property which had starred Katharine Hepburn.

"Okay, yes," said Leo.

Now David was taken a little aback by all this, and he had to think very quickly about what he should ask for next. So he managed to think up two more properties owned by RKO and each time Leo said, very politely, "Okay, yes."

And finally David asked, "Do you really want to pay out all this to buy Ingrid Bergman?"

"I'm so happy that Ingrid is for sale," said Leo.

And he paid, and I was so happy that the picture was a great success, just as successful as *Going My Way,* and that David was completely wrong.

Of course from the minute I played in *The Bells of St. Mary's* everybody knew what I should do forever afterwards. I should be a nun—oh sure, a very funny nun, but a nun just the same. The only really good thing I found about being a nun was that all I showed was my face. The rest of me was shrouded in large black drapes. I could eat ice cream forever. No one worried about my weight.

I loved doing my first comedy scenes, because no one knew I could play comedy before this. It was also such a delight to be directed by Leo. But I didn't get to know Bing Crosby at all. He was very polite and nice, and couldn't have been more pleasant, but he was always surrounded by a little group of three or four men chattering away and protecting him from everybody else. I asked who they were and I was told they were his gagmen.

Actually I played an extra gag on Bing and Leo at the end of the picture. It was the very last scene, the last shot we had to do. Sister Benedict is very unhappy because she is being sent away to some health resort, and she thinks it is because she is not good at her job, and no good with the children. Everybody else knows it's because she has TB and until she recovers her health she can't work with the children. In this very last shot, Father O'Malley thinks it better she be told the truth.

So Bing tells me, and my face lights up with joy because—in Sister Benedict's terms—TB is nothing compared with thinking that I can't look after the children. I say, "Thank you, Father, thank you with all my heart." And Bing answers, "If you're ever in trouble, sister, just dial 'O' for O'Malley," and I reply gratefully, "Thank you, I will." I walk away, and that's the end of the picture.

"Fine," shouted Leo. "That's it. That's great. Wrap it up."

But I turned to him and said, "Do you mind? Could I do that scene just once more? I think I could do it just a little better."

Leo looked surprised because he knew that the scene was as good as we'd ever get, and the film was finally finished; but being such a nice man he said, "Okay, okay . . . if you want to. All right, fellas. One more take, here we go. . . ."

So that time I said, "Thank you, Father, oh, thank you with all my heart." And I threw my arms around Bing and kissed him right on the mouth. Bing nearly fell down with shock. Everybody stood up. "Cut! Stop the cameras! Cut, for heaven's sake, cut!" The priest acting as consultant came running up, actually running, in a great state: "Now this is going too far. Miss Bergman, we simply can't allow that. A Catholic nun kissing a Catholic father . . . you can't have such a thing in a movie. . . ."

I was already grinning all over my face. Bing was just recovering from the assault, and I looked around and, of course, Leo had caught on and he was laughing his head off. The crew got the joke, too, and now even the priest realized it was all a big joke.

———————— • ————————

It was a happy film, punctuated halfway through by the 1944 Academy Awards at Grauman's Chinese Theater. Ingrid had been nominated the year before for her performance in *For Whom the Bell Tolls* and had lost to Jennifer Jones for her part in *The Song of Bernadette.* Now she had been nominated for *Gaslight.* Before the best actress was announced, Bing Crosby and Leo McCarey received Oscars for the best actor and best director, respectively, for *Going My Way.*

When Ingrid too won an Oscar, she made her polite reply at the microphone: "I am deeply grateful for this award. I am particularly glad to get it this time because I'm working on a picture at the moment with Mr. Crosby and Mr. McCarey. And I'm afraid if I went on the set tomorrow without an award, neither of them would speak to me."

Chapter 9

When I arrived in Paris on June 6, 1945, to start a tour of Germany with Jack Benny, Larry Adler, and Martha Tilton to entertain the troops, the war had ended less than a month before. Paris was wonderful. In spite of all its shortages and black markets it had such a spirit. I hadn't been in Europe for eight whole years. It was like starting to live all over again.

The Ritz Hotel was the headquarters for the American war correspondents, the press corps, and all the entertainers. And the very afternoon I arrived I found a note pushed under my bedroom door. I found it very funny.

Subject: Dinner. 6.28.45. Paris. France.
To: Miss Ingrid Bergman.
Part 1. This is a community effort. The community consists of Bob Capa and Irwin Shaw.
    2. We were planning on sending you flowers with this note inviting you to dinner this evening—but after consultation we discovered it was possible to pay for the flowers or the dinner, or the dinner or the flowers, not both. We took a vote and dinner won by a close margin.
    3. It was suggested that if you did not care for dinner, flowers might be sent. No decision has been reached on this so far.

4. Besides flowers we have lots of doubtful qualities.
5. If we write much more we will have no conversation left, as our supply of charm is limited.
6. We will call you at 6.15.
7. We do not sleep.
   Signed:
   Worried.

Well, naturally you know what I chose. I preferred to eat rather
than to sit in a room in the Ritz Hotel staring at a bunch of flowers.
I'd never heard of Irwin Shaw or Bob Capa, but when they rang I
went down and met them in the bar and found that Bob was an
accredited war photographer, and Irwin Shaw a G.I.

And I got on so well with both of them. It was a great evening.
We had a wonderful time. We ate at a little restaurant. I met their
friends. We all laughed, we all danced.

From that very first evening I liked Bob Capa very much. He was
Hungarian, amusing, and with much charm. It was a marvelous
start to the tour I was going to make.

We set out on the tour to be as funny as we could and get the
boys laughing again, because they hadn't had much to laugh about
for the past few years. Jack Benny had his jokes, Larry Adler played
his harmonica. Martha sang, and I did several "pieces" out of a new
play *Joan of Lorraine* which I was going to do on the New York
stage later in the year, and a skit with Jack Benny on *Gaslight.*

I met Capa again in Berlin. The city had been blown to bits: it
was absolutely unbelievable. No roofs on the houses, everything
outside. Capa found a bathtub in the street. He said this was going
to be his scoop: for the first time, Ingrid Bergman photographed
in a bathtub. I laughed and said "Okay." And so there I was, sitting
in the bathtub out in the street . . . fully clothed. He was so excited
about what he'd done he rushed back to develop his films, and
somehow in his hurry the negative was ruined. So the famous scoop
—the future center-page pull-out of Bergman in the bathtub—
never did make any magazine.

There were often no roads left in Germany, so we drove over
fields. We lived in private homes and we lived in barracks. We were
the first group to come in; at least, we had thought we would be the
first entertainers in the field, but when we arrived at the Ritz Hotel
in Paris there was Marlene Dietrich on her way out. She said, with

a big smile, "Ah, now you're coming, when the war's over." She was the bravest of them all because she was right in there during the war. She went from one front to the next and she entertained the American boys and Allied troops while the fighting was still going on. She told me about having to wash her hair in gasoline in a helmet because there was no water. I didn't have her kind of troubles, but it was an enormous experience.

For weeks and weeks we traveled all over Germany and into Czechoslovakia. As we drove toward the towns in our big black German Capitan cars, we could usually see a church sticking out of the ruins. If the church had also been destroyed, there was always _something_ that told us this had once been a place where people lived. But it was terrible to see.

Wherever we went the G.I.'s put up a platform and sat on the ground around us. Our units always had some sort of orchestra or band. We'd rehearse a little bit with the musicians and then on we'd go. Then we'd pack up, dance with the boys, have drinks with them, talk to the officers. We tried to be very fair, not to give all our attention to the officers. Someone had complained that the officers got all the entertainment after the show and the boys didn't—the same complaint we had had in Alaska the year before. So we talked with the boys, and they showed photographs of their wives or sweethearts or sisters and told me, "She looks just like you," which was very sweet. The fact that I was female was what really mattered.

One of the most beautiful sights I ever saw was in Heidelberg. It was Jack Benny's idea. We were performing in an amphitheater there, when Jack Benny said: "Now listen! When I count to three, all of you strike a match or flick a lighter . . . one, two, three!" And it was the most wonderful moment—this enormous place suddenly lit up with what seemed like a million little lights, a great bowl of light, suddenly alive.

We had such luck with our little group. Jack Benny was one of the nicest human beings I ever met. The kindness of that man. The generosity, tired as he was, talking to the boys, talking to the officers.

We were being transported quickly. Only one show in each place. We could get a little nap in the car but that was about all the rest we got.

And of course there were occasionally dreadful shocks. They

all, except me, went to see a concentration camp. We were playing in the neighborhood, and General Eisenhower was there and he invited the whole troupe to come and see it. Everybody said you should see these things, but I stayed behind. When they came back they were all sick. They didn't want to talk about it. I can imagine what they saw from the photographs I've seen. I just didn't want to see it. I didn't want to have it in my brain. There are certain things you wish people had never told you. I know they exist, but don't put the picture in front of my eyes. It stops you even working again. It numbs you, it freezes you. You can no longer operate.

Then there was the time they "killed" Larry Adler. All the young soldiers were a bit trigger-happy. Especially the sentries. They were so used to shooting they said "Halt" once and, the second time if you didn't obey, they shot you. So there was this guard standing at a roadblock as we drove up. He said something to our chauffeur about seeing our papers, but our chauffeur was a German boy and he drove straight through. Then we heard a shot. I heard the shot very clearly and so did Larry. Larry felt the shot in the back. He fell on his knees in the car and he screamed, "I'm shot! I'm shot! Oh, my God!" I took him in my arms, held him against me, and he wailed, "Say good-bye to my wife and to my children." And I said, "I will, I will, Larry, don't die." I looked at the back of him, and I said, "Larry, Larry, I see no hole." There was silence from Larry. I looked again, and I said, "The bullet should have made a hole, shouldn't it? And you're not bleeding or anything?" So he calmed down, and we took the jacket off, and there was no sign of a wound. Of course by that time the chauffeur had stopped and the guard had come and everybody was yelling. Jack Benny had been in the other car; but he had heard the shot and raced back to our car. We looked at the back of the seat and found the bullet trapped in the stuffing. It had hit a spring and the seat spring had broken, shot forward and hit Larry in the back. Larry kept the bullet.

Back in Paris again with Jack Benny, Larry Adler, and the others, there was Capa. And I suppose that's where I began to fall in love with him.

We were there on V-J Day when Japan surrendered. That was another celebration with great crowds in the streets. I'd seen newsreels of how all the girls threw themselves at the soldiers and kissed them on V-E Day and I said to Bob Capa, "I'm going to do that, I'm going to throw myself at somebody and kiss him."

We were sitting in a Jeep in the Champs-Elysées and Capa asked, "Which one?" I said, "Him—over there." I dashed out of the car, threw myself at the soldier, and kissed him on the mouth. He didn't think twice about it. He kissed me back.

———— • ————

It was in Paris, shortly before the war started that Robert Capa first began his career as a famous photographer. Born in Hungary, he emigrated to Germany in 1932 when he was eighteen to improve his education, and with the sudden burgeoning of photo-journalism and the arrival of the new photographic marvels, he decided that this was where his future lay. But Hitler was gaining in power. When the Führer's dislike of Jews became maniacal—Capa was Jewish—Robert skied away to safety across the Alps and chose Paris as his home-town.

By this time his interest in photography was obsessive. Speaking the normal Hungarian complement of five languages, Capa was once asked which of these languages he thought and dreamt in. "Pictures," he replied immediately. Had he reflected, he might have added, "dangerous pictures". He foraged where he could in the world. In the Spanish Civil War he took one of the most famous and dramatic pictures: a Spanish Republican soldier falling at the moment of death.

When France was overrun by the Nazis, he escaped to America. In New York, as a Hungarian stateless person, he was about to be interned as an enemy alien when he got himself an assignment with *Colliers* magazine to take pictures in bombed and beleaguered Britain. One of his first jobs was to photograph a squadron of young United States airmen on their first Flying Fortress mission over Europe. Very pleased with one particularly apt picture of a young American lieutenant whose nose visually matched the Perspex cone of his Fortress, Capa photographed the squadron of twenty-four planes taking off. Six hours later, only seventeen returned. The lead ship, its undercarriage shot away, was given priority to land first. Capa photographed first-aid personnel carrying the dead and wounded into ambulances. The last man to emerge was the wounded pilot. He looked at Capa contemptuously, and said angrily, "Are *these* the pictures you were waiting for, photographer?"

The scar that insult left on Capa's self-esteem remained with him for the rest of his life. The wide divergence between the civilian bystander and the fighting man had been made painfully clear. On the train back to London, Robert Capa was very thoughtful indeed. If he was to continue in his chosen profession and maintain his self-respect, there was going to be no more waiting on the airfield for the planes to return, no more reporting hostilities from safely behind the lines. From now on there were going to be no easy compromises. Where the action was hottest, his camera was going to be clicking. The sort of pictures he had just taken, he wrote, were "Only for undertakers and I didn't like being one. If I was to share the funeral, I swore I would also have to share the procession."

Economic needs also being what they were, he sold the Flying Fortress pictures to *Illustrated* magazine. The grateful editor informed him they were featuring the nose-cone shot on the front cover. But three days before publication, Capa found a more subdued editor and a group of highly irate United States security officers in his bedroom. Was he aware that while he had revealed the lieutenant's nose in the Perspex cone, he had also photographed one of the most closely guarded and vital secrets in the Flying Fortress bomber: the Norden bombsight? All four hundred thousand copies of the picture magazine were recalled and destroyed. Capa left for North Africa with a feeling that he had only narrowly escaped the firing squad.

There, following his newly acquired determination, and encouraged by the commander of the Eighty-second Airborne Division, Capa, with no parachute training whatsoever, stepped into space one dark night over Sicily. He spent the rest of the night dangling in a tree some fifty feet above the ground, aware that the romantic Hungarian accent which gave him such an advantage with the girls, left him with an even chance of being shot by either friend or foe.

He transferred to *Life* magazine as a staff photographer and photographed his way with the Army across Sicily and up through Italy in the midst of bitter fighting. He arrived back in England in time to be offered the doubtful distinction of being one of only four photographers to land on the Normandy beaches with the first wave of the United States invasion forces. Capa's philosophy was now decided: "If my son should ever ask 'What is the difference between the war correspondent and any other man in uniform?' I would say that the war correspondent gets more drinks, more girls, better pay, and greater freedom than the soldier, but that having the freedom to choose his spot, being allowed to be a coward and not be executed for it, is his torture. The war correspondent has his stake—his life —in his own hands, and he can put it on this horse or that horse, or he can put it back in his pocket at the very last minute. I am a gambler. I decided to go in with the 'Company E' in the first wave."

On June 6, 1944 in the gray-blue light of dawn, their landing craft ran aground on Omaha Beach, and Capa and "E" company were dropped on to the flat shelving sand under a crossfire of heavy machine guns and mortar shells. The beach was littered with steel stakes, barbed wire, and wrecked amphibious tanks. Capa crawled through the floating dead and wounded, trying to take pictures and stay alive. Pinned down on the beach, he experienced the most terrifying moments of his life. He arrived back at Weymouth the next morning on a boat laden with dead and wounded in a state of emotional shock.

The one hundred and six pictures he delivered were probably the best ever taken of the landing at Omaha. They illustrated the savage drama of those terrible moments on the beach as no others ever did. But his laboratory assistant, excited and eager, tried to dry the negatives too quickly. The emulsion ran. Only eight were saved.

Capa was back on Omaha Beach on D-Day plus two. He rolled into Paris on top of a tank for the greatest liberation party of the war, photographed action all across France, at Bastogne, and into Germany. He dropped once more by parachute in the invasion across the Rhine, and saw the war end with the Allies joining up with the Russians. By the greatest good fortune, he happened to be staying at the Ritz Hotel with his colleague Irwin Shaw, when Miss Bergman crossed the foyer and went up to her room, quite unaware that she was about to be waylaid by an "influence" that would change her life. Most certainly Bob Capa had no idea what he was starting when he collaborated with Irwin Shaw in sending up the note that evening.

When Ingrid met him, Robert Capa, at age thirty-one, a year older than Ingrid, was an arresting and original human being. Vigorous and challenging, he was an international man, worldly and wise, and yet, despite the sardonic banter, still vulnerable. The bright dark eyes under heavy brows, the engaging accent, the lively sense of humor, his ability to manipulate people or authorities to match his mood made him immense good company. He had a gambler's sense of priorities: He was intensely aware that he had but one short life to live, and that he should not leak it away conforming to a set of standards which did not amuse him. On the other hand, he agreed that it was necessary to make a living.

He told Ingrid: "You're mad. You have become an industry, an institution. You must return to the status of human being. Your husband is driving you; the film companies are driving you; you let everybody drive you. It's just work, work, work. You don't take the things you should out of life because you've got no time for living. You're like a cart running on three wheels; you don't realize you've lost the fourth wheel, but at any moment now you are going to topple sideways."

She disagreed. "No," she said, "I am fulfilling myself. I'm going to make more films in Hollywood. I'm going back to the theater to do more plays, especially the one I've always wanted to do, *Joan*. I need the discipline of the theater. . . ." But underneath she thought, Is he right? Could he possibly be right?

Ingrid knew that Capa had his problems too. Behind the cynicism, the audacious smile, the cloud of cigarette smoke, the hand that welcomed an unending flow of glasses, lay a watchful, questing uncertainty. Like many correspondents of that era, and, indeed, like his good friend Papa Hemingway, drink had become something of a "machismo challenge" as well as an anodyne. On occasions, life took on the aspect of being not much more than a series of boring intervals between drinks.

In 1945, also, he had to decide how he was going to change gear and return to the pedestrian speed limits of peace. He could, predictably, chase more wars. But would the kissing, boozing, matador existence become just a bore?

Yes, he could criticize Ingrid for allowing herself to drift down the plush alleyway of her film and stage career without giving herself breathing space for a wider, fuller existence. But like so many young men returning from the wars, he now had to find a new direction for himself. And what part, if any, was Ingrid to play in that?

Chapter 10

In the list of Ingrid's relationships, few—at first sight—were more unlikely than her long and sustained friendship with the chubby genius of a British director, Alfred Hitchcock. Some of it was due to their mutual inclination to drift toward a martini after a hard day in the studio, but Ingrid found Hitch's dogmatic British attitude toward drinking rather odd:

———————— • ————————

The clock had to strike six before he'd race for the martinis. He just adored keeping your glass filled. He awarded me the honorary title of "The Human Sink."

One night he was cooking dinner for the two of us, and we were drinking away and laughing and having fun. But at length I said, "Hitch, I'm getting sleepy."

"Well, go and lie down on the sofa and recover, while I finish the meal," he ordered. I went into the living room and I woke up in the middle of the night. I looked across the room to the other sofa and there was Hitch curled up and sleeping like a baby. At that moment he opened one eye.

I asked, "What happened to our marvelous meal?"

"Dammit," he said, "you passed out on me. And then, dammit, I must have passed out on me."

The lovely dinner was stone cold.

———————— • ————————

She was once asked by an author who was preparing an article on Alfred Hitchcock to send him a few words regarding his qualities.

She wrote:

> He is a magnificently prepared director. There is nothing that he does not know about the picture he is going to do. Every angle and every set-up he has prepared at home with a miniature set of what is being built in the studio. He does not even look into the camera, for he says, "I know what it looks like." I don't know any other director who works like this. Of course he wants everything primarily *his* way, but if an actor has an idea, he is willing to let the actor try it. Sometimes I thought I got through, and that Hitchcock was going to change his set-up. But as a rule he used to get his way by simply saying, "If you can't do it my way, fake it." It was a very good lesson for me, as many times in the future when I couldn't win a battle with a director, I'd remember Hitch's words and, "fake it."
>
> His humor and his sharp wit are a delight. He likes, I think, very real people. If someone on the set was a phony he was liable to start a sort of double-talk, which sounded like absolutely normal conversation but turned out to be nonsense. That is how he got rid of visitors.

Inevitably the man who got Ingrid and Alfred Hitchcock together was David Selznick, even though by these middle forties David's astonishing career was beginning to lose momentum.

Between 1924 and 1940 he had employed practically every great star in Hollywood, produced sixty films, many of them huge international successes—and *Gone With the Wind.* At the age of thirty-seven, with this enormous movie for which he was predominantly responsible, he reached a peak he was never to achieve again. It made him world-famous, a fortune, and it exhausted him. It also dispirited him to realize that he could never do better.

He had offered his film expertise to the war effort, but the generals he approached were neither cooperative nor impressed. He flirted with the idea of entering politics, but the closest he ever got to any sort of political appointment was to become Chairman of the Hollywood Committee for United China Relief. At heart he was always a film man, and he could never desert the trade and the craft he loved.

———— • ————

He had such enormous enthusiasm, and such enormous energy. He really burned his candle at both ends. Of course he rented me out for large sums as soon as I returned to Hollywood, and a lot of my friends said, "What an interesting agent you have. The roles are reversed. He takes ninety percent and you get ten percent."

———— • ————

From 1940 until the end of 1945 Ingrid had made only eleven films and her yearly salary had worked out at sixty thousand dollars a year. But from *Adam Had Four Sons* onward, David was leasing her to other film companies. From Warners, for *Casablanca,* he received one hundred and ten thousand dollars; from Paramount, for *For Whom the Bell Tolls,* one hundred and fifty thousand dollars; for *Saratoga Trunk,* one hundred thousand dollars; and the price became astronomical when he haggled over *The Bells of St. Mary's.*

———— • ————

I laughed about it. I didn't really mind. I'd signed a contract. I earned a lot more money than I ever had in Sweden. David didn't know I was going to be successful any more than I did. If he could make money renting me out, good luck to him. We made some great pictures and I loved working.

He produced *Spellbound* himself with Hitch as director.

———— • ————

In *Spellbound* Ingrid played a young psychiatrist working in an expensive sanitorium who discovers that the newly appointed head of her department is as emotionally "disturbed" as the rest of the patients. Ingrid herself was also very slightly disturbed to find that for the first time in her career she was playing with a leading man who was slightly *younger* than she was. He had already appeared in *The Keys of the Kingdom,* and was rated in the movie magazine columns as "one of the most promising young male prospects on the screen." Gregory Peck certainly fulfilled that prophecy.

With Selznick and Hitchcock working together, the film world expected originality. They almost got it. David Selznick engaged the surrealist artist Salvador Dali to design an elaborate dream sequence to match Gregory Peck's nightmares. It opened with four-hundred human eyes glaring down at him from black velvet drapes. Then a pair of pliers fifteen times taller than Peck chased him up the side of a pyramid, and finally he was confronted by a plaster cast of Ingrid as a Grecian goddess with a face that slowly cracked, emitting streams of ants.

Ingrid was coated in plaster but the ants were banned. And practically the whole of the scene was "lost" in that limbo of the film world known as the cutting-room floor. Salvador Dali's relationship with David O. Selznick cooled rapidly.

Time magazine said: "Hitchcock's deft timing and sharp, imaginative camera work raise *Spellbound* well above the routine of Hollywood thrillers." The *New York Herald Tribune:* "Compelling performances by Ingrid Bergman and Gregory Peck, the work is a masterful psychiatric thriller."

The film made a lot of money. So much money that David Selznick almost immediately began to put together the ingredients for a second Hitchcock thriller, *Notorious.* David sold it as a package to RKO in a deal that included Hitchcock as director, Ben Hecht as scriptwriter, and Cary Grant and Ingrid as stars. David received eight hundred thousand dollars and fifty percent of the profits. As it grossed eight million dollars, everyone was very happy indeed.

Cary Grant was a United States secret agent who suspected Ingrid —daughter of an already convicted Nazi spy—of a lack of loyalty, but who fell in love with her. To prove her patriotism she married the villain, Claude Rains, and helped Cary uncover the secret of the locked wine cellar, and the bottle containing, of all surprising deposits, the almost unheard of ore, uranium. The cameras zooming down from above the chandelier of a crowded ballroom to the precious key clutched tightly in Ingrid's hand as she danced with Cary Grant was one of the most spectacular shots of Hitch's spectacular career. And the use of uranium as a plot motive around the time the first atomic bomb was detonated attracted the attention of the FBI. Although

Hitch rolled his eyes and protested no interest whatsoever in such nasty chemicals, the security men who kept him under surveillance for several weeks were not amused.

Outwitting the "establishment" was a natural Hitchcock technique. He delighted in overcoming the censorship of the Johnson office by filming a kiss between Cary and Ingrid which lasted five times longer than that permitted:

———— • ————

A kiss could last three seconds. We just kissed each other and talked, leaned away and kissed each other again. Then the telephone came between us, then we moved to the other side of the telephone. So it was a kiss which opened and closed; but the censors couldn't and didn't cut the scene because we never at any one point kissed for more than three seconds. We did other things: we nibbled on each other's ears, and kissed a cheek, so that it looked endless, and became sensational in Hollywood.

———— • ————

Notorious was the start of a continuing friendship between Cary Grant and Ingrid. And it was shortly afterwards that Cary was to utter the immortal phrase: "I think the Academy ought to set aside a special award for Bergman every year whether she makes a picture or not!"

And with the end of *Notorious* came the start of negotiations for the role Ingrid had sought for years.

———— • ————

Joan of Arc always obsessed me. I don't quite know where this deep compulsion came from, perhaps from way back in my childhood dreams, but when David Selznick sent me that cable at the beginning of the war I was divinely happy. Then of course the war intervened and David didn't think it the right time. Nevertheless, every time I was at a cocktail party, I used to walk around and see if I could catch some director or producer, and say, "Now what about Joan of Arc?" It didn't do me any good. Nobody wanted any part of Joan. So little by little, the whole thing faded out, but I never gave up hope.

Then I got a telephone call in Hollywood from Maxwell Anderson in New York. I didn't really know anything about Maxwell Anderson except that he was a playwright. I didn't even know how he got me directly without going through an agent, but there he was on the phone, and he said: "I've written a play, and I was just wondering . . . I know you are doing a lot of movies, but I'm just wondering maybe one day you might like to come to Broadway to do a play?"

I said, "Yes, of course, I'd like to do that. Tell me, what is your play all about?"

"Joan of Arc," he replied, and I almost dropped the phone.

"Joan of Arc! Good heavens, send it out immediately. Of course I must read it first because everyone will think I'm mad if I accept it without reading it, but I can almost swear to you I'll do it. Please send it quickly. I'm very excited by the idea."

Well, he got all excited because I was excited, and he said, "Miss Bergman, I shall bring the script out to California myself as soon as I can possibly get there."

He came out. I read the play. In his version the curtain rose on a stage in New York, and the cast was just about to start rehearsals of *Joan of Arc.* The actors got all churned up about how they should play their parts, and the stage director got into it too. There was an awful lot of modern politics and stuff about the freedom of the theater intertwined with the Joan of Arc story. To me, there was not enough of Joan and far too much of this political thing, but I thought I could work on Maxwell and sort that out later. The main thing was that at last I had Joan.

I went to Selznick: "David, I have a perfect play for me. I've finished *Notorious.* You don't have another movie lined up for me right now. Can I do it?"

David didn't seem to have any objections. My contract was going to run out with him soon anyway, so perhaps he was trying to humor me because he never believed that I might leave him. We figured out that doing the play would take about nine months altogether: rehearsals, out-of-town opening, and then into New York for a limited season.

The contractual negotiations started and everything went on and on—forever. The discussions were endless. One day Maxwell Anderson, who was still waiting in Hollywood, came to me and said, "I can see that you're not going to do the play. I realize now that I should never have gotten involved with people in the movies, because they have far too many problems and demands upon their time. I know it's not your fault but from now on I am going to stick to people in the theater. So I'm going back to New York tomorrow. I've very much enjoyed meeting you, and if you could do me one more little favor, I'd love to see the Pacific Ocean once more."

Off we went in my little car out to Santa Monica beach. We left the car, took a walk, and we sat in the sand. And I said, "Max, do you have the *Joan of Arc* contract with you?" He looked at me and said, "Here in my pocket." "Give it to me," I said, "and I'll sign it."

So there on the sand of Santa Monica beach I signed his contract, and he looked at me and said, "You know what you've done? You're stuck now."

I said, "That's good. That's it. I don't care. I'm determined to do this play."

The next day with the discussions still going on and on, Maxwell Anderson winked at me and I winked at him, and off he went, back to New York. Eventually Petter came home and said, "Now they're ready for you to sign the contract," and I said, "I already did. I guess I just anticipated their decision."

I've never worked just for money. I've always worked for the pleasure of doing what I thought was the right thing at the right moment. If I can then get a good deal, that's fine. But the part not the money is what comes first.

Nevertheless, when my contract with David expired, I felt I had a right to some of the money he was making by renting me out. I said to him, "Now the contract's up, David, I'd like to earn some of that money myself." Then he got angry with me, because he always felt—as he once wrote to me in a very long memo—that he had lifted me from "obscurity to great stardom." I was very unhappy about his anger because I looked upon David as my father, my guide and leader, and I hated the fact that he wouldn't even speak to me anymore, and said very nasty things about how ungrateful I was.

———————— • ————————

In 1946 Ingrid made her first film as an independent artist, *Arch of Triumph.* The New York rehearsals and opening of *Joan of Lorraine* were not scheduled until that fall.

The backing came from a new group, Enterprise Films. Its directors were full of high-minded intentions to make quality films and share the profits among management, writers, directors, actors, and technicians—if there was any profit to share, that is. This was their very first film, and they had assembled a very starry group indeed to make it. The film was based upon the novel by the famous German writer, Erich Maria Remarque. Remarque, author of the world-famous best seller, *All Quiet on the Western Front,* had moved to Paris and by 1946 was contemplating American citizenship in New York. He was a writer of great talent, and the affection he felt for the tall laughing Swedish girl was demonstrated in every letter he wrote her. And he wrote many:

> These days of September. They go like arrows through one's heart. Floating, full of nameless goodbyes, sustained hopes and promises, golden and quiet without regrets. To keep the intensity of youth clearer by experience comes the mystic ninth month of the year: the beginning of the second life—conscious, but without resignation. There exists a wine like it. A 1937 Oppenheimer of which I snatched in a lucky hour, a few bottles. I have them here. Please do call me when you are here, and tell me you will stay—and let us have one of these September wines.
>
> But don't do it too late—life and wines don't wait— October is still another wonderful month. After that the hard facts and the endless rains of November.

The rains came early for *Arch of Triumph.* The film was a sad and depressing story of a Paris of rain and lamplight, its citizens unresolved and uncertain on the eve of the Second World War. The part of the refugee surgeon Ravic, played by Charles Boyer, fleeing, as Remarque himself had done, from the evil excesses of Germany's new rulers, was divided and confused. It was difficult to reconcile Ravic's tender and elusive love affair with Ingrid's Joan Madou, a sexy, amoral nightclub singer, with his determination to murder the gestapo chief who had tortured and killed his wife.

———————— • ————————

Arch of Triumph was one of the few films in my life that I felt "wrong" about. I really didn't want to do it and I told them so, but they persevered and there was Charles Boyer in it and Charles Laughton, so I decided it was ridiculous not to do it. But I was always unsure of myself, concerned that I would not be "believable." Then it came out very long and they cut it to pieces, and it didn't make sense.

———— • ————

Box office and common intelligence indicated that bringing together the two stars who had been so brilliant in *Gaslight* made success inevitable. Not so. In *The New York Times,* Bosley Crowther wrote: "From within Lewis Milestone's roving camera, we watch love as it is made by two of the movies' most able craftsmen, repetitiously and at exceeding length. And to the inevitable question, 'Is that bad?' we can only say that too much of a good thing—even of Bergman and Boyer—is too much."

———— • ————

Bob Capa came to Hollywood not only because I was there, but also because many of his friends were there, and he thought he might give it a try. I was doing *Arch of Triumph,* and Capa said, "What about me coming on the set and taking a few pictures?" So I asked the director, Lewis Milestone, and he was pleased to have Capa because he was very famous. Bob Capa took many very interesting photographs of me but somehow Hollywood wasn't his scene. . . .

———— • ————

The dilemma, however, was not Hollywood. The dilemma was that they had fallen in love.

———— • ————

That part was not easy . . . not easy at all, because I was so moral, so prudish you might say. It was difficult for him too, somehow, I think, because he also knew it was very important. But I wanted very much to be with him. He was an adventurous, freedom-loving man. Money didn't mean anything to him, he was terribly generous. Once in Hyde Park, London, I'll never forget, we passed this old tramp asleep in the grass. And Capa said, "Let's surprise the old bum when he wakes up by putting a fiver in his hand." And he gave him a five-pound note. You know, coming from my background where every dollar was counted, to me this was such generosity . . . this was so marvelous. When I was collecting clothes for a French orphanage and the poor people in France who had suffered during the war, I put a big basket outside my dressing room and people went by and put in their old shoes and sweaters and clothes. Capa dropped in a suit, and I said, "My God, you can't give me a suit, you need it." And he said, "I have *three* suits, what do I need three suits for? Two's enough. Take this one." Yet when I approached a famous actor friend of mine who had at least two hundred suits, and suggested he might like to give one away, he said, "Well, you know, Ingrid, I never know when I need them . . . you know, they're so useful. . . ." And of course that was the difference between Capa and the rest of the world.

———————— • ————————

If Capa had said to Ingrid, "Come away with me, let's take our chance, hit the world, drink deep of the good red wine of life," she might have gone, but it is unlikely. If he had said, "Come marry me and be my love, and we will all the pleasures prove," she would probably have been at his side. But he didn't say that.

———————— • ————————

He told me, "I cannot marry you. I cannot tie myself down. If they say 'Korea tomorrow,' and we're married and we have a child, I won't be able to go to Korea. And that's impossible. I'm not the marrying kind."

In my mind and according to my background you marry the man you love. So there was the difficulty. He went away, and came back again, he went away and came back again, but nothing was ever going to change. . . . I understood that.

———————— • ————————

Ingrid, dedicated and indoctrinated by her craft, could understand Capa's point of view entirely. Eventually their association left them both slightly worried. Capa was never going to live in the shadow of a great star; Ingrid was never going to venture more than ankle-deep into the muddy waters of intrigue. But Capa influenced Ingrid deeply.

They let things float, and floated with them. And while Capa took the pictures, Ingrid completed *Arch of Triumph,* and went off to New York to start rehearsals of Maxwell Anderson's *Joan of Lorraine.* Capa went off to France to write the book of his wartime experiences. He wrote to her:

> Today I bought a typewriter and a house. The typewriter is small, the house a little bigger. It is in the forest ten miles from Paris, and it has a kitchen with a big table, a room with a big bed, and a studio with a skylight and a big fireplace. The Ritz bar, the El Morocco and the corner of the place on the Vendôme are asking about you. I do much more. Please write one word and say that you will be good and heartbreakingly pretty and that you will cool a bottle of champagne for the fifteenth of March. Tomorrow am climbing into the small BMW, filling the car with cigarettes and books and brandy. This time I am going out to ski, and be thin and brown inside, and thin and brown outside.
>
> I hope you did not sign hundreds of contracts to become less and less of a human being and more and more of an institution. You have to be very careful because success is much more dangerous and corrupting than disaster, and I would hate. . . .
>
> Now I stop. That was emerging as a very difficult and nearly pompous sentence. My ink is dry and I have just talked to you on the phone, you dear maid from Hollywood via Sweden. I'll see *Joan* around the middle of March if the Gods and your guardians allow it.
>
> I do love you very much.

Capa wrote a very good book. It was published in 1947 and entitled *Slightly Out of Focus.*

———— • ————

Just before I was going off to New York to start rehearsing *Joan of Lorraine,* I met David Selznick at a party, a big party with people dancing. He didn't come near me. So while most of the people at his table were dancing and he sat alone, I went over and sat down with him. I said: "I hate to leave Hollywood knowing that you are angry with me. I want you to wish me good luck before I go off to do *Joan.*" So he looked at me and said, "Good luck." And the next week he announced in the papers that he was going to do a *Joan of Arc* film with Jennifer Jones!

But we did end up as friends. Eventually he wrote:

> I am informed that even Dan O'Shea has reluctantly and at long last come to the conclusion that no new deal with us has been seriously envisaged as part of your future plans. This conclusion comes as no surprise to me, despite our final reliance and faith that I expressed in our conversation and in no way lessens my sorrow over our "divorce" after so many years of happy marriage. You once said you had "two husbands." But Petter was the senior, and of course he knew all the time that his will would prevail. I do regret all the futile gestures and elaborate "negotiations" but that is all I do regret in a relationship which will always be a source of pride to me. I am sure you know that I have the greatest confidence that your career will go steadily up to new heights, achieving in full the promise of your great talent; and that my good wishes will always be yours no matter what you do. So long Ingrid! May all the New Years beyond bring you everything of which you dream.

Chapter
11

Maxwell Anderson was nearing sixty, mild-mannered, big and broad with a gingerish moustache; his smile was slow, his hair thinning, and he was gentle and rather shy. During the run of *Joan of Lorraine* he wrote that Ingrid possessed "the incandescent genius that transcends technique."

But Ingrid, with Ruth as co-conspirator, used her technique on him to make the play into what she wanted.

———— • ————

During the rehearsals and even before the rehearsals, we started to do a little work on Max. Every day Ruth and I had lunch with him. I thought I knew everything there was to know about Joan, having studied her all my life. So I'd come along with my little book full of notes on Joan, and I'd say, "Look Max, at this nice thing Joan said here. That's not in your play is it? Don't you think that little bit would be wonderful in your play, Max?" And Maxwell would say, "Well, I haven't heard about that. Where did you discover it? Did you! I see. Well, I guess we could find room for it here, couldn't we? Yes, we could definitely put it in here."

Then Ruth and I would be sitting innocently over our coffee next day and we'd say, "Now what about this little line here, Max? Did you know that is the actual line Joan used at her trial? Yes, it's in the actual transcript. That would come in very well in our first act, wouldn't it, Max?"

Maxwell was very good. He listened. Some things he was stubborn about, but he did change an awful lot. The play became much more about Joan of Arc than his original conception. In the end, it was about seventy percent Joan, and thirty percent of talk, which was a complete reversal of how we started out in the beginning. Maybe I was wrong, but I don't think so, and I admit I only thought about Joan.

Almost as soon as we arrived in Washington I heard the astonishing news that black people were not allowed to attend the theater there. Here we had come to the capital of America, with a play about freedom and the right of man to do what his conscience dictates, at the end of a big war about freedom, and black people were not allowed to buy a seat and come to the theater. I couldn't believe that a man could come up with money in his hand, put it on the desk and not be able to buy a ticket. It made me furious. I said to Maxwell Anderson, "Shame on you, coming with this play to Washington, knowing this would happen. If I'd known black people weren't allowed in, I'd never have put my feet in this town."

Max was very worried.

"I know, I know, it's too bad, too bad, but you can't alter things overnight; it will alter eventually. Now don't go on about it in your interviews. . . ."

I said, "I certainly will if I get the chance."

"But you'll only stir up trouble and ruin the play. Leave it. We can't change anything at the moment. It's only two weeks in Washington and then we go to New York. Leave it. . . ."

I knew I couldn't leave it. I had to say something. So we came to the press reception the day before the opening, and I was waiting for the right question to lead me into the subject. Maxwell Anderson and the publicity man were so nervous they were chewing their nails. But the press did not ask the right question. They had no reason to bring the subject up.

Everybody was getting up to leave, saying, "Thank you, Miss Bergman, good-bye, Miss Bergman," and I said, "Thank you too, gentlemen, but I shall never come back to Washington again."

That made everyone sit down quite smartly in their seats again. Poor Maxwell just put his hands over his face. The newsmen said,

"Not come back to Washington? Why won't you come back to Washington, Miss Bergman?"

"Because," I said, "I would not have set foot in this place and performed had I known that black people were not allowed into the theater. I am bound by my contract, so I must continue. But I will not come back here again until black people, just like white people, can come to the theater. We play for everybody. Everybody!"

Well, they wrote that in the newspapers, and Maxwell Anderson was nearly hysterical. But people crowded in just the same and it was a huge success. Certainly I was criticized by many people. Outside the stage door people spat at me and called me "nigger lover."

But that did not make any difference. How could I go out there on the stage every night crying Joan's words that Maxwell Anderson had written: "Every man gives his life for what he believes. Every woman gives her life for what she believes. Some people believe in little or nothing, nevertheless they give up their lives for that little or nothing. One life is all we have, and we live it as we live it, and we believe in living it, and then it's gone. But to surrender what you are, and to live without belief—that's more terrible than dying—more terrible than dying young."

Joan was eighteen years old and was burned to death. All I had to put up with was a bit of spit. I got letters from all over the world, from actors and many people, even from actors in Sweden, supporting me. But it took seven more years before they did finally admit black people to the theater.

Naturally that opening night in Washington was a bit tense because most people thought I'd put the kiss of death on the play at that press reception. There were pickets outside the doors protesting, but it all went pretty well. After all the kisses, and the "You were marvelous" and, "Well done, you were great," I went off to bed. There was no party that I can remember—maybe we had something to eat and drink—but I was in the bedroom and there was a knock on the door. I called, "Who's that?" and a voice answered, "It's Maxwell." It was Max and Mrs. Max and their son Allan, who was the stage manager, and they said, "Sorry to disturb you, but we thought you ought to know, we've just sacked the director."

"Sacked the director! But why? Surely Margo Jones has been doing a very good job? . . ."

"No, we were not pleased at all with her. She will be getting

— 171 —

the production credit in New York, but we were not pleased at all."

I thought, How cruel can you be? On opening night to fire someone just like that. But I remembered Irene Selznick's warning when I first arrived in Hollywood: "Be wary of all of them. It can happen to you . . . to anyone. Yes, everything is lovely they say, you were great, and then out of the blue they are plotting behind your back, and you're fired."

Margo left at once, never said good-bye to me or anyone. She just took the next train out of Washington. I can imagine how she must have felt.

Sam Wanamaker took over. He was very young and I kept saying, "Listen Sam, you're only twenty-seven and you mustn't talk like that to all those older actors out there. They won't like it." And Sam said, "Hell, I've been sitting out on stage for every performance since we started"—he played the double part of stage director and Joan's inquisitor, and was on stage all the time. "I can see what's wrong . . . and a lot's wrong." Sam was very bossy, arrogant even, and this was his first directing job. But the play—I have to admit it—had got rather static. It was floating out and disappearing and Sam put life back into it and vitality.

We opened in New York. I suppose that was one of the greatest theatrical nights of my life.

———— • ————

According to many theatrical purists, Ingrid could be described as "only a film star." In November, 1946, she was therefore putting her reputation and her skills firmly on the line and squarely at risk in front of a certainly sophisticated, often bored, and inevitably critical New York audience. She had her own credo to sustain her: "On the stage you are another person. You are playing another person and you become that person, and in some ways this is a great release from your own problems. But you must go out and do a *job*. Don't do it halfway, thinking, I was forced to do this, so what the hell, I don't care. No-o-o! If you are going to open your mouth, open it well, as well as you can. Don't do a half-kind of job. Do it to your very limit. Otherwise they will never believe in what you are doing."

To become Joan of Arc, to inspire belief in her, requires gifts of a quite extraordinary nature. But Ingrid had always been able to inspire in her audience a *belief* in what she was doing. And the critics believed her now.

In the *New York Herald Tribune,* Howard Barnes wrote: "The radiant Ingrid Bergman brought theatrical sorcery to a discursive script in *Joan of Lorraine.* Her Maid of Orleans is a figure to be remembered with gratitude and deep satisfaction. A celebrated actress of the screen has served notice that she is with few peers in the whole realm of make believe."

The New Yorker: "A performance that may be incomparable in the theatre of our day." And Robert Sherwood, one of America's finest playwrights, said simply: "She *is* Saint Joan."

———————— • ————————

I've never forgotten that evening. It was just glorious, unbelievable. I remember getting ready to go to the party at the Astor Hotel. I put on my evening dress, left my dressing room, arrived at the hotel, and went into the ladies room. There, I sat down on a chair and cried and cried and cried. I said to myself, "Is this it? Is this the reaction to success? I sit in the ladies room and I cry?" And everybody went by me and said, "What's the matter with you? You have a big success tonight?" But I went on crying.

I learned so much about an audience during that run of *Joan of Lorraine.* The public comes to the theater not because they want to heckle and see things go wrong. They come because they hope it's going to be wonderful, and they're going to join in that one special occasion, that special night. The night things *did* go wrong, I was dressed in my armor, I was talking to my heavenly voices. I had to sit down on a narrow wooden bench with four small legs. Well, either I miscalculated or the bench wasn't in its proper place. Anyway, instead of sitting in the middle, I sat on the end. The bench tipped up, and bang, I sat down on my behind with a clash of armor. I sat there waiting for the laugh that was going to lift the roof off. But no. All I heard was one great breath of dismay . . . "Oooohh" . . . a marvelous sound of pity. Then complete silence. I learned at that moment that the audience doesn't want anything to happen to you—they're sorry for you; they're on your side; they don't laugh at you; they weep for you. Yes, they laugh when it's funny—when you ask them to laugh—but when it's serious they hold their breath waiting for you to take hold again.

———————— • ————————

Capa wrote, perhaps sensing that her work and her life were taking her away from him:

> Do not go away. There are very few precious things in life—not life itself—but the merry mind. It was, it is, your merry mind that I love, and there are very few merry minds in a man's life.
>
> Loving, loving, Capa.

His intuition was correct. Telegrams and letters of congratulation flooded in. From Petter who had come to New York for the opening night but was now back in Los Angeles on hospital duty, a telegram: "You made me cry." And another from a busy schoolgirl: "Lucky you, lucky Joan, lucky me. Pia."

To the outside world, her marriage was stable and happy even though Ingrid's love for Capa had shown her how much was missing from her life. Both she and Petter covered that reality with a complete immersion in their work.

Ingrid wrote to Ruth:

> This week was a week of misery. Last week of 1946. It seems almost right that the last week was bad. It started very bad. I lost my voice Monday; it came back Wednesday. Then I got some dirt in my eye one day walking. My eye swelled up, and Thursday and Friday it was horrible. Then that disappeared and Saturday I came down with a horrible cold. I could hardly be heard beyond the first row. Now I am in bed hoping that I will be well tomorrow night and then New Year's Day. May it be a wonderful year for us both. If it is for you I have a feeling it will be for me too. . . . Steinbeck and Hemingway saw the show. Hemingway said I was the greatest actress in the world. Many came backstage but I don't remember who.

But one of those who came backstage was Victor Fleming. Her affection for him during the making of *Dr. Jekyll and Mr. Hyde* still survived. But during the whole subsequent period, Victor Fleming had remained remarkably detached. Now he saw the show and burst into the dressing room.

He'd come to New York with a book which he wanted to film and he wanted me in it. But he came sweeping in, threw the book in the corner of my dressing room, grabbed me in his arms, embraced me and said, "This is it. You should play Joan forever and ever . . . You must play Joan on the screen." So there it was. The words I'd been waiting for as long as I could remember, certainly for the last six years since David Selznick had said we were going to do it. I was so happy. At last it was serious. Victor Fleming and Walter Wanger were going to form a production company with me as one of the partners.

Maxwell Anderson began work on a film adaptation of his play. Victor Fleming began his commuter existence between Los Angeles and New York. The fact that she was now a partner in the production of a movie stirred Ingrid with a sense of responsibility she had never experienced before. She wrote to Ruth:

> I'm terribly distressed about our script. God, what is Maxwell thinking about? The things he agreed to do, and liked here when he talked at Hampshire House, he has forgotten. Why do we have a writer who only breathes Anderson? Capa suggests the title, *The Witch.* A very good name for a picture, but I am not for it this time. I have a feeling Joan would say, "But Ingrid, you know I was not a witch." I am really longing to get out to you in California.
>
> Nothing seems to help the play. David Selznick was out front yesterday and still I didn't "fly." I gave as good a performance as I possibly could, but *that feeling* isn't coming any more. I am very tired. Too many people. Too much food and drink lately. Maybe that's what kills the feeling. But I have only three more weeks and I am trying to do everything I can to use the time. Then I'll go back into the cage, sit in the sun, obey Petter and be sober and look eighteen years old.
>
> Capa has finally found something that excites him. He and John Steinbeck are going to Russia. Capa will take his

16 mm camera and write short stories while Steinbeck will find a new book. I am happy because I am sure it is the right thing for both of them.

Capa had tried to settle down, tolerate peace and come to terms with it. Without war there was travel, strange places, new people. The trip to Russia was postponed. Instead he went to Turkey to make a documentary film. On the way he paused in England and wrote Ingrid:

London is so quiet and empty, but still Europe and so much more real and refreshing after the States. Every time I go to a bar, to a play, for a walk in the foggy streets, I want you to be there next to me.

From Istanbul he wrote:

This is Sunday afternoon and I am sitting on this terrace of my room looking over the Bosphorus and minarets and seeing only your face. I told you last time that I wanted to know how I would feel when I would be far away, isolated and alone. Now I know. I talk to myself. In our world the values are false and we cannot afford to have defeats. Now I say something again which I cannot explain with the pen: you have to wait for a bottle, for a floor, for a fireplace, for a cigarette. I am a newspaperman again, and it is all right. I sleep in strange hotels, read during the nights and try to grasp the problems of a country in a short time. It is good to work, to think, and to be lonely. I had to make out the bill for my last year, and to do it, I had to go away. Now I am pleased and happy that I stayed in Berlin, that I went to Hollywood, and that I got out when the time came, you see I'm writing to myself. There is no champagne in Turkey at all. All I can drink is Arak which is a kind of absinthe or pernod. I am a very good boy. How are you? Are you behaving under your armor? I hope you can hurry up your Joan film project and begin to shoot next summer in France. *Please* listen to my voices.

Ingrid wrote to Ruth:

> I get so angry when I read Fleming's letters. He seems to
> have to spend day after day with business people: everyone
> trying to find out where and how to get the last dollar out of
> the picture. I know Victor has talked business much more
> than story, but it is important I guess to get these things
> organized after all. He said, last time we spoke on the
> phone, that now he is only concentrating on story. If only I
> knew what I wanted, Ruth. I am sure I could drive it
> through. But you see I am not sure. I listen to Capa and the
> others, but I don't know how to put ideas into dialogue and
> scenes. Also I have an idea that their viewpoints would not
> go through censorship and Cardinal Spellman. If only I
> knew *myself* what I wanted instead of always listening to
> others. When I get out of New York to California, I'll listen
> to you and as I believe in you I'll fight for your ideas. I'll be
> the bridge for everyone who wants to come to Victor with
> ideas. Don't think for a moment I believe I can turn Victor
> round my little finger, but I'll try to talk like an angel, be
> strong like a god, and dangerous like a devil. Forward my
> friends. Now starts the battle for Joan!

There was also, at that moment, another battle going on of a far
different nature. She knew she could not "turn Victor round her little
finger," but she knew very well she had considerable influence with
him—for one overwhelming reason. Victor Fleming was now in love
with her.

His first hesitant declaration arrived in an envelope on which he
had scrawled:

> This was in my pocket when I arrived. Several more I
> destroyed. The *Lord* only knows what is written here, and
> no doubt His mind is a little hazy because he had not a
> very firm grip upon me at the time I was writing—we were
> slightly on the "outs." I was putting more trust in alcohol
> than in the Lord. And now I am putting all my trust in
> you, when, without opening this, I send it, for you may
> think me very foolish.

Inside the envelope the letter was brief:

Santa Fe (The Chief)
Just a note to tell you dear—to tell you what? That it's evening. That we miss you? That we drank to you? No— To tell you boldly like a lover that I love you—cry across the miles and hours of darkness that I love you—that you flood across my mind like waves across the sand. If you care—or if you don't, these things to you with love I say. I am devotedly—your foolish—ME.

Yes, she did care. She cared very much for this tall, handsome, vital man. Perhaps being half in love gave an edge, a drive, and a direction to the huge task they had set themselves: the task of adapting that flood of drama, passion, and belief ignited on the stage of the Alvin Theater and enclosing it within the confines of the cinematic process.

———— • ————

So many books have been written about Joan, analyzing what was right with her and what was wrong with her. Was she in love with the Dauphin of France? Did she ever love a man? Did she enjoy, actually *enjoy* being out on the battlefield? George Bernard Shaw made her a shrewd, plain, pugnacious little girl, a sort of fifteenth-century political agitator. Maxwell Anderson's Joan was sweet and shy and very feminine, but in his theatrical terms he used her to help illustrate his own arguments about faith and modern problems, and I didn't think that came into our story at all. What we tried to do in the movie was the real Joan, from the documents and the trial, the girl who went out onto the battlefield and cried when she saw the terrible horror of medieval battle. I've always thought that the real character of Joan is revealed by her own words, the words she spoke at her trial.

We tried to please everybody, especially about the religious content, and about her "voices." There is always argument about her "voices." Some people say it is only in her imagination she heard them. You couldn't just play the voices alone on a sound track, because Joan said she both heard the voices and *saw* Saint Catherine, Saint Michael, and Saint Margaret. And again you must remember she testified in those medieval days of great superstition and fear. I don't care if she heard them or didn't hear them. The main thing is she *declared* she heard them and *that* inspired her to take the actions she took. That seems to me to be important.

———— • ————

"Angel," wrote Victor—he had called her "Angel" ever since Ingrid had shown him a description of Saint Joan as "a drunken angel."

> About the script. It is not good. Much too long. Max has not done what he said, has not stayed on the story line, keeps on *Joan of Lorraine.* What's wrong? Walter Wanger and I have talked to several writers—we are going to put someone on at once. Yesterday I spent with Walter trying to bring him up to date on the story and the business. Today I came to the Roach studio. Our gang are all hard workers, like beavers and all seem happy. Monday we have—or rather you have our new corporation business manager to see. He comes very well recommended having had charge of Columbia Studios. Walter and I hope he will keep the Corp on their toes and get the picture started on time.
>
> Angel—Angel—why didn't I get a chain three thousand miles long with a good winding device on the end. Better quit now before I start telling you I love you— telling you Angel I love you—yes—yes—yes—it's ME.

She did not for one moment protest against this declaration of love. It was all part of the flood of creation. What she did not accurately perceive was that Victor was not merely half in love, he had toppled over the edge, and his fall, deep into an emotional crevasse of his own making, was far closer to agony than ecstasy. Already he was identifying himself as "the snake," and his feelings of guilt—from his very first letter—were already tearing his conscience. He made no demands upon her. He was a very honorable man.

> Dear and darling Angel. How good to hear your voice. How tongue-tied and stupid I become. How sad for you. Then when you put the phone down, the click is like a

bullet. Dead silence. Numbness and then thoughts. Thoughts that beat like drums upon my brain. My heart, my brain. I hate and loathe both. How much they hurt and torment me—pain my flesh and bones. When they have had their fill of that, they quarrel and fight each other. My brain beats my heart into a great numbness. Then my brain pounds my heart to death. All this I can do nothing about.

For Victor it was all too late. He was nearly sixty. She was half his age. That fact was irrevocable, and it broke his heart. He was confounded with ideas of duty and responsibility; he could hear the mocking words: "old enough to be her father."
He wrote:

> In Arabian Nights it says: "Do what thy manhood bids thee do. From none but self expect applause. He best lives and noblest dies, who makes and keeps his self-made laws."

Victor had broken all his self-made laws. Victor Fleming, the strong man, the man of action, the man who made his own decisions and blamed no one but himself, now stood outside himself, observed his own weaknesses, his own inability to solve his problem, ease the pain or assuage the despair. After his last train journey back from New York, and before Ingrid closed in *Joan* and moved back to Hollywood, he wrote:

> Time stopped when I got aboard that train. It became dark and in the darkness I was lost. Why I did not think to do some drinking I don't know. I went to bed for fourteen hours and I slept fourteen minutes, forgot to order breakfast on the Century, and had no food or coffee until one P.M. That much I remember. Someone met me at the train. I'm very much afraid she found me crying. A hundred years old and crying over a girl. I said, "There's no fool like an old fool."

Back in Hollywood, Victor did not write her any more letters. He was married, with a wife and children. Ingrid was back with Petter and Pia at Benedict Canyon. During the weeks it took to make *Joan of Arc* they met every day on the set, and the intensity of their work gave them no time for anything else.

———————— • ————————

Vic Fleming wore himself out on the picture. He was here and there and everywhere. I loved just to watch him: he moved beautifully, he was so graceful and he had this great warmth toward everyone, always pleasant and helpful. And such a hard worker. He'd started as a cameraman long ago with D.W. Griffith and Douglas Fairbanks, and been a director since 1919, and union practices very often got on his nerves. He could never wait for the man who was to come and do it to arrive; if a plug had to be put in, he put it in himself; if something needed carrying, he carried it. They were all union jobs, but he did them himself, and got away with them, so obviously they all liked him. But it was a very tight budget we were working on, and it was difficult because there wasn't much belief in Hollywood that the picture was going to be any good, even though it had been a good play and we had had a success in New York. Nobody thought there was any box office in a young girl saving her country, especially with no love story. I think the pressures got to Victor Fleming. He was so anxious to make this a great success because he knew I was in love with Joan and her story.

Before *Joan of Arc* was released, our publicity people thought it would be a good idea if I did a tour following the exact journey that Joan made. During the making of the film we had two priests, wonderful Father Donceur who had come over specially from France, and an American priest, Father Devlin, who sat on the set all day talking Latin together. So with Father Donceur as guide and instructor we started off in France at Domrémy where Joan was born. It's quite a big place now, a bit like Lourdes. They closed the schools and had the kids lining the streets throwing flowers; I saw Joan's home, I saw the church. Then we traveled the road she took to Reims where she met the Dauphin. And then to the place of the fighting at Orléans.

It was unbelievable. Wherever I went, they treated me as if I were the reincarnation of Joan of Arc, as if they were waiting for her to return. And maybe they were. I was mobbed, not because I was a movie star but because I was Joan of Arc—it was most moving. We ended up at Rouen, and there was the last photograph of me on my knees placing flowers on this slab of stone where she was burned.

And for years after that, for at least fifteen years when I came back to France, the customs and immigration men looked at me and said, "Ah, Jeanne d'Arc . . . welcome home."

I thought that not only was it very nice of them, but it was quite remarkable. Here I was a Protestant and a Swede, doing a technicolor movie in Hollywood, written by an American, and they were good-tempered about it, flattered even. Though I did get one open letter to a newspaper, written by Jean Delannoy, the French director, saying Anouilh had written a screen play for another Joan of Arc, and I should stop our production of Joan because the French had the cultural and traditional rights to their folk saint. But since our picture had already started they were a bit late.

———————— • ————————

The premiere of *Joan of Arc* was held in New York. Ingrid was escorted by Victor Fleming. When it was over Ingrid knew, and Victor Fleming knew, that in terms of their highest ambition they had failed.

Most of the critics were kind and polite. Several, like *The Times* of London, were very flattering about Ingrid's performance, writing of the "radiant tenderness of the moments when her voices speak to her." *Time* magazine observed: "Bergman's passionate fidelity to her part saves the day."

Erich Maria Remarque wrote to her:

Strange, I know that having seen Joan on the screen, I will not be able to recall her face back from my imagination. It will be from now on always your face. Already, looking at the crucified photo in your letter, I believe she looked like you. This is not an accusation of mental murder; it is a story of death and resurrection.

From now on nobody will ever think of her in other forms than in the storms, lightnings, and landscapes of your face, and I, wanting it or not, will be included in the magical exchange. So hail and farewell. She died a beautiful death in your arms.

———————— • ————————

Shortly after I returned from France, Father Donceur sent me a parcel containing a small wooden figure of the Madonna. It had been damaged in transit and there was a note from the post office attached: "Virgin arriving Hollywood. Slightly damaged. Lost her head." And I thought, "Well, that's Hollywood!"

I glued her head back on and she's been with me ever since.

———————— • ————————

Some weeks after the première of *Joan,* Victor Fleming was sitting in a chair in his own home when he suddenly slumped forward. He was rushed by car to the hospital. He was dead before he reached the emergency room. The post-mortem indicated a severe heart attack.

Deeply grieved and shocked, Ingrid attended his funeral. In Ingrid's terminology you are either "in love" or "you love." She had been "in love" with Bob Capa, and she had "loved" Victor Fleming as she loved so many other of her friends. She had no premonition that Victor would create such traumatic storms in his own heart. Nevertheless, she felt a certain responsibility. Had the recent pressures of the film contributed to his death? No one would ever know.

But now it was her turn to stand back and look at herself. For some time she knew she had been stepping out of line. And she had already made a decision. She had to look very carefully at her association with Capa and probably end it. She had to pull herself together and return to the role of mother-of-a-delightful-daughter, sharer-of-a-beautiful-home, and faithful-wife-of-a-hard-working-surgeon.

But she was still concerned with the reality of her art and increasingly annoyed by the artificial quality of the Hollywood back-lot movies. As soon as she saw the Rossellini movies she knew she wanted to do a picture like *Open City* or *Paisan,* a truly realistic film.

———————— • ————————

When I saw *Joan* recently on television—it's hard to realize it was made more than thirty years ago—I saw it had that smooth, glossy quality of Hollywood. All the battle scenes were done in the studio: the towers of Chinon and the French villages were painted backdrops. I didn't think I looked like a peasant girl at all. I just looked like a movie star playing the part of Joan. Clean face, nice hairdo.

I can't blame the hairdressers and the costumers for doing their job, although sometimes they used to drive me nearly crazy. At the very last minute they'd be rushing up, brushing my hair perfectly into place, and this one is fiddling with my clothes, pulling this and pushing that, and another one is powdering my face—and there I am, mouthing my lines and thinking of my entrance. Usually I could concentrate and ignore them; it's all part of the process of making a film. Though I will admit—as I did when I saw *Joan* —I've looked at myself on the screen and been quite put out at such a beautiful hairdo, such perfect makeup, when the part called for an appearance not a quarter as glamorous.

I suppose when I look back, this is where my instinctive rebellion and resentment began—where I began to change my vision. *Arch of Triumph* looked beautiful on the set but it was still not real. With *Joan* I would have liked to go to France and have done it there. When I visited Domrémy, Joan's home, I had the feeling that it should start there, realistic and true. Before this, when I did *Notorious,* I had asked Hitchcock, "Couldn't we go to South America where it is set and film there?" He had said, no, it has to be on the back lot. But now the war was over and the next picture I was to do after *Joan* was *Under Capricorn,* another picture directed by Hitchcock. So I began to work on Hitch again: "Now look, it's set in Australia. Let's go to Australia and do it there." I couldn't get Hitch to go that far, but he did agree on England. Fine, at least a lot of new faces and new backgrounds. I just wanted to get out of the back lot.

At the time she played in *Anna Christie*.

"Here's looking at you, kid."
Humphrey Bogart and Ingrid Bergman in *Casablanca*.
(JACK WOODS FOR WARNER BROS.)

Paul Henreid, Ingrid, and Sidney Greenstreet in *Casablanca*. (JACK WOODS FOR WARNER BROS.)
With Gary Cooper in *For Whom the Bell Tolls*. (COPYRIGHT 1942. PARAMOUNT PICTURES. INC.)

For Whom the Bell Tolls. The famous haircut. (COPYRIGHT 1942, PARAMOUNT PICTURES, INC.)

Ingrid between Gary Cooper and Katina Paxinou in *For Whom the Bell Tolls.*
(COPYRIGHT 1942, PARAMOUNT PICTURES, INC.)

Off to Alaska.
(U.S. ARMY SIGNAL CORPS)

On tour in Alaska.
(U.S. ARMY SIGNAL CORPS)

Addressing
a war bond rally.

In *Swedes in America:*
a documentary film.
(WAR INFORMATION
PHOTO)

With Charles Boyer in *Gaslight*. (M-G-M)

John Warburton, Jerry Austin, Gary Cooper, and Ingrid in *Saratoga Trunk*.
(JACK WOODS FOR WARNER BROS.)

With Bing Crosby in *The Bells of St. Mary's*. (RKO RADIO)

Three Oscar winners, Leo McCarey, Ingrid, and Bing Crosby,
on the set of *The Bells of St. Mary's*.

With Gregory Peck in *Spellbound*. (SELZNICK PROPERTIES)

Salvador Dali depicted Ingrid as a Greek goddess for the dream sequence in *Spellbound*.
(MADISON LACY FOR SELZNICK PROPERTIES)

With David O. Selznick. (SELZNICK PROPERTIES)

With Cary Grant and Alfred Hitchcock discussing *Notorious.*
(GASTON LONGET FOR RKO RADIO PICTURES)

In *Joan of Lorraine,* the Maxwell Anderson play. (GJON MILI, LIFE MAGAZINE, TIME, INC.)

With Charles Boyer in *Arch of Triumph.* (ENTERPRISE STUDIOS–UNITED ARTISTS)

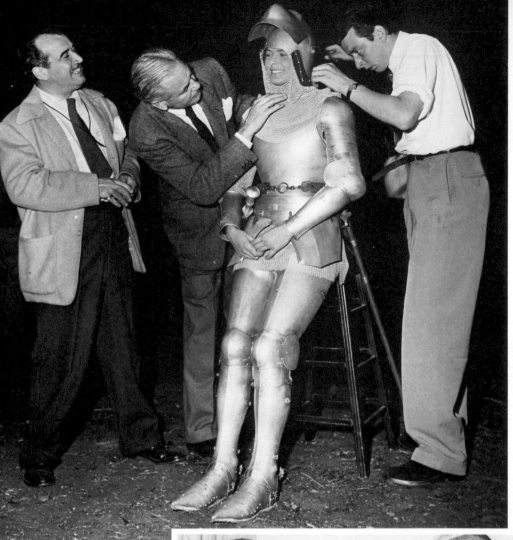

Being fitted into armor for *Joan of Arc*. (SIERRA PICTURES–RKO RADIO)

Discussing *Joan of Arc* with Father Donceur and Victor Fleming. (SIERRA PICTURES–RKO RADIO)

As *Joan of Arc*. (SIERRA PICTURES–RKO RADIO)

Photograph Ingrid had taken to
send to Bob Capa during her
tour of Joan of Arc country.

With Michael Wilding in
Under Capricorn.
(TRANSATLANTIC PRODUCTION
FOR WARNER BROS.)

Chapter 12

Dear Ruth (At the studio. August 6, 1948) Oh dear! This is my seventh week waiting. The picture started O.K. the 19th, but with Hitch's ten-minute takes they were behind one week after one day's shooting. The technicians here have very little or no experience. And they don't seem to care. I have been waiting and waiting, but every day it is the same: "We didn't get the shot today, but for sure we'll have it tomorrow morning." Finally after four days I was told Hitch had abandoned the shot and would start with my entrance. I was so happy, rehearsed and at two o'clock the same day had the first take. During the second take all the lights went out, the electricians walked down the ladders and left. Strike! All afternoon we waited for them to finish their meeting, but they never came back. This morning I was up at six; at nine I was told they had not come back yet: "Just relax in your dressing room!"

I am outraged but the others seem to take it relaxed. Nothing new. After the war they always have a couple of strikes. The reason for the strike was that two men were fired because of bad work and coming late to work several times.

Hitch is trying to find an entirely new electricians' crew. Until then, we'll have no peace. This is their second walk-

out. The camera crew and sound crew are nice. But it is
a hostile feeling on the set that just kills you. People hardly
look or speak to you. When I had the first test, the crew
were whistling and making funny remarks. I was stunned
because you know how very good people have always
been. Don't think everybody is bad but you know if it is
just a few they color the whole set. The script is interesting
now, we've got a pretty good end, but Hitch's new technique I don't like. I have had no experience with it yet, for
my first entrance was just a normal shot. But I have
watched him with the others. It is so frightening for actors
and crew. If the least bit goes wrong, you know . . . I think
Hitch and I will have some arguments. He wanted to
shoot a whole roll of film, the camera following me everywhere and the sets and furniture being pulled away. It
meant we had to rehearse a whole day without shooting
and then shoot the scenes the following day. It made
everybody nervous, but he insisted. We already had one
little argument about my entrance and I got my way. I
know I always can with him, but I dislike the argument.
. . . To top the rest of the mishaps I have a *slow* hairdresser. I have to be here at seven thirty. Makeup is very
fast, hardly any, and very gray: no lipstick, no ice-towels,
and the rest of Jack Pierce's fun. All the time is for hair.
So already at nine a.m. I am sore, not only my behind.

I saw Noel in Paris. [Noel Howard had been technical
adviser on *Joan of Arc.*] He was going with Capa to Capri,
and was worried about Capa's light view on money. Noel
is as broke as a painter should be. Too bad. Capa I don't
worry about. He is working on a new book, sold the old
to the movies. Television is on-and-off, and much gambling on, so I guess he'll carry Noel on his gay gypsy
shoulders.

Look what a long letter the strike will give you. It is now
eleven thirty. No move in any direction. I fear I'll be here
until Christmas. Pia and Petter arrive from Liverpool
eleven o'clock tonight. Poor child. What a trip. Train Los
Angeles to New York. Boat eight days. Five hours train
journey to London. I didn't want her to fly across. I
wanted her to know how big the world is. Now she knows.
I'm going to be in trouble. I smoke all the time. I drink
more than ever. I have put on at least ten pounds. I am

just ready for Petter! Now my pencil is disappearing, so it's no use starting a new sheet of paper. Give my love to Hollywood. . . . lovely place where you can work despite a strike. Next time I'll tell you about my meeting with George Bernard Shaw.

That meeting began with a phone call. It was Gabriel Pascal, the colorful, ebullient Hungarian producer who had arrived in England as an immigrant during the thirties and had quickly climbed to success. In those early days Gabriel, rather pressed for funds, had raised the railway fare to the Hereford village of Ayot St. Lawrence, and arrived at Shaw's front door by taxi. The housekeeper answered his knock.

"I have come specially all the way from London," said Gabriel, "to see Mr. Shaw on very important business."

"How unfortunate," replied the housekeeper. "Mr. Shaw is sleeping. He will not be available until three o'clock this afternoon."

Gabriel paused. "Ah," he said, "that raises a small personal problem. Do you think you could lend me the taxi fare back to the village so that I can return at three?"

Slightly surprised the housekeeper handed over a pound.

Shaw, informed of the transaction, was highly amused by the foreign gentleman who had had the impertinence to borrow the taxi fare from his housekeeper. On Gabriel's return he invited him in to his study.

"What makes your journey so urgent?" he asked.

Gabriel reached across and laid his hand on the great playwright's knee. "Mr. Shaw," he said with utter sincerity, "I have come to make you famous!"

At the end of a long and absorbing afternoon Gabriel Pascal left the cottage at Ayot St. Lawrence authorized to handle the film rights of all of Bernard Shaw's plays.

———— • ————

Gabriel Pascal had come to see me in California a couple of times. He wanted me to do *Candida* as a movie, and if I didn't like the idea of *Candida* as a movie, he wanted me to do it as a play. But I didn't like that idea either, so I was slightly surprised when he said, "Mr. Bernard Shaw would like you to come to tea with him at his cottage at Ayot St. Lawrence."

"That would be very nice. I would love to meet Mr. Shaw."

"He wants to meet you," said Gabriel warningly, "because he understands you've done a Joan of Arc in America that wasn't *his*. And he sent you *his* play."

We drove to the cottage in Herefordshire and there was Mr. Shaw, ninety-two years old, grinning like a leprechaun, already hanging over the gate, waiting. I got out of the car with Gabriel. Mr. Shaw hadn't even opened the gate for me when he said, "Why didn't you do my play?"

"Well, hallo, Mr. Shaw. Could I come in first?"

He opened the gate and said, "Certainly you can come in. We're going to have tea. Why didn't you do my play?"

I said, "I didn't do your play because I didn't like it."

Mr. Shaw stopped absolutely dead. I thought he might be thinking of pushing me out through the gate again. I had the feeling that no one on earth had ever said to Mr. Shaw that they didn't like *Saint Joan.* Maybe they had said it about other plays but not *Saint Joan.*

He stared at me. "What are you saying? Don't you know it's a masterpiece?"

"I'm sure it's a masterpiece, but it isn't the Saint Joan of the real French girl. You've made her far too clever. You've rewritten her speeches. You've made her say a lot of things which the real Saint Joan wouldn't have dreamt of saying."

We were still outside his cottage, still walking toward the front door, and I thought, He's going to get so mad at me that we'll never get inside at all, let alone have tea.

But he started to laugh and he took us inside, and he went on laughing and laughing while we had tea. And he said, "No one would dare to say anything like this to me. You, a little girl from Hollywood, what is your name again? Oh, and you're a great actress they tell me, and you didn't want to do my *Saint Joan.* Now, what other of my plays have you done?"

"I haven't done any of your plays."

"My dear girl, you haven't even begun yet."

We sat there and we talked and talked about different plays and the actresses he had known—and what had I done?—and who was this Maxwell Anderson? Certainly we discussed Joan very seriously.

I said, "I made Joan a simple peasant girl. Your words are marvelous, but they're George Bernard Shaw's words, not Joan's. I know Joan of Arc's words by heart because her answers at the trial were transcribed and are historical documents. She had no education and only her inborn common sense to give her courage. She was not afraid of any one of those men who first instructed her and then put her on trial. Yes, they were learned and wise and had been taught to read and write, and she couldn't do any of those things, but she *did* stand up to them and answer them. You have her saying 'I love to be with men. I hate to be dressed in skirts and sit and spin at home.' But that was exactly what she did want: to stay at home and watch her sheep, and do her spinning and weaving. She didn't want to run in front of the soldiers in battle."

Finally it came time to say farewell. I could see that Mr. Shaw had great difficulty in getting out of his chair, and I said to myself, I'm not going to help him. He's a proud old man. That's the last thing he will want.

So he struggled and struggled and up came Gabriel to give him a lift, and he was furious, furious. As he walked toward the car he said, "Will you come and see me again?"

"Yes, I would love to. Next week my husband is coming, and I would just love you to meet my husband, and we will come out again and see you over the weekend."

He looked at me with those wicked little gleaming eyes of his, and said, "I am not a bit interested in seeing your husband. It's you I want to see again."

And his eyes were so flirtatious and sweet, and so intent upon getting *this* woman back. He was ninety-two! I'm so sorry I never saw him again.

———— • ————

Bob Capa had written to Ingrid often during his lengthy stay in Turkey:

> I am taking pictures and when we have finished I will try and sell the story to my London paper for a return ticket to New York, and to a New York paper for two weeks living there. That would be between the twenty-first of January and the tenth of February. How are your plans? Do you still learn French? What are you doing with your days now that you fill in your routine? How is it to be a stage actress? Who is taking you to bistros? How is the shape of the fine young girl from Lorraine? Merry

Xmas to you. Last year it was no New Year, this year no Christmas. I will have to live on last Christmas for this year. The second year is well on its way. How about Spring in Paris? Tonight I'm going to the Champagne Room in Ankara, where the pianist Sacha was the partner of the pianist from El Morocco in Vienna a long time ago. Are you a champagne-room girl? There are a great many places I see alone.

Merry bottle and a great New Year to you.

God, how I would like to see your face.

Domestic harmony between Petter and Ingrid had not improved in 1947 when they were on a short skiing holiday and Capa arrived. On the slopes it quickly became clear to Petter that he was a far better skier than Capa. But it also became clear to him, watching Ingrid and Capa laughing and drinking together, that something more than friendship existed between them. Ingrid did not deny the accusation.

———————— • ————————

We were skiing in Sun Valley, and Capa was there too. I wanted to show off how good I could ski, and I wasn't a very good skier, so I fell almost immediately and twisted my ankle; that was the end of me. I was taken off back to the hotel room where I lay with my leg up. And Capa came in to see me one evening because he was going down to gamble; he loved gambling. He came up a little later with his winnings and put them by my side and said, "Look what I've won," and "Now I'm going back to win some more." A couple of times he came up with some small winnings, not very much, but he had won something.

Then Petter came up and said, "I've just been looking in at the gambling room down there and Capa is losing an awful lot of money. He's just going mad down there."

"Well that's the way gambling is," I said, "you win some and you lose some."

Petter went away and returned a little later and said, "Capa is just foolish. The money he's losing. Someone really should stop him."

I said, "All right. I'll go down and see what I can do."

I hobbled down on my one foot. It was late at night then, maybe one or two o'clock. I talked to Capa, but it made no difference. "I'm going to win it all or lose it all," he said.

I went back to bed, and in the morning of course Capa looked a wreck. And he'd lost everything. Two thousand dollars, all he had saved. But he said, "What difference does it make? It's very good for me. Now I have to work harder."

———————— • ————————

Capa's idea of going to Russia with John Steinbeck had now been revived. And it was now that Ingrid decided their relationship must be resolved. She wrote to Ruth who had always been disturbed and concerned by Ingrid's involvement with Capa:

> I know the Hungarian influence; I'll always be grateful for it. I don't know but I feel sure that it changed much in me. The future I must face—I think for the good, but of course there are those who think for the worst. But he knows we are closing the chapter. It is a bad thing when all other things around him are bad too. But then you can't choose your time. We are drinking our last bottles of champagne. I am tearing a very dear piece away from my life, but we are learning and also making a clean operation so that both patients will live happily ever after . . . What an Easter . . . Lucky only one a year. Love and more love to you my very best friend.

Capa and Ingrid remained great friends. Occasionally he dropped back into her life, but their relationship was different now. And it remained so until the final bitter tragedy.

At the end of August 1948, Ingrid wrote to Ruth:

> Petter and I went to Paris for the weekend of my birthday. We had a most wonderful time. To bed at five in the morning two days in a row. . . .
> *Under Capricorn* is half finished. The other day I burst. The camera was supposed to follow me around for eleven whole minutes, which meant we had to rehearse a whole day with the walls or furniture falling backwards as the camera went through, and of course that couldn't be done

fast enough. So I told Hitch off. How I hate this new technique of his. How I suffer and loathe every moment on the set. My two leading men, Michael Wilding and Joe Cotten, just sat there and said nothing, but I know they agree with me, and I said enough for the whole cast. Little Hitch just left. Never said a word. Just went home . . . oh dear. . . .

A month later in another letter to Ruth, Ingrid was prepared to concede that maybe there was some good in Hitch's new method after all.

The picture is nearly finished. Some of those damned long scenes work out very well. In one nine-and-a-half-minute take, I talked all the time; the camera never left me and it worked fine. I must say much better than being cut up and edited . . .

I heard from Mr. Rossellini again that his proposed film now had a title, *Terra di Dio, God's Earth.* [*Stromboli* as a title hadn't even been thought of then. It became *Stromboli* because of the great scandal: they even named a cocktail after it.] I answered that I thought the idea was very interesting, but where was the script? how long would it take to shoot? what language would I speak? And surely it would be better for us to meet and talk about it. Roberto replied that he was going to Amalfi to film, but that he would like to come to Paris where perhaps we could meet at the Hotel George V at a date convenient to me. I sent a telegram to his hotel in Amalfi offering a date when I could come to Paris with my husband and we would meet at the hotel.

On September 23, she wrote to Ruth:

. . . Over the weekend I'll meet Roberto Rossellini. I look forward to it so much.

——————— • ———————

Of course when I sent my telegram to Amalfi to Roberto Rossellini, I'd no idea that I would be creating something of a domestic explosion. I didn't know that Anna Magnani was with him, and she knew very little or nothing about me. For reasons which are quite obvious now, he'd kept very secretive about the whole thing. But she was a woman. And she knew that something was in the air.

Roberto Rossellini left Rome with Anna Magnani. Upon arrival in Amalfi he quietly informed the head porter at his favorite hotel, the Albergo Luna Convento, that any letter bearing English stamps or any telegram should not be given or shown to any "other people," but delivered to him discreetly and unobtrusively. The dining room at the Albergo Luna Convento is long, formal and old-fashioned, filled with closely ranked tables, hemmed in even tighter by high-backed chairs. At lunch that day it was packed with holiday makers seeking relief from the heat of Rome. The head porter picked his way conspiratorially through the noisy eaters, mistakenly believing that the instruction "other people" did not apply to a relationship so obviously intimate as that of Roberto and Anna. He bent his lips toward the Maestro's ear, his stage whisper audible enough to be heard in the subterranean kitchens.

"Signor Rossellini . . . you say if you receive a telegram from England, I must give it to you privately. Here it is."

"Ah, grazie," murmured Roberto with a show of complete indifference, and without bothering to glance at it, slipped the telegram into his pocket.

A dark flash of Anna's eyes marked the transaction, but she went on mixing the mountain of spaghetti with oil, pepper, salt, and thick tomato. Rome being a city where gossip is as prevalent as sunshine, the inaudible humming of Roberto's association with this new Swedish actress named Ingrid Bergman had already registered in Anna's small and delicate ears.

"Now," she said affably, spooning in more tomato from the large dish, "Is this all right—eh, Roberto?"

Roberto's face wore its faraway look. It didn't fool Anna for even a micro-second.

"Ah, sì, sì, grazie."

"Good. Here you can have it."

Without pause Anna grasped the serving dish in both hands and tossed the heap of spaghetti straight into Roberto's face.

I suppose you could call that moment the start of our actual relationship. I didn't know much about Anna Magnani. I only knew she played the leading lady in *Open City* and that she was magnificent. I suppose he must have had a terrible fight with her after that incident, but they were always fighting each other. It was part of their life together. But at that time I knew practically nothing about him or her. I didn't know if he was married. I simply thought he was a great director and I wanted to do a picture with him. That was my honest feeling as I went to our first meeting.

We went across to Paris, Petter and I, and we all met at the Hotel George V. Roberto had two other men with him, one to translate and one had something to do with finance. We were introduced and Petter said something to me, and I didn't hear him. I was looking at those dark eyes of Roberto's.

I guessed he was about ten years older than me. He was very shy, and he didn't look like a movie man—not the sort I was used to anyway. And the questions and answers were so different from the ordinary Hollywood dialogue.

For example, I asked, "How long will the picture take? How many weeks?"

Roberto looked puzzled. "Weeks? Well, four, five weeks?"

"How is that possible? Every Hollywood movie is three months. That's always the minimum you sign up for, then a contractual prolongation for another ten days, if it's necessary."

He looked a bit unhappy at that and said, "Well, if you want me to, I can try and prolong the picture and make it last that long. I don't know how to do that, but I can try."

I thought what a funny answer that was. Then I asked, "What language shall we use?"

"Language? Any language you feel at ease with. Wouldn't Swedish be the easiest thing?"

I suppose I got a bit irritated by that. "But how can I do it in Swedish? *You* don't even understand what I say then. What language will you write the script in?"

"I shall write it in Italian, but the dialogue doesn't matter. You can say whatever you like because it will be dubbed anyway."

I thought about that, then I went on: "What about clothes?"

He just shrugged, "Clothes? Of what importance are they? We buy the cheapest sort of clothes, the sort of clothes this poor woman would buy . . . the sort of clothes she would buy if she lived in a displaced persons' camp."

Later I learned that he had worked out the first idea with Anna Magnani, and then I came along and he gave it to me. No wonder she threw the spaghetti at him. But I liked him from that very first moment, probably because he was completely the opposite of those fast-talking movie types in Hollywood. You couldn't say he was a strikingly handsome man, but he had a fine head and a very intelligent, very mobile face. And more than anything else I liked what he *said*: those words and the images he inspired were so different from the words of anybody else.

Petter came into the picture—not about the contract, the agents handled the contract afterwards—but asking about the living expenses.

He was getting very hard, so I broke in and said to him in Swedish, "Can you come into the next room for a minute so that I can talk to you?" We went and I said to Petter, "I beg you, don't make the deal too hard on him because I want to work with him. I so love to hear this man, he's so different from anybody else. Don't make the deal hard and difficult because who cares? What I want is just to go to Italy and make this movie. Don't make me lose the picture."

Petter said quickly, "You won't lose it, but I want you to have a good deal. I mean, it's silly they should get you cheaply when you are Number One in America; it would be ridiculous for you to go to Italy to do a picture for nothing."

"I know that, Petter, but you know about all the difficult clauses."

"They're necessary."

"Well, remember I want very much to make this movie."

We all said good-bye. I returned to England with Petter, finished *Under Capricorn* with Hitch and then went back to California.

Still no contract, but I did get a letter early in November:

Dear Mrs. Bergman,

I send you as promised a short synopsis of my story: I can't call it a real full-length story, because it is not a story. I am used to following a few basic ideas and building them up little by little during the process of the work as the scenes very often spring out of direct inspiration from reality. I don't know whether my words will have the same power of the images: anyhow, I assure you that, during this work of mine, my own emotions have been strong and intense as never before. I wish I could speak to you about Her and He, the Island, the men and women of the island, that humanity so primitive though so antique, made wise by experience of centuries. One could think that they live so simply and poorly just because of that knowledge of the vanity of everything we consider civilized and necessary.

I am sure you will find many parts of the story quite rugged, and that your personality will be hurt and offended by some reactions of the personage. You mustn't think that I approve of the behaviour of HIM. I deplore the wild and brutal jealousy of the islander, I consider it a remainder of an elementary and old-fashioned mentality. I describe it because it is part of the ambience, like the prickly pears, the pines and the goats. But I can't deny in the deepness of my soul there is a secret envy for those who can love so passionately, so wildly, as to forget any tenderness, any pity for their beloved ones. They are guided only by a deep desire of possession of the body and soul of the woman they love. Civilization has smoothed the strength of feelings; undoubtedly it's more comfortable to reach the top of a mountain by funicular, but perhaps the joy was greater when men climbed dangerously to the top.

I beg your pardon for the many diversions, I am filled with so many thoughts and I fear that you cannot understand me completely only by a letter. I am anxious to know your impression after you have read this story. I beg you to consider that the translation was made in a great hurry by people who have not the complete mastery of the language.

I want you to know how deeply I wish to translate those ideas into images, just to quiet down the turmoil of my brain.

Waiting to know your judgment, I am,

Yours very truly and devoted
R. Rossellini.

———— • ————

Roberto was awarded the New York Film Critics Award for *Open City* as the best foreign film of 1948 and invited to New York to receive it. As no contract had yet been signed for the Italian film, it made sense that Roberto should visit the Lindstroms out in California, and that discussion about financing generally should continue. Ingrid thought it an excellent idea.

From New York Roberto wired: "I just arrive friendly." Ingrid smiled when she received it and replied: "Waiting for you in the Wild West."

———————— • ————————

By this time I still didn't know who was to put up the money, who was going to do what, so I felt that the best thing would be that when Roberto came to Hollywood we could discuss everything.

Sam Goldwyn wanted to make a picture with me. I knew him through David Selznick. He liked me, he grew very fond of me. We talked a lot, and I used to come by his office sometimes, and sit and talk and have a drink with him; he was always saying, "I've got to make a picture with you. Let's do it now, let's get a story." Then he'd call in his story writers and say, "David Selznick has got this girl, and I can buy her from David, but I haven't got a story." But the story writers never did write a story for me and he never found one. So now I called up Sam Goldwyn and said, "Sam, I have a story I like. Would you like to do this one? It's by an Italian named Roberto Rossellini."

Sam said "Sure," and he looked at those first few pages Roberto had sent. "Sounds very artistic," he said, and I could sense he liked the idea of backing a prestige film. "Let me talk to this fellow."

So they talked. Roberto, first with his French—I'd learned a little of that language by now—and then, very quickly—very smart he was—in English with a terrible accent. Since he knew Latin, he just took the Latin word and cut off the end and now it was an English word with the wrong accent. But you could understand what he meant. So he was able to talk to people. And he talked to Goldwyn who fell absolutely in love with him. Everything was fine and Goldwyn was going to do the picture; it was going to be a big Sam Goldwyn picture. We had a press reception. I have photographs of us with Goldwyn smiling and signing the contracts and everybody happy, we, sitting there, as in school, on a platform with the press below staring up at us. I felt so stupid sitting up there like a schoolmistress. Anyway, there we sat with Goldwyn in the middle and Roberto and myself on either side. And they asked questions:

"Mr. Goldwyn, what is the picture about? How much is it going to cost? And where will it be shot?" Goldwyn was answering all the questions wrong.

I finally got so fed up I said, "Sam, you're telling the wrong story. That's not the movie, and that's not what we're going to do. We're going to be on an island called Stromboli. Please let Roberto talk, he knows what he's going to do. Let him say something."

It started off very badly.

When we got off the press reception platform, Sam said, "I've seen *Open City*, but I would like to see another picture of Roberto's. Has he got one?"

Certainly he had one. So Roberto brings out *Germany Year Zero*. It was the third of the trilogy with *Paisan* and *Open City*.

I once said to Roberto, "I don't understand; the others are so warm and human, and you make me cry, but *Germany Year Zero* doesn't make me cry." And he replied, "Well I couldn't make you cry because after what Italy had been through I detested the Germans. I went over there just as the war was finished, and I shot with what I saw. I didn't like what I saw."

So the picture he made is very cold, very brutal, but extremely interesting, and it has a relationship with the other two pictures.

Sam Goldwyn had a dinner party to give the first showing of *Germany Year Zero*. He invited a lot of people from Hollywood. After dinner we saw the movie. The picture finished and the lights came on. *And no one said a word.* Not a word. No applause. Complete silence. Twenty people. Not a sound. This freezing cold silence from all these people. Instinctively I stood up and walked to Roberto, threw an arm around him and kissed him on the cheek, to show everybody—something—I didn't know what I wanted to show—but I had to protect him. And then started the discussion.

"Well, it wasn't actually what we expected." "When did you shoot it?" "How long did it take?" I knew that Roberto was unhappy because they didn't understand his picture.

A couple of days later Sam Goldwyn called me up and said, "I'm sorry, I can't do the movie. I can't understand the man; I don't know what he's doing, what he's talking about. He doesn't know anything about budgets; he doesn't know anything about schedules. This kind of movie, I won't put money into it."

I had to come home and tell Roberto that we didn't have a deal.

It really is quite funny sometimes how ridiculous little incidents cause so much trouble between people. When Roberto arrived in

America in January, 1949, he could bring very little money with him because of the Italian currency restrictions. In Hollywood he'd stayed at the Beverly Hills Hotel, and that was far too expensive, so we invited him to stay in our guest house at 1220 Benedict Canyon Drive.

Just before Christmas I'd been shopping with Pia to select some of the Christmas presents I had to buy. Pia was now getting her new bicycle. We went into the toy shop and there, standing in the corner, was a huge silly toy cow called Elsie, wearing an apron. Pia stared at Elsie and fell in love with her; that's what she wanted for Christmas, and the bicycle was forgotten.

Elsie was seventy-five dollars! I went to Petter and said, "Can I buy Elsie for Pia for Christmas, because that is the one thing she wants."

Petter said, "Absolutely not. Ridiculous! A cow for seventy-five dollars? To stand in the corner? A cow standing in a corner with an apron?"

"Well—you're right—yes, you're right," I said. "A bicycle makes more sense." So Pia got her bicycle for Christmas and nobody bought Elsie.

Then Roberto came to stay with us and he had no money, so he borrowed three hundred dollars from Petter. He wanted to take back to Italy a present for his son Renzo, by his first wife. "I know what I want," he said, "cowboy boots and hat and one of those Indian feather headdresses."

Off we went to my toy shop, and there was Elsie. Roberto took one look at her and he fell in love with her too.

"That cow," he said, "that's for Pia."

I thought, Oh, my God! Petter will think I brought him here just to get him to buy Elsie. So I said, "Oh no!" But once Roberto Rossellini made up his mind, nothing but nothing was going to change it. The fact that he spent seventy-five dollars, which Petter had just lent him, on something as useless as Elsie had nothing to do with it. Money never had anything to do with any of Roberto's decisions. He wanted to thank us for looking after him and putting him up in the guest house, and what could be nicer than to give our daughter a present which he knew she would love?

———— • ————

Ingrid's resolve to become a good wife and mother was now peeling away. Ingrid had known in her heart for a long time that if the right man came along and said the right words, she was ready and willing to go. In one short month, Roberto Rossellini did that. He did not equivocate. He did not seek justification. He did not say, "We must think of Petter and Anna Magnani." He said simply, "Come away with me."

To make a film on the barren island of Stromboli they were about to set out on a great adventure together. Why should they not also adventure with their private lives?

Ingrid's diary, which on Tuesday, January 25, 1949, reported briefly, "Rossellini here," also revealed that they had dinner together that evening, and that on Wednesday they drove to the Pacific Ocean and had dinner with Billy Wilder, the celebrated film producer and writer. And so it went on: lunches, dinners, drives along the coastline, more often than not alone; meetings, parties, script conferences.

On Tuesday, February 4, a diary entry recorded that work had begun on the Lindstroms' long-contemplated rebuilding of their house. Two months later, on her way to Rome, Ingrid was to confess to Kay Brown that "every time a workman hit the roof with a hammer, it was like a nail going into my head."

———— • ————

But meanwhile another urgent problem had arisen. With Sam Goldwyn out, who was going to finance the picture?

I asked Petter what to do and he said, "Why don't you call Howard Hughes of RKO? He'll do the picture."

"No. I don't want to." And a shiver went through me. "You know I'm afraid of that man."

Then Petter said, very coldly and abruptly, "I'm sure you can handle him."

I had met Howard Hughes through Cary Grant and Irene Selznick when I was in New York. I suppose it must have been the year before. Cary and Irene had suggested that we make up a foursome with him. So we all went out together and ended up dancing at El Morocco. He was very nice. We danced and talked, and I remember him saying: "I'm so lonely, I'm so terribly lonely. You know I have no friends."

I thought, what a silly thing for a man to say. Here's this very rich and famous man—I'd read all about him being a daredevil flier in the papers, and about the famous movie stars he'd escorted—and he's lonely? I laughed and said, "Then it must be your own fault, because you don't go out and look for friends. Anyway, I'm having a good time; you're not lonely tonight, are you?"

He obviously decided I was going to be one of his friends, because the phone kept going, and it was usually Cary Grant saying, "He's just dying to see you again." Eventually I said to Cary, "I'm not interested in seeing him again. And why are *you* bothering with him? Can't he ring me himself?"

Then, for some reason, Joe Steele got mixed up in the action, and I was told that Hughes wanted to fly Cary, Joe Steele, and me all the way back to California. I learned later that he'd bought up every available seat ticket on planes flying to California that day, so if we wanted to fly that day we had to fly with Howard Hughes.

Cary, Joe, and I slept most of the way across, but at dawn Hughes woke me up to give me a guided tour at rim level of the Grand Canyon. It was a fantastic experience and I said, "Thank you very much, that was marvelous." And that, as far as I was concerned, was the end of it. But no, it wasn't. Howard wanted to give a party for me, and I said I didn't want to go to his party. Then, Joe Steele tried to influence me, saying, "You like the food at the Beachcomber. And there'll be lots of other people you know, you won't be alone with him."

I said, "Joe, I don't want to meet him again, I don't want to see him again."

I was simply not at ease with him. I knew what he was after. Everyone was trying to make me more interested. I wasn't. And I didn't intend to be.

———— • ————

It is doubtful if any American millionaire in the long history of American millionaires has ever been more eccentric than Howard Hughes. And what Howard Hughes wanted he usually got. Money bought everything. Well, it nearly always bought everything. Certainly it was meant to buy Ingrid Bergman.

And Howard didn't give up easily.

———— • ————

One day who rings me up but Howard Hughes himself. It was funny. I'd just washed my hair and I was sitting on the floor drying it. I picked up the phone with one hand, and I was using the dryer with the other. The voice said, "This is Howard Hughes, and I've just bought a film studio for you."

I turned off the hairdryer and asked, "What have you done?"

"I've just bought a film studio for you. I've bought RKO. It's yours. It's my present to you. Are you happy now?"

I said, "You've bought me a film studio. Well that's very nice. Thank you."

I didn't really know if he was joking or not, but as he was Howard Hughes, he probably wasn't. If he had bought a studio and could get a good script, and if we could get one of my favorite directors and one or two leading men I thought rather good, then why shouldn't I do a movie? So I said, "But that isn't enough."

"Not enough!"

"I don't know what to do with a studio. What I need is a good script and a good director. . . ."

"Okay, okay, just give me the names of the scriptwriters and directors you want, and I'll get them."

I suppose if I'd been serious and really wanted RKO, I'd have been asking him around for martinis that very evening. But I wasn't serious. Not about Howard Hughes anyway. Anyway, I'd practically forgotten the whole episode when Roberto Rossellini entered my life, and Petter came up with his name to finance our picture.

"All right," I said, "I'll call him."

In those days he was living in a bungalow at the Beverly Hills Hotel next door to Arthur Miller and Marilyn Monroe, and not much more than fifteen minutes from our house. He didn't take any longer than that to get there.

He was in white tennis clothes, and wearing white shoes. He sat down, looked at me, and said in that sort of low, clipped Texan voice of his: "Sure, okay, I'll do the picture."

Roberto was there too, so I introduced him, but Howard Hughes hardly knew he was present. Roberto didn't exist as far as he was concerned.

"How much money do you need?"

"Listen," I said, "don't you want to hear the story?"

"No, I don't want to hear the story. I'm not interested. I don't care what sort of story it is. Are you beautiful in it? Are you going to have wonderful clothes?"

I began to laugh. "No. I'm playing a DP in some horrible camp. I'm going to wear the worst and cheapest things you ever saw."

"Too bad. The next picture you're going to do, you'll look great. It's to be a marvelous picture with RKO and you can make it with whatever director you like"—this with a glance at Roberto. "But have your little fun and then you'll come back to me, and we'll make a great movie."

Of course I never did come back to him, and I think he hated *Stromboli* since he reedited it the way he wanted it, and by that time he had the whole worldwide scandal on his hands.

Despite this he wrote to me, but I put away his letter and didn't discover it went unanswered until twenty-five years later. That was when I decided to leave the house at Choisel in France for good. I was going through a lot of old letters, and there—I could hardly believe my eyes—was a letter from Howard Hughes, sent to Italy to me, in the middle of all that great scandal. It was such a dear letter from a man I'd disappointed and brushed off in every possible way, and I felt so sad that I hadn't given it the attention it deserved.

———————— • ————————

The letter came from 7000 Romaine Street, California and was dated February 10, 1950, eight days after Robertino's birth.

He told her he had hesitated at first to write her because "I have never been fortunate enough to know you very well or consider myself a close friend of yours."

He was not trying to judge her decision but instead to tell her how impressed he was with her "courage, utter simplicity, and lack of guile or subterfuge," and by the way she had faced the issue and not blamed anyone else.

"Reality is a matter of intent," he told her; it comes from within, not from legislation or legal documents.

It was his hope and belief that by the time Robertino was old enough to comprehend, the world's attitude might be "a little truer and broader." Her son would carry no stigma, he said, but instead the heritage of a mother who "though she may not have been so terribly clever, shrewd, or wise, is one of the most brilliant and courageous women of our generation."

———— • ————

Now twenty-five years later, I didn't quite know what to do about it. Then I heard that he was staying at the Inn on the Park in London. So I just wrote that after all these years I was moved to tears by his letter, that I would always keep it, and I had never realized how kind he really was. I never heard from him. I didn't expect to. I just hoped that if he had moments of awareness, someone might tell him I'd written. I didn't think there was any point in trying to see him.

———— • ————

On Monday February 28, 1949, Petter and Ingrid left for a skiing holiday at the mountain resort of Aspen, and Roberto Rossellini left for Rome. But the catalytic process had begun.

———— • ————

When I was with Petter at Aspen, I kept pleading with him to let me leave for Rome early and he said, "But you're not going to start the picture for weeks." And I said, "I know, but I'd like to be in Rome. I'd like to learn the language. I'd like to be with those people. . . . I think it's better if I get there a bit early."

I plagued Petter to let me go, because I was just longing to listen to Roberto, to hear what he had to say, and how he said it.

———— • ————

His telegram from La Guardia Airport said only, "I leave now. Good-bye. Roberto."

But Ingrid was grateful for any communication:
Aspen. March 4, 1949.

> Thank God your wire came that you had arrived. I was expecting it yesterday evening and when it still had not come this morning I began to look in the newspapers for accidents. I ski and the mountain is so big. I try to be careful so I can come to you in one piece. I'd like to come now. I am all right, no trouble, but Petter thinks the 19th is early enough. I told him about our trip—Capri, Amalfi,

Messina—but Petter got angry and said I was not going out to make a pleasure trip. It was out of the question that I travel with you. We'd better start the picture on time, as RKO begins to pay me on April 1st.

Five days ago you left. We have fifteen more. Write a letter about all your troubles. I think we will leave Aspen on the 7th. I am glad you are home.

I.

On March 7 she wrote again:

We are leaving today. I am very ungrateful, for the snow is wonderful. I have learned a lot with a good ski teacher. But my mind is elsewhere. Please write me the news.

When I get home I can wire you. I eat all the time and will become as fat as you like. If I don't work soon, I'll go crazy. If I don't go soon. . . . Please hurry up with the preparations.

J'ai fini! My last run down the mountain and I have not broken everything! Now I'll call for a double martini and celebrate and pack. Today is Monday, next Monday I am in New York and same week, with best plane I am in Rome. Are you ready? Your son must have been happy with all your gifts. I want to talk to you.

On March 7, 1949, the Lindstroms left Aspen, arriving back in Beverly Hills on March 9. Two days later on Friday evening, Ingrid took the train to New York. She didn't take much baggage with her, and only three hundred dollars in travelers checks. If anyone could have prophesied that it would be seven tumultuous years before she returned to the United States, she simply would not have believed it.

Her cablegram to Roberto was ecstatic:

CAN'T HEAR, CAN'T UNDERSTAND, CAN'T SPEAK. ARRIVE NEW YORK THE TWELFTH HOTEL HAMPSHIRE HOUSE. LEAVING NEW YORK NINETEENTH ON BEST PLANE ARRIVING ROME 11.20 SUNDAY NIGHT THE TWENTIETH TWA FLIGHT 916.

On March 12, Roberto called the Hampshire House from Italy. As soon as Ingrid put down the receiver she began her letter:

Hampshire House, March 12, 1949 Saturday. After the phone call.

For God's sake telephone ten times a day if you want to be that stupid! I like to stay up in the evenings and talk —just like you do. And where is that freedom you talked about, if I have to be home by two every night? It is also stupid to call a hotel that is in close contact with the press. There has already been so much written about us, I discovered when I came back from the mountain. My marriage was finished—from now on *all* my pictures are to be made by you—we hear in town. I followed you to New York, people say—a new triangle drama has hit Hollywood. On and on went the gossip columnists. I am very unhappy about it and don't want to add any daily telephone calls. Please understand me and help me.

I didn't have time to say good-bye to people and get sentimental—not until I saw Petter stand at the airport, so lonely and silent. Again, I realized my selfishness, and now when I am here I have nothing else to do but go to the theaters and wait, again.

Everybody asks me about the gossip about us, so I went home to look at your picture. I am still looking.

Roberto cabled:

EVERYTHING SETTLED. I AM VERY HAPPY. ANXIOUS THESE THREE DAYS ARE TOO LONG. I GO TO NAPLES FOR PREPARATION FILM. MY ADDRESS IS HOTEL EXCELSIOR. I RETURN ROME SATURDAY. DIO, DIO, ROBERTO.

In Ingrid's diary for March 20, 1949, is the single word *"Roma."* It is underlined twice.

Chapter 13

Arriving in Rome was just like something out of a dream. I've never experienced a welcome like it anywhere else in the world. It was a fiesta—everyone laughing and shouting and waving and going mad. There were so many people at the airport you'd think it was a queen arriving, instead of just me. Roberto shoved a big bouquet of flowers into my arms and we forced our way into the cars. Roberto pushed me into his sporty red Cisitalia, and drove off into Rome, straight to the Excelsior Hotel. And the crowds were there, too. We just couldn't get through them to the front door.

Roberto immediately started fighting the photographers; that was his normal behavior with photographers. There he was hitting out with his fist and trying to smash a way through to the door. He tore one photographer's jacket right off at the arm, and the next day he felt sorry about it and sent him a new jacket. We finally managed to get inside Roberto's apartment where a party was waiting. All Roberto's friends were there. Frederico Fellini had put marvelous little caricatures on the walls: drawings of Roberto and me and the island of Stromboli. And there was champagne and everyone was laughing and chattering. Roberto had put little gifts everywhere. I was simply overwhelmed.

———— • ————

More than anyone else perhaps, Liana Ferri, who had translated Ingrid's first letter to Roberto, understood exactly what was happening:

"To understand how the people of Rome were behaving, you've got to understand what they went through," Liana said. "We had endured a war of which we had wanted no part. We had been cascaded into war by that idiot Mussolini. We had been under German occupation, and we had listened night and day to the sound of German boots tramping through the streets, and we were frightened, very frightened. For nine months the roads to the south and north, the roads everywhere out of Rome were bombed daily, and we were completely cut off. Especially from food. We needed the food from the north and the south, and we didn't get it. So we starved; we literally starved. For the first time in our lives we understood completely the second line of the Lord's Prayer: 'Give us this day our daily bread.' And we were never given it. Oh, I don't suppose the historians will lose any sleep over the fact that Rome starved for nine months and I lost nine kilos in weight. I suppose the Allies might think that is good for me."

Liana Ferri smiled. "And of course we expected the Allies to be different from the Germans. In some things they were. In the first place the Americans wore boots with rubber soles, so we got to sleep at nights. But the charm soon wore off and we were soon repeating the familiar complaint of liberated Europeans about the Yanks . . . overfed, overpaid, oversexed and over here. They occupied hotels —whole streets of hotels—told us what to do, what they liked—an entire red light district sprang up near the Spanish Steps. A lot of Fascists, looking humble and contrite and reformed, were put into positions of power. The Roman women went to bed with every American soldier; every woman in Rome was in love, it seemed, with an American soldier.

"It was against this sort of background that young Roberto Rossellini had made his great films, *Open City* and *Paisan.* Then he had captured Ingrid. This great actress was in Italy to make a picture and she was in love with our Roberto Rossellini! 'Bravo, Roberto, bravo!' She had left that cold Nordic husband of hers. Now she would find the true meaning of life and love. 'Bravo, Roberto, bravo, Ingrid!'

"It was compensation for all we'd gone through, all the hunger and humiliations. Oh, yes, we cried, 'Hurrah, Roberto.' But I didn't say 'Hurrah, Roberto,' because I knew him so well. After all, I'd translated all his letters back to Ingrid, and I was there when she arrived at the airport and at the party. I was struck by her simplicity and honesty. She was in love and she was without any malice.

"I said to Roberto, 'I know you. I know your story with your wife, with the Greek-Russian girl, the German dancer, and with Anna Magnani. I know your tricks. Listen to me, I am a good friend of yours, but if you treat Ingrid badly, if you take advantage of her simplicity and shyness, I shall not be your friend, and I shall not speak to you anymore, because it is not allowed for a person like you, shrewd as you are, foxy as you are, to take advantage of a woman who is completely harmless, completely without defense. That I won't stand and I am very clear!'

"And Roberto answered, 'You are always criticizing other people. You are always cautious and pragmatic. I love her, do you understand? I love her.'

"He was always involved with problems: money problems, contract problems, women problems. He was always in a turmoil, he couldn't live without turmoil. If he lived in peace, he was dead. He needed storm weather. Unless there was a hurricane blowing and he was building barricades and fighting battles, he was bored—just plain bored. Life was a battle: films were a battle. He didn't get out of bed unless he had to fight a battle. Without one he just stayed in bed complaining, 'I have a headache, my stomach hurts, I feel sick.' "

Liana continued: "I once wrote an article about him for an Italian magazine and I called him a Renaissance man. He had all the faults and all the qualities of the Renaissance types. He was a revivalist, a man for all seasons, a dilettante; he would start one tremendous episode and go mad with enthusiasm and forget it the next day. He would love you, kiss you, fall over backwards for you, and next day he'd stab his best friend in the back just for the pleasure of doing it.

"His personality was impossible to understand because one minute he'd be doing the nicest thing for someone he hardly knew and two minutes later he would have forgotten all about him.

"Ingrid knew absolutely nothing about Roberto," said Liana. "She arrived there in Rome like a little innocent lamb. And someone had to stand up for her. I intended to stand up for her."

Like Petter Lindstrom, Roberto Rossellini was a remarkable and original man. If the command had been issued: "Will the real Petter Lindstrom stand up?" Petter would have stepped forward without hesitation, firm, resolute, assured. If the same command had been issued to Roberto, it would have required at least twelve different individuals to obey the summons. To his bankers, lawyers, and backers, he showed one face. To his children, he was a fortress of love, warmth, and affection; to his film colleagues, he was the man who alternately screamed abuse, larded them with praise, or simply ignored them; to Anna Magnani, he was the man who steered her through great film parts, with whom she conducted a passionate battle of opposing wills. To Ingrid, Roberto was first a great director who could give her career fresh impetus and a dynamic direction, and possibly—possibly, someone who might requite the barely understood yearnings within her. But one thing is certain. If any wise and impartial judge had, at that moment, been asked to adjudicate as to whether Roberto Rossellini was in love with Ingrid Bergman, and Ingrid Bergman with Roberto Rossellini, the verdict would have been a positive and resounding "Yes."

To Roberto, Ingrid was a challenge. She was beautiful. She belonged to someone else. She was vital and amusing, yet at times she had a solemn intensity of purpose which he could not understand. Unlike Roberto, she never tossed ten balls in the air at the same time, uncertain whether she could keep them airborne, uncaring if they fell. Ingrid concentrated on one job at a time; it was impossible for her personal happiness ever to do anything else. Her smile lit up her entire being, and her sudden laugh was joyous and unaffected. Like all male Italians, Roberto needed no reassurance that he had anything to learn about women; Ingrid, however, constantly managed to surprise him.

It was not in Roberto's character to try to qualify love. He didn't spoon it out in little measures. He didn't care or wonder if he was going to make a fool of himself; he was completely devoid of any Anglo-Saxon doubt or caution. Love took him by the heart, scattered his wits, and drove him to the side of his beloved. Roberto was the boldest lover in the world; would risk all that he stood for; was ready to sacrifice, win or lose, for love. He was desperately, passionately in love with Ingrid. He wanted her. He was not prepared to let her out of his hands or his sight.

———————— • ————————

I think that deep down I was in love with Roberto from the moment I saw *Open City,* for I could never get over the fact that he was always there in my thoughts.

Probably, subconsciously, he offered a way out from both my problems: my marriage and my life in Hollywood. But it wasn't clear to me at that time, even though I wrote those letters. If people had looked suspicious when I mentioned Italy, I would certainly have said quite indignantly, "I'm going to make a movie—that's all I'm going for."

I knew that he liked me. Afterwards he insisted that he'd told Petter he loved me, but of course he spoke so little English in those days that he probably said it in a language that Petter didn't understand. I realize now he was certain he could win me over once I was in Italy. He always got what he wanted. And at that time he wanted me!

———————— • ————————

On the day following Ingrid's arrival, it seemed as though all the citizens of Rome had decided to show how overjoyed they were by massing outside the Excelsior Hotel. The Via Veneto was jammed solid. No one could move into or out of the hotel foyer, and Ingrid was marooned in her bedroom.

Roberto and the hotel management were experts at circumvention: "If Miss Bergman would come this way, slip down these back stairs, out through this back door, and into this narrow street . . ." a few twists and turns and Ingrid and Roberto were strolling through the streets enjoying the sunshine. Of course they were soon discovered by the photographers. And naturally the crowds collected. But they were manageable crowds and everyone was good-tempered and happy to see Ingrid.

Rome overwhelmed her; its noise, traffic, and people; its narrow, twisting streets, hemmed in by tall, pale terra cotta walls, suddenly opening into graceful squares of heavenly proportions; the water splashing from fountains; the sense of antiquity. Nothing had pre pared her Nordic soul for such a place. She surrendered to the color, the music, the gaiety, and the great affection which engulfed her everywhere she went:

———————— • ————————

Roberto wanted me to meet all his friends; he wanted to show me Naples, and Capri, and Amalfi, and a dozen places I'd never heard of. Everything was so new to me: the country and the people, their outgoing way of living, the beauty of it. And Roberto seemed to know everything there was to know.

————— • —————

At the end of the week they sped southwards out of Rome down the Appian Way in the booming red Cisitalia, over the old flagstones, past the little temples by the roadside, the ancient shrines of pagan Rome. Ingrid was conscious of the speed of the car, the wind in her hair, the sunshine on her face, conscious that the word "ecstasy" was not big enough to mirror the intensity of her feelings.

They sped on down the road south, passing Monte Cassino high on its peak, the bombed abbey which marked the graveyard of young men from a dozen different nations. They reached the spring-green fields leading to Naples, rode past the peasants in their slow, high-wheeled carts. They halted at the quayside fronting the wide blue bay before crossing to Capri in a churning, rolling ferry boat smelling of garlic and cigarette smoke, noisy with the screams of seabirds, the slap of waves, and the raucous amplified music of Italian tenors celebrating *Amore.*

On Capri, she stood at Roberto's side looking down at the blue sea swirling and sucking at the gray and shattered cliffs which had entranced Tiberius. And life exactly matched her private dream.

————— • —————

I have a sweet photograph in which I look so happy it is unbelievable. We are in a little place where people go dancing. I think it must be the only time I ever danced with Roberto, because he's just not a dancer. But that evening he danced. I think he was doing everything to win me over.

He was wonderful at recounting the history of Italy; he knew everything that had happened throughout its history. And if he didn't know it, I think he made it up. He knew all about the history and the monuments and the ruins; he knew all about the legends; and he knew practically everybody in Italy as far as I could see.

As we walked around, the photographers followed us everywhere, and Roberto was so calm and quiet and happy that he didn't even bother to punch them. And then came that famous photo—which *Life* magazine printed—on the Amalfi coast as we climbed the steps toward one of those round towers. We were hand in hand, and that went all over the world showing what a loose woman I was. . . .

—————— • ——————

If one had to select a stretch of rugged coastline of singular beauty, legendary historical association, designed by nature to stupefy the eye and entrance the soul, then the Amalfi coastline would be as good as any.

In 1949 very little traffic moved around its hairpin bends or through the tiny towns tucked into its tiny sheltered bays. The road going south rises steeply out of Amalfi, and on the crest of the hill no more than a hundred meters from the town stands the hotel known as the Albergo Luna Convento (Convent of the Moon). From the twelfth to sixteenth centuries it served as a Capuchin monastery and today still maintains much of its monastic simplicity; functionally, the ancient cloisters surround what is now the bar. It had always been one of Roberto's favorite hotels. Anna Magnani had anointed him with spaghetti there. With Ingrid he had no such trouble.

Ingrid's wide window showed a vista of a broad smooth bay, hemmed in by mountains falling steeply into deep dark water. When the moon was full it sailed across the mountain tops and hovered above the glittering sea.

Roberto was driven to recall the ancient legends of this promontory: how bold Ulysses, returning from the Trojan Wars, his ship driven by unfavorable winds against this very coast, had chanced upon an island inhabited by the beautiful sorceress, Circe.

Ingrid smiled at Roberto's yarns, unconscious of the parallels: she was herself as beautiful as any Circe—and just as famous. It seemed as though life and love had not changed all that much over the past ten thousand years.

There were, of course, occasional rifts between the lovers, differences of opinion or emphasis. Horses, for example: skinny, mangy beasts, pulling heavy loads, and beaten indiscriminately by their equally underfed owners. It happened several times on the narrow roads, and on each occasion the horrified Ingrid would indignantly order Roberto to stop while she leapt from the car.

"How dare you do that," she would shout in English at the driver. "Stop it this minute! Look at the poor animal! He's so weak and undersized, how do you expect him to pull that load? You should be ashamed of yourself . . . ashamed, do you hear me?"

The peasant, slightly stunned by the onrush of this golden Saint Joan and only half aware that such a normal activity as his beating his horse had occasioned this outburst, would stare open-mouthed. His eyes would eventually move across to the *commendatore* who sat behind the wheel of the automobile for help or explanation.

None ever came. Impassive and silent as an oriental Buddha, Roberto waited for Ingrid to rejoin him in the front seat. Then he would let in the clutch and move slowly away, allowing the final words of Ingrid's exasperation to flow past his head.

"What do you think of that? Have you ever seen anything more cruel or disgusting in your life? That poor animal! You could see its ribs sticking through the flesh."

Roberto's expression would not change. His philosophical statement was always the same:

"Don't you understand. The man is beaten too. How else does he get back at the beating he's taken from life? Who else is there to beat except the horse? How else does he let the anger and frustration out of his soul?"

It was a reply which never satisfied Ingrid, and she would retort, "Then he should find some other way," and stay on the alert for the next unfortunate animal she might have to rush to rescue.

There were other occasions when Ingrid simply could not believe —and certainly did not take seriously—what Roberto was doing. The time when they passed through the coastal town of Salerno, and Ingrid was treated for the first time to Roberto's documentary method of casting. He pulled up near a beach where a number of fishermen were working by their boats. Ever since Ingrid's arrival in Rome, she and Roberto had been conversing in a mixture of basic French and English. Now when he announced disarmingly, "You wait here, I just go find you a leading man," Ingrid took this as a joke and laughed merrily as he walked down toward the boats. Twenty minutes later he got back into the car. "I got you two," he said casually, "a tall, good-looking young man and a short one. You can take your pick when we get to Stromboli."

Ingrid still took it as a joke. Not until she got to the island did she realize that he was most certainly not joking. He had put both young men on the payroll, and given them the name of the hotel where they were to join the camera team passing through Salerno that night.

In 1949 the coast road was narrower, the villages and towns in that astonishingly beautiful region of high peaks and wide fertile valleys, remote and backward. They turned inland toward the tiny town of

Cantanzaro where Roberto had decided to spend the night. Obviously the Mayor had been warned of their coming by the Maestro's lieutenants, and the inhabitants were packed six deep down either side of the narrow main street to welcome them. The Cisitalia crept through a human funnel to the front door of the small hotel:

———————— • ————————

It was unbelievable. The schools were all closed. The kids had been given a holiday, and everyone was lining the streets to wave and cheer us. It was like a royal visit. We stopped at the hotel. There were flowers everywhere; the foyer was packed, and as we went up the stairs, people stood three deep on either side. My bedroom—you should have seen the bedroom, a huge bed splendidly laid out with marvelous silk sheets trimmed with lace. And there was the Mayor explaining that these were the very sheets upon which he and his wife had enjoyed their wedding night, some years before. And would I be good enough to autograph them and leave them behind tomorrow morning?

In those days in those small Italian hotels there were no rooms with bathrooms. So after the mayor had made his little speech and left the room I'd closed the door. Then I decided to go to the bathroom. It was now getting a bit late and I expected them all to have left the hotel. But when I peeped out, there they were, all still standing in rows, and they all began to applaud as soon as they saw my face. So I smiled and went back into the room. Waited another ten minutes and tried again. But they were still there. More polite applause. So I smiled and closed the door a second time. Well, another ten minutes and I was becoming desperate. So I just opened the door and walked out into the corridor. And they were marvelous. I was applauded all the way to the bathroom and all the way back again. First time it had ever happened in my life.

———————— • ————————

It was a momentous and eventful journey. Although there were many precedents to reassure her, for Italy is a country notably indulgent toward lovers, Ingrid's conscience, hammered into shape by the uncompromising churchmen of the Swedish Lutheran faith, was already ticking uneasily by the time they reached Amalfi.

During her stay in Rome, Petter's letters had been arriving regu-

larly. At the beginning of March he wrote to her reminding her of
his warning that she had no hope of slipping into Rome unobserved,
and was pleased to hear that she hadn't been crushed to death. On
March 31 he wrote thanking her for the letter which had described
her stay in Rome, adding that he hoped the money he had wired to
Roberto had already arrived, and that everyone was waiting anxiously for a report on how the production was proceeding.

In Amalfi Ingrid knew the moment had come to be completely
honest with Petter, even though the letter was the most painful and
difficult she ever had to write. She attempted several drafts. And at
last on notepaper emblazoned with a picture of the Albergo Luna
Convento, she began:

> Petter lilla:
> It will be very difficult for you to read this letter and it
> is difficult for me to write. But I believe it is the only way.
> I would like to explain everything from the beginning, but
> you know enough. I would ask forgiveness, but that seems
> ridiculous. It is not altogether my fault, and how can you
> forgive that I want to stay with Roberto?
> It was not my intention to fall in love and go to Italy
> forever. After all our plans and dreams; you know that is
> true. But how can I help it or change it? You saw in
> Hollywood how my enthusiasm for Roberto grew and
> how much alike we are with the same desire for the same
> kind of work, the same understanding of life. I thought
> maybe I could conquer the feeling I had for him, when I
> saw him in his own milieu, so different from mine. But it
> is only the opposite. I had not the courage to talk about
> him more than I did with you; I didn't know the depth of
> his feelings.
> My Petter, I know how this letter falls like a bomb on
> our house, our Pia, our future, our past so filled with
> sacrifice and help on your part. And now you stand alone
> in the ruins and I can't help you. I ask only more sacrifice
> and more help.
> Dear, I never thought this moment would come after all
> we have gone through together, and now I don't know
> what to do. Poor little Papa, but also poor little Mama.

Under Italian law, if Petter Lindstrom had flown straight to Italy and shot, if not Ingrid then certainly Roberto, through the heart, he would probably have been found guilty of murder but innocent of any crime except that of deep and understandable human emotion.

But Petter was not like that. Petter was sane and level-headed and decent. He worked things out clearly in his mind, and when his mind was made up he acted. Already the newspapers were full of rumors of romance between Roberto and Ingrid. But as he walked through the bright California sunshine, he could not believe what Ingrid had written. It was not that he did not *want* to believe it; he did *not* believe it. Ten years of good marriage—with ups and downs, but who doesn't have them? A lovely house, a beautiful baby girl, a nursery specially built for a sister or brother for Pia. . . . Something must have gone wrong with Ingrid. He knew his own wife. He had to see her. If she was truthful in what she said, then she had to come back and tell Pia herself that it was all over. Then he would accept it. He sent off a cablegram and caught the plane to New York.

Chapter
14

I wanted Petter to know I was leaving him, that I was unfaithful. So I wrote that letter to Petter telling the truth, and a little later a second one that said, "I have found the place where I want to live, these are my people, and I want to stay here and I'm sorry. . . ." I felt that I was free. That was my divorce. I had been honest. If the church insisted that I was still married, that didn't really tie me down because I had already asked three years earlier for a divorce, which Petter wouldn't accept for one minute. And I had no reason to leave then, because at that time there was no other person that I wanted to marry. There was no other person I wanted to live with. So nothing happened.

There were so many years when I was just waiting to find somebody who would *make* me leave. Roberto did that. I didn't think it would upset the whole world. . . .

———————— • ————————

It was a hopeful and facile self-deception. It ignored the fact that in the twentieth century, the world press had the power to shatter all romantic daydreams and turn life into a nightmare. Ingrid did not think that she and Roberto were important enough for that sort of treatment. After all, hundreds of other couples got divorced.

So in those first ten days that the lovers drove in their scarlet chariot across enchanted terrain, she was radiant with a happiness that made all else irrelevant.

Few journeys' ends can compare to those last few miles of Calabria, to the heel of Italy, and the Straits of Messina. The car swung along the black thread of the coastline road down from the mountains, crossing rocky headlands above an ocean of crystal clarity which shallowed to palest green. Villages were encrusted at the water's edge like barnacles on the hull of a galleon. High in the mountains they clung like swallows' nests. It was a fusion of natural and man-made beauty overwhelming in its antiquity, and Roberto talked of mythology and love.

Then there, beyond the wide Straits of Messina, stood Sicily. The wind was warm crossing on the ferry. Behind lay the blue-gray shape of Italy, blurred and almost lost in haze. Messina, a low waterfront of fawn and white-colored buildings, curved along a crescent bay, mountains behind.

On Monday, April 4, with their film gear already stowed aboard the sturdy, forty-foot fishing schooner, the bows littered with boxes of tomatoes, coils of wire, camera equipment, bags of flour, toilet rolls and the battered suitcases of the film technicians, they left Sicily. The *San Lorenzo,* with its clanking trouble-ridden engine, its smelly evidence of the daily fishing routines, chugged out into the Tyrrhenian Sea heading for the Lipari Islands and the most northerly of them all—Stromboli.

These days, fast hydrofoils slice over the waves in constant crossings to all the Lipari Islands, but in 1948 they were remote from all forms of tourist traffic, and the weekly mailboat from Naples was their only regular link with the mainland.

Two hours at sea saw the *San Lorenzo* chugging past the first small island of Volcano, where a smoldering and intensely competitive Anna Magnani was shortly to make a rival film spectacular, complete with matching shots of the near-by and eruptive Stromboli.

They crossed open sea for two more hours before the high cone of Stromboli, smeared with white smoke, rose up against the horizon. As the *San Lorenzo* drew closer, they could stare two thousand feet upward to the black gullet of the live volcano. A semicircle of crimson lava curled like a bloody lip around the smoking cone, and a vast chute of recently spewed pitch-black rock spilled downwards at a steep angle to plunge directly into the bright seas below. And they were thrown off balance both physically and mentally.

Good God, who would want to live in this desolate and dangerous spot? And more to the point, how *could* they live here? It was spectacularly dramatic, yes; but surely there were plenty of empty places on the mainland offering a demi-paradise compared with this?

And easier places to film in? But when Roberto Rossellini said "documentary," he meant "documentary," not a set decked out to look like the real thing.

They found the village of Stromboli around the next lava headland. The gullet of the volcano had tilted away from that side of the island. Above a black and inhospitable beach, the more ancient residues of lava had settled into tolerable slopes, and the centuries had covered them with undergrowth, sparta grass and clumps of feathery bamboo. Gardens were planted in this rich volcanic soil. Vegetables, flowers, fig trees, vines, bougainvillea, geraniums grew there even though a thousand feet higher, the green vegetation was abruptly cut off. On these lower slopes the villagers had built their square, white, Moorish-style houses, with short chimneys and barred windows. They crowded side by side along narrow lanes, sometimes only three or four feet wide, that twisted upward to the open square and the white church with the tall spire. But the cone of Stromboli dominated every aspect of life. At certain hours it blocked out the sun. At night it was a sweeping segment of darkness against the bright stars. Day and night from its subterranean belly came gurgles and muffled explosions. Indeed, while they were there, it put on a display of eruptive violence which kept the delighted film crew out on the *San Lorenzo* until dawn filming the scene.

When they first arrived, they dropped anchor in deep and choppy water a hundred yards off the powdery, coal-black beach. The actors and technicians, followed by equipment and stores, were lowered into small rowboats and ferried ashore. Wading up onto the beach, Ingrid looked around at the island in some perplexity. It did not look at all like paradise. But it provided a spectacular setting for a movie.

———————— • ————————

As soon as we got to Stromboli and began to film, people realized that Roberto and I spent more time together than was really necessary just to shoot a movie. Then the newspaper people arrived and started inquiring: talked to the people here and there, counted the number of toothbrushes in my bathroom. And where did Roberto sleep? And where did his sister sleep? And was I alone in my bedroom? First the Italian newspapers and then from everywhere, from England and America.

———————— • ————————

So Ingrid's hopeful assumption "that it wouldn't upset the whole world" was short-lived. The Italian press scenting *amore* as sharks scent blood, were already dispatching reporters disguised as fishermen, tourists, and on one occasion even as a monk, to the island.

Speculation had begun as soon as Ingrid had reached Rome and looked at Roberto with eyes of love. It had increased as they journeyed to Capri, and was given impetus by *Life* magazine's full-page photo of them holding hands in Amalfi. As far as Petter was concerned, it exploded when he received Ingrid's letter.

The letter crossed one of his, the normal friendly letter that a husband writes to his wife. He thanked her for the telegram that she had sent before she left Rome, asked her how the filming was going. Most of the letter was devoted to how good Pia's skiing was: she'd only been on skis once before and yet she'd used the rope lift, and was "shooting down the hills like a veteran."

But on April 9 and 12, cables from Petter arrived in Stromboli asking her to telephone him immediately. Petter was unaware there was no telephone on the island. And then before she could call him, his reply to the letter she had sent from Amalfi arrived. He started, "Katt," his pet name for her. He wrote that since he had received her letter he had been sick to his soul, but he was hoping to come out of all this a better man.

One thing he wanted to make clear: "A wife that does not want to stay with me is no good to me," but he was not prepared to sit back and allow her to behave so scandalously. She must realize that the only way she could get a divorce was to return to America and discuss it with him; why this sickening display of publicity?

He was convinced that when she went into her affair she did not think of its implications: that Rossellini was a married man in a Catholic country and she would simply replace Anna as his mistress. No marriage to Rossellini would ever be sanctioned in Italy.

She had said that she wanted to stay in Italy. This would be a moral blow to Hollywood and to the country that had accepted her.

She, Petter, and Rossellini alone knew about the intimate letter she had sent him. How could its contents be known to a New York newspaper? Thanks to the stories coming out of Italy a scandal of tremendous proportions was brewing. He had had to close his office to get away from the "hyenas." He had sent Pia to Minnesota with Mrs. Vernon, the wife of Ingrid's business manager.

Roberto Rossellini—Petter usually referred to him as "your Italian"—might have charm and talent but how trustworthy was he?

Hadn't he immediately tried to raise money on photocopies of the first letter she had written saying she wanted to work with him?

She had known Petter for fourteen years. She knew he was absolutely truthful. Now he swore on his mother's memory that the day "the Italian" had left their house in Beverly Hills he had assured Petter that his only concern was to make a great picture. He could be trusted with Ingrid; he would protect her from any possible gossip. He liked Petter "as his own brother." He would, as Petter requested, introduce Ingrid to Anna as soon as possible.

Instead, Roberto had managed to get Anna away to London before Ingrid arrived in Rome. He had also cut Ingrid off from all her friends and outside contacts, and had betrayed Petter, who had carried breakfast to him every morning and had raised money to pay his personal debts.

Petter was convinced that this affair was not for a woman who was "originally good and fair." But he told her she would have to think of people other than herself, that it was "about time you grew up." Did she ever consider him, for example? He had spent all their married life together trying to help her; he had shouldered all her responsibilities and burdens. Probably he would have been wiser to let her face them herself. He complained that she never stopped to think that he, too, could have doubts and mental agony. He had always had great need for her: "No man that loved his wife gave her more freedom than I gave you." Only a few weeks before in January 1949 she had admitted how happy she had been; she had planned the new kitchen and nursery with the architect, ready for the "new arrival." But after only two weeks in Italy she had pulled the world down around his head. Now only God could help him and Pia and her.

Ingrid wept when she read the letter. If only she could make Petter understand that this was the most difficult and heartbreaking thing she had to do in her whole life. She didn't want to hurt him. The idea of harming Pia filled her with agony.

Pia herself says she remembers little about her early life with her parents, but she has a vivid memory of the day her mother left for Italy. As she tells it:

"I have very few memories of my childhood in relationship to my family. Either this is a suppression of memories or it's a fact that they really weren't around very much.

"I really don't remember seeing my mother much. I think she

went to work very early in the morning, at six o'clock when they started, and I think she came home in the evening and then said good night to me or something. I don't think we spent too much time together. At least I'm assuming that, because I don't have any memory of it. . . .

"And then I remember we moved to Benedict Canyon in Beverly Hills, and I remember that house very well because that is where I grew up, and we were there until I was about twelve, I guess.

"Of course, my mother was just in the upswing of her career, so I don't think it was just the work that kept her away. In the film industry, you've got a lot to do after the working hours—promotion and such.

"I think they were both very active in their professional lives, and I remember there were people in the house, and I remember there was a woman who looked after me. But by and large, I was alone. We had dogs, but I don't remember them actually being with me very much. I had no brothers or sisters, nor did I live in an area where I was likely to have children around. But I think you develop a tremendous attachment for a house and for the physical things, I mean, I remember that house in detail. I loved that house and I loved the garden—I can remember the garden, which is odd because I can't seem to remember any people in it. It was like an empty house somehow: there were very few people there.

"Of course it was a big house with a fence around it. If you wanted to get in you had to telephone at the gate and say who you were and then be buzzed in. So it became a little fortress. I was very conscious of this because in the beginning I could get my hand through the gate —my hand was small enough—to open it, but after a few years my hand got too big, so I had to be buzzed in too. That wasn't unusual among the people who lived in the film business. That is the way Maria Cooper—Gary Cooper's daughter—and the other children whom I knew lived. We were very guarded. It was natural, because there would be tour buses coming through and sightseers to point at your house, and you wouldn't want them to come right up and ring the doorbell and say, Hi, we just wanted to see your bedroom or something.

"I got up in the morning. Someone drove me to school, or I took the school bus, and I went to school all day. When I came home, there wasn't anybody there and I would play outside and then I would go to bed.

"I mean, I had no idea about anything. I never saw any arguments.

I was completely cut off from my parents: I had no idea what might have been going on.

"I do remember mother leaving when she was going to Italy. I do remember distinctly the day she left, and it was a big farewell. I remember her driving down the driveway because it was a long driveway and I remember her waving, and it was very sad. I thought she was coming back. I'm not sure she didn't think she was coming back herself.

"I can remember my father in some sort of discussion telling me that she wasn't going to come back. It was a tremendous shock. I don't remember the sequence of events after that very much. I remember I had a governess who left at exactly the same time. I had the feeling that everybody was leaving."

Roberto wrote to Petter:

Dear Petter,

You remember that I promised you I should always be sincere with you. I believe the moment has arrived that you, Ingrid and I are facing each other and I hope we are able to look each other straight in the eyes with esteem and human understanding (comprehension).

The three weeks I spent in Italy after my departure from America, my torment, the responsibility to return to Anna gave me the measure of my sentiment for Ingrid, the sentiment of which I told you. And after the arrival of Ingrid, our emotion, her tears gave us the profound certainty. And now Petter I want to talk to you with humanity.

What to do? If I didn't have the deep estimation and respect for you, all would be very easy. But Ingrid and I are above all preoccupied not to betray you and do not want to hurt you more than is necessary. To tell you nothing? Take time—no, that would surely betray you and be inhuman. Between the lines in your letter and telegram, your doubt and torment is clear. It is therefore good that you know everything right away. It is good for you and for us. I know that I give you great sorrow, but believe me, your sorrow is also for me a great torment. I remember very clearly all that you told me the evening we spoke to each other. You told me that Ingrid is easily enthusiastic, sensible but not intelligent, and that she has a temperament that makes her thoughtless. Believe me you make a very serious mistake if you think that. We have meditated very seriously and with unbelievable clarity. During two months Ingrid and I have hidden our love and that because immediately after we saw each other in Beverly Hills we understood it was something very big and solemn and we felt that if we told each other we would be bound forever. And not to harm you we said nothing until the situation was clear even without words. And at present, we are here, powerless, because we are dominated by an extraordinary love and we suffer to be obliged to give you pain. You are wrong to judge Ingrid like you have done and you are wrong to be so hard and authoritative with her who has fear of you and the fear estranges her from you. . . . I want to tell you clearly that I will defend Ingrid in her fear for you. It is unjust that you have made her frightened. . . . I hope that you will understand that one cannot condemn a big love and it is impossible to do anything against it.

I have begun my divorce, and now Petter, please let us be human, understand and have mutual respect.

Roberto.

Petter is sure he did not receive this letter. The newspapers quoted him as saying that Ingrid must have been under the influence of drugs and didn't know what she was doing. That made Ingrid angry: "There was no man on earth who hated drugs as much as Roberto; he was furious with people who took anything—he wouldn't even take a sleeping pill. He did not drink, not even wine."

The Italian press was now howling and clamoring with hypocritical indignation, happy innuendo, and sheer delight. The magazine *Travaso* featured a full-page colored cartoon depicting Joan-of-Arc Ingrid, clad in her full armor, tied to the stake above a heap of celluloid film, with Roberto Rossellini trying to prevent Anna Magnani from putting a match to the bonfire, he protesting: "Do you realize you're trying to burn a million dollars?"—and Anna saying "What do I care. To hell with Stromboli."

Anna Magnani was photographed by *France-Soir* arriving in

Paris, her mouth stretched wide to show her beautiful teeth. The banner headline declared: "Rossellini-Bergman—let me laugh!"

In answer to questions, Anna was reported as saying: "I was never really the director's mistress, but in any case I never interfered with his love life. My relationship with him was always a veritable nightmare. The only thing I regret is that Rossellini dropped me to rush off to America leaving me without a director for my next picture."

"When he was in America, what were your relations with him?"

"He talked with me on the telephone every day. When he was living in Ingrid Bergman's household, he sent me secret cables."

"And when you were in London?"

"He telephoned me every day until the moment that Ingrid Bergman announced her intention of getting a divorce."

"But shouldn't *you* have gone to Stromboli?"

"I never expected that. And all I want to do now is to live for my work and child. And I am certain that Ingrid and I will become the best of friends."

They never did become the best of friends. In fact they never met.

Ercole Grazadei, one of Rome's most famous lawyers who knew everybody of consequence in the Italian film world, a friend of Roberto's and Anna Magnani's, and later of Ingrid's, always declared that Anna behaved impeccably. "She kept silent," he said. "She never uttered a word of criticism against Roberto or Ingrid. This woman, whose origins were certainly rooted in the squalor of Rome during a bitter war, was certainly a great actress and certainly great in the way she behaved."

Ingrid looking back on those years agreed.

———— • ————

I don't think there's any doubt that Roberto Rossellini was the great love of Anna's life.

They didn't talk for years as far as I know, but when she became ill in the seventies, and Roberto heard that it was serious, he sent a little note and some flowers to the hospital. And she wrote back and asked if he would come and visit her. He did, and he was at the hospital regularly until the day she died.

When I heard about this, I telephoned him from London, told him how glad I was that he was doing this. The circle was closed; she had the man she loved more than anyone else in her whole life near her again.

Her funeral was something extraordinary. There were great crowds in the streets and around the church and they were in tears —she was so loved by the Italian people. So many people they couldn't all get into the church. And when the coffin was carried out they applauded. I think that's so moving. You could only do that in Italy; I mean, Swedes would never even *think* of applauding at a funeral. And then, there was no place for her to be buried— she had not bought a plot in a graveyard or anything—so Roberto brought her to his family grave, and she's there now . . . near Rome, with Roberto and all the rest of the Rossellini family.

————————— • —————————

On Stromboli the discomfort of trying to film in a place with no hotel, no telephone—only a tiny post and cable office—little sanitation, no running water, no transport but one's own two feet, never-ending flies and midges, and dreary food made life almost insupportable. The small population consisted mainly of children and the very old. Most of the young men were away earning a living on the mainland, or in Germany and France, sending back a proportion of their wages to wives or parents.

It was a strange island, without gaiety. The old men had spent their lives trying to wrest a living from the meager soil and the impoverished sea; they knew nothing but endless, backbreaking toil. The women, young and old, matched the black volcanic background, with their dark clothes, dark eyes and hair.

The film community which had been so lively and gay in Sicily and on the mainland was influenced by this somber atmosphere. It began to split into wary, indifferent, or contentious groups. Roberto, Ingrid, Roberto's sister Marcella, and Ellen Neuwald, Ingrid's secretary (Ingrid never quite knew what she was doing with a secretary, but it was in the RKO contract, so Ellen lent a hand with a dozen different jobs), shared a modest four-room, pink stucco house close to the sea. Roberto had returned from Hollywood adamant that a bathroom was mandatory for all film stars, so a special building was erected against the old house, and bath, lavatory, and bidet were transported to Stromboli. The islanders had never seen such contraptions and none was ever connected up with much success. A funnel, pushed through the roof into Ingrid's bathroom, served as a shower; when she was ready to bathe she hollered to a man stationed on the roof who poured buckets of sea water down the spout.

Hollywood's interests were represented by Art Cohn, a writer despatched by RKO to inject a modicum of recognizable dialogue into Roberto's treatments. Art's wife, Marta, was also a writer, and both of them fell in love with Ingrid and Roberto, and defected immediately to their side.

RKO also sent in a British publicity man who took one look at the situation, departed to a small house overlooking the sea at the end of the island, and made the most of his chore by mixing gin and tonic, swimming in the warm sea, keeping out of everybody's way, and making copious notes for future reference.

———— • ————

He was supposed to help us, but all he did was to spy. The world's press came to Stromboli to see what was going on. The movie? They couldn't care less. . . . What about the love affair? That was the big news. So when our publicity man eventually left, he wrote stories for one of the British Sunday papers, and when I read them I couldn't believe it, they were so absolutely false. Made-up dialogue between Roberto and me: he was the one who'd even been to my bathroom to see how many toothbrushes were there. Practically everything was fiction. I was so mad I got a lawyer and I said: "I'm suing him, I'm suing him!" The lawyer said, "Okay, but understand that's just what the paper wants, a big lawsuit. You'll have to go to London and appear in the witness box and they'll ask you a lot of questions which will be very embarrassing to you. Are you sure you want to go through with that?" I thought for two seconds and said "No." So he sold the stories and I suppose the world believed all of them.

———— • ————

RKO, in Roberto's eyes, was now becoming Enemy Number One. The film company's chagrin at the scandal surrounding Ingrid, the fear that the film might even be banned, caused them to dispatch writers, publicity men, and production managers in order to try to protect their investment.

In all his previous productions, Roberto had been the sole arbiter of what went on. And he intended that happy state to continue. Writers might be allowed to initiate the fundamental creative processes, but he, Roberto, *wrote* with his camera. Through his juxtaposition of angle, light, shade, and emotional reflex, he revealed and illumined the conflict, pity, and passion inherent in the human condition. So what did he need writers for? Actually he grew very fond of Art Cohn and almost forgot he was a writer, but Art was never allowed to make any impact upon the film. Publicity men? Publicity men were as commonplace as reels of celluloid in the industry. He could ignore them. But a production manager! Production details and the pace of the shooting were the absolute preserve of Roberto; they depended entirely on the condition of his digestive juices, the state of his headache, boredom, exaltation, or need for contemplation. Roberto's credo was always that an equitable balance must be sought between life and film-making: the importance of spear fishing must be weighed against that of climbing to the top of the volcano to shoot a few feet of film—especially if the day was hot and the water was very clear.

Ed Killy, the first production manager sent by RKO, lasted a month. He was replaced by Harold Lewis, a noted Hollywood trouble-shooter. Big and physically powerful, tough and aggressive, Harold was renowned for bringing home the bacon and to hell with art. His was the ability to drive film production forward, to maintain the flow of work so that completed reels of film were piled into stacks ready for shipment to America.

To Roberto, great films were a product of the imagination and the soul. When his soul was inspired he would work like a maniac, but a daily conveyer belt? No! But Roberto sidestepped Harold's roar of efficiency with the delicacy and finesse of a gifted matador. In the flash of an Italian eye, he dreamed up a thousand reasons for lack of completed film footage in the can. With consummate politeness, he enlisted Harold's aid. Perhaps Harold could arrange to have reserves of fresh water available at the top of the volcano for his poor exhausted film crew and cast? Perhaps Harold could arrange to get the great silver tuna running from the Atlantic through the Mediterranean and around to Sicily to hold themselves available for slaughter and therefore filming? Perhaps Harold had a personal line to God and so could arrange volcanic eruptions on cue, make the sun shine at the right moment?

Roberto was a man of infinite variety: evasions, truculences, outbursts, passionate gestures, engulfing rages, and sweet reasonableness. No one could handle him except by giving way to him. No one ever had, though in those early days on Stromboli, Ingrid gave it a good try.

Her diary for April 7, 1949, records hopefully: "Start of film." The page for Friday, April 8, is a blank; Saturday, April 9, indicates a more cautious approach: "Try start film." Sunday reports: "Start film."

Much of this stop-go technique was the result of Roberto's action in engaging Stromboli villagers to masquerade as actors. Roberto referred to them as "amateurs." But before long Ingrid ceased to believe that they were entitled even to *that* charitable description.

———————— • ————————

The fact that Roberto disliked actors was now made clear to me. Oh yes, he had many friends among actors because he found them amusing, but he refused to believe that a man could have so much vanity that he could go out and perform on a stage; be like a rooster out there; comb his hair and put on make-up. "You watch any actor pass a mirror," he said. "I don't mind women because they always look in mirrors anyway, but an actor can't bear to pass a mirror without adjusting his tie or brushing back a strand of hair or doing something to himself."

From the very first, I didn't have any difficulty in working and communicating with Roberto. Sometimes he had a bit of trouble explaining what he wanted, but after that it was a communication by thought process. I could read his eyes. Even when he couldn't explain in words what he wanted, I felt *what* he wanted. . . .

But on Stromboli during those first few days, God Almighty . . . we had no professional actors, we only had *these* amateurs. I've never forgotten the first real blazing row I had with him. I stood it day after day, and then I went up to him, and I blew up. I was absolutely shaking with rage. "You can *have* these realistic pictures," I shouted. "To hell with them! These people don't even know what dialogue is, they don't know where to stand; they don't even *care* what they're doing. I can't bear to work another day with you!"

There was a long silence. So much for the two great lovers. Even the Italians stopped talking for a minute. I mean, these people Roberto had got were peasants. I've nothing against peasants: I love peasants, but to expect them to act! . . .

They couldn't have cared less, they'd just stand around laughing, and Roberto would say, "Now you walk up that line toward that place. That's where the camera is. Understand?" And they'd reply,

"Oh yes, this line here? Is this all right?" Then Roberto would give them an idea of what to talk about and they'd chatter away, and I'd stand there like an idiot, because I didn't speak any Italian, so I didn't know what they were saying. And I didn't know when they'd finished; they didn't even know themselves, for that matter, for Italians go on talking forever. So I stood there saying, "Have you finished yet?" or "What do I answer to that?" Absolute chaos.

So to solve it, Roberto attached a string to one of their big toes inside their shoes. Then he stood there, holding this bunch of strings, and first he'd pull that string and one man spoke, then he'd pull another string and another man spoke. I didn't have a string on my toe, so I didn't know when I was supposed to speak. And *this* was realistic film-making! The dialogue was never ready, or there never was any dialogue. I thought I was going crazy.

And the volcano . . . the volcano! The first time I had to try to climb it, we slogged for four hours upward. After I climbed for two hours, I just sat down, gasped and said, "I'm sorry, I can't make it." But after a rest I did make it, and at the top I could have just lain down and died. At this rate I knew we'd never get the film started, let alone finished.

But of course Roberto just accepted my outbursts as normal movie-star temperament. You see, I fell in love with him because he was so rare; I'd never met anyone like him before; I'd never met anybody with his kind of freedom. He made everything larger than life; life took on new dimensions, new excitement, new horizons. And he gave me courage which I never had before. I was always frightened of everything, and he said, "Frightened of what? What is there to be frightened about?" Roberto wasn't frightened of anybody or anything . . . except sometimes he was superstitious about certain days and black cats crossing the road in front of him. If a black cat crossed the road in front of the car, he'd stop and wait for another car to pass us so that the other driver would take the bad luck.

———————— • ————————

So, despite the storms, Ingrid never doubted Roberto, never fell out of love with him. At the end of a long day, his charm, his concern, his vulnerability always won her over. More than that. In her opinion, and that of many of his contemporaries, Rossellini was one of the foremost film pioneers of this century. She had an obsessive belief in his genius. And she knew he had used this same documentary technique for *Open City*. She had heard the whole story of how that masterpiece was made.

The small band who made *Open City* had had little money but a compelling idea based upon the fierce realities of their own lives and a passionate determination to record their moments of history. So they had borrowed and begged from anyone they could find and when things had got really tough the director had pawned his furniture. They had hired a cameraman and crew who knew that their chances of anything more than subsistence payments were negligible.

Film stock at the end of the war was as scarce as brotherly love, and though they occasionally managed to "liberate" some from co-operative technicians in the United States Forces Film Units, often Roberto Rossellini was reduced to buying strips of 35-mm film from Rome's street photographers. This meant, of course, that much of it was of poor quality, the reason why sometimes a scene was misty. Often, because they had no lights, shots looked as if they had been filmed on a foggy day. Frequently, there was no sound because the recording apparatus was on the blink, but then, Rossellini had no great conviction in the power of dialogue to enhance any aspect of a film. He believed that what the audience *sees,* it remembers, and what it *hears,* it forgets.

His was an operation which had sucked its life from the indestructible Italian capacity for regeneration in a city searching feverishly for a philosophy to elucidate its despair and match its rebirth.

Ingrid has always marveled at the chance happenings that brought Roberto and her together: for example, the arrival of her first letter at Minerva Studios which immediately burned down, the letter then raked from the ashes. *Open City* owed its American debut to similar, almost incredible luck.

In Italy it was a flop. Critics disliked it, audiences stayed away. Its immeasurably important United States distribution was due to the bizarre fact that an American G.I., Rod Geiger, crossing a street in Rome one night, a little the worse for wear, caught his foot in an electric cable and fell on his face. The only reason Rossellini had an electric-light cable that night was because an ingenious electrician in his crew had plugged in—totally illegally—to the power source feeding the presses of the United States Forces *Stars and Stripes* newspaper. Getting to his feet, Rod traced the cable back to the source of action, and was amazed to find himself in the middle of a movie shot.

Rod convinced Rossellini that moving pictures were his life's blood and that he had the greatest movie contacts in the world. When he was discharged from the army a few weeks later, he departed for New York with one of the precious copies of the film in his dufflebag.

In New York he arranged for film distributor Joe Burstyn to see the film. Joe arranged distribution, but Roberto and his aides never saw a dollar of the reputed half-million the movie made in the United States. But Joe arranged the deal which financed Roberto in the making of *Paisan.*

In *Open City* Joe did not immediately recognize a work of startling and original genius, but his experience told him this was "the real thing." With bitter reality, Rossellini had dramatized a shabby, weary, decadent Rome at the end of a preposterous dictatorship and a desperate war: a background that few knew existed. *Open City* tore at the heartstrings. It throbbed with love and disillusionment. And a quarter of a century later, critics defined it as a key film in the history of world cinema.

There is a strange sidelight to this film made long before Roberto met Ingrid Bergman. As she first noticed when she saw *Open City* again with him, he had used both her names in it: Ingrid for the evil German woman and Bergman for the SS captain.

Ingrid knew that Roberto was obsessed by man and the adventure which is life, that his dislike of studios, sets, and make-up arose because they induced artificiality. She understood why he felt that the presence of professional actors with their special skills and marked personalities blurred the original characters he was trying to create.

Most important to her, he shared her total disbelief in the Hollywood concept that to be successful you must maintain your prototype-image, endlessly repeat your familiar performance.

It is perhaps possible that Roberto, in his early days as a director, suffered from the happy misconception that all people were like Italians, to whom life was one continual acting performance. No Italian needed residence at a National Dramatic School, or a method-school of acting. They were born "naturals."

"Neorealism does not stop at the surface," Roberto said, "but seeks the most subtle aspects of the soul." He also said: "I am not a pessimist at all. I am only a realist, and I am quite prepared to portray a world full of joy and serene happiness, if only we could create such a world first. That is why I turned back to the world of

Saint Francis, who despite the wickedness of the world, found joy where nowadays nobody seems to seek it, in humility and service."

Nevertheless, there were many moments of filming on Stromboli when exhaustion, rather than contemplative thought processes, was the main ingredient of Ingrid's life.

———————— • ————————

Roberto gave me a dog, a little black bulldog. That was all I needed. I put him down on the black lava sand, and he disappeared; he matched the sand so closely you couldn't see him. Dear little Stromboli—what else could we call him?—stayed with me for years afterwards and barked at all the photographers.

And, because I was exhausted, Roberto sent to the mainland for two donkeys. Lots of people on Stromboli had never seen a donkey. They'd never seen a film show either, so at the same time Roberto imported a few films and showed them on a screen rigged up in the square. The old people simply couldn't comprehend what was happening. Oh, it was a primitive island.

Anyway, now Roberto and I had donkeys, but everybody else walked. Those poor men who pulled the generators up to the top of the volcano: it was agonizing to watch them. They cried with exhaustion; cried. I suffered watching these people work; I've never seen people work so hard. The Italians in those days on those islands didn't seem to expect anything different. They just worked like slaves. It was heartbreaking.

The two men whom Roberto had picked up off the beach in Salerno worked just as hard carrying things as everybody else. They had no idea Roberto was going to use one of them as my leading man. Roberto used to say, "Now, you see why I use amateurs. If I'd used actors they wouldn't carry all that stuff."

Both young men were fishermen; they thought they were going to play the parts of fishermen in the picture. So they carried lights and cameras and equipment, and Roberto made them do all sorts of jobs, but all the time he was studying them both very closely. He thought at first that the taller, the better-looking one of the two would get the part, but eventually he said to me, "Sorry, but the shorter one is more intelligent; he will be your leading man."

I think Mario Vitale almost fainted when Roberto gave him the news. But as soon as Mario was sure he'd got the job, he asked, "And when do I kiss her?"

"You don't," Roberto said sourly. "But you get seventy-five dollars a week. So that should be good enough."

The taller boy was given another part in the movie.

———————— • ————————

The weekly mail boat from Naples brought batches of letters from friends, enemies, and well-wishers. From 180 Central Park South came a sweet letter from Mr. J. Fred Coots who assured her that the "hostility to your apparent romantic sympathies with each other are not condemned by millions of us, and as a song writer I am composing a beautiful new song for you both. I shall mail the manuscript —words and music—as soon as it is ready. My title for this song is: 'My Sicilian is One in a Million No wonder I love him so.' " Ingrid preserved the letter.

Then on April 22, 1949, Ingrid was shocked by a letter that came from the Motion Picture Association of America, a body invented by the movie-makers themselves to act in a film-censorship capacity and to insure that before the end-credits rolled, the good beat the bad, and that the morals and standards applicable in a Christian society were maintained. The letter was signed by Joseph I. Breen, Vice-President and Director of the Production Code Administration, and its dramatic implications to a woman of Ingrid's vulnerability were alarming:

> Dear Miss Bergman,
>
> In recent days, the American newspapers have carried, rather widely, a story to the effect that you are about to divorce your husband, forsake your child, and marry Roberto Rossellini.
>
> It goes without saying that these reports are the cause of great consternation among large numbers of our people who have come to look upon you as the *first* lady of the screen—both individually and artistically. On all hands, I hear nothing but expressions of profound shock that you have any such plans.
>
> My purpose in presuming to write to you in the matter is to call your attention to the situation. I feel that these

reports are untrue and that they are, possibly, the result of some overzealousness on the part of a press-agent, who mistakenly believes them to be helpful from a publicity standpoint.

Anyone who has such thoughts is, of course, tragically in error. Such stories will not only *not* react favorably to your picture, but may very well *destroy your career as a motion picture artist.* They may result in the American public becoming so thoroughly enraged that your pictures will be ignored, and your box-office value ruined.

This condition has become so serious that I am constrained to suggest that you find occasion, *at the earliest possible moment,* to issue a denial of these rumors—to state, quite frankly, that they are not true, that you have no intention to desert your child or to divorce your husband, and that you have no plans to marry anyone.

I make this suggestion to you in the utmost sincerity and solely with a view to stamping out these reports that constitute a major scandal and may well result in *complete disaster personally.*

I hope you won't mind my writing to you so frankly. This is all so important, however, that I cannot resist conveying to you my considered thought in the matter.

> With assurances of my esteem, I am,
> Very cordially, Joseph I. Breen.

The letter not only threatened her career as an actress but her livelihood, and also the success of *Saint Joan,* now on general release in the United States and Europe. It also threatened her last picture, *Under Capricorn,* awaiting release in the autumn, and indeed, the future of the film which had brought about this scandal which they were now making in Stromboli. Given the power of the Hollywood moguls and the organizations they had created, it was possible that all three films might be banned or withdrawn from distribution.

The cable from Walter Wanger, who had produced *Saint Joan,* did nothing to reassure her:

THE MALICIOUS STORIES ABOUT YOUR BEHAVIOR NEED IMMEDIATE CONTRADICTION FROM YOU. IF YOU ARE NOT CONCERNED ABOUT YOURSELF AND YOUR FAMILY YOU SHOULD REALIZE THAT BECAUSE I BELIEVED IN

YOU AND YOUR HONESTY, I HAVE MADE A HUGE INVEST-
MENT ENDANGERING MY FUTURE AND THAT OF MY
FAMILY WHICH YOU ARE JEOPARDIZING IF YOU DO NOT
BEHAVE IN A WAY WHICH WILL DISPROVE THESE UGLY
RUMORS BROADCAST OVER RADIO AND PRESS THROUGH-
OUT THE WORLD.

WE BOTH HAVE A RESPONSIBILITY TO VICTOR FLEM-
ING'S MEMORY AND TO ALL THE PEOPLE THAT BELIEVE
IN US. ASSUME YOU ARE UNAWARE, OR NOT BEING IN-
FORMED OF, THE MAGNITUDE OF THE NEWSPAPER STO-
RIES, AND THEIR CONSEQUENCES, AND THAT YOU ARE
BEING COMPLETELY MISLED. DO NOT FOOL YOURSELF BY
THINKING THAT WHAT YOU ARE DOING IS OF SUCH COU-
RAGEOUS PROPORTIONS OR SO ARTISTIC TO EXCUSE
WHAT ORDINARY PEOPLE BELIEVE.

CABLE ME ON RECEIPT OF THIS WIRE.

It seemed to Ingrid that people simply did not understand her true
position. Yes, she had certainly brought this upon herself, but
couldn't she at least claim some sort of private life? Couldn't they
see that she had a point of view, that she hadn't committed a crime
of major proportions? But news cuttings, letters, cartoons, and jeering, taunting, indignant criticisms arrived by the boatload, and her
confusion and sense of guilt became almost intolerable. In despair,
she drafted a letter to Father Donceur, the French priest who had
acted as adviser on the *Saint Joan* film, and for whom she had the
highest regard:

Stromboli, May 1, 1949.

My dear Père Donceur,
How deeply I have hurt and disillusioned you! How
ridiculous I have made all your good words about me!
And when people have a good opinion and with their love
put you high up, how much harder is the fall! Of all the
gossip and stories that circle the world right now, I believe
many are lies and malicious peoples' inventions. But also
true information. I have been shocked that my private
actions have been made public, that all I have done or said,
telegrams even, and telephone calls, have been given to the
newspapers. I can well imagine how my husband has suffered, and how I have hurt and humiliated both him and

Pia. It is true that I wrote my husband and asked him for a divorce. I believed it was better and more honest to tell him right away.

It never occurred to me that I, by giving him my thoughts, also gave the world this sensational scandal. Petter is in Italy now hunted by the press. I have not been able to leave the island to meet him because of the bad sea. I am heartbroken over the tragedy I have brought upon my family and the people involved in my films. I realize how I have hurt our *Joan.* It is impossible to deny these rumors, impossible to keep peoples' respect. It is too difficult for me to solve the problem; too difficult to be in the public eye. I therefore hope that if I give up my movie career and I disappear, I might be able to save *Joan* my disgrace. I have written to Mr. Breen in Hollywood about my decision, hoping that the pictures I have already made will not be banned and the people concerned with those films will not suffer because of me. With all my love.

Ingrid.

Chapter 15

For some reason unknown to her then and still a mystery to her today, Ingrid did not post either the letter to Joseph Breen or to Father Donceur. (On May 2, 1951, she found them again, clipped them together and placed them in her files adding the note: "Two years later. How much I felt like a dog. How lucky these letters were not sent, as I feel so completely different about these happenings today.")

From many of her closest friends letters of encouragement started arriving. From New York, Irene Selznick wrote:

> I know that moderation cannot be lent to one's feelings, but it is vitally important for your self-esteem, for protection of Pia, and for your welfare that your external behavior be marked by restraint and conformity. I mean this regardless of which path your life takes you. If this is not ultimate and permanent, then surely the price is needlessly excessive. If this is to be your way and your life, then don't let it be launched under the auspices of a scandal! If it is *this* important to you, I beg you to walk with dignity and discretion.
>
> Forgive me for sounding as if I'm standing in a pulpit —but darling I love you so very much, increasingly if the truth be told—that I want for you only what will be your happiness, and in a way which is worthy of you.

You are pure in heart and so healthy emotionally, that what is right for you must and will prevail. I know I don't have to tell you that anything I can do for you is yours for less than asking—now and before and always. . . .

From Villa Aprile, Cortina d'Ampezzo, Italy, Ernest Hemingway wrote in pencil:

Dear Ingrid: Here's your contact, daughter. How is Stromboli? How is Calabria? I have a sort of idea how they are. (Beautiful and Very Dirty.) But how are you? That's what's important. (Maybe you are very beautiful and very dirty too?)

Your letter with Petter's fine P.S. came here to hospital in Padova where I have been with an infected eye. I got it the day you arrived in Italy. How's that for long-distance contact?

Am on my fifth million units of penicillin (they punch my derriere like a time clock every three hours) but fever now is normal and the infection which turned into erysipelas (no relation to syphilis) but knocked it finally. . . .
(Continued on June 5 from Finca Vigia, San Francisco de Paula, Cuba:)

What happened was that I got sicker after I wrote that first part and I had to use a lot more penicillin and my eye was too bad to write.

Then I read all that stuff about you and Rossellini and Petter and I didn't know what to write. Now I've had time to think it over (still knowing nothing of what goes on) and I do know I love you very much and am your same solid true friend no matter what you ever do, or decide or where you ever go. The only thing is that I miss you.

Listen daughter, now I have to make speech. This is our one and only life as I once explained to you. No one is famous nor infamous. You are a great actress. I know that from New York. Great actresses always have great troubles sooner or later. If they did not they would not be worth a shit. (Bad word you can delete it.) All things great actresses do are forgiven.

Continue speech: Everybody reaches wrong decisions.

But many times the wrong decision is the right decision wrongly made. End of speech.

New speech: Do *not* worry. It never helped anything *ever.*

Finished with speeches. Daughter, please don't worry and be a brave and good girl and know you have, only this short distance away, two people, Mary and me, who love you and are loyal to you.

Let's be cheerful now like when we used to drink together. . . . Remember this is Holy Year and everybody is pardoned for everything. Maybe you can have quintuplets in the Vatican and I will come and be a first time godfather. . . .

If you love Roberto truly give him our love and tell him he better be a damned good boy for you or Mister Papa will kill him some morning when he has a morning free.

Ernest.

P.S. This is a lousy letter but we live in the lousiest times there ever were I think. But it is our one and only life so we might as well not complain about the ball park we have to play in.

We had a wonderful time in Italy. I love Venice in the non-tourist time and all the country around it and the Dolomites are the best mountains I know. I wish you had not been working and could have come up and stayed with us in Cortina d'Ampezzo. I tried to call you up from the hospital, but they said you were in some place without a phone.

Maybe this will never get to you. It certainly won't if I don't send it off. Good luck my dear. Mary sends her love.

Ernest (Mister Papa).

The letters from her friends helped. But they couldn't counter her reaction to the criticism. Petter's letter—sincere, truthful, despairing —had grieved and upset her. And she had begun to agonize about the pain all this would inflict on Pia. She had rushed happily into a relationship which seemed to answer all her problems only to find herself confronting a heartbreaking dilemma.

It was absolute hell. I cried so much I thought there couldn't be any tears left. I felt the newspapers were right. I'd abandoned my husband and child. I was an awful woman. . . . But I hadn't meant it that way. I'd written that letter to Petter to say, "I'm not fooling you. I'm not coming back. You won't want me any more anyway. Let's get a divorce." There were phone calls and cables and Petter came to Italy to see me. The final outcome was a meeting arranged in Messina, Sicily.

Then I had trouble with Roberto. I really didn't know it, but at the time the storms started, Roberto was determined never to let me go back to Petter again, not even for a single hour, if he could help it. Of course I know now that this was foolish. If I had gotten together with Petter and we had talked it out like two reasonable people, so much drama and unhappiness could have been prevented. Roberto with his sense of *fantasy* thought that Petter would take me away for good; we would elope in the middle of the night. He couldn't believe that a man just comes to talk to his wife and says, "Let's talk this over."

I suppose Roberto had reason to some extent. He knew I was frightened of Petter.

He'd seen all the tears I'd cried on Stromboli. . . . People thought I was having such a marvelous time being in love when all I did was cry because the real guilt of my offense was now grinding me down. I felt terrible about all the people who wrote me: I'd ruined their movie; I'd ruined myself; my career was finished forever. . . . Everyone got into the act to lecture me and here I was stuck and didn't know what to do about it. . . .

Petter's idea was that I should finish the picture to which I was committed and then go back to America so we could talk this whole thing out. And of course from a commonsense point of view I agreed with that.

But there wasn't any common sense about our meeting that afternoon in the hotel in Messina. There was this immediate confrontation, because when I talked to Roberto he argued one thing, and when I talked to Petter he argued another, and I thought, I can't cope with them both! And I said, "Can't we three talk together, sit down and see who's saying what?"

It was so dreadful that I can't remember all of it—I have blacked it out of my mind, drawn a curtain down. Then it was night and

Petter had booked a double room, and having come all that way from America he obviously had a right to talk to me, so we went in, and Petter locked the door, and Roberto went mad.

———————— • ————————

Kay Brown was also there. She was at that time working for MCA in New York, and Ingrid was their client and Kay's personal responsibility.

As she tells it: "I was in the middle of it all, and of course in my terms it was pure and quite unbelievable Italian melodrama. I remember in New York the telephone ringing out of the blue and it's Lew Wasserman, the head of MCA in Hollywood.

" 'Pack your bags,' he said.

" 'What for? Where to? I don't want to go anywhere.'

" 'The island of Stromboli. Your girl's going to wreck herself. She's talking too much. She's simply got to stop talking.'

"So I fly off to Italy, and I catch a night boat . . . only a small fishing boat down to Stromboli, and I arrive at six o'clock in the morning in my high heels and mink coat, and it's like arriving at the end of the world. The fishing boat is surging up and down, and there's another boat next to it, also tossing up and down, that we're supposed to get down into, and a third even smaller boat which is to row us ashore. Apparently there's no way, no ladder, to get me down into the other boat safely, so they put me in a canvas fish chute, and I'm slid down that, mink coat and all. Then I'm placed in the small rowboat and we row ashore, where one of the seamen tosses me over his shoulder like a sack of coal and deposits me about three yards from the beach in a foot of surf. And there, standing on the beach with his hands outstretched, is Roberto saying 'Good morning, Miss Brown,' and I'm wading ashore like a missionary come to convert the natives.

"The whole thing is crazy and depressing. When I see Ingrid, she's not the girl I know. She's very remote, she's not happy to see me. . . . I didn't realize at this time that RKO and MCA, in fact all things American, were taking over as 'the enemies' as far as Roberto and therefore Ingrid were concerned. I was so torn. I knew that Ingrid had every right to do what she wanted to do. If she'd decided to live on the Solomon Islands with a cannibal chief, I would still have loved her, still have been behind her, still worked for her; but that did not necessarily mean I felt that Ingrid was right. Our conversations were so useless. I would say, 'Ingrid, this is ridiculous, you'll lose your husband and your daughter and your career and everything,' and Ingrid would simply reply, 'Yes, I know.' To me she looked so lost and wan and bewildered.

"I couldn't do much good. I went back to Rome after a few days, and then I went down to Messina for the meeting which was to take place between Petter and Ingrid. And it was so theatrical. It was May Day and the place was full of Communists, and I'd just left America where McCarthy was scaring the pants off everyone about Communists. I expected them all to have horns growing out of their heads. In our hotel, the Italian contingent—Roberto and his associates—were the ones who arranged everything. They'd been overwhelmed by the press ever since Ingrid arrived in Italy, and I think they thought they were going to be driven mad in Sicily, so everything was secretive. I was taken through back alleys, then through a courtyard, then through more corridors, and finally my guide tapped on a door, and I thought, Good God, what am I doing this for? I've got two children, and I live in New York and what am I doing here? Then the door opened, and there was Ingrid and I was back in the scenario. My job was to take Petter secretly round to Ingrid's bedroom—they gave me the number—which I did, and then I went back to my own room. Of course, I didn't know anything about the row I'd started though I heard that damn car all night long. . . ."

———— • ————

Roberto had told me a dozen times that if I left him he'd kill himself, and often he was waving a revolver about. Another thing was his fixation about death in his car: he always had a tree picked out into which he was going to crash it. The terrible thing was it might not have been an idle threat. With Roberto, you never knew what he might do. When he had made up his mind, he had a strength which was unbelievable. If he really wanted something, nothing would stop him; he wouldn't for a moment say, "I'm tired" or "Is it really worth it?" He'd just go on and on until he got it. It was the same with his film-making; if he said "I'm going to get that scene!" he got it.

Sometimes he would get into such a rage that he frightened me, really frightened me. But as fast as he got angry just as quickly it would go away. He was as gentle as a little lamb when he was good-humored; when everything went his way and he got what he wanted, then he was a very nice person. I remember saying to him once, "How can I understand the Italian temperament? In the streets they jump out of the car, and yell and scream, and look as if they're going to kill each other, and then get back in and drive off as if nothing had happened. Those things scare me very much, because I really think they mean it."

Later on in Rome, I'd come out in the kitchen because of the noise, and I'd see the cook and the maid grappling with each other with knives in their hands and I'd almost drop dead. I didn't realize it was just normal fun, Italian style, that they were just having a dramatic time threatening that they would cut each other up, and yelling and screaming because it gave them a kick. I was terribly worried, but I had no need to be because it was just the Italian way of handling things. . . .

Once I said to Roberto when he was good-humored, "You know, you frighten me when you get so angry." He said, "Well, you'll have to help me. Do you think I want to get that angry? " And I asked, "What do I do?" "Just throw your arms around me," he said. "Hold me close, hold me close so I can feel you and your warmth and your love." And I said "All right, all right, I'll try that."

Well, the next time he had one of his seizures and things were flying, I rushed up and I took him in my arms and I started to say . . . and bang, he threw me against the wall so hard I almost broke in pieces. Well, I mean, I couldn't do anything. Even to get near him was to risk your life.

So that night in Messina, Roberto had all his plans worked out. He was certain that Petter was going to induce me to leave with him, or kidnap me, and he knew that there were only three entrances to the hotel. So he had stationed a friend at each of them, and then off he went circling the block in his car —round and round—ready to chase us if we came out. Petter and I were in the room and Roberto was circling around and around every thirty seconds—vroom—vroom—vroom—with me saying "Here he comes again . . . here he comes again!" He never stopped all night long, hour after hour, and I just sat at the window and stared out and listened to Petter talking until the dawn came up. It was a nightmare.

I said, "I can't possibly leave, I must finish the picture because RKO has all this money in it."

He agreed. He understood that. But he said, "Immediately after the picture you must promise to come back to America, and we'll talk the whole thing out." I thought that would be the best idea, and I thought I would be able to do that.

———————— • ————————

Kay Brown took up the story: "I was supposed to pour oil on troubled waters, but there just wasn't enough oil in Italy to smooth out these troubles. I tried to help things along by writing a statement that we were going to issue to the world's press to keep them quiet: a simple statement coming from Ingrid to the effect that she had clarified the situation with her husband, that she was returning to Stromboli to complete the picture, and that upon its conclusion she would be meeting her husband either in Sweden or the United States. Everything I wrote, Art Cohn rewrote, and what we got out was not very credible. There was also an agreement that to end the disastrous publicity, it would be better if Ingrid did not share the house with Roberto and his family, and that they should behave as if nothing but a director-actress relationship was between them. I realized later that could be no more than a charitable hope, because there was about as much chance of Roberto doing this as there was of Ingrid swimming the Atlantic. However, the agreement was made. The farcical drama attached to the entire episode was really quite unbelievable. Everything had to be done to fool the press and the photographers. But actually the press and the photographers hadn't even caught up with what was going on in Messina. Nevertheless, various friends of Roberto's sidled up to tell me of the hush-hush plans which were to cover our secret dash from the hotel. On the stroke of two, we were all to gather in the upstairs corridor, then we'd follow a line of white markers down through the back stairs and passages to where the cars were parked; and then we'd leap into these and rush off at full speed.

"We all met at the specific time. But, of course, no one had told Petter Lindstrom of the arrangements and he was having nothing to do with them. He said coldly, 'I do not intend to slink out through any back door. My wife and I are going down the main staircase and out of the front entrance as usual.' So Roberto had to rush around rearranging the cars, and when we went down the only photographer waiting outside was a sixteen-year-old boy with a camera. Ingrid and Roberto jumped into their red racing car and zoomed away. I squeezed into the back of a small Fiat with the Italian lawyer, and I made sure that the driver ignored Roberto and drove slowly.

"After we'd gone about a mile or so, there were Ingrid and Roberto broken down at the side of the road, or maybe Roberto had run out of fuel after driving around the hotel all night. Fiasco. So they had to squeeze into our car and I sat on Roberto's lap and Ingrid sat on the solicitor's. How I managed to keep a straight face, I'll never know but, of course, at that moment Ingrid was far too unhappy to see the funny side of anything."

———————————— • ————————————

I hated everything about that meeting in Messina, and I was just as mad at Roberto because I thought he behaved very badly too. I looked at these two men fighting about me, and I thought both of them were awful. I went aboard our boat with a face like stone. I sat on that boat that took us out and back to Stromboli, and I didn't say a word to Roberto; I said, "I'm not going to talk to anybody ever again. I'm just never going to talk. . . ."

———————————— • ————————————

Ingrid was bewildered and desperately unhappy about what was going on. Petter believed he had left with various fundamental points agreed upon. If Ingrid returned to America and faced Pia, he would divorce her. The letters that passed between them were the reasonable ones of two adults who thought they understood each other, who had lived together and been in love, and were now trying to establish a measure of coherence and understanding in their relationship. But letters took days and weeks to arrive while the world's press could flash reports and statements and innuendos to every edition within seconds, many of which were totally untrue.

Petter wrote constantly, sometimes reprovingly from Rome and Paris. He had no more advice to give her he said; she was on her own now; he was very relieved that he was not having to get mixed up in her "contracting business" any more; he was going to clear up their present commitments then turn away to medicine and surgery; now was her chance to grow up. Sometimes his letters were full of concern and memories of the past. From Sydney Bernstein's house in Kent he wrote reminding her that the next day was the anniversary of their engagement. He was sorry he had been in such a depressed state for the past few weeks when she really needed his affection and help. Whatever happened they must maintain their friendship and be able to discuss things privately and sensibly.

He still felt "lost and numb." He was trying to reconcile the past, present, and future which all seemed a bit blurred, and he hoped as she did that things would get better later. He ended, "If only I knew where the letters go."

Ingrid wrote back:

We have been waiting in Stromboli in the rain. No one will ever understand the physical effort in this production. Now I left Messina after our meeting giving you three promises:
1. Roberto moves out of the house.
2. Finish the picture.
3. Talk with people in Rome to get first-hand information on R. I also promised not to discuss anything more or give further statements to the press.

But I read several of yours: "No divorce now or in the future."

It hurts me that you are hurt, but one fact remains: You beg me to grow up. You are hoping this terrible situation I have made for myself will teach me and give me a chance to grow up. I'd like to grow up but you won't let me. I know we discussed not to break our relationship until I had thought it over, until after the picture, but it seems useless and unnecessarily cruel for all concerned.

I don't like to be hard, because I know you suffer, but I must fight with your weapons. I am sending a lawyer to London to ask for a separation. I have thought, Petter, I have figured, and I see no other way out of it. Your two last letters were so sad and kind and moved me very much, after the others I have read. We have many many good memories and I thank you with all my heart and with all my tears that have flowed when I have thought of our past. And we have Pia. I don't know why you stay so long in London. I fear you are planning another Messina meeting, which I am afraid I cannot take. I am afraid I don't have the strength for more arguments. I am afraid of more tears, and I am afraid of going crazy.

Pia is alone so long. I wish she were with you. She has never before been without us both for so long a time. Take care of her, go home to her, or bring her to you in London. . . . Take her with you if you go to Sweden. Or let me see her a little. I have not forgotten her, as you may think. I write her one or two times a week. I am glad you spoke with her on the phone and explained the post. She might not receive the letters as I have only got one out of those twenty you said she'd sent.

Dear Petter, let us not linger any longer in this situation. My mind is made up. What has happened cannot be erased. It will be impossible to go back and live together again. What must be done, do fast, so we can begin to think about the future. So we can maybe find some peace of mind again. Please, realize a hopeless fight and stubborn refusal to see the reality hurt us more in the long run.

This is my destiny and I am tired, too.

Katt.

Petter's reply of June 23, 1949, said he needed time to think it over, that they shouldn't force the situation. But he assured her that all he had said to the journalist was "No comment," that he had never mentioned divorce or "never divorce." And he reminded her that there was no reason to believe he would be quoted correctly any more than she would. He would always defend "Pia's mother" when the press attacked her.

He assured her again he didn't intend to try to force her to stay with him, that he would try to see things from her point of view. But before he left Europe, he wanted to see her again "alone and at peace and then leave you as a friend." He had "no hard words or reproaches and you won't see my tears." She was just to tell him how she wanted things and what he should say to Pia. As for him, he wanted to remember Ingrid "as the little girl in the gray collar."

———— • ————

I tried saying to Roberto, "Look, I'll go back and talk to Petter and get a divorce, talk him into it, explain it to him. I hate just to run away and never come back."

"No," said Roberto, "Petter will never let you come back. He will lock you up or put you in an insane asylum or something; you'll never return to Italy." And, of course, I was afraid that I would break down if I saw Pia.

So I thought, best thing is to stay, and sooner or later I'll get a divorce. But, of course, Petter didn't go back to America. He stayed in Sydney Bernstein's house in England writing me letters and asking why couldn't we meet? And I wrote letters back, and it was all hell . . . hell. . . .

Dearest Petter,

First: I don't hate you. How can you believe that? Nobody tries to make me hate you and nobody could, even if they tried. Dear Petter, don't worry like that. In your loneliness you have built up a lot of fantasies. For example: I am never going to take Pia away from you. How can you think that I am so inhuman and that I want to rob you of both your little girls? If you let me have her and she is with me some vacations I would be grateful, and that would, I am sure, be good for her too.

You shouldn't think that Roberto is so cruel that he is trying to kill you. Naturally he is mad and sore over the things people and newspapers say and the way they have tried to ruin him. He knows that you, Kay Brown, and RKO talk and gossip all the time, saying what a pig he is. He has, through me, lost his whole prestige as a person and an artist. I receive daily clippings from America, so terribly nasty and unfair, ridiculous and condescending about him. You remember what wonderful notices he got in Hollywood after *Paisan*? How we called him "the little giant"? Now they say he didn't even make that picture, that Burstyn cut a lot of impossible newsreels together. And *Open City* is also not his work! And he lived on the money of Anna Magnani when in reality he has given her one hundred percent of the picture *L'Amore*. I have never heard of a more generous gift to an actress.

Here in Italy he has also lost friends and possibilities of work. And you ought to know, after all the years with me, how we poor animals who make headlines suffer when things are done and written unjustly and only to kill. It is for that reason I feel we must break and try to stop the flood of insults. I am terribly sorry, but the picture is far from finished. I have been worried many times it would never be. We have had too many problems, both personal and professional. . . .

You say you defend me, but don't you think I defend you too? You must think that I have grown into a monster.

I agree, I wish you to be with Pia when the separation is declared. But as you see, we won't be in Rome for a long time. In the meantime we all wait and suffer. If we have another meeting we will tear at each other's heartstrings and end in despair.

I will write to you, I'll write to Pia. But before we go crazy, let us try to break immediately and see what can be done with the future. I want naturally not another scandal. Therefore if it can be settled in friendship and without noise it is best.

Dear, don't worry about me. I'll be alright, you see. Try to remember the Roberto you first got to know in Hollywood. I see so much good in him. He has made mistakes like all others, and maybe now he is not always reasonable because he feels like a wounded animal.

Think of your own future. Your work that is so great and important. Stay in the house (until the money is finished!) if you like or move to wherever your work takes you. All we have in California is yours and Pia's. Go home as fast as you can, go home to child and dog. Take a long steambath because there you think the best. Many people have had great sorrows but they live and sometimes become better and richer human beings.

Time heals all wounds and I am always your

Katt.

She grieved for Petter but she was in love. She was making a film with the man she loved. They were on a lonely island and every day the sun shone. It seemed a romantic situation, yet Ingrid's list of charitable contributions during those months on the island illustrate more than anything else perhaps the real background to that period:

"To two churches on Stromboli . . . 50,000 lira; contribution for ruined fishing net: 20,000; clothing for two children: 70,000; hospital expenses for maid: 15,000; wooden leg for man: 30,000; sick woman in bed: 10,000; woman alone with several children: 20,000; contribution for eye operation for child: 30,000; candles, cigarettes for internees and children at the DP camp at Farfa where picture was shot. Contribution to funeral expenses for crew member who died on volcano: 60,000 [he was overcome by fumes and died of a heart attack]; contribution toward fund for his family: 600,000 lira."

Petter replied from London that he was awfully disappointed that she would not take his "extended hand." Certainly for the sake of Pia and himself he was not going to humiliate himself further. And he was certainly not going to Stromboli.

He reminded her that Roberto's divorce had not gone through, that it might take two years to ratify, and that she too was still married. She had to think of Pia.

He declared again his love for her, said that in his quiet way he had loved her "as much as a man can love—at least as deeply—but I was born in the far north of Sweden, and the nature there is barren. . . ." And he asked himself why they ever left Sweden for a Hollywood that was "rather an unnatural place for us." It was a poignant letter, which ended, "We poor little human beings."

Ingrid replied:

Dear Petter,
    Again and again I have written to you of my free and definite decision to have a separation and clarity in a situation all the world is peeking at and ridiculing. Petter, what can I say and do to make you understand it is not possible to play for time? You seem to think you are the only one who suffers in this situation. A clear break is the only thing that can save us. The press will quit harassing you at home and in your office. Pia will have peace at school when she starts again, and we here won't have to be hunted like animals all the time. . . .
    Please, Petter, I realize that to break up a marriage is a tragic thing, but it hasn't killed anyone. I thought it quite amusing that in the four months I have gone, Paulette Goddard has divorced, Ann Todd in England divorced her husband after twelve years and married the director David Lean, Viveca Lindfors, Ginger Rogers, Joan Fontaine, and Alida Valli have sued for divorce. Don't think this is the end of the world, your life, and your work.

How long do you think you can "protect" Pia? Talk to her with sincerity, give her my letter, ask her to write me and I'll answer immediately. We'll take good care of her. You might not believe it possible at this time, but you'll see. It will work out, we'll talk and discuss and help each other, Petter. It is only for you to take the first step which naturally is the most difficult: to realize and agree that our marriage is finished. . . .

She wrote to Pia:

Darling, I wish I could take a big bird and fly home to talk to you instead of writing. But I'll have to talk to your photo which is in front of me.

Our life, Pia dear, will change. And that is difficult to tell you because we have such a nice and happy life. The difference is that you'll stay more with Papa, and Mama will be away like so many times before, but this time she'll be away for an even longer time. You remember Mr. Rossellini and that we liked him so much when he lived with us. During this picture I realized I liked him more and more and I wanted to stay with him. It doesn't mean we'll never see each other. You'll come to me for your vacation. We'll have fun and make trips together. You must never forget that I love Papa and I love you and I will always be with you. After all, we belong together and that cannot be changed. But sometimes people like to live with somebody else that is not their proper family. That is a separation or a divorce. I know we talked about how many of your friends had divorced parents. It is nothing unusual but it is rather sad. You have to be for Papa both daughter and "wife," and you'll have all the time with him that I used to have. Take good care of him. Your friends will naturally talk to you because as you know with me it is out in the newspapers. There is nothing you have to be ashamed of. Just say, yes, my parents are separated. You have always been so good with answers to people who go too far and make curious stupid questions. Write to me and I'll write to you, and the time will go so fast—I hope —until we meet again.

Love Mama.

Meanwhile, events were reaching a crisis point in Stromboli. On June 21, 1949, Ingrid received a letter from her respected Beverly Hills lawyer, Mendel Silberman, expressing his concern:

> If you will remember in the original discussion it was suggested that the picture could be finished in six weeks. . . . Since it has now gone beyond the ten-week limit you can understand just how disturbed the RKO organization is becoming. . . .

Ingrid could. On July 5, she replied:

> It makes us all unhappy the film takes so long, but there is no possible way to speed it up. I don't feel RKO has a reason for great worry as in the end they will have a film for 600,000 dollars—maybe we will be somewhat over budget, just like the schedule, but it can't be very much —and you know what the last three Bergman films have cost. They also get a picture which is quite the opposite to *Joan of Arc.* The scandal probably has helped, I think; there can't be a man, woman, or child who won't be curious to see *what* happened in Stromboli, even if the picture is bad. We have some extraordinary scenes of the eruption of the volcano, of the tuna fishing, and of the very dramatic end in an unusual atmosphere on this desolate island. We are working as hard as we can here. . . . Give my agent Lew Wasserman my best regards and this advice: I don't intend to work again for a very long time. I am afraid he has engaged his people in England and America in a vain search for stories. It is entirely useless as I have found lately that being a movie actress with a successful career can almost kill you. . . .

By the middle of July, both Harold Lewis's patience and that of RKO's European office was exhausted. Harold delivered his ultimatum to Roberto: "Finish the picture in one week or funds will be cut off and the picture abandoned." Ingrid, Roberto, the Cohns, Joe Steele, who had just arrived, and a few others went into conference to frame a cable. It was dispatched under Ingrid's name to Silberman.

INCLEMENT WEATHER, ILLNESSES AND INJURIES HAVE INCREASED THE PROBLEMS ON THIS PRIMITIVE ISLAND. IMPOSSIBLE TO BELIEVE RKO HAS BEEN INFORMED OF THESE DIFFICULTIES. OTHERWISE IT WOULD NOT HARASS US AT A TIME WHEN WE ARE WORKING NIGHT AND DAY TO FINISH AS QUICKLY AS HUMANLY POSSIBLE. WE CAME HERE TO MAKE THE BEST PICTURE OF WHICH WE ARE CAPABLE. DESPITE MANY DELAYS WE HAVE HARDLY EXCEEDED THE ITALIAN BUDGET, ALTHOUGH WE HAVE BEEN OBLIGATED TO MAKE TWO COMPLETE VERSIONS OF THE PICTURE AT ADDED COST IN TIME AND MONEY. WE HAVE NEVER BEEN GIVEN AN ACCOUNTING OF THE AMERICAN BUDGET NOR EVEN CONSULTED ABOUT SEVERAL COSTLY EXPENDITURES. . . . ENTIRE TROUPE HAS UNDERGONE MANY PRIVATIONS, ONE OF OUR MEN DIED OF SULPHUR FUMES ON VOLCANO. NEVER IN MY EXPERIENCE HAS A COMPANY UNDERGONE SUCH HARDSHIPS. NONE OF US EXPECT ANY PRAISE FOR THIS, BUT NEITHER DO WE EXPECT THE DEFAMATORY STATE-MENTS THAT HAVE COME. PLEASE APPRISE LEW WAS-SERMAN OF THIS CABLE AND ADVISE ME IMMEDIATELY WHETHER I SHOULD SEND A COPY TO HOWARD HUGHES.
REGARDS.
INGRID BERGMAN.

Mendel Silberman's reply on July 26 was soothing:

> Have contacted RKO who are cabling Lewis suggesting Stromboli shooting continue until next Saturday if necessary. They point out original estimate shooting time entire picture six weeks, and contract time ten weeks and after sixteen weeks picture still unfinished. I feel everyone's interest to finish picture without controversy. . . . They do know of the tremendous difficulties and hardships that shooting this picture on Stromboli has entailed. . . .

On August 2, 1949, Ingrid's diary records briefly: "Left Stromboli." She had never departed from any location or finished the main shooting of any picture with a greater sense of relief.

In four short months she had abdicated her position as "Hollywood's First Lady," and was feeling wretched and dejected. In her own mind, she was certain she had let down or betrayed all her friends and all the people who had worked so hard to finance and produce her pictures. She had abandoned her husband and ten-year-old daughter. Petter's relatives and his parents, all of whom she greatly respected, must detest her. Her confidence was at its lowest ebb. Her depression and tears rarely ceased. If nothing else, Ingrid had a conscience which worked overtime.

She had also made a public declaration to the press that her movie career was now at an end. It was the prerogative of actors and actresses to make such statements, and then re-emerge from retirement when it suited them. But in Ingrid's mind lurked the terrible suspicion that this announcement might not only be true but inevitable. Her body had signaled an inescapable physical reality: she was pregnant. She was pregnant by a man not yet divorced from his wife. There was no way she could face a ten-year-old daughter and explain this sequence of events. A divorce was plainly going to take many months or even years. She had already experienced the outraged reactions of many public institutions and the world's press over the present scandal. The birth of her child seemed likely to result in a publicity explosion of even greater proportions.

Ingrid was completely correct in her analysis. On the day that the New York press blazoned the news that an "out-of-wedlock" Ingrid Bergman had produced a beautiful baby boy, Robert Anderson, author and playwright, whose life would cross dramatically with that of Ingrid's in future years, left his apartment to buy a newspaper. At his nearest newsstand, a man was scrutinizing the headline. As Robert Anderson arrived, the man said bitterly to the world in general: "So she *was* just a godamned whore!"

Chapter

16

On August 5, 1949, Joe Steele presided at a conference in Rome to issue Ingrid's press release: "It was not my desire to make any statement until the conclusion of the picture I am now making. But persistent malicious gossip that has even reached the point where I am made to appear as a prisoner has obliged me to break my silence and demonstrate my free will. I have instructed my lawyer to start divorce proceedings immediately. Also, with the conclusion of the picture it is my intention to retire into private life."

A day later, the Rome newspaper *Giornale Della Sera* announced that Ingrid Bergman was pregnant. Three days later, Hedda Hopper appeared in the skies over the Rome airport, established herself at the Excelsior Hotel, contacted Joe Steele and peremptorily demanded an interview with Ingrid.

Roberto pugnaciously refused to be interviewed. Politely, Joe pointed out that it was not Roberto Hedda wished to see. Joe also advised that Hedda had flown a long long way to do her job, no matter how repulsive some people might find it, and for Ingrid to refuse to see her would be discourteous and serve no useful purpose. Joe did not know, or believe, that Ingrid was pregnant.

Ingrid agreed to the interview. Hedda was not actually blindfolded, but she was certainly taken by a circuitous route to the Rossellini apartment. Ingrid smiled cheerfully, answered all the questions, said all the right things, hoped that her divorce from Petter could be arranged speedily and amicably, and did not even blush when Miss Hopper, just before she left, popped the significant question. "What's all this I hear about a pregnancy, Ingrid?" Laughing politely and standing up to say good-bye and reveal her slender figure, Ingrid answered, "Good heavens, Hedda. Do I look like it?"

Hedda returned to Hollywood to reassure her readers that there was no truth in the rumor, and that Roberto and Ingrid were about to sue the paper concerned.

There was of course a most important reason behind Ingrid's evasion of the question without actually telling a lie. If news emerged that she was indeed expecting a baby, Petter's reactions would be those of any other husband faced with a similar situation: disbelief, shock, and then fury. And if he received such information through a newspaper headline, he might be totally unforgiving. Ingrid, therefore, had to establish a relationship with Petter as quickly as possible and enlist his cooperation in getting divorce proceedings not only started but completed before the baby was born.

Roberto, being a man immersed in litigation, was of the opinion that this could only be achieved through the process of law rather than by mutual persuasion. Lawyers would jolt Petter into action.

"All right," said Ingrid, "let's get things moving through a lawyer."

There was one handy. Munroe MacDonald was an American who had worked in the legal department of the United States forces of occupation. He had settled in Rome with an Italian wife. Forty years old, personable, eager to be of help in such a highpowered controversy, he seemed to be the ideal person. Naturally, he needed briefing before he set off for the United States on his important mission; naturally he sat in on their intimate and guarded meetings. Naturally, he needed complete power of attorney to enforce any action he might take, and to help him in these matters Ingrid sat down and typed a document of many thousand words giving details of her background, her life with Petter, and the sequence of events which had led up to the present dilemma. Mr. MacDonald stowed it carefully in his briefcase and set off for New York.

Within hours of landing in New York, he, or some agent, had arranged an interview with gossip-columnist Cholly Knickerbocker, and within twenty-four hours the Hearst newspapers were on the streets throughout the nation proclaiming that they, for the first time, could tell "Ingrid's Real Love Story." Revealed were the confidences, intimacies, and clever but inaccurate twists of events which could only have come from the documents Mr. MacDonald carried. Blandly, he explained to Roberto over the telephone some time later that he had been party to such things because he thought it was in their best interests.

From Ingrid's document, one fact which had been buried in her subconscious for a considerable time emerged: "Deep down in my heart I was still the wife of Petter, and he knew it. He often said, no man ever gave his wife more freedom. That is true, but I was always free away from him and not with him."

Munroe MacDonald continued happily to Hollywood and began issuing statements with the prodigality of a press agent. In essence he announced that although Miss Bergman did not know what share of the community property she owned, as Dr. Lindstrom handled practically all her financial affairs, she was prepared to offer Dr. Lindstrom half of it in return for a divorce and part-time custody of their daughter. . . . MacDonald also reported that Roberto Rossellini had instructed him to make it clear that he wanted no part of Miss Bergman's property; he had never yet lived on any woman's earnings and did not intend to start now.

On September 22, 1949, Sydney Bernstein sent Ingrid news of the opening of *Under Capricorn* in New York: A mixed press . . . more disappointment over the story than in the artists. . . . Warner Bros. very optimistic and saying this is one of her best pictures. . . . Why didn't she come to England for the gala performance? . . . The visit would help her personally . . . a visit to England would be a bridge between Italy and America.

Ingrid gave two reasons for refusing. The first, there was too much trouble brewing with RKO over *Stromboli*. The second: "I don't intend ever again of my own free will to see the press and answer questions. If I encounter a newspaperman, it will be an unavoidable accident. In Sweden we have a proverb: 'Burned child avoids the fire.' I know the English press has been the most human and dignified, but still . . . I am burned. Right now I have the worst storm raging in the United States. I didn't think it could be worse at this time, and I really believe this will be the end of me. I am perfectly willing to pay for my own faults—but I don't need a bridge to America, Sydney, for I have no intention of going back. . . ."

On December 14, 1949, a letter from the Belgian RKO representative in Brussels reached Roberto and Ingrid. The night before, he had

had the privilege of screening the first print of *Stromboli*. He was ecstatic:

> *Stromboli* is overwhelming. Here is a picture which will satisfy the taste of the most discriminating movie-goers (including the most refined film critics) and which will have at the same time irresistible appeal to the general public. *Stromboli* is the best Rossellini picture. *Stromboli* is the best Bergman picture. *Stromboli* is *The* picture of 1950. Ingrid Bergman's performance in *Stromboli* is without question and by far the best of her brilliant career.
> . . .
>
> In short *Stromboli,* the first of our all European releases for the 1950–1951 season, will be the sensation of Europe, and I want you to start talking to exhibitors right now.

It was not hard to see why the Belgian representative was a salesman of the highest rank. For he was completely wrong.

Whatever else he did, Munroe MacDonald certainly succeeded overwhelmingly in one direction. The sensational publicity he had managed to arouse completely alienated Petter Lindstrom. From now on, officially and privately, he was to treat Ingrid and Roberto Rossellini with the maximum caution. Petter believed that they were making untrue and malicious statements about him and conducting a trial by newspaper. He had talked to Ingrid by phone before he read the MacDonald news. Now he wrote her a letter saying that it had been nice to hear her voice, and that he had been sad to hear of all her difficulties and, indeed, had fallen back into his old habit of wanting to help her.

Then, Petter's letter went on, Mr. MacDonald had got into the act through his newspaper interviews stating that Ingrid had told him personally that she had informed Pia that she was not coming home. Petter found this intolerable. How could she have as her representative a person who immediately communicated all her private affairs to the press?

Mr. MacDonald had had the nerve to present a long statement about their married life together, and done his best to blacken Petter's name. If she was, as she said, now making decisions on her own, were these the tactics she wanted?

Petter had heard that Roberto Rossellini was alleging in Stromboli that Ingrid had arrived in Italy without a penny, and that Petter had never given her furs or jewels or dresses. And Mr. MacDonald's interviews contained the same nonsense. What did she expect to achieve by throwing dirt of this nature? Was she simply trying to make him angry?

Dear Petter: I feel really like Don Quixote fighting against the windmill. You are my windmill and probably you are hoping to hit me one day with a big blade and kill me.

Granted, MacDonald shot his big mouth off, told tasteless stories that he had not been given the right to do. But he IS my representative as I told you on the phone. Why don't you believe it is I who chose an *American?* It was hard to find in Italy. For your sake I didn't want an Italian even if he spoke the best English. And so we have again scandal and ruin and disaster in the press, more sleepless nights and intolerable suffering. Whose fault is it? Do you have the stomach to say it is mine—even if MacDonald is my man, even if I have to be his springboard to fame and pay for his blunders. Is it MY FAULT ALONE, Petter? After six months of trying to get a divorce, after all I have written and all I have warned you of, you are on the phone with your laugh and sarcastic answer, "Sure I'll see your lawyer." You know very well we can't afford the expense of these men traveling all over the world trying to talk to you while you play hide and seek.

You say my lawyers have offered you a fortune for my liberty. And in headlines. It is not their fault what the paper makes headlines of. Probably the paper people were as surprised as the lawyers. It is not usual for a woman not to ask for anything. Probably they think I am a fool to give you all I have. Half of what I have earned is mine. But I want to leave it for you and Pia.

I am tired of writing, but my anger drives me on. . . .

You believe only Petter. And you don't like anything or anybody against Petter. As you used to say: "When have I ever made a mistake?"

Your good health and sleep well. . . .

— 261 —

Ingrid was horrified when MacDonald enlisted Gregson Bautzer to act as her lawyer in Hollywood. She had been hoping for a wise old legal expert; all she knew about Bautzer was that he was often featured in Hollywood magazines as the handsome escort of such famous film stars as Ginger Rogers, Lana Turner, and Joan Crawford and was referred to as "the most eligible bachelor in the entire film community." Hardly what she wanted as her representative and adviser.

But events proved her quite wrong. Greg Bautzer handled the complex and seemingly never-ending litigation shrewdly and efficiently. At the close of the whole sorry affair, Ingrid sent him a letter thanking him for all he had done and also thanking him for the extreme modesty of his fees.

———— • ————

I had a small problem with Joe Steele. He was in Rome when the newspapers came out with the first stories of my pregnancy, and he was outraged and insisted we should sue them. I think he was a bit shocked when Roberto took it all rather calmly. Then, when he went back to Hollywood, he got all agitated about the disgraceful newspapers and radio columnists continually making these allegations. He was going to sue them, he was going to give them hell. So as a postscript to one of my letters, I added: ". . . for your eyes alone. I want your family and friends and everybody except your God kept outside. Just say, 'I don't know. All is possible.' After all you *didn't* know when you left Italy." Then I told him the truth.

———— • ————

Joe Steele reacted almost as if he were going to be forced to have the baby himself. "It was," he said, "like having my leg blown off."

For a few days Joe agonized over the burden he was carrying. Journalists and radio commentators continued to pester him with demands for confirmation or denial. Eventually it became too much for Joe. He had to talk to someone. With the most honorable motives, he decided to confide in Howard Hughes. He rang Johnny Meyer, Hughes's lieutenant, and obtained the unlisted number of Hughes's Beverly Hills Hotel bungalow. Within minutes he was talking to Howard. He was, he said, about to communicate something in the very strictest confidence. If Ingrid knew what he was doing she would never forgive him. . . . But he had thought about it, had nightmares about it and, well, Ingrid was pregnant!

Howard Hughes was interested. When was it due? Joe guessed about March, and then got to the point he wanted to make. Howard had to make an immediate decision. Undoubtedly, the news would blow the picture sky high. Ruin it. It would probably be banned. Ingrid and Roberto Rossellini were broke. If Howard could rush the picture to completion, release it in, say, more than five hundred theaters, nationwide, Ingrid and Roberto might have a chance of making some money. Ingrid deserved such a chance.

Howard Hughes thanked Joe and said he would follow his advice. Joe went home not quite certain whether he had blundered or not. When he woke up the next morning, he knew he had. The *Los Angeles Examiner* blazoned thick, black, front-page headlines: "Ingrid Bergman Baby Due in Three Months at Rome," followed closely by the *Herald Express's* "Report Ingrid Bergman to Have Baby Shocks Filmdom," and a day later by the *Examiner's* follow-up: "Rossellini Says Baby Story Invades Rights."

Mr. Hughes had decided there was more profit to be gained from exposure than from secrecy. The story was exposed to the reading public under the byline of Louella Parsons: "Few women in history or men either," gushed Louella, "have made the sacrifice the Swedish star has made for love. . . ."

She then went on to broaden her theme into romantic comparisons with Mary Queen of Scots and Bothwell, Lady Hamilton and Nelson, the Prince of Wales and Mrs. Simpson.

It is doubtful if any person in modern times, innocent of royal title, not guilty of stealing ten million dollars, or of some vile and ruthless murder, has ever had to face, as Ingrid did, not just the normal "invasion of privacy," but a twenty-four-hour-a-day-siege behind locked doors and shuttered windows, to protect herself from being submerged under a deluge of newsmen and photographers.

In a large portion of the American press for a period of some twelve days, immense drama such as President Truman's announcement of the invention of the hydrogen bomb and all it presaged for mankind was used as feeble bottom-of-the-page material fit only to support the black and bulging headlines charting the arrival of Ingrid's baby.

Just before the baby was due, with the scandal at its height and life never blacker, Ernest Hemingway telephoned.

"What's this? America's gone crazy. Scandal because of a baby! Ridiculous! I hope you have twins. I'll be their godfather, and promise to carry them into St. Peter's, one on each arm. Now what can I do for you?"

Ingrid said, "Can you put that in the paper, Ernest?—because every newspaper is full of such hatred and dark things. Say it to a newspaper. Nobody else does."

"I will, I will," he said. And he did. And the following week there was a photograph of Papa on the front page saying, "What is all this nonsense? She's going to have a child. So what? Women are always having children. I'm proud of her and happy for her. She loves Roberto and he loves her, and they want the child. We should celebrate with her not condemn her."

———————— • ————————

The phone rang in our apartment. It was getting on toward noon and the date was February 2, 1950. I remember that date very well. It was Mrs. Lydia Vernon, the wife of our business manager, and she was ringing from Beverly Hills. She started right in: "What's the matter with you? You really must pull yourself together and come back and see Pia. Do you understand that? You have to come back to America to see Pia. She is crying for you all the time. She's dreadfully unhappy. Get on a plane and come back at once."

I was so upset I was crying, and kept trying to interrupt, "But I can't come now. Don't you understand? As soon as I can, I'll arrange something."

But she went on and on just raving at me, and when I finally managed to put the phone down, I felt the first contractional pain of the birth starting. And I had this terrible presentiment. I was going into the hospital to have this baby and perhaps I wouldn't come out of it alive. It had something to do with being brought up on movies, I think. I had to pay for my sins: you either died or went to prison if you sinned.

I had to write, I just had to write to Pia to tell her I loved her, that even at this moment, if it should be my last, she would know I had been thinking about her. I had to have some document to prove that. So I got to my typewriter and put in carbon and paper: if the letter got lost at least the carbon copy would get to her somehow. And now what did I say? How to tell a ten-year-old child that I was expecting another baby, why I couldn't come home and

have the baby with her and Papa. How to tell her I'd fallen in love with another man; he was the father of the child, and I would stay in Italy, and she would come and visit me and I would visit her.
. . .

Then Elena Di Montis, the maid who'd been with me ever since I first arrived in Italy, rushed in and took one look at me, all curled up and typing away, and cried, "For pity's sake, we can't have the baby *here!* I can't handle such things. We must call the doctor. Please call the doctor." And I was saying, "No, No, I must write this letter first."

I looked at the clock on the wall. I knew from Pia's birth that these contracting pains come regularly, every four minutes for the first period, then three minutes, and so on, and between them peace and you feel absolutely fine. So I plugged away at the letter and then I glanced up at the clock and oh . . . oh . . . oh . . . oohhhh, here we go again. Every four minutes I was literally hanging on to the chair, and then back to the typing. Now the spasms were coming every three minutes and Elena was hopping round going mad, moaning "Signora, the doctor, the doctor! Please call the doctor! I can't help you . . . I have no experience."

"I haven't finished the letter yet, I haven't finished the letter. I must finish the letter."

"But you'll have the baby here, and I don't know what to do. Let me call the doctor. I'll call the doctor? . . ."

I finally finished it, literally hanging over the chair. I wiped the sweat away and said, "All right, call the doctor now."

Roberto was away in the mountains outside Rome shooting *Flowers of St. Francis,* so he was also telephoned. I expect he jumped into his Ferrari and might even have got to the clinic before I did.

The car arrived. I sneaked into it and off we went. Then when we were halfway there, I suddenly realized I wasn't wearing my green emerald ring which Roberto had given me, and which I never took off. I had washed my hands and left it in the bathroom. That really threw me. In the hospital I rushed for the phone. Poor Elena; there I was raving at her again: "I can't have this baby without that green ring on my finger! It is in the bathroom! Throw yourself in a taxi and rush it to the hospital. I shall not have the baby without it. Hurry! Hurry!"

The pains were now arriving so regularly that all my time schedules had gone astray. And I had gone astray too because the last thing I remembered was dear Elena slipping the ring on my finger and smiling at me. Then I was in the delivery room and Robertino was born at seven o'clock in the evening.

———————— • ————————

The letter to Pia, considering the conditions under which it was written, was a marvel of exposition:

February 2, 1950.

> Dear darling mine:
> Today is ten days since I spoke on the phone to you and I have not written since. Isn't that just awful. What happened? I know for a couple of days I did not feel so good. I guess I ate too much candy. Someone sent me a box from America and as I have not seen American candy for such a long time I swallowed all. I guess Papa wouldn't have liked that, but it was so good. . . .
> Dear Pia, I can understand that the children in school ask a lot of questions. I wrote you before to find out what they said, but I guess you have not had time to answer that. I wish so that I could help you. I will try to write a few things, though, that might clear some dark spots. First: You know that long before I went to Italy we always had newspaper people curious and writing a lot. At that time we used to laugh because they were so silly in their many stories, true and untrue. Now they never could find something *really* bad to write about Papa and me because we stayed at home, we were happy alone, and it was hard to find stories about us. Now this has happened and because they have waited for the day when they could say something sensational about Mama, they are all crazy for joy. I don't know why, but human beings seem to enjoy much more the bad stories than the good ones. Very few newspaper men ever wrote anything about the many people from Hollywood who went out to entertain soldiers and lived in difficult situations just to make some soldiers happy. And all of us have gone to hospitals to cheer patients, all of us have given money to the poor. But that does not interest the newspapers. This story, after all Papa's and my years together, that I want to leave and that

I want to marry Mr. Rossellini, that is something that will interest all readers and therefore they write all, even without checking if it is true or not.

I have outside my apartment house here a whole lot of people. I have tried, as I told you in an earlier letter, to keep my address secret, but it is not possible. The milkman tells the groceryman. He tells his wife, she tells her hairdresser, who tells her children, who tell their friends in school and so on. The doorman is very good. He is a little thin man and sometimes I feel so sorry for him because he gets so afraid when a big strong American newspaperman threatens him; he wants to see me and he is going to send the police after the doorman. But the little doorman tries all he can.

I had not left the apartment for five weeks because I saw that a car of photographers was waiting all day in the street. I took Stromboli to the terrace on the roof, we had nice walks there and I could sit and read and take sunbaths. I didn't need to go out. We used to look down into the street and see those cameras and we spit, just a little, down upon them. That is, I spit, Stromboli was not able to, but I know he wanted to. Then one day, and this is five weeks later, I did not see them any more. I thought they must have given up; I'll go to the corner just to have a walk and get out a bit. I came out and two seconds later a camera was in my face and there was a man that had taken my picture. I screamed at him in English, but he happened to be Italian and just smiled back. Later I had to smile too because he was so happy. Imagine, he had waited all that time and finally I came out and the sun was shining and this picture turned out so well. Now his boss was happy and he probably got some extra money for his work. I smiled when I thought of that but in the street I started to cry like a baby.

Pia, I want you to know that all the stories about what I have said and so on are invented. I have NEVER NEVER said that I would give up my child, that means you, and that I would never see you again. They write that I don't know why, to show what a silly mother I am or something. I love you Pia, sweetiepie, and if it now is a long time we have not seen each other and it might still be some time as you have to go to school, it does not mean that we never see each other. I am going to have a little house here and I am going to have a little room called Pia's room, and whenever you come, it is there ready for you, with your things, and you will see that after a while it won't seem so strange to you to have two homes, one with Papa and one with Mama. And we will make trips together, because now you are so big you can travel with me like a grown-up person and we will see much of the world. I will also come to America so you don't have to do all the traveling. We will share it.

I think you will find it very interesting to have two homes. I don't say, darling, that it is better than one. Oh no, I realize that for you, one home with Papa and Mama is the very best. But as the very best did not come our way, this we have to see with the best light and discover what good things there are. Believe me, it is not all so terrible. You will find friends here. There is an English school with only English children. So you won't feel so alone. And when I have another child you will play with it and we will teach "it" good English. My Italian is worse than my French and you know how bad my French is!

I said to you before that Papa is Papa and we don't hate each other. During this time when you discuss a divorce there are always a lot of things to settle and decide. Naturally, we discuss, but we don't fight. I wish I knew what it is bad they say about Papa, for then I could explain to you what it means and why certain things are said.

Please write me. Don't be afraid to talk to me openly as you do with Mrs. Vernon. She is of great help but some things you might like to hear directly from Mama.

I am so so sorry that you have to go through all this. But Life is long and this is only a short period in the shadow. The sun will shine again and we will all be happy.

> With all my love and kisses,
> Mama

Ingrid quite unwittingly ruined the gala première of Anna Magnani's film riposte to Roberto, *Volcano!* The Fiamma Cinema was packed. The journalists were there in great numbers. The opening credits flashed up on the screen; there was a pop and the screen went blank. A bulb in the projector had burned out. There was no replacement. A boy was dispatched on a bicycle across Rome to get a new one. The bulb was replaced, the film started, and Anna Magnani was suddenly startled by the fact that half the audience—all the journalists—seemed to be leaving. "What's going on?" asked Anna.

"Ingrid Bergman's just had a son," whispered one of her friends. "The press are all rushing off to the hospital."

"It's sabotage," muttered Anna. She was far too experienced an actress to try and compete for publicity with a newborn baby. She made a dignified exit. Both the première and the film itself were flops.

In another part of Rome, the first version of *Stromboli* was being shown to a selected audience of several hundred priests and a sprinkling of bishops to illustrate that its ending was inspired and uplifting and had little in common with the hurriedly edited version slapped together by RKO and released across the United States.

The usually sedate and peaceful maternity home staffed by smiling nuns was now in a state of bedlam. Within seconds, the Italian press knew that the moment of truth had arrived and phones began to ring all over the hospital like minor fire alarms. Alerted by Roberto as to what to expect and the action to be taken, all iron gates into the hospital grounds were locked and the medical personnel alerted to repel invaders. The American press tried to obtain confirmation. One member of the Associated Press managed to attract the attention of a nun unaware of the arrival of their famous patient. When he demanded that she swear on the Bible that Miss Ingrid Bergman was not in the building, she answered, "Ah, but you must mean Borghese. Yes the Principessa Borghese has given birth to lovely twins this evening, but there is no reason to tear the gates down because of that."

By midnight, all the hospital staff, and the expectant or nursing mothers, were being disturbed by the noise. The hospital director called the riot police. Lights flashing, sirens screaming, they arrived on the scene, their steel helmets adding another ingredient to the proceedings. The newsmen and photographers retreated a few yards. It was a bitterly cold February night and they collected wood from a nearby park and lit fires. Combining forces, newsmen and police stood around to warm their hands.

The hospital director, at first outraged by the invasion, had by morning decided that it was foolish to ignore such a golden opportunity for free publicity. He made the cautious announcement that at five in the afternoon he would admit newsmen—no cameras—into the downstairs reception rooms *only* where they could admire the clinical efficiency of his establishment. It was like opening a meat market to a pack of hungry wolves. Polite and admiring gentlemen in heavy overcoats filed in, and once inside tore concealed cameras from their undergarments and raced in every direction pursued by nuns and angry attendants.

Only the *Life* photographer made it to the second floor and the locked door of Suite 34. Behind it, Ingrid lay in bed, the steel shutters at her window pulled tight and locked, and Robertino secreted in a deep cot by her side. The photographer was captured and hustled back down the stairs, and eventually the hospital was cleared.

Balked, the photographers took up siege positions and prepared to await their opportunity. This they did for twelve days. They draped themselves in the trees and, like monkeys, walked around the top of the wall enclosing the maternity home, while the police tried to pry them off. One did fall off and broke his arm, causing no grief in Roberto's heart and little in Ingrid's. They rented one apartment facing the hospital and from every window trained their cameras in the hope of snapping anything remotely usable. They bribed hospital attendants to deliver letters. Their pleas were simple: "My job is in peril." "My chances of promotion are receding." "My wife can't stand me being out late at night; perhaps she will take a lover."

One arrived with flowers sent specially from Maxwell Anderson —"look, here is his signature"—but they *must* be delivered personally. The first prize should have been awarded to the American photographer who wrote in to say he had heard that the baby had been born a monster. Out of pure altruism, if only Miss Bergman would grant him a few seconds of her time, facing his camera with the baby in her arms, he could prove to the world that this was a foul lie.

———————— • ————————

They tried to bribe innocent nuns, offering them a million lire just to open my bedroom door a couple of inches so they could take one quick snapshot of me in bed. One Italian cameraman with a pregnant wife padded her a bit and got her admitted to the hospital. He carried her suitcase up to the bedroom. There, a nun opened it and, hallo, instead of baby clothes, cameras! She was weeks away from her event. Both were shown the door. Another climbed a drainpipe to my balcony, but couldn't force open the shutters. They even managed to persuade Dr. Sannicandro, the clinic's gynecologist, to answer questions on Italian radio: yes, I'd had the same anaesthetic as Rita Hayworth—that sort of stuff. The papers were using old photographs and trying to fix them to suggest they had something to do with the birth.

And one weekly paper came out with a photograph on its front cover which made us gasp. There I was sitting up in bed smiling happily with the baby in my arms. There was Roberto standing proudly by my side. There was the nurse and there was a man who was pretending to be a doctor, with a balloon coming out of his mouth saying: "It's a boy." And inside the paper tucked away in very tiny letters, which prevented them from being sued, was a line saying, "The picture on the front cover is a photo-montage." They'd taken a photograph of me shot on Stromboli and replaced the head of the woman in bed with my head; they'd taken a "head" of Roberto when he was signing the contract, and they'd mocked up the rest. Of course they sold millions of copies. But it was not a harmless little prank. Lots of people wrote, and thousands of people everywhere said, "So they allowed that child to be photographed in the hospital? The nerve of it! How shameless! And they're not even married!"

But one generous gesture from a woman I hardly knew pleased me very much. In America the Hearst press was printing the worst possible stories against me. Yet the very first basket of flowers to arrive at the hospital had a telegram attached which said: "I love and admire you." And it came from Marion Davies, William Randolph Hearst's mistress.

Roberto and I didn't want our child to be abused by the press. He had a right to privacy also. We wanted peace for him in those first few days of his life. Roberto was adamant about that. So Roberto worked out our escape from the hospital. In the middle of the night he suddenly said, "We go!" So at four A.M. I got up, picked up Robertino, and raced down the stairs with Roberto. Not even the nurses knew I was leaving. They tore after us, crying, "Oh, you can't go! You can't go!" We said, "Just watch us." We jumped into Roberto's car, which was waiting at the entrance, and off we sped.

He had a friend in a car who drove behind us, and then suddenly stopped and turned across the road, blocking off the photographers. So I managed to get back to the house without a single photograph being taken.

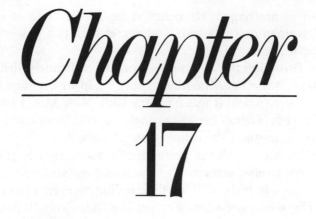

Chapter 17

On March 14, 1950, the Honorable Edwin C. Johnson of Colorado stood up in the Senate of the United States and delivered the most astounding and vitriolic attack against an actress and a film director ever made in that august assembly. He began: "Mr. President, now that the stupid film about a pregnant woman and a volcano has exploited America with the usual finesse, to the mutual delight of RKO and the debased Rossellini, are we merely to yawn wearily, greatly relieved that this hideous thing is finished and then forget it? I hope not. A way must be found to protect the people in the future against that sort of gyp. . . .

"Mr. President, even in this modern age of surprise it is upsetting to have our most popular but pregnant Hollywood movie queen, her condition the result of an illicit affair, play the part of a cheap chiseling female to add spice to a silly story which lacks appeal on its own. To bolster the box-office take, *Stromboli* simply has to have a private scandal on the part of the leading lady. . . ."

He outlined his contempt: "The disgusting publicity campaign . . . the nauseating commercial opportunism displayed by this corporation . . . the vile and unspeakable Rossellini who sets an all-time low in shameless exploitation and disregard for good public morals . . ."

The bill he was about to introduce, he said, "demands the licensing of actresses, producers and films by a division of the Department of Commerce." Ingrid Bergman had perpetrated "an assault upon the institution of marriage." He believed her to be "one of the most powerful women on earth today—I regret to say, a powerful influence for evil . . .

"When Rossellini the love pirate returned to Rome smirking over his conquest, it was not Mrs. Lindstrom's scalp which hung from the conquering hero's belt; it was her very soul. Now Mrs. Petter Lindstrom and what is left of her has brought two children into the world —one has no mother; the other is illegitimate."

Printed in his speech for permanent preservation in the Senate Record were twelve extracts from newspapers and magazines, all scathing, about Ingrid and Rossellini, including even a piece of criticism by *The Washington Star*'s critic, Jay Carmody: "It is a miserably inept work, meaningless as to story, grotesque in performance, confused in direction, and profoundly dull. . . . As Miss Bergman's swan song, it is one best forgotten as quickly as possible."

Mr. Johnson admitted that Miss Bergman had once been his own favorite actress. . . . "She was a sweet and understanding person with an attractive personality which captivated everybody on and off the screen. God has been very good to Ingrid Bergman." But was she suffering from "the dreaded mental disease schizophrenia?" Was she the victim "of some kind of hypnotic influence? . . . Her unnatural attitude toward her own little girl surely indicates a mental abnormality. . . . Under our law no alien guilty of turpitude can set foot on American soil again. Mrs. Petter Lindstrom has deliberately exiled herself from a country which was so good to her." He ended, "If out of the degradation associated with *Stromboli,* decency and common sense can be established in Hollywood, Ingrid Bergman will not have destroyed her career for naught. Out of her ashes may come a better Hollywood."

———— • ————

So there I was. Holy Year in Rome with a newborn baby. And everywhere—especially in America—these waves of hatred generated against Roberto and me. Rome, full of tourists and pilgrims, with carpets and flags hung over the windows, and I the scarlet woman among them.

It became a matter of sheer physical and mental survival. I'd got a new family and a new life. I was determined to be an ordinary woman taking care of her home and child. I'd got Roberto's family too. There was Marcella, his sister, and Fiorella, Marcella's daughter who was a little older than Pia and became like a daughter to me as well.

In that boiling hot summer Fiorella was with me when I was up in the mountains outside Rome at Fiuggi to escape the heat. She did her best to help by throwing stones at all the photographers who tried to take pictures, and she became such a good stone-thrower that I had to try to stop her by saying, "Fiorella, darling, they're really only doing their job." But Fiorella kept throwing stones.

Roberto bought Santa Marinella, a big house on the sea about sixty kilometers from Rome, but I wasn't allowed to go there, because all the collected generations of old Italian mamas insist that young children should not be raised near the sea. It was supposed to do something harmful to their ears or brains or something. I thought it was all nonsense, but I was a newcomer so there was no point in starting off with arguments. Roberto was still working like mad on *Flowers of St. Francis* so we didn't see much of him, but we could always hear him coming up the mountainside, the vroom—vroom—vroom of the Ferrari, then he'd kiss me and Robertino, fall asleep almost immediately, and race back to Rome early next morning.

Petter had had to become an American citizen to be able to open an office of his own, and he was accepted on November 1, 1949. But I'd never really wanted to give up my Swedish citizenship. Petter hadn't been able to understand this when he was making his own application. "Why?" he said. "You don't want to go back to Sweden and live there do you? You love America, so what's the reason?" I said, "I don't know what it is. I just know I'm not going to be a happy person being an American when Sweden is still there." Anyway we had left it for discussion until after I finished *Stromboli,* and of course after *Stromboli* it never came up in conversation again.

I was a married Swedish citizen hoping to divorce and marry an Italian who had had his marriage annulled, and my husband was now an American citizen living in California. I suppose lawyers were invented for such complications.

First, the birth certificate. As far as I could see, everyone in the whole wide world knew that I'd given birth to a seven-pound baby boy and that the father was—as he'd admitted in headlines—Roberto Rossellini. But could we put that on the birth certificate? No! I was still married to Petter, so if my name had been put down,

Petter would officially have been the father of the child and Roberto would have torn the office down. If we could get a divorce before the time limit for registering a birth elapsed, it would be all right, so that is what we tried to do first.

Petter wasn't in any hurry. He would get his divorce in California when he was certain all the settlements were right and suited him. Petter could also contest any European divorce we got as illegal. We tried everywhere but our only hope seemed to be Mexico. So back to the lawyers and through them I petitioned for divorce on grounds of cruelty, nonsupport, and incompatibility. On February 9, I got a cable saying that the divorce had been granted and that Roberto or I could marry anybody we chose.

But February 9 was too late for the birth certificate. Roberto had had to register himself as the father of the child and they put me down as the "mother whose identity will be revealed later."

The next thing was how to get married? Sweden didn't recognize a proxy, Mexican divorce, any more than America did, so in Swedish terms I was still married to Petter. Italy wouldn't allow a civil marriage unless I could produce documentary evidence that I had a Swedish divorce. That was impossible so it was back to Mexico again, and the lawyers. A great friend of ours, Marcello Girosi, also a film producer in Rome, flew out to Mexico to be me—to represent me there, and with a lawyer turned up at the marriage ceremony. So there was this absurd situation of two men acting as bride and bridegroom, with one saying to the other, "I take you, Ingrid Bergman, as my lawful wedded wife," and the other one saying, "And I take you, Roberto Rossellini, as my lawful wedded husband."

The day the marriage ceremony was to take place, Marcello telephoned to give me the exact time, because I wanted at the very moment that they were saying "I do," to have the feeling that these words spoken so many thousands of miles away would somehow come across to us in our little church in Rome. I'd already chosen the church, a very pretty little place with a boat outside.

I had invited some friends for that evening; they didn't know why they'd been invited; they thought they were just coming to dinner as usual: Amidei and Fellini and Liana Ferri. And the phone rang and it was Roberto: he was delayed at the studio as usual. I was almost in hysterics because we had to get from our apartment to the church before they closed it up for the night. By the time Roberto finally arrived, it was closed. But we found another one, a little one, a very sweet tiny church near the Via Appia, and in that church I knelt down and Roberto held my hand—and then we went home and told all our friends that now we were married, and drank the champagne.

Of course all this time I'd been having trouble with the language. Roberto and I spoke French together, although my French wasn't very good, and I spoke French to Roberto's friends and his sister, but then, of course, they got tired of French and fell back into Italian. I'd let them speak for a while, then I'd say, "Come on, I want to be in on the jokes." So they'd go back into French and then away they went in Italian again. . . .

But then, one day, to my complete surprise I just followed the conversation and I said, "My God, I thought they were speaking French, but it's *Italian*, and I can understand it." Then I started grammar with Marcella, and I started to practice; I never took any real lessons, I learned it all by ear, but I suppose my speaking four languages—Swedish, English, German, and French—helped a lot.

I liked Roberto's mother very much. She was a small woman, she wore thick glasses, she didn't hear very well, and she liked me because she could always hear my very strong voice—she hadn't heard her other daughters-in-law so well. We became enormously good friends. She was a charming woman, very well educated, and she had married Roberto's father, a handsome young architect, when they met in Venice when she was very young. They were very wealthy, and the father completely spoiled the four children, Roberto being the oldest. Roberto had had a succession of English governesses to teach him English, but being Roberto, he took over: all the governesses went back to England speaking perfect Italian, and Roberto remained without one word of English. There was money for holidays, money for governesses, money for everything: Roberto came in one day and said, "Papa, can I have money for the taxi that is waiting outside?" Papa said, "Certainly, where have you come from?" Roberto said, "Naples," which was a hundred and fifty miles away—and Papa laughed and gave him the money.

Roberto always enjoyed a very rich life-style. He was mad about racing cars and became a passionate driver. Then his father died at an early age and the children, who had never been given a single instruction in their life as to how to *make* money, went on spending it until it was practically all gone.

Once upon a time there'd been this huge house just off the Via

Veneto with carriages and servants and guests at every meal, and Mama Rossellini not knowing half the people there at breakfast, lunch, or dinner. Roberto was absolutely the same, and at Santa Marinella very often I didn't know who everybody was. Mama used to say to me, "You do very well. Sometimes I just couldn't stand it, and I'd run back home to Venice to my mother."

Oh, she was very sweet, Roberto's mother, and a great help to me. She was a practicing and devout Catholic who went to church every Sunday, and said her prayers every morning and every night. When Roberto was a small boy, he became very ill and had to have a dangerous operation; he had pleurisy. She was quite a young woman, about twenty-eight years old, and she went to the church and she made a vow that if Roberto got well, she would wear black for the rest of her life. He did get well and she wore black for the rest of her life.

She believed absolutely in the power of God and the Church. When Roberto and RKO had their great row which started on Stromboli with Roberto holding some of the film back, and went on with Roberto suing them about the money and the profits and the way they ruined the film by editing it so badly, she tried to help him in the only way she knew. She went to church and made another vow that she'd never eat fruit again if Roberto won. And she loved fruit. We told her that she'd better forget it and eat some fruit when she felt like it, because we were pretty sure that RKO was going to win, and that was the way it turned out. So at least Mama could go on eating fruit.

She was the one who said to me, "I do hope you're going to let the children become Catholics, because they're living and will be brought up in a Catholic country." I saw the sense in that, and for her sake I said, "Yes." Not that Roberto exerted the slightest pressure. But I saw no reason why I should insist on the children becoming Lutherans or Episcopalians when our home was Catholic Italy. I've never had any strong feelings about different religions. Roberto had no great feelings about religion either. I remember in Holy Year he was trying to get the Ferrari through crowds of people in the narrow streets and getting very annoyed and I asked, "What's going on?" "Oh, they're probably making another of those damned saints," he said. That made me laugh. He had a sort of practical realism toward religion: many of his closest friends were priests and monks; he admired them, and liked to be with them and talk to them, and he never looked down at or ridiculed religion in any way.

He believed in "reason—reason. I admire people who have the *will* to believe in miracles," he said. "That's already a religion in itself."

Eventually we lived in the big ten-room apartment on the Viale Bruno Buozi in Rome in the winter and out at Santa Marinella on the coast in the summer. I didn't have all that much to do, for the household went on by itself because the place was full of servants. I didn't have to worry about buying the food or cooking it. I didn't have to do any cleaning or making beds or anything like that, but I went around scrubbing things they didn't see, because having Swedish eyes I saw more dirt and dust than they did.

Roberto, as always, went on living like a millionaire. He sold this film right and that film right, he raised money here, and spent it there. Fiorella told me once about some banker he'd sat across from at dinner; Roberto had looked across at him with his hypnotic eyes and at the end of dinner had managed to secure a loan of twenty million lire for some project or other. The banker forever afterwards refused to sit anywhere near Roberto: he was certain he'd been hypnotized.

Santa Marinella had a huge garden shaded with palms and pines. There were long verandas for escape from the sun, usually four or five cars in the garages, and dogs and chickens and servants everywhere. And never-ending guests. There was a railway line which ran along the coast at the back too, and all the passengers would crowd to one side to wave and shout to us as they roared past. We were part of the tourist scene, and we'd wave back.

I don't know how Roberto managed to handle it all; he was always so generous to everybody. I'd go to Roberto every Monday morning and get the household money. Perhaps I'd say, "And I need a new pair of shoes." He'd say, "Well, don't get *one* pair, get *six* pairs, it will save time in the long run."

He was very generous when he had money, but if he didn't have any money he was just as generous. He would give away the shirt off his back. The trouble was he'd give away the shirts off everybody else's back too.

That was a strange contradictory thing about him. He adored the working classes, made most of his pictures about the working *people*, but when it came to paying little bills, and doing for little people what the little people really needed, there was no hurry. Plenty of time. And what stirred me up was that they didn't *want* to do anything about it. I would say to some of our small creditors, "Why don't you send him the bill? Why don't you sue him? If I were you, I'd sue him for not paying this." "Oh, but I couldn't do that to the *Commendatore* Rossellini."

Roberto would get angry when he was called "*Commendatore.*" "I'm *not* a *Commendatore,*" he'd say. "But you deserve it, *Commendatore,* you deserve to be one." What's the answer to that? You couldn't send the "*Commendatore*" a bill. They would rather starve than send the "*Commendatore*" a bill. I'd get so mad. I'd run around and try to get their bills paid, all these people who depended on him.

And of course there *was* something in Roberto's nature which made you grateful. If he made a gentle gesture toward you, if he looked at you in *that* way after you'd said something funny, and he too thought it funny, you felt as if you'd won an Oscar. Most of the time he exuded such warmth that people just fell apart.

But he could be so aggravating that it was unbelievable. Take the Arthur Rubinsteins, for example. Back in California when I was with Petter and we were living at Benedict Canyon Drive, the Rubinsteins were our next-door neighbors. Pia and I were terribly impressed. We used to stand quietly behind the hedge and listen to him practicing. Then we got to know them and Petter and I were invited to dinner. I was living in Rome with Roberto, Arthur Rubinstein arrived to give a concert. I went to the concert, and afterwards went backstage, and he and his wife seemed very pleased to see me again. So I was bold enough to say, "Would you like to have supper with us at home one night?" To my surprise, they said they'd love it.

"Oh yes," they said, "we're so tired of these big banquets every night. It would be great."

"Good, good. Roberto's brother, Renzo, is a composer. I'll invite him and his wife along too."

"Great, great."

So I told Roberto and he loved the idea. I did my best with the dinner. Renzo and his wife arrived. Arthur Rubinstein and his wife arrived. And Roberto did not arrive. So we had one drink, and we had two drinks; at the third drink I got very nervous, and called the studio, and Roberto said, "Yes, what is it?"

"Have you forgotten that the world-famous pianist Arthur Rubinstein and his wife are here for dinner? We are waiting, and we're on the third martini, and you must come home."

"Home!" snorted Roberto. "I'm busy. I'm cutting the picture. I'll come as soon as I can."

Met by Roberto Rossellini as she arrives in Rome. (WIDE WORLD PHOTOS)

In a cafe in Capri. (D'ELIA)

With octopus and Mario Sponza in *Stromboli.* (ROD TOLMIE FOR RKO RADIO PICTURES, INC.)

Mario Vitale as her Sicilian husband in *Stromboli.* (RKO RADIO PICTURES)

The volcanic island of Stromboli. (RKO RADIO PICTURES)

Roberto Rossellini in his skin-diving equipment.
(DAVID SEYMOUR/MAGNUM PHOTOS, INC.)

The first day on the new
film. (©KING FEATURES
SYNDICATE, INC.)

Ingrid and Robertino.
(©KING FEATURES
SYNDICATE, INC.)

Ingrid and Roberto with their twin daughters, Ingrid and Isabella.

Two basketsful.
(DAVID SEYMOUR/MAGNUM PHOTOS, INC.)

Italy, 1967. (DAVID SEYMOUR/MAGNUM PHOTOS, INC.)

Irene Selznick in Rex Harrison's Jeep. Ingrid holds Robertino.
(PUBLIFOTO–SANTA MARGHERITA LIGURE)

With George Sanders in *Journey to Italy*. (TITANUS–ROBERTO ROSSELLINI)

Journey to Italy. The museum in Naples. (BBC HULTON PICTURE LIBRARY)

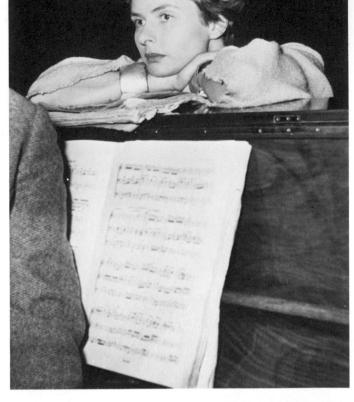

Ingrid in rehearsal for *Joan of Arc at the Stake.* (VESPASIANI)

Joan of Arc at the Stake. Ingrid with writer Paul Claudel, choreographer Serge Lifar, composer Arthur Honegger, and Roberto at the Paris Opera House.

Joan at the Stake. (DAVID SEYMOUR/MAGNUM PHOTOS, INC.)

Family group.
(FLERTZMAN–ERICSSON)

With Mathias Wiemann
in *Fear*. (LARS LOOSCHEN)

With Gregory Peck at Santa
Marinella. (DAVID SEYMOUR/
MAGNUM PHOTOS, INC.)

Jean Renoir, producer,
director, and writer of *Elena
et les Hommes*, greets Ingrid and
her children. (MARCEL FOURNES)

Ingrid in *Paris Does Strange Things. (Elena et les Hommes).* (WARNER BROS.)

Ingrid in Stockholm,
showing her son his
grandfather's
photographic shop.

Roberto Rossellini
in India filming the
monkey sequence that
so affected Ingrid.
(TONTI)

With Yul Brynner in *Anastasia*, for which she won her second Oscar.
(20TH CENTURY-FOX)

The Alvin gang greets Ingrid on her first return to New York.
Warren Thomas, center.

Anatole Litvak, director of *Anastasia*, and his star celebrate the New York Film Critics
Award at Sardi's. (UNITED PRESS INTERNATIONAL PHOTO)

I went back, trying to look like a hostess who's got everything under control, and I said, "Roberto's a bit delayed. Shall we go in and start, and he'll catch up with us?"

We trooped into the dining room, and we got through the prosciutto and melon. We were into the spaghetti, and I was sitting there looking at the empty seat. . . . So I called again, and said, "Look we're already at the table. Forget the movie. This is *Arthur Ru-bin-stein.* You can't do this to such a famous man who's come here on his one free evening, and is looking forward to meeting you."

"All right, all right, I'll come as soon as I can." We went on sitting at the table, and we ate the main course and the sweet, and the conversation was getting thinner and thinner. I didn't know what to talk about any more. And they kept saying politely, "I wonder what's keeping Roberto." I made futile excuses . . . this dubbing . . . so important . . . delays at the studio—and it was getting awfully sticky at that table. We left the table and we were going into the living room for coffee. Just then, we saw Roberto come in; he crossed the hall and went straight up into the bedroom.

I was so relieved. "Here he is, at last. . . . Let's go and have coffee." So we had coffee . . . and no Roberto. . . . At last I said, "I'll just go and see. . . ."

He'd gone to bed. "I have a headache," he said, "don't disturb me."

I said, "I'm going to die. I cannot go back now, after dinner and tell them you've gone to bed with a headache!"

"Well, don't tell them anything. Tell them I didn't come home."

"But I told them you came home. They saw you come home."

"I'm ill. Tell them I'm ill."

I went back, and any acting ability I ever possessed was now drained. I said, "I'm terribly sorry, but he isn't feeling well."

"Oh," they said sympathetically, "that's too bad. We *are* sorry."

I was sitting there, knowing that my lies must now be showing very plainly on my face, and then, suddenly, the double doors to the living room were pushed wide apart, and there stood Roberto —penitent—his arms stretched wide for the embrace.

"Maestro!" he cried.

He threw his arms round Rubinstein, and Rubinstein did the same thing. They just fell into each other's arms, and they sat until four in the morning never pausing for breath; they adored each other, I couldn't tear them apart. . . . I thought I was going to have a heart attack. . . . I thought I might even *enjoy* a heart attack. . . .

Then there was that never-to-be-forgotten time, the second time that Hedda Hopper paid us a visit. She wanted to come out and see us at Santa Marinella. I discussed this with Roberto. I said, "It could stop the papers from writing how unhappy I am, and how awful everything is, and what a beast you are, and how you have destroyed my career. She can see what a marvelous home life we have, and what a lovely place it is in the country and on the beach, and she can meet the children. We'll give her a very good meal with fresh sea food. . . ."

"Okay," said Roberto, "if you think it will do any good."

"But you must be nice to her," I said, "and talk to her of course. You must show what a charming person you are."

"Sure, sure, I'll talk to her."

He sent his Rolls-Royce to pick her up, and she arrived. Roberto took one look at her and disliked her immediately. Completely. So he decided not to open his mouth. He sat and looked at the sea as if there were something enormously interesting out on the horizon. She was talking to me, and then she tried to talk to him but all his answers were, "Hmm? I didn't understand the question." Or, "I don't know," and back to looking at the sea. Then she'd try another question. "What? . . . I don't talk about those things." "What? . . . I don't know." Whatever she tried—questions about the marriage, the situation between the two of us, were we hurt? Were we bitter? Would we ever go back to America?—he never heard the question; he didn't answer it; he didn't know what she was talking about. And finally *he* left.

I was stuck with her alone. She went away and she wrote a very nasty article, because she started in about how unhappy I was, how I cried, how I longed to be back in America, and the last thing she saw as she drove away was "grieving Ingrid" behind the curtain. This wasn't in the slightest bit true. I was outside bawling out Roberto for not having played his part well enough. And he simply said, "I don't talk to women like that. I didn't know she was such a bitch."

"I did warn you, didn't I?" I said. "I did say we should do this to get a nice article in America. Now you've made it worse."

"I don't care," he said, "what do I care what she thinks or what she writes?"

So that was that.

Chapter 18

By the middle of 1950, I had made an important discovery. I had to go back into films because we needed the money. I had to go out to work and Roberto had to work with me because he just couldn't go out and find another *Open City*. People criticized him about my retirement from films: "Are you crazy? You're like a man with a big beefsteak in front of you"—that was me—"and you've lost your teeth. But you can raise all the money in the world if you and Ingrid work together."

———— • ————

As the long hot months of Holy Year ebbed away, Ingrid had slipped from her position of Number One at the box office into something approaching "Box-Office Disaster." She was setting a record for the number of companies she helped put out of business. *Arch of Triumph* failed. After *Joan of Arc*, Enterprise Studios went into liquidation. Sierra Pictures, pioneered by Walter Wanger and Victor Fleming, associated with Ingrid's own company, EN, folded. Transatlantic Pictures, formed specially to back *Under Capricorn*, slid quietly under the waves. And certainly no one in the Rossellini entourage was going to make a fortune out of *Stromboli*.

Early in 1950, she had written to her agents, MCA, saying that she had no need for an American agent as she had no intention of visiting or working in America in the near future, and therefore was not renewing her contract. She added, "Nobody at RKO has had the courtesy to inform me or Mr. Rossellini about their opinion of *Stromboli,* but through the grapevine we hear that they think the film great and at the same time they are cutting and changing and chopping it up to a fine 'Grade A' RKO hamburger. . . ."

When *Stromboli* finally opened in New York in the edited version totally disowned by Roberto Rossellini, *The New York Times* called it ". . . incredibly feeble, inarticulate, uninspiring, and painfully banal." The *New York Herald Tribune's* opinion was that ". . . there is no depth to Ingrid Bergman's performance, no vitality in Roberto Rossellini's direction. There is neither sense nor sensation to be found in it. *Stromboli* profits only from notoriety: as a film drama it is a waste of talent and a waste of time."

Variety reported that American exhibitors had declared that they would screen *Stromboli* in the movie theaters, and if it *made* money they would continue to show it. But if the picture did not make money they would ban it "upon grounds of morality."

Ingrid said to Roberto, "This world is not to be believed."

Still, Ingrid's prime concern at this time was not her image as a film star but her baby son and Pia. She knew that in the eyes of the world she had abandoned Pia—a judgment she would not accept. But she was desperately anxious to end Pia's unhappiness. This was going to be very difficult as Petter was suing her for an American divorce, so the newspaper stories would continue.

Letters from Peter Wegner, a Czech refugee who had lived with Petter and Ingrid as Petter's medical protégé, did not help Ingrid's conscience:

He told her how beautiful the house looked, that the flowers were blossoming, the dill growing. He enclosed pictures of Pia to show how she had changed in the past months. He said that she looked happy and did not speak about what was happening, but that she was filled with "underground emotions" and reserve. One night, after having spent a happy day swimming and bicycling with the Vernons on Catalina, she had started to cry and asked them why she could not be doing those same things with "pappi and mammi."

Some weeks later Wegner wrote saying he simply could not send her the letter Pia had just written because Pia was so bitter at the continued newspaper stories, and had said so many nasty things about Ingrid.

Ingrid did her best to keep calm in her response to him:

I wish I could explain to you my feelings in regard to Pia. I am NOT afraid of her bitterness or hard words against me. I am not even afraid of her hatred. It is Pia, and she is my daughter. There is nothing concerning her, and her reactions, that I cannot take. You understand, you don't have to protect me from what she writes me. If I was allowed to know what goes on in Pia's mind maybe I could help her. Her "bitter" letter that you did not mail was maybe the first connection Pia and I would have had; maybe we could have begun to talk like "grown-ups." . . .

You write now "You who were so sensitive to everybody's opinion are now so indifferent." Yes, I am that, and I thank God who slowly dressed me in a heavy skin, otherwise I would now be dead. I have enough enemies who send me every unpleasant thing the newspapers have said all over the world. Just now came another batch of clippings. . . . I don't know if my skin is heavy enough, but in time I am sure God will give me a fur coat.

There is, however, another obstacle in any divorce matter: the child. I shall try and be as generous as any mother could. But it is useless to try and take her away from me. I have never thought of taking her from her father. He should feel the same about me. If he doesn't it will only hurt him in the long run. A child will not forget her mother. Whatever that mother has done, she is the MOTHER. I have great faith that all this misery will end and end well. Without that hope it would be hard to go through these days. When it has ended we will have gone through hell, but perhaps that was what we needed.

If you can manage to make Pia write to me, you know I am grateful. But don't force her. Let the time pass; maybe she only suffers by inventing letters to me. Let her play and dance and the day will come when she WANTS to write to me.

My best wishes to you. I hope that your work is going well and I hope you don't feel that also you would have been better off without me.

She had asked, to no avail, that Petter allow Pia to come to Italy for a holiday that summer. Ingrid wrote:

Naturally we will discuss how and when Pia can come. I would sure hate to have her while I was working. This time I shall be WITH her. When the great heat comes to Rome I have to take the baby up to the mountains. Then I can have her. We are going to talk about it and you ought to understand that I will do only the very very best for her. If Pia comes now or in ten years, we will always have the newspaper men chasing us, but this is the easiest place to escape.

If I hear of anybody leaving Hollywood to come to Italy I'll ask you to give them a few things to bring back to me. The paintings of Papa and Mama I have missed so much, and I love Pia's. Someday I will ask you for all those awards. I have a lot of empty shelves. I'd also like to keep the Madonna Father Donceur gave me. But it can wait like the clothes and the other personal junk I have in my drawers. The only thing that will be a problem is our 16-mm film. I guess you will let me borrow it sometimes to let me see what I looked like in my youth!

--- • ---

Of course the newspaper men and photographers did keep after us all the time. We'd be sitting in a restaurant, and someone would pass behind Roberto and whisper a remark I couldn't understand. You see, it's so easy to provoke a quarrel in Italian. And Roberto was very easily provoked. Every photographer knew that. It was much more interesting to take a photograph of him when he was angry—yelling and screaming—instead of just eating dinner with me in a restaurant.

Some of the letters from America were impossible to answer. How could I do this to *them*? *They* had set me on a pedestal, put me up as an example to *their* daughters. Now, what were they going to tell their daughters? I fall in love with an Italian and they don't know what to tell their daughters. I didn't think I should take all the responsibility. It was a climate of such hysteria, so unbalanced.

Somebody who tried to cheer me up said it was because I was so loved, a love which had so quickly turned to hate. Perhaps it was Ruth. She wrote me some very wise letters.

Ingrid dear . . . in each letter you upset yourself about all the publicity. . . . I know it has been bad but it isn't good for you to mull it over so. . . . Ingrid dear, people fall out of love as they fall in love. The best treatment is to honestly put yourself in the other person's place . . . and being an actress it should be easier for you. . . . It isn't that I am saying that you should change anything . . . except your attitude . . . but I can tell you to look at it with your usual fairness, clarity and broadness . . . and you will be happier about the whole thing.

You ask me how Petter behaves. . . . I can tell you; very well . . . he is quieter . . . settled and very busy with his work. . . . I have seen him a few times . . . and then he talked chiefly about Pia . . . and he does *not* talk about anything I might believe or disbelieve. He knows how I feel about you and he respects that. . . .

Ingrid dear . . . I know it is hard going right now but it will straighten out. One day leads into another and in that way we can meet anything.

———— • ————

Roberto and Ingrid visited Venice for the film festival. While the Swedish press was headlining its views that the scandal was a blot on the national flag, both *Stromboli* and the first showing of Roberto's *Flowers of St. Francis*—which he had been making while Ingrid was producing her son—were loudly applauded. They heard, also, that Petter was going ahead with his divorce petition.

From Santa Marinella on October 6, 1950, Ingrid wrote to Petter with Pia still uppermost in her mind:

I think you can just as well know that however you try to explain what are or are not my rights to Pia, I know as well as you that I cannot lose her. She is too old to forget me. The more you try to keep us apart the more she will desire to see me and be with me. I have my rights on paper just as you have yours. But I guess that can be read as you do, upside down or something like that. It doesn't matter, Petter. In the long run you will only lose the child you try to take. It has been proved again and again. And I have your letters. Whenever she wants to she can read the whole story. You say she is independent and intelligent, and "can trace the truth and motives behind words and actions." That's very good and I am happy for that.

On November 1, 1950, in a Los Angeles court, Petter Lindstrom's divorce from Ingrid Bergman was granted. Asked if he had any bitterness in his heart regarding Ingrid, he answered, "No, I have no bitterness. I feel sorry for the awkward predicament she has placed herself in. I think she has many good qualities besides being very beautiful."

Petter also said: "I certainly was proud of her successes and was not jealous of her companions. She participated in about nine movies in Sweden and one in Germany, certainly without any interference from her husband. During all her film work in Hollywood I never set foot on a movie set except twice for a few minutes when I had to leave a message. From 1943 to 1950 she probably did not spend more than three to six consecutive months at our house in California. She had all the freedom to visit and associate with anyone she wanted. She did not spend much time with her daughter since I took care of Pia's needs and schooling and I regularly attended sessions at school and meetings of the Parent-Teachers Association."

As for allowing Pia to see her mother, he said flatly, "I would be glad to take Pia to Europe to see her mother. But I have no intention of taking my daughter to Italy." He also added that boats sailed both ways between Europe and America, and it was quite possible for Ingrid to catch one from Europe.

The findings of the court regarding Pia were simple. She would stay in California under the custody of the father and receive her education there. Only in the United States could Ingrid have Pia for one-half of her school vacation while Petter had her for the other half. It was a ruling that did not satisfy Ingrid, but one that, for the time being, she could do little about.

She wrote to Petter: "I hear you are selling our house in California. What a pity. But it is possibly the best for you even though you like it and the steambath. To try and live a new life against *our* surroundings must be very trying. . . ."

Her lawyers were conferring with Petter's about property settlements and "accounting of funds," a process which was not helped by the fact that John Vernon, who had handled Ingrid's financial affairs since before Ingrid's departure to Italy, had suddenly disappeared. He was finally discovered in a San Francisco hospital suffering from a nervous breakdown and amnesia. Not long afterwards, Greg Bautzer's office uncovered an unaccounted-for balance of some eighty thousand dollars in John Vernon's name in an obscure Los Angeles bank. But it was many months before it was reported that a man identified as John Vernon had committed suicide in a downtown hotel—leaving a bitter note.

Ingrid pressed Petter by letter and telephone to arrange a meeting between her and Pia, but it was July 1951 before he felt he could take time off from his medical duties to take a holiday in Sweden. After more telephone calls and cables, he agreed that if Ingrid felt she could not come to Sweden, he would arrange to bring Pia to London so that they could meet there.

But there were still difficulties to be resolved. Pia had been part of the recent divorce settlement. For her to be allowed to leave the United States meant that application had to be made to the relevant court. Judicial permission was also necessary to withdraw two thousand dollars from the trust fund set up for her by Petter and Ingrid to pay her expenses. The judges who heard the application asked whether, if it was granted, there was any chance of the California courts losing jurisdiction over the child's custody. The lawyer acting for Petter Lindstrom replied that "special precautions would be taken to prevent anything happening, and that Petter Lindstrom would be accompanying his daughter to both Sweden and England."

It was an inauspicious beginning. The visit was doomed from the outset.

———— • ————

Petter said I was not allowed any publicity and the press must know nothing whatsoever about the visit. That would be very difficult, and even more difficult for me, unobserved, to leave Italy, cross Europe, and arrive in London. But my good friends Sydney Bernstein, who had produced *Under Capricorn,* and Ann Todd and David Lean whom we'd met in Rome, and who were now married, agreed to help us. I took a train from Rome to the ferryboat in France. On the cross-channel steamer I sat all muffled up in a private cabin after asking the captain not to reveal that I was aboard. He kept my secret. Sydney Bernstein met me at Dover with his car and rushed me straight up to Ann and David's house in Ilchester Place, London. Petter arrived a little later with Pia.

It was two years since we had seen each other, and we were both a little shy, but we were both very happy. But that happiness did not last very long.

————————— • —————————

David Lean offered his account of what happened at that meeting in an affidafit for the visitation-rights hearing in California the following year:

> Mrs. Rossellini, Dr. Lindstrom, Pia Lindstrom, Mrs. Lean and I all had dinner at our house that evening, and we had made arrangements for Mrs. Rossellini and her daughter to occupy one of our bedrooms for the night. Dr. Lindstrom asked me whether there was a bedroom for him since he was not going to let Pia sleep alone with Mrs. Rossellini. I advised Dr. Lindstrom that we did not have a bedroom for him and I asked him if there was anything that Mrs. Lean and I could do that would set his mind at rest and permit him to leave Pia with Mrs. Rossellini in our house. Dr. Lindstrom told me that his chief worry was that if he left the house he might not be admitted again. He explained to me that a situation could be created by protracted litigation in England whereby he could be deprived temporarily of Pia's custody while the litigation was in progress. In order to alleviate his fears I asked him whether he would be willing to leave our house for the night if I gave him the key to the front door. Dr. Lindstrom accepted the key and thereupon agreed to let Pia stay with her mother for the night.
>
> Some time after we had gone to bed, although the exact time is unknown to me, Dr. Lindstrom re-entered the house and at seven o'clock in the morning the cook found him sitting in the hall which has a view of the stairs and the front door.
>
> At approximately seven thirty A.M. I came downstairs and found Dr. Lindstrom in the hall. I asked him if he would come into the sitting room and have some breakfast sent in to him. Dr. Lindstrom replied that he wished to remain in the hall.

Petter was not feeling charitable toward Ingrid or to any of her friends. He felt that there was a very real risk of Pia's being spirited off to Italy. Furthermore, he had been on the brink of being offered a professorship in neurosurgery and had been turned down by the Dean because of the scandal associated with his name.

An affidavit from Ann Todd declared:

> At the request of Mrs. Roberto Rossellini on approximately the 24th day of July 1951 I interceded with Dr. Petter Lindstrom to permit Pia Lindstrom to visit her mother again or to allow her mother to take Pia to see the film *Alice in Wonderland*.
>
> Dr. Lindstrom finally granted permission after considerable insistence by me that there would be no "tricks" and that if Dr. Lindstrom permitted Pia to go to the film with her mother Pia would be returned to him. This permission was granted only upon condition that Pia and Mrs. Rossellini should be accompanied by my daughter, my secretary and myself, together with a friend of Pia's who had just arrived in London.
>
> On the following day we all had lunch and then saw the film and after the film we all went to our home at No. 1 Ilchester Place, London, and within a few minutes Dr. Lindstrom arrived to take Pia away announcing that he had a taxi waiting outside.

———— • ————

It was then I asked him if I could be alone with Pia. Petter said, "All right, we'll drive out to Sydney Bernstein's place in the country; you can be alone with her there." We went down into Kent and Sydney was there with his wife and friends and obviously they knew something was up, but they were very kind and left us alone. There was a television in one room, so we put Pia in to watch it, and Petter said, "You can go into the television room and be alone with Pia; and I'll be in this room next door."

I said, "But Pia will find this so very strange."

I wanted to make everything as natural as possible for Pia so that she wouldn't get frightened. But we both sat there watching television, and Petter sat in the next room, and eventually I went in and said, "It's so silly, you sitting in here." And in a minute or two he came in, and came up behind me, and said to me quietly, "I'm going to take Pia away with me. Say good-bye to her. I've decided we're leaving."

I said, "But I was promised a week with her. One week after two years, that's not much."

"Well, I've changed my mind."

"But you can't do this. Please let's go out and discuss this in the corridor, not in front of Pia."

She was so absorbed in the television I don't think she heard us, so we went outside into the corridor. I remember it so well, my saying, "But I've only had her for two days in the city, and one day down here, and you're taking her away. Please, you can't."

"I've changed my mind. I want to go to Sweden. I told you in the first place to come to Sweden."

"How could I come to Sweden, to Stöde and meet your father? It would be a tragedy for him. I can't handle that. I can't cope with it." I was beginning to cry, and I didn't want to cry because I knew that would upset Pia. Then Petter began to say I'd ruined his life, that he should have had a professorship long ago but was stopped in mid-career by all the scandal. And all the things he'd done for me, and all the terrible things I'd done to him. All the time I was saying, "Please stop, please let's not upset Pia."

So we all drove back to London, and Pia and Petter stayed at a hotel in Mayfair; I stayed at one in Half Moon Street close by so I could visit them. Petter doesn't remember any part of this visit the way I do. It was all so impossible. I remember the last time I saw Pia. She was trying to be so nice and light as if nothing had happened, trying to cover up what she really felt, and I was trying to cover up what I really felt. I kissed her and said, "We'll meet again soon." And I remember staring at her, thinking it would be soon, but it was six long years before we did meet again.

It was all so unnecessary. I keep telling everybody now who gets a divorce, "Please stay friendly. Don't take it out on the children. You can part, but don't make the children go on suffering because of the arguments."

———— • ————

Ingrid wrote to Irene Selznick from Santa Marinella on September 10, 1951:

The child was wonderful. So calm about it all. So serene. She talks about Roberto and the baby without any strain. It all seems natural and simple when you listen to her. She loves me (I pray) but she loves maybe her father more because she has to take care of him. And she is beautiful. I was moved to tears when I saw how sweet she was. She has nothing against coming here, in fact she would love to, but she understands that it hurts Petter, so she has asked me to be patient!

———————— • ————————

All through those years I wrote Pia letter after letter, without knowing whether she received them or not. I kept copies of all of them so that perhaps one day she could get them and understand; letters about what life was like, and about Robertino and the twins.

I would hear from her sporadically. In December she wrote me about her Christmas party at school, that she bought a new dress, that she was reading *A Christmas Carol* to her father, and that Walter Wanger had shot the man he thought was his wife's lover!

Sometimes her letters to me were accusing, which I understood.

In February 1952, she thanked me for a sweater I sent her, but then accused me of giving inaccurate information and even a personal letter to *Look* magazine. She said the article made it sound as though it were all her father's fault and reminded me that I was the one who left, not he. She admonished me: "Think of what they say in school." But by Mother's Day Pia had apparently got over what they said in school. In a card she wrote me that her bird had four eggs and her kittens were almost cats.

———————— • ————————

In the cold autumn of 1951, Roberto, with the backing of a Ponti-De Laurentiis production, had started to make *Europa '51*, entitled in some countries *The Greatest Love*. It told the story of Irene, played by Ingrid, and George, by Alexander Knox, two Americans living in Rome whose young son kills himself because he believes his mother neither loves nor understands him. The *New York Herald Tribune* called it a brave try. Bosley Crowther in *The New York Times* observed that it was notable that Ingrid had grown older very gracefully, with more beauty in "her eternally interesting face." But the picture did nothing to advance her acting career. And Ingrid knew she was pregnant again.

———————— • ————————

We were in such a hurry to get through that movie *before* it showed. And then, of course, I grew terribly big. Pia was now thirteen, Robertino two, and having had two children before, I didn't understand why I looked like an elephant. I went to the doctors and they X-rayed me because they couldn't hear two hearts; they thought the child was maybe misplaced.

I sat and waited and the doctor came out with a smile up around his ears so I knew nothing was wrong. I asked, "How many?" He told me he thought only two; he had seen four feet and four hands but they were behind each other so he could only hear one heart.

I just couldn't wait to get home. I telephoned from the hospital and told Roberto. And he telephoned *all Rome*, he was so proud of what he had done—two at a time. My first reaction was worry: how in the world did you take care of two babies at the same time?

I got so big I couldn't sleep at all, and I couldn't get into any clothes. Finally I couldn't eat, so eventually I spent the last month in the hospital. They fed me intravenously, and I was exercising on the roof, walking around in a big robe. The press was down below keeping watch and I kept waving to them. They could only photograph my face with a telephoto lens as I peered over and laughed at them. They shouted up, "When?" And I said, "I hope soon, because I'm tired of this."

Anyway they never *did* come, and the doctors began to get very worried because twins should come ahead of time. Mine were now *beyond* the time that they were supposed to come. So they wanted to induce the birth. I called Roberto—he was working on location —and I said, "How can we allow this? We choose their birthday. That is not right. All the stars, the astrological signs, the moon, and the constellations will be confused. Your birthday is supposed to have some meaning in the scheme of things, isn't it? Their horoscopes will never be right if *I* decide what day they come. I want to wait."

Roberto agreed with me, but then the doctors got on to Roberto and convinced him—to hell with the constellations. It was just

getting too dangerous. So he talked to me and I saw the sense in
that. Came the morning, the doctor arrived with his injection, and
I said, "Let me ring Roberto."

"It's the eighteenth of June," I said. "Do you think that's a good
day?"

"Eighteenth of June? Sure that's a good day. Go ahead."

———————— • ————————

While Ingrid was waiting to have her twins in the hospital, another
drama was taking place on the other side of the world: the visitation
rights fight over Pia. The London episode with Pia had distressed
Ingrid so much that she had decided she must regularize her position
in law. She instructed Greg Bautzer to petition the courts to allow
Pia to visit Italy during her holidays in 1952 and stay at Santa
Marinella. To Ingrid, it seemed a simple, normal, maternal request.
To Petter, it appeared a possible first step to losing Pia altogether.
He did not trust Roberto. How would he ever get Pia back once she
set foot in Italy? He opposed the petition. The case was heard in July,
1952, before a woman judge, Mildred T. Lillie.

The verdict turned entirely on Pia's own reactions. Gregson
Bautzer questioned Pia on some of them:

"When you told your mother that you loved her and missed her
when you saw her in England last summer, you said it only to be
polite?"

"I don't believe I said I missed her. I—I guess I did. We saw each
other several days. Mother asked me, 'Are you happy?' "

"Didn't you say you had missed her and would like to see her?"

"I don't believe I really ever said that. She never really asked me,
'Do you miss me?' And I never said, 'Yes, I do.' Even if she did, I
couldn't very well say, 'No, I didn't love her.' "

"Have you ever written your mother letters in which you told her
that you loved her?"

"I always sign them 'Love Pia.' "

"And does that express the way you feel about her?"

"No, it's just the way I end the letter."

"Miss Lindstrom, you do understand what this case is all about
as to what your mother seeks to do?"

"Yes. She wants me to come to Italy. And I don't want to go to
Italy."

"But you must realize, do you not, that your mother is not asking
you to come and live with her?"

"But I just saw her last summer."

"But you realize, do you not, that your mother is not making a request of this court, or of you, to live with her?"

"Yes."

"Now, I take it when you signed your letter, 'Love Pia,' you didn't actually love her?"

"I don't love my mother. I like her."

"And you don't miss her?"

"No."

"And you don't have any desire to see her?"

"No. I would rather live with my father."

"You love your father very much, don't you, Miss Lindstrom?"

"Yes."

"You met Mr. Rossellini when he was living in your house?"

"Yes."

"Did you have any conversations with Mr. Rossellini at that time?"

"Well, he lived in our house so I guess I talked to him, but I don't remember anything we talked about."

"Did you find him to be a considerate, gentlemanly man?"

"I don't remember. I didn't find him anything."

"During the times you saw him, did you observe anything about him that you objected to?"

"Well I didn't eat with him. I ate by myself, I went to bed earlier than he did, so I didn't observe much."

"But during the times you did see him, you didn't dislike him?"

"I didn't like him, I didn't dislike him."

"What generally has your father said, and what have you said about Mr. Rossellini?"

"I don't remember what we discussed. We discussed that he used to stand in front of the fireplace and tell us how religious he was. He borrowed money from my father and then bought presents for me."

Judge Lillie intervened to ask:

"Do you feel that your mother doesn't care about you now?"

"Well I don't think she cares about me too much."

"Why do you say that?"

"Well she didn't seem very interested in me when she left. It was only after she left and got married and had children that she suddenly decided she wanted me."

Gregson Bautzer returned to the questioning:

"Miss Lindstrom, whether or not you know your mother very well or whether you will have the opportunity in the future to know her well, do you love your mother?"

"No, not very much. I mean I have seen her enough, and I know I have met her, but I haven't seen her enough to really love her. My father has mostly been taking care of me, I lived with my father mostly."

Judge Lillie summed up, deploring the world-wide publicity which had followed the case and considering the reactions of both Ingrid and Petter. She found them both at fault for their pride and selfishness. She censured Dr. Lindstrom for assuming that he had to do nothing more than required under the law unless the court ordered him to, and Miss Bergman for insisting on the rights she had "bought and bargained for." She also took into account Pia's unfavorable opinion of the defendant's husband, Roberto Rossellini. She added, "There is no obstacle under law, or court order, preventing Miss Bergman from exercising her right to visit Pia here if she so desires. Miss Bergman had gone to Italy voluntarily in 1949 and has since remained, and the record is silent as to when, if ever, she will return to the United States." There was a need for caution in ordering a child to visit a parent in a foreign country, particularly when the child was a minor and would be going against her will and against the will of the parent having custody of her. "Children are not chattels to be passed back and forwards between parents to satisfy their pride, convenience and desires at the expense of the welfare of the children."

Judge Lillie's verdict was that: "The court believes there should be a reconciliation between the child and the defendant as soon as feasible. At the present time it is not in the best interests of the minor child that she should be ordered by the court to leave her home in the United States and travel to Italy by July 15, 1952 to visit her mother. Therefore the motion of the defendant to require the child to be taken to Italy for a visit with her mother is denied."

Long-distance, Ingrid could not counter any of the evidence raised at the court hearing, so Roberto had planned to attend the session for her though he was furious that he could not just send an affidavit. Ingrid wrote from the hospital to Mollie Faustman, one of her oldest Swedish friends:

> Roberto has applied for a visa to go to the U.S. We couldn't see any other way out. In Washington they say there are no obstacles, but it will still take some

time to arrange. Petter said quickly that he wouldn't be *admitted*.

Of course Roberto won't be able to be there before the end of the court case. Petter's lawyer has refused adjournment—the case has already been delayed enough! Selznick and a lot of other friends have given testimony of our home and Roberto. Selznick talked about Roberto as if he had been a God—or at least Superman. Everybody has been extremely kind. Unfortunately the judge refused to allow Roberto to send affidavits from Italy or from friends here. She wanted him and any witness to appear in person. But for God's sake, he can't take half of Italy with him to Hollywood to testify that he does not take cocaine. In other words, your sweet, wonderful letter probably won't do much good. Still, I'll keep it and thank you with all my heart—we may need it one day. I do wish that Papa Lindstrom could read it.

Roberto has spent two million lire in ten days in telephone charges and telegrams. One telegram to the judge cost one thousand dollars!

I'm sorry I have so many sad things to report but my heart is full.

———————— • ————————

I wanted a girl very much because Roberto had had two sons previously with his first wife and one with me. So this had to be a little girl and the name I had chosen was Isabella. But now there was going to be a second baby and that name was not chosen because it might be a boy. So I was rolled into the delivery room and eventually Isabella arrived, and I told the doctor, "Go at once and tell Roberto he has a daughter." Then the doctor came back and said, "Yes, he is very happy." The doctor sat down on a little stool near me and said, "Ah, well, now we just have to wait for the next one." And I remember thinking, God Almighty, do I have to go through that *again!*

And then they said, "One more girl." Two baby girls! How wonderful! It was Roberto who chose her name: Isotta Ingrid. But from the beginning we called her Ingrid.

I was sad to know that Pia was not coming that summer because I missed her so much. It was a sort of agony of missing her, but

I listened to other people who came to see me who all said, "Wait. Wait. The children come back; they come back."

———————— • ————————

She wrote immediately to Pia to give her the news:

> Dearest big girl—Oh, now it's all over. Think, two babies in one sweep—but really it is a little difficult to believe. The babies are well and eat, sleep and scream just as they should. I didn't have too bad a time. When the first one was born it seemed so funny with all the doctors and nurses sitting down around me waiting for the second. It was like in the theater: intermission between the first and second acts. The two girls look completely unalike, and I think as they grow up they will prefer it that way, not always being compared and confused with each other.
>
> Did you get my telegram? You were the first one of course I wanted to tell. But as I hardly ever hear if you received what I send, I must ask you now and then.
>
> I saw a clipping of you on your graduation and you had *high heels*! I almost fell out of bed. And your mother doesn't wear high heels yet. I hope you'll send me a photo. Do you know you have never sent me a photo after England. I read Papa took pictures of you. Please send me one. Did you like the dress I sent? I made it bigger than the measurements we took in England, and you really look even bigger. Would you tell me one day, sweetie, Pia, if you received the flowers at school-graduation and also the letter I wrote on your confirmation day? There are some letters you'll be glad to have when you are big. I know because I had no mother at all, and when my mother's friends send me the letters she wrote to them I am so happy. That way I have learned to know my mother.
>
> How I wish you could see these little babies. I know you would love to know them when they are so tiny. Robin is already a big boy. That's why I wanted you to come this year. I suppose I have to have a new baby later on and hope you'll be with me then. I am awfully sorry you are not coming—I am sure you understand all that, and you must know that I understand all about you. I don't think

anybody needs to explain between us. What you said to the judge couldn't hurt me deep down in my heart, it hurts just on the surface for a time. Because a child can't hurt its mother, for that love is too big and protecting. But I must continue to fight for my right to have you in my home. There is nothing I hate so much as injustice and I'll fight until my last drop of strength. Lots of love and hope to hear from you soon.

P.S. What about the gold cross for your confirmation? Did you wear it with the medal?

In July Pia wrote that she had worn the cross at her confirmation, and told of moving to Pittsburgh. She wanted to stay in Pittsburgh that summer to get acquainted. She did not want to go to Italy. As she put it, they need not have a court case over it. She could have told Ingrid she didn't want to go that summer. But she kept her mother up-to-date on the animal population and all of her hobbies.

———————————— • ————————————

As I have said, now that I look back at it, I suppose I know I should and could have gone back to America in the first place to talk Petter into a divorce and then to see Pia. But no one will really understand the force and the fury of Roberto's will. Marta Cohn once said to me, "Of course you could have gone. You could have borrowed money, bought a plane ticket, and borrowed more money in America." Which was true. The point was, I wasn't capable of leaving against Roberto's wishes. Steal or borrow the money, yes, but what would have happened when I returned? Riots would have broken out. Of course I would have come back to him. I had three children in Italy. But Roberto never believed that. Somehow if I left him and went to America, it would have been a deep act of unfaithfulness, and I would never return . . . or when I did return it would be to a situation I had damaged irreparably.

———————————— • ————————————

Ingrid spent the summer of 1952 at Santa Marinella, and as a by-product of that period made one of the short sequences which made up the film *Siamo Donne (We, the Women)* concerning the loves, lives, and day-to-day problems of various famous actresses:

Ingrid, Anna Magnani, Alida Valli, and Isa Miranda among them.
Ingrid's part of the story concerned a vendetta waged by her against
a neighbor's cheeky hen with an appetite for Miss Bergman's beautiful roses.

In August there was a birthday letter from Pia telling of a needle-
work dish towel she had made and sent her mother and telling how
much she liked Pittsburgh despite the smoke—the kids were nicer
than in Beverly Hills.

With so much time to spare, Ingrid wrote to all her friends, but
more than anyone else she wrote to Pia. On August 25, 1952, she
filled two long pages asking Pia about her tennis, Spanish dancing,
politics, Pittsburgh, and all the pets. She finished:

> I love you an awful lot and I hope this winter will go very
> fast so summer will be here again and you with it! Now
> I'll go and jump in the sea—Splash!

On September 13:

> Darling dear daughter—another time I'll just say: D.D.D.
> Many happy returns. I hope you have the most wonderful
> birthday and of course that all your wishes come true. You
> are getting so old my sweetiepie, my little girl, so big. I
> must be pretty old myself to have such an old daughter.
> I remember that when I had reached my last teen year—
> 19, I felt so old and afraid to leave and become twenty. I
> remember I made a wish that I would never feel older than
> 19 and I believe my wish came true. Until this day I don't
> feel older than 19 despite my looks. I hope it will be the
> same when I have gray hair. On the 20th I'll be thinking
> of you all day and placing flowers in the frame of your
> picture and I and all your friends here will be blowing
> kisses to you. So if you feel a terrible draft you'll know
> what it is.
> You made me very happy with all the lovely presents
> for my birthday. The towel you have embroidered is so
> cute and far too nice to use. But I shall find an honor place
> on the wall somewhere. . . . Again all my love and much
> happiness.

October 27:

Dear silent Pia, I am waiting and waiting. I don't even know where you live except the hospital address. Couldn't you soon tell me where you live and also give me your phone number so that I could call you again. I haven't spoken to you for so long, this time I won't really know what to say. You know how it is when one never speaks, one has nothing to say because one has too much to say. Do you follow my funny reasoning? If I could speak to you every day I would have a million things to discuss. Now I will be overwhelmed by your voice and start to cry. Well, give me the number anyway! . . .

On New Year's Eve, 1952:

Dearest Pia, sweetheart. It's eleven o'clock New Year's Eve. We have all the family with children here and I have run away to my little studio to send you a written thought. All the time I have you in mind; no matter how many are around me makes no difference. In another hour I'll raise a glass of champagne to you and to my other children, to all the people I love, to the whole world, and I'll hope and pray for a good year, good for the world, good for you. . . . Do you remember when Papa and I used to wake you up at 12. Then you were bigger and stayed up with us. Now you are so big it's incredible. At midnight we'll all say, "To Pia." And I with all my love say, "To my darling daughter far away." Your Mama.

Rome, January 22, 1953:

It was wonderful to talk to you on the phone. I could have gone on and on it was such a good connection. But I was sad about what you said; but I'll wait for you, always, always, you know that. I can't help many of the things they write, Pia. I have told you that as long as I am Ingrid Bergman, I'll always have these things happen. You can't expect me not to be written about or photographed. Also you have no idea how many newspaper people I turn down every day who want to write. I'll try to be very careful and give them even less but I am unfortunately NEWS still and will be until I get so bad as an actress that no one ever talks of me again.

. . . I must tell you this too. I called off all my lawyers in California. You know I had three of them. But no one will move. Don't worry, my sweet little baby. I don't want to hurt you. I just want to have you with me once in a while. How can I do it? If you think it can be done, fine. The last lawyer that we found is such a nice person. He is finally what I wish I had all along. He is the father of four children and he is an understanding person. I asked him to stop in Pittsburgh on his way back from Italy. But he sent me a wire saying Papa couldn't see him this time. I wish he would one day. . . . But remember Pia I'll never do anything you don't want me to do. Why should I when I love you and think of you and want you to be happy? Why I fight so hard is, you see, because I think you would be happier if you knew my life here, if it wasn't just something that people tell you about, but something you can judge for yourself. And I would like you to know your half-brother and sisters only because I think it would make you very happy. You would go back to your Papa and Pittsburgh happier because you would feel us much closer and we would have so much more to write about until next time we see each other. . . .

Pia remembers these times quite clearly:

"I remember my father in regard to this early situation—this whole situation—as being just devastated. And it was a very sad thing to see what he went through; I mean, it was just awful for him to somehow maintain himself, going to work, and the hospital, and operating and being a dignified surgeon on the one hand and, on the other hand, reading all of this in the papers: the worst kind of gossip and salacious journalism, and innuendoes. It was a sort of soap opera. Your whole life becomes a joke, and that was particularly terrible because his profession was such a serious one. If he'd been in the theater or been a writer, maybe it would have been different, but if you're a brain surgeon you're in a closed society. A hospital is run a certain way, and it has a code of behavior. You still have to get there at six o'clock to scrub up with the other surgeons; I'm only imagining what it must have been like. I saw the results when he came home; he was truly in a terrible depression, and it was just a tremendous blow to his whole life. It affected him in so many different ways. He is a very strong person and he's a very unusual human being. He's very intelligent, he's very funny, he can be very outgoing, and he's a marvelous dancer . . . the best dancer I know of. He did in his own right achieve a tremendous amount. I mean, for a boy born in North Sweden on a farm, you know, who became this very fine brain surgeon. Recently psycho-surgery has been outlawed in the State of California, but they made a special provision in the law for him: he has his own clause in the state law which says: except for the surgery of Dr. Lindstrom. He gets patients from all over the world; his patients fly to him from everywhere; he usually operates on people who've been to many other surgeons without any success.

"I can't help but see a great deal of it from his side. I did happen to stay with him, and Mother left. A whole new life opened for her which was dramatic and glorious and a passionate love affair so romantic and marvelous. Well, that was grand for Mother. But on the other hand, what was left behind was not. I didn't happen to live with the part that was all that glorious; I mean, I was left with what was left, so I see this from a completely different point of view. I was part of what was left so I couldn't help but associate myself with my father and feel that Mother left *us*. Father didn't discourage me from feeling that, because in fact that is what she did do."

Pia's answer to Ingrid was sealed with three small blobs of green wax:

She thanked her mother for the presents she had sent, but reminded Ingrid that she had asked her not to "make any more noise in the paper" and to "stop with suits and lawyers." It had been on television that a new lawyer was coming over and so was Ingrid. Pia resented what she called the "scandal against my father all the time" and asked if he was so bad, why did Ingrid marry him? Pia did not want to go to Rome and wouldn't be forced to. She ended by reminding her mother that Ingrid had three other children to worry about and suggested she concern herself with them and leave Pia and her father alone.

March 3, 1953:

Dearest, my Pia: It has taken me some time to get up enough courage to answer your last letter. It hurts to answer almost as much as it hurts to read it.

Had my letter arrived a little sooner explaining the visit of my lawyer, you would not have had such a shock. Now you know that it was meant as a FRIENDLY visit. As a matter of fact, I was told Papa had a friendly talk with him over the phone. So there is nothing to get upset about. I have no other lawyer; I don't intend to take another.

I have told you many times that what is said over radio or television or written in the papers I can't prevent. I can refuse to give interviews about my private life. I have done so after I spoke to you. But when you make a picture there is always a certain amount of publicity about it. A picture is sold not only on its merits, also on its publicity. I can therefore not prevent newspaper men to come on the set. It has been like that all my life. What you hear over radio or television is GOSSIP. Papa has chosen, since I left him, not to believe this. If you now, too, refuse to believe me there is nothing I can do—except repeat what I have said.

I shall not bother you again, Pia. It seems I am incapable of showing you that I won't force you to do anything. If you had been younger I might have tried. But now you are old enough to decide. You ask me to leave you alone. All right, I'll do that. I have fought hard for almost four years just to be able to have the smallest part of you. I have never asked for much so as not to hurt Papa. But I have failed. Still, you are my child and I love you as much as I love the others. One child can't take the place of another, as you think. I love you, my funny monkey, I kiss your blond hair, I kiss your silly nose. With all my heart I love you, I'll always be near you even if you don't see me. . . .

Chapter 19

Ingrid was deeply hurt by Pia's letter, and she wrote to the lawyer who had tried to intercede in Pittsburgh:

> She must know that I love her and that I have fought for her. She can't say what I feared most: that I have abandoned her. She herself does not want me. Okay. I'll go off into the woods and cry out my pain. She has rebuffed me. I shall not take that by falling on my face and pleading at her feet. She wants to be left alone. I shall leave her alone.

During the latter half of 1953, with money getting tighter, and Roberto declaring that he wanted to make many movies and lots of money, they planned another movie of greater scope and ambition: a film version of the French writer Colette's novel *Duo,* the story of a husband-wife relationship. For this they needed an international male star to play opposite Ingrid against a background of Italy's beautiful scenery and ancient monuments.

Roberto had always liked George Sanders, the Russian-born actor who had played the hero in Ingrid's third Hollywood film, *Rage in Heaven,* and who later won an Oscar for his part as the cynical theater critic in *All About Eve.*

When Rossellini's cable arrived in Hollywood inviting him to play opposite Ingrid, he was married to Zsa Zsa Gabor, the beautiful

Hungarian who had not yet appeared in any Hollywood picture; she was very hurt and bewildered that when George received his Oscar she wasn't given one too.

George Sanders made a career out of seeming suave, but that was a façade. Behind the flippancy and urbanity and the impeccable plum-velvet syllables, there was a deep disquiet, a never-ending desire for a reality to make life coherent and therefore bearable. Strung somewhere along the genetic chains which bind us from birth to death was a Russian gene of the deepest and darkest gloom.

Still he accepted Roberto's invitation happily, waved good-bye to Zsa Zsa sitting imperturbably under her hair dryer, and set off for Rome.

———— • ————

George Sanders had been told by Roberto that he liked his type, and that he was going to fit in absolutely with the husband and wife story of Colette's *Duo*. Unfortunately, by the time George arrived, Roberto had discovered that the rights were already sold. So now he had an actor and he didn't have a story. Of course that didn't bother Roberto. He would write another script.

George Sanders looked at me and said, "What is this? I'm coming here to do *Duo* and now it's going to be something else? He's changed his mind?"

I said, "Yes," because I knew Roberto was making up the story as he went along so as not to lose George Sanders. I was quite bewildered too, but I thought Roberto is Roberto; he might do another magnificent *Open City*. After all, we're going to Naples and he'll be inspired there.

———— • ————

But even Ingrid began to have doubts after the first two weeks shooting which consisted of her staring at ancient statues in the Naples Museum while an equally ancient guide bumbled on about the glories of Greece and Rome.

—— 307 ——

———————— • ————————

Roberto wrote the script day by day and George had a series of nervous breakdowns. He was on the phone every night talking to his psychiatrist back in Hollywood.

Roberto just couldn't believe this. "Fifty dollars an hour just to talk to a psychiatrist! In Italy you go to confession and the priest says, 'You will repeat twenty-five Hail Marys and go in peace, my son.' "

Roberto didn't know whether to send for the psychiatrist or Zsa Zsa Gabor to cheer up George; finally he settled for Zsa Zsa. She looked beautiful, and sat there and played the piano, and we put them together at Ravello where an American company was shooting a John Huston picture with Jennifer Jones and Robert Morley. We thought George Sanders would be happier there. But he wasn't.

Of course he couldn't get used to Roberto's habits. Like me, he'd been trained in Hollywood: shooting schedules, prepared dialogue, efficiency, speed. I remember when I first started working with Roberto in Italian studios, I arrived at the hour work was due to start. But, no Roberto. "You can't start shooting before I get there," said Roberto. "I'll go anyway. I'd rather wait on the set than in our hallway." I learned to accept that sort of thing. George Sanders never did.

———————— • ————————

George did learn about Roberto's passion for skin diving, for Roberto needed little persuasion to move from Naples to wider and bluer locations in Capri where skin diving was no more than a quick run and a fast dive away. When the sun became too hot, the work went on too long, or the cameraman had a hangover, it was the signal for a crew member to hurtle onto the set as if bearing news of a second coming of Christ, shouting that a shoal of fish were converging on the bay. Within minutes, Roberto would be encased in his rubber suit, his eyes gleaming behind mask, spear-gun at the ready, his flappers beating a slow flurry across the Mediterranean. The crew would pull plugs, extinguish lights, swig from Chianti bottles, and head for their buses. Ingrid would sit back, light a cigarette, and try and think of another way of cheering up George.

It simply defeated him. I remember in Amalfi, in the hotel room we used as a dressing room, the tears were just pouring down his cheeks, and I said, "What's happened to you? What's the matter?"

"I am so unhappy in this movie, that's the matter. There's no dialogue. I don't know what's going to happen tomorrow. It's just impossible. I can't take it."

"Look, we'll write our own dialogue for the next scene. We'll write it now, and then we'll rehearse it."

"But what good does that do? It won't be any better tomorrow because we rehearse it."

———————— • ————————

It was only when *Journey to Italy* was finished and George went off to get his plane to rejoin Zsa Zsa who had already left for Paris, that he was ready to admit, to his own astonishment, that he had really enjoyed the experience. Where else would the director put a fatherly arm round his shoulder and say, "My friend, it isn't the first bad movie you've been in. Nor will it be the last. So cheer up." He admired Ingrid. He even liked the peculiar assistants whizzing away in all directions. Yes, on reflection, he had really had a good time.

The critics, as usual, hated the film.

But Ingrid was quite happy. The misunderstanding with Pia had been cleared up. They were corresponding again and Ingrid was telling her all about the oratorio *Joan of Arc at the Stake.*

———————— • ————————

I think it all began when we were in Naples and Capri filming *Journey to Italy.* Paul Claudel and Arthur Honegger's oratorio had first been performed in the middle thirties. The Director of the San Carlo Opera Company, Pasquale Di Costanza, sent Roberto the oratorio asking why didn't he direct it, and why didn't I play the leading role? Well, that was a new challenge.

I knew the piece well. I'd been given the whole set of five records by Joe Steele and Ruth Roberts while we were working on the film of *Joan of Arc.* I found it exciting then and exciting now. I could learn the words in Italian and learn to recognize every phrase of the music by ear.

But what about Roberto? Now he was going to leap in and direct a cast of a hundred, including ballet dancers plus a choir of fifty? It didn't seem to worry him one little bit. I kept saying to him as we got closer to the time for rehearsals, "Aren't you going to think about the way you're going to do it?"

"Sure, as soon as I have time."

So time went on, and I said again, "You know directors *do* figure out things on the stage before rehearsal starts. They do their homework."

"I'm thinking."

Okay, he was thinking, and one day he said, "Just give me one of those old envelopes, will you?"

I handed one over. We had dozens. He never opened envelopes. He never opened a letter and he never answered one. The wastepaper basket was full of unopened letters. So now he was scribbling on the back of the envelope. After a few minutes he handed it over.

"There's my scenario."

I said, "On *that* envelope?"

"Yes, yes, that's the way I'm going to do it."

I looked at it and couldn't make any sense of it at all, but as we started to rehearse it all became clear. As he was working, other ideas were emerging: a film idea, back projections so that we could change the backcloth from a landscape to a church in seconds, lantern-slides. Roberto got quite enthusiastic. And the best thing was that in Naples we had plenty of time for rehearsals.

Fortunately for me, Roberto took hardly any notice of Paul Claudel's stage instructions. They call for Joan to be standing at the stake in the middle of the stage as the curtain rises. She never moves. She talks, she recalls her childhood, while the trial and the whole thing is dramatized by the singers and chorus.

I said to Roberto, "I can't stand there for a *whole hour* just tied up! I want to move! And he got what I thought was a brilliant idea. The curtain rises, and another girl, a small child, is tied to the stake at the back, and she is Saint Joan. The flames rise and she is dying; then, out of the darkness I rise up on an elevator to my first position. I'm dressed all in black, only my face showing. That face represents my mind, the mind that can look back at my life and my experiences. There are big gangways sloping up here and there, and on one of them I meet Brother Dominique who tells me of what I am accused. Then the gangways are lowered to the floor and I'm free to run around.

It sounds complicated but it worked very well, and with the jostling crowds, and the singers and chorus it was a great success. Both the audiences and the critics liked it in Italy. We played at the opera house in Palermo in Sicily, at La Scala, Milan, at the Paris and Stockholm opera houses, and in Barcelona and London. We played in four languages in five different countries.

But Roberto, who didn't like actors, decided he liked opera singers even less. "It's all this talking about the voice and the notes and the tones—oh God, they're so boring," he said. "And they have no idea what's going on in the world. They have no idea if a war is going on, or if we're being attacked by the Martians. They just don't care. It's all this tra-la-la-la! The only thing in their lives is the sound of their voices and the next aria."

———————— • ————————

Around this time some very unhappy news reached Ingrid about Bob Capa.

He had ignored the Korean War, stating that he was very happy to be an unemployed war photographer, and hoped that he could stay that way to the end of his life.

But in 1954, *Life* lured him out to the guns again by asking him to cover the French colonial war in Vietnam. The first week of June, he and two other correspondents set out at dawn with a French armored column to push deep into Vietnam territory. Capa sat with his flask of iced tea and bottle of cognac in the front seat of the Jeep. Often the column was bogged down under enemy fire. In one lull in the firing he went forward with his camera, saying, "Look for me when you get started." They did. They found him lying in the roadway, dead. He had stepped on an enemy land mine.

At a small ceremony afterwards, General René Cogny awarded him a posthumous *Croix de Guerre* with palm leaf and said, "He was the first war correspondent to be killed in these battles. He fell like a soldier. He deserves a soldier's honors."

It was a little more than ten years since Capa had made his big decision to take his chances along with the other warriors. He was forty years old.

Ingrid wrote to Ruth:

> Thank God for *Joan at the Stake*. We have now signed up
> for Spain. Too bad it brings very little money so we have

to get a picture in now and again. I am now frantically looking for another opera or play. It is true how little people write these days. We are such a dried-up generation inventing atom bombs.

Thanks for the clippings on Capa. So strange and terrible he has gone. Strange also they printed in most magazines here all Capa's pictures and his life, and by this odd coincidence the next pages are all about *Joan at the Stake* and my life.

———————— • ————————

Since we were on the opera circuit, many agents wanted us to perform in opera houses all over Europe.

As we needed the money, off we went to various cities in Europe.

Barcelona was an unforgettable experience. It wasn't really the pleasantest month of my life because everything in Spain starts so late, and goes on so late, and in the theater everything was so dusty and dirty. We couldn't understand what was the matter with the lights until Roberto cleaned them with his handkerchief. My dressing room was very beautiful with all sorts of drapes and everything, but they were all so dusty.

I couldn't keep the door closed. The bathroom smelled so badly I couldn't even go into it. Every day a man came and put a bucket of disinfectant down the toilet bowl, and I said it would probably be better if they just cleaned it out with soap and water. Then I got an infection in my eyes, and in the mornings I couldn't even open them. I had to go to a famous eye specialist every day, and on the night of the opening I looked like an owl because I couldn't use make-up. Anyway I was supposed to be playing a saint and a dead saint too, so that was all right.

And as far as rehearsals went, the cast had all been recruited locally, and we never had a full rehearsal *ever*. The electricians were working on other jobs in the daytime because they were so badly paid; they just had to have two jobs. We never could get the soloists together: they were singing in this concert and that concert. If we got the piano player, we could rehearse some of the ballet, but then some of the big stars of the ballet would be missing. Or the solo singers would arrive to find the chorus had all gone home. I've never seen anything like it. I never want to see anything like it again.

The conductor, Señor Mendoza, never could get the orchestra together either: they were all out playing at nightclubs and cafés to make ends meet. He worked separately with the soloists, the chorus, the ballet, and with me and Brother Dominique, who had the other main speaking part. But getting everyone together and having a full dress-rehearsal? It was not possible. We planned one for the same night as the opening . . . to do a full dress-rehearsal and then go straight on into the real thing.

I sat in my dressing room, and never in my life have I felt so miserable. The lavatory smell, my aching eyes, no rehearsal. And I said to myself, "I must just behave like a horse, with blinkers, go forward in the way I know. Don't look at anything technical. Don't worry if half the scenery falls down. Just remember your lines, look at the conductor, and keep your talk in tempo with the music so that you end up in unison with the chorus. . . . But *they* haven't been rehearsed properly. . . . Oh, God!"

The opera house at Barcelona was enormous, and it was packed to the roof. We started off, and soon I noticed there was a new monk on the stage whom I'd never seen before. He was running here and running there, and pushing this lot in that direction and the other lot over there. As he came past me, he looked up under his cowl, grinned, and said, "By the way, you're no good either!" It was Roberto. He was directing the whole thing on *stage*! "More *fortissimo* . . . that's better, . . . now ballet, ballet—animation, animation! . . ."

The audience seemed to love it. It must be the generous heart of the Spanish people because they applauded and cheered. But to me it was pure agony.

We were traveling as a big party now together with the children. And as we were now in Spain Roberto *had* to take Robertino to a bullfight. I hate bullfighting. I wouldn't go. I was so upset, I was so mad. "He's too young to see such a spectacle," I said. "I can't see how they kill these beautiful animals for the enjoyment of the people. They don't ask the bull if he likes to be killed. It's fine for the bullfighter—he knows he risks his life and he's very courageous—but no one asks the bull what he thinks about the whole thing." I'd heard about the blood and the horses being gored. The Spanish people and their involvement with death, the drama, the anger—even the dancing with its stamping of feet is anger—is not in my character. I can't even bear killing a fly. I always say,

"Excuse me," before I hit them. So I tried to prepare Robertino for the ordeal he was going to go through, but I think I rather overdid it. I made the bull sound like a dragon with fire gushing from his nostrils. When Robertino came home he was just as normal as always, much more interested in running his little car around and making noises like a Ferrari. He didn't look upset and he didn't tell me anything. I thought that maybe it was deep down in his subconscious. So I asked, "What did you think about the bullfight?" He didn't answer, just went on "vroom-vrooming" with his car. I tried to sound even more offhand.

"Did you like it?" I asked.

"Mama," he said, "do you know what a bull is? D'you know what comes rushing through that gate out there—the husband of a cow."

So that was his big discovery. A bull is the husband of a cow. I'd over-dramatized again. And Robertino went on playing with his cars.

Years later I went to Spain with Isabella and Ingrid, but then the publicity was too much. The photographers ruined the Prado for us because they followed us in hordes. We were trying to look at a beautiful Velázquez and the flashbulbs were blinding us. All the guards were scampering around saying, "It is forbidden to photograph in the galleries," but a fat lot the photographers cared. We ran in front of all of them so that we might glimpse a famous painting or two before they caught up with us, but it wasn't any good. Then we asked at the hotel where we could go for the evening to see some Spanish dancing and listen to the castanets. But as soon as we got there, we became the show: there were spotlights on us, and I was asked to come up on the stage. I went up and took a bow and smiled and waved. But that didn't satisfy them; they wanted my two daughters also. It was then I said, "I came here to be entertained, not to be the *entertainment.*" So it all ended sadly with the three of us leaving.

We arrived in Paris for our gala oratorio opening at the Paris Opera House. That was going to be the big one. But it was also going to be the big trouble because we knew that Paul Claudel lived in Paris, and that he had heard we had not followed all those strict stage instructions he had written.

We were invited to tea. He was very stern. He talked at great length to Roberto about the *purpose* of the oratorio. It was vital for its success that Joan be fixed, he said, tied at the stake throughout the whole performance, dying right there in front of your eyes for the whole hour. So when I confessed that I ran around quite a lot, he was aghast and said, "I can't imagine how you could do such a thing, make such a mistake. *And I will not have it.* You cannot perform my oratorio at the opera house doing all these strange things. I cannot allow it."

We were very gloomy. "Well, the only thing we can do is show you a full dress-rehearsal, and hope that you like it," we said. "But if you disapprove . . . well?"

If he disapproved? Absolute disaster! We were opening in a few days. We were sold out—every seat for the entire period—and if Paul Claudel came along and said, "I don't like this . . . it is *off*"? The director of the theater was nearly hysterical at the thought. "I shall have to return all the bookings, pay all the cast. We have absolutely nothing to put in its place at such short notice. I shall have an empty theater and I shall be ruined."

Everybody in the cast, the orchestra, the chorus, and the ballet knew this, and it was a very shaky rehearsal indeed. Paul Claudel sat there in the stalls with his chin in his hands and in the dark I could see his eyes following me, following everything I did. So I came to my last line, where in the flames I break my fetters and cry out: "It is joy that is strong. It is love that is stronger. It is God that is strongest of all." And we stood there, waiting for the verdict of just one man.

Those seconds passed like years. Then he walked forward and he said, "And Ingrid is even stronger."

Oh what a relief! The whole cast knew we'd won. Claudel was wonderful. He said he was absolutely delighted at seeing his own play produced in a way he'd never seen it played before. He said, "My God, you play it like a peasant girl, you really play it like a simple peasant girl." And I said, "But she was a peasant girl, a simple maid. She didn't know she was going to be a saint. She never stepped outside her own character." And he sat down again, and said, "Oh, what a relief. Oh, how touching." He was full of praise for Roberto and me.

We got to know each other very well, and later on I asked him on one occasion, "Why did you think it necessary at first to keep your Joan tied up at the stake all through the whole oratorio?" He smiled, and said, "Revenge."

Then he explained the history of the oratorio. In 1933, a group of students at the Sorbonne were performing a selection of medieval mystery plays. Ida Rubinstein went to see them and was entranced. Ida was a famous actress, dancer, and mime. Gabriele d'Annunzio and Claude Debussy had written *Martyre de Saint Sebastian* specially for her; Ravel had composed his *Bolero* for Ida; André Gide and Stravinsky had collaborated on *Persephone* for her. Ida approached Honegger and commissioned him to write the music for a similar sort of subject. They chose the theme of Joan of Arc. At first Paul Claudel did not want to write the text—he was Ambassador in Brussels at the time. Then he changed his mind. If Ida was famous for her mime, dancing, and statuesque poses, he would test her by tying her to the stake for the full seventy minutes. "Then we would find out if she had a good voice as well as dancing feet."

I was fascinated by the story. Especially the commissioning part. I said, "Why doesn't someone commission something specially for *me?*" And Paul Claudel looked at me with his eyes twinkling, and said, "Because, my dear, you do not have a wealthy lover."

Arthur Honegger, the composer, was sick and living in Switzerland. He didn't think he could come to the opening, but he sent us telegrams. He also sent me a photograph of himself—a big, handsome dark-haired man with a wonderful face—and he wrote on it: "To the interpreter of my opera." I kept that photograph always in my dressing room.

I sent him photos of the opera, showing how we had produced it in Naples and Milan. Honegger wrote back: "You know I am sick, and there is no hope of me getting any better. But you have kept me alive for longer by all these photographs which I have all around my bedroom. I looked at them and I could hear the music of our opera ringing in my head. And I have decided. I said to my wife, 'We are going to Paris for the opening.'"

I shall never forget when he first came to rehearsals. The orchestra stood up and applauded and applauded. It was so moving. And there was this little shrunken old man being helped down to his seat. But where was the big, dramatic dark man of the photograph? I went down and shook hands with him, and kissed him on the cheek, and later, when we spoke privately, I said, "That photograph you sent me? . . ." He smiled and said, "I never thought I would ever meet you. So I sent you a photograph taken when I was about thirty-five to make an impression on you. I didn't want you to know I was an old man."

I went to their Paris house in Montmartre several times because he wanted to give me various intonations, and he was in every way sweet and kind, saying, "I love the natural voice you use. Every other actress has declaimed so heroically, but you talk like an ordinary girl. And you do that little dance and sing with the children. That is the real Joan."

It was a wonderful night, a great success, and we all went to the Tour D'Argent for supper afterwards. Honegger was enjoying himself immensely, laughing and eating and drinking. And after dinner he actually had a cigar. That horrified his wife. "His health," she said, "Really, he shouldn't do these things."

I said to his wife: "But he is so happy. I cannot understand why you should be so careful. I mean, why not let him have a good time and have his cigar, have a drink? Better surely than pulling away and saying, 'Don't eat and don't drink, don't go to Paris, don't see the play, just stay home and wait to die.'" I'm not sure she approved of my viewpoint, and it is true he died not long afterwards, but he did have that last memorable evening.

Then Jack Hylton came across from England. I did not know who he was, but I heard he used to be a band leader and now he was an impresario, and he wanted to bring us to London. We were really unwise to accept, but we both wanted to go to England.

Everything was much more difficult there. The translation was difficult. The oratorio was written in French and you cannot get the same vowel sounds in English that you can in French and Italian. The English words did not match the music and much was lost. And then we had to go into the Stoll Theatre, which is vast, but the stage was not big enough for us. We had this enormous orchestra, so many instruments that we had to put some of the musicians in the boxes, so the sound became lopsided. People who sat on one side heard only the percussion; and on the other side, they heard only the violins. We should have been at Covent Garden—they could have handled our orchestra and cast. And we played as if we were in an ordinary theater, six nights a week, for a month, instead of appearing as we did elsewhere as one among other operas in an operatic repertoire.

Certainly Jack Hylton didn't make any money out of it. But he was very nice about that. I don't think he ever expected to make any money out of it. When I asked, "Why in the world did you ask us to come?" he laughed and said, "This is the best and most dignified production I have ever put on in my whole theatrical career. This is the feather in my cap."

———— • ————

The British public welcomed Ingrid with love and affection, but the reviews were mixed.

Louis T. Stanley in *The Sketch* said: "In the engulfing darkness and piercing shafts of light at the Stoll she suggests the spiritual statuesque calm of one who has climbed to the summit high above the gross world. She evokes the sadness of things supremely well. . . . The quality she possesses is more than beauty: it is strangeness in beauty."

It would be in her native Sweden three and a half months later that she would get her worst reception.

———— • ————

After all those years, when I finally came home to appear on the Swedish stage with this oratorio I loved, my joy was enormous. After the long journey we had made through Italy, France, England, and Spain, after working in three foreign languages, I would at last speak my own. People stood in line all night as they do in England; they stood in the snow outside the opera house trying to get tickets. During the sixteen years I had been abroad, I had never stopped loving Sweden, never stopped hoping to return one day.

At the opening, our first appearance at the opera, the applause poured over me. I could feel the warmth that came to me from the public, and my happiness was very big. My dream had been fulfilled. I said to Roberto afterwards, "Now I can lie down peacefully and die."

Perhaps that was what I should have done. The critics said it was the worst thing they had ever seen. There wasn't one day after the opening night that some newspaper or magazine wasn't out to kill me.

But despite the critics, we had a wonderful welcome in Sweden. Roberto and I were invited to a ball attended by the King of Sweden. But Roberto didn't have any tails. They said, "Can't you rent tails or put on a uniform or something?" Roberto said he couldn't, but he'd come along and hide behind a potted palm or a pillar and watch me being presented. So with two other ladies I went up and we made our curtsy, and the King smiled and that was that. Then after everyone had been presented, an equerry said that the King would like a word with me, which was very flattering. The King was very charming, but really he was more interested in Roberto than he was in me. "Where is your husband?" he asked. "Well, he's hiding behind a pillar over there, your Majesty," I said, "because he hasn't got tails." "Well, isn't that ridiculous, isn't that stupid?" said the King. "I was looking forward to having a discussion about Ferraris with him. You just go across and bring him over here to have a word." Roberto was brought over and he and the King chatted about Ferraris until they had to be pried apart.

I was invited to dinner by a group which was called "The Swedes." Years before, my father had sung with them and been on their tour of the United States. They talked about him and they sang the songs that he had sung with them; I was so moved I cried in my napkin.

———————— • ————————

The press campaign began as soon as the Rossellinis arrived in Stockholm with the children. They were pursued everywhere. The front pages were full of descriptions of the family, of Ingrid's clothes and jewelry, of Roberto's figure and receding hairline, and the children's reactions to everything. And soon the less favorable comments began to appear: "Ingrid demands more money than Jussi Björling for her appearance at the Opera—ticket prices reach a record high —Ingrid Bergman can't even sing!" Then came a clutch of derogatory articles about Ingrid's parents which irritated her. One journalist was very annoyed because he heard Ingrid say she hoped she could speak Swedish "without an accent after all these years." "*She,* who keeps emphasizing her aptitude for foreign languages as soon as she gets the chance!"

The opening night notices were uniformly bad and often spiteful. They accused her of being robust, cheerful, unspiritual, cheap, and almost comic in her role as Joan of Arc. "This egocentric woman didn't look for a moment as though she was suffering—but nor would I if I were paid as much as she is a night." "She lacks magnetism and intensity," said another. On the other hand everyone praised her Swedish male lead, Anders Näslund. Rossellini was given his share of the blame: his direction was superficial and banal. They also made unfavorable comparisons between Ingrid and other actresses who had played Saint Joan. "Why import Ingrid Bergman and pay through the nose to see her when we have X and Y who are much better in every way."

One critic used the oratorio as the vehicle for an attack on her. Stig Ahlgren, writing in *Vecko-Journalen* under the title *"To Show One-self for Money,"* said:

> Ingrid Bergman is not an actress in the official sense. Her career has been enacted on quite a different level. It is both malicious and unfair to compare her to professional actresses, as has been done.
>
> It just happened that, after making one film failure after another, nothing else remained for Rossellini and Ingrid Bergman but to travel from one city to another, from one country to another, showing Ingrid Bergman for money.
>
> Should they be heckled for this? Absolutely not! "If you got something people want! . . ." Ingrid Bergman is merchandise, so far merchandise in demand, offered on the open market. She charges and is paid according to the general price guides, just like herring and crude iron.
> . . .

The provincial press reported gleefully that Ingrid Bergman's opening in Stockholm had been a near-fiasco. It was also reported that in the early morning after the first night, a journalist had broken into the hotel suite where they were sleeping and taken photographs of the children. Rossellini rang the police to report the intrusion, and the paper claimed that his actions were motivated by the bad reviews they had received, or were about to receive. The Rossellinis had to put up with this sort of thing. What else were they after but publicity?

Roberto stayed only long enough to iron out any snags in the production.

Ingrid faced it all:

———— • ————

I hated the bad notices, but well, that's one thing, because I feel that if you're putting yourself in front of an audience they have the right to say, "We don't think you are any good. I'm not going to spend my money on you." And people who are critics as a profession have a right to say, "Don't go to see them, it's a waste of your time and money." So that wasn't what I objected to. I objected to the attacks on my personal life.

As in Spain, and France, and England, we had the children with us, and we traveled like gypsies, Italian style. Loads of baggage, one maid, one nurse. And the Swedish press seemed to find this disgraceful. "She's come here with only *two* people to look after the children. She has three children, surely she should have *three* nurses." That sort of thing. Then Roberto driving his Ferrari—he'd already raced it in Sweden—and there was the Rolls-Royce. "How dare they have two cars waiting outside the hotel, that's the height of ostentation!"

I was criticized for not wanting to have the children photographed. Oh, why not? Were they misshapen or something? So, trying to be cooperative, we said, "Okay, come along and take pictures. We don't want to be standoffish, but we do feel it better that the kids don't start thinking they're out-of-the-ordinary by having their photos in the papers all the time." So pictures of the kids and Roberto and me, smiling and looking happy were printed in every magazine and newspaper. Was that all right? "Look at her posturing with the children, pretending to be a gracious and lovely mother. Doing it for publicity obviously."

Really, it was unbelievable. I went with my old friend Mollie Faustman to see Anna Norrie on her ninetieth birthday. She was a teacher of mine when I left the Royal Dramatic School; she was the one who taught me all about movement. I took her a bottle of champagne. And the photographers were there waiting. "Please no photographs," we said. "Oh, just one, Ingrid." So when that appeared, again I was criticized for trying to cash in on somebody else's publicity to get my face in the papers.

Then I heard that soon after Honegger's death, Paul Claudel had died. I loved those two old men. So I told the management of the theater, we should do something that night in Claudel's memory. Perhaps some flowers each side of the stage tied with black ribbon? No, we couldn't do that. Whoever heard of flowers tied with black ribbon. Silly! So I said, "Then can't I say something as a mark of respect before the curtain goes up?" "What are you going to say?" "I don't know, just a few words to tell the audience that tonight we are the only company in the world playing this oratorio and it is a specially sad occasion. I've just got to say something." So they agreed. The curtain rose and I said, "Tonight our opera is in mourning. Earlier today the poet and author of *Joan of Arc at the*

Stake, Paul Claudel, died. We feel a great sense of loss and a deep sorrow, but he lives on in our minds as a great author and a man of wit, poetry, and spiritual strength. He has left us. But he has also left his words behind. We dedicate this performance to his memory."

The following day the papers bawled me out because I'd had the nerve to come out front with my crocodile tears, pretend I was sorry, and try to make a little extra personal publicity by showing off in front of the curtain. No one had ever done such a thing before. It was very embarrassing to the audience. A lot more in that vein.

The final straw came a week or so later. One of Stockholm's papers rang me up and asked me to appear in a Sunday charity performance for polio victims. It was to be held in an enormous concert hall, and lots of actors and actresses had donated their services free and would dance and sing and tell stories. Naturally I said, "Yes." Then they asked what I would do. I said, "Well I don't want to do anything out of the oratorio, but I'll talk or do something. Ask the compère—the man who introduces us—to ask me a question, and I'll never stop talking." "Oh good, you'll tell some jokes."

So that was fine. And then on the very morning—that Sunday morning—of the charity show, I opened that paper, and what did I find. An editorial, attacking me, a leading article which took all honor and everything away from me. And this was the paper which was using my appearance to help fill its hall. I was so mad. I rang up Mollie Faustman and told her what I was going to do.

"Ingrid, you can't do this, you just can't," she said.

"I can and I'm going to."

"If you do it, you've planted your last potato in Sweden."

That's a Swedish saying we have which means you're finished for good.

"Yes, I have planted my last potato," I said.

"It will be the end of you in Sweden."

"It's already the end of me in Sweden. I'm bawled out every solid day in the newspaper. I can't open a magazine, I can't even put on the radio without hearing how awful I am. You know the line from Strindberg's play, 'If I say "No" they beat me. If I say "Yes" they beat me.' That is how it has become for me in Sweden. Now I'm going to answer."

"Well it takes a lot of courage. I haven't even the courage to come and listen to you. I'll meet you afterwards."

"Yes, wait for me at the Königs café. We'll have a coffee."

So I arrived at the charity show. And my old friend Edvin Adolphson, who directed my very first picture in Sweden twenty years earlier, was introducing the performers. "Edvin," I said, "you just take me out on to the stage and say, 'Here's Ingrid back in Sweden. Ingrid, how does it feel to come back to your own country again?' That's all I need. From then on I'll talk."

I was on stage and I started. "It's not you the audience here tonight I want to talk about. You come and fill this hall; you come and fill the opera house; you queue up through all these nights of cold weather to attend a performance, and never in my life have I received so many flowers and so many lovely letters. No, I am talking about the newspapers and the press generally. What have I done to get such a beating? It's not my fault that I have been invited to a lot of different parties. It's not my fault that whatever I do I must be photographed. That is the newspapers."

I told them about the photographs, I told them all the things I had stored up in my heart. "What I resent is not that anyone criticizes my performance, but that they should constantly criticize my private life. Many of my colleagues say, 'You shouldn't care what the papers say about you,' and 'What is said today is forgotten tomorrow. No one will remember.' Well, I will remember. No one will stand up to them and say we've had enough. Well, I've had enough. The minute you become of any importance outside Sweden the papers immediately try to discredit you. . . ."

I know I was very emotional about what I said. It was just a concert hall with spotlights, so I could see the people in front of me, and some of them were crying, and I said, "Thank you very much for listening to me, but this is how I feel about coming back to Sweden, and probably I shall never come back ever again."

I walked off the stage. I didn't say good-bye to anybody, I picked up my coat and went out into the street and around to the Königs café where Mollie was waiting. She asked, "You did it?" I was still shaking, I was still trembling, and I said, "Yes." And she said, "Oh, my God, I wonder what they'll say tomorrow?"

But the papers the next day were very nice to me. Everybody turned to help me, but I remembered what Joan of Arc once said, "Help yourself and God will help you."

———————— • ————————

In her column the next morning, Mollie Faustman made clear whose side she was on:

> One of the most ridiculous claims is that Ingrid Berg-man is a clever businesswoman. If anyone is stupid in business it's her! I don't think she can be blamed for accepting the high fee she is offered—it seems her slander-ers would have acted otherwise in her situation—but the claim that she is avaricious is complete nonsense, which I feel ashamed even to mention. Let me tell you about one episode: As a young girl, Ingrid had made her first film and an old man wrote to her from Småland. It was a little letter where he told her that his cow had died and could she send him the money for a new one? We both agreed that, unfortunately, there was nothing we could do about it. Neither of us had any money to spare in those days; the salary Ingrid earned was quite modest. But the following day Ingrid brought the money to me. "I've thought about that poor man and his cow all night. Send this in your name please." I sent it anonymously. Ever since then In-grid's life has continued along similar lines. What a busi-nesswoman! If all the people whom she had helped were to step forward, it would be a very long row indeed.

Her old friend Bang, who had hidden in the bushes at Ingrid's wedding, also wrote in her defense, although Bang could see the viewpoint of many of her colleagues. Yes, they should have come to Ingrid's aid, but they did not wish to start a great row and contro-versy while Ingrid was still in the middle of her *Joan at the Stake*. She ended with a touch of irony: "But I do agree that it is really awful of this Ingrid Bergman to celebrate her son's fifth birthday in flat shoes and well dressed. Surely one has a right to expect a sly bitch like Ingrid Bergman at least to appear slovenly, in high-heeled shoes! And of course it must have been a publicity stunt to arrange Rober-tino's birthday while she was actually in Stockholm."

On March 19, 1955, Ingrid wrote to Ruth:

> Roberto has been away from Stockholm most of the time. I think he is planning a film in Spain, then France. I don't know what will happen to me.
>
> I'd love to work in France. Hope someone has an idea.

Funnily enough, in these last days I have had four proposi-
tions from America. One film with Gary Cooper and Billy
Wilder. . . . Oh, how I would love that—but not in Hollywood. Leo McCarey called me, still about that *Adam and
Eve* idea, now with John Wayne. I can't see how the
picture could be good. I'll read the script carefully when
I get time, but I doubt it. Then Kay Brown wants me to
do *Anastasia,* and Bob Hope has a story, *Not for Money.*
These all to be made in Europe, but I think all of them will
fall through.

They have made many offers here to stay for films and
theater, but the press is so disgusting that I don't want to
remain. I have made such a fuss that they don't persecute
me any more, and the papers are full of how brave I am
that I *dared* to tell *them.* But it is a rotten press atmosphere here. The public is wonderful. I have thousands of
lovely letters and flowers every day. The theater sold out
22 performances instead of 10. (I am so rich I bought
furniture at Svenskt Tenn—the most beautiful shop in the
world—at four times ordinary prices.) We could sell out
20 more performances but I must go to Palermo in Sicily,
opening the opera there for Easter. Here the public yells
like Italians after each show, but the newspapers continue
to say "polite applause." Hopeless! I have made a radio
speech that will be heard next week just as I leave to tell
them some more. Then I won't come back. Maybe. The
children loved the snow after they got used to it. It is so
beautiful, lots and lots of snow. I have met *everyone* from
my life in Sweden. My piano teacher when I was ten. My
mother's friends (when I was two), my schoolfriends, my
dramatic-school friends, and all through my film days. I
have so many old and new friends. They've been wonderful to me. With me here is Roberto's sister's daughter
Fiorella who I love so much. She is like Pia for me. Then
my aunt from Germany is here. We have taken a *floor*
again in the hotel. Even Petter came. Big headlines, but he
didn't call me, nor any of his friends. Too bad I can't send
a greeting to Pia. She would be happy to have one through
her father. Think what a relief to know that Papa and
Mama are friends. But no! So we'll just have to stick to
letters. All my love. Ingrid.

The European tour of the Rossellinis in *Joan of Arc at the Stake* lasted until the spring of 1955 and was interrupted by two films. The first, *Joan at the Stake,* was made because they felt Claudel and Honegger's oratorio should be preserved. But Roberto had great difficulty in getting it released and it did not recoup its costs. *Fear* was a Minerva Film Production directed by Roberto, financed by German money, and made in Munich.

———————— • ————————

I remember that *Angst (Fear)* was quite difficult because we had the children with us, and we were doing two language versions, one German, one English, and I suppose my emotions were showing through a bit. I always felt a little resentful that Roberto wouldn't let me work with any other director. There were all these wonderful Italian directors: Zeffirelli, Fellini, Visconti, De Sica; all wanted to work with me and I wanted to work with them; and they were furious with Roberto that he wouldn't let me work for them . . . but in Roberto's terms, I was his property.

Roberto couldn't work with actresses except Anna Magnani. Maybe that was because they were the same stock, a good mix. We weren't a good mix. The world hated the Rossellini version of me, so nothing worked. And he was stuck with me. What did he want with an international star? Nothing. He didn't know what to write for me. And, of course, by this time we both knew it. It was something we did not talk about. But the silences between us grew longer—the silences when I didn't dare to say anything because I would hurt his feelings. Roberto would take whatever I said, and, unhappy as he was, would make a scene about it. He liked to fight. And besides the traumas of our artistic life, our increasing debts worried me enormously.

Mathias Wiemann, the German actor who was playing my husband in *Fear* felt this unhappiness in me, and one day he said very quietly, "You are being torn to pieces. You'll go insane if you continue like this. Why don't you leave Roberto?"

I stared at him with a terrible sense of shock. Leave Roberto? "How can I do that?" I said. "It's impossible!" And it was impossible.

———————— • ————————

It is possible however, that *Fear* will be remembered only because of the damning criticism it received from Angelo Solmi, one of Italy's most respected critics, in the magazine *Oggi*: "Roberto and Ingrid," he wrote, "will either have to change their style of work radically— or retire into dignified silence. The abyss into which Bergman and Rossellini have plunged can be measured by *Fear*. This is not because this film is any worse than their other recent motion pictures together, but because half a dozen tries with negative results prove the inability of the couple to create anything acceptable to the public or the critics. Once the world's unquestioned Number One star and successor to Greta Garbo, Miss Bergman in her latest pictures has only been a shadow of herself."

Chapter 20

Many people accused Roberto Rossellini of almost ruining the career of Ingrid Bergman. To Ingrid, the truth is that the positions were reversed: in those years she ruined him. In order to work with her, he went against his own precepts and introduced a Hollywood star into his documentaries. It was a combination that simply did not work.

Ingrid grew to maturity in those years with Roberto. There were periods of intense happiness. But as partners in films aimed at a commercial market—a success to which Roberto only halfheartedly aspired—they failed abysmally. Every picture they made together was unsuccessful. The golden oil of Italy and the pure, sparkling snow-water of Sweden resolutely refused to mix.

———————— • ————————

It was really my old friend Jean Renoir who rescued me. When we had our great friendship in Hollywood, I would often say to Jean, "We must work together. When shall we do it?" Jean would look at me wisely and say, "No. The time is not yet ready, Ingrid. You're too big a star for me now. But I shall wait until you are falling. It happens in all careers in Hollywood. You go up and you go down. Now you've gone up as high as you can possibly go and you will stay there. But I shall wait until you are falling and then I shall be holding the net to catch you. I shall be there with the net."

So Jean Renoir came to visit us in Santa Marinella, and he said, "Ingrid, now is the time, and I have the net ready. I want you to come and do a film in Paris with me."

I said, "Jean, it is not possible. Roberto will not let me work with anybody else."

Jean looked at me and smiled again. "I shall talk to Roberto," he said. And to my intense surprise Roberto said, "What a great idea. Certainly you must work with Jean." And that's how I went to Paris to make *Elena et les Hommes.* Roberto was making long-term arrangements to go to India to do a film there. Maybe that had something to do with his change of heart. Then, too, Jean was one of the very few directors in the world whom Roberto admired.

It was stimulating to work in Paris with Jean directing, and Mel Ferrer, Jean Marais, and Juliette Greco. They said it was the coldest winter they'd had in Europe for a hundred years. But the children were with me and I enjoyed it. The movie was a big success in France—the critics loved it—but when it came out in the United States under the title *Paris Does Strange Things,* the critics declared it a disaster.

For Roberto, things were not going well. He was having great difficulties getting money together for any film in Italy because we'd had so little success.

———————— • ————————

And Roberto and Ingrid were having severe marital problems as well, as revealed in a letter Ingrid wrote from "Paris—late at night, January 19, '56" to Gigi Girosi, a close friend in Rome:

> My very dear Gigi: This is a letter to ask you to be a witness on this trial. Roberto has just left for Italy and says he will never come back. He has with him a letter from me that says I agree to the separation and that the children should be allowed to live only in Italy or France. He took the children's passports with him. As I told you before I don't know if it is serious or not. It has gone on for so long I don't know what to believe anymore. But still, after all these years, I become frightened and I think this time maybe he means it. Today he told me that if I did not write the letter he wanted, he would take the children with him and leave tonight so that when I came back from the

studio—*Elena et les Hommes*—they would all be gone. I did not believe it of course but still when he gets like that I am afraid that lacking train tickets he will put them all in the car and drive off. I promised to sign. If it is necessary I want you to tell Mama Rossellini this as I have told her I would not agree to any such thing. But Roberto actually threatened that he would put up such a scandal if I did not agree. I don't quite understand what scandal he wants to create. But I had to go to the studio and I did not have the time to do more about it.

After you left, dear, all was peaceful for a few days. Then he decided that we would write this letter on Sunday. We would spend the whole day figuring out what to do about the future. All Sunday I waited. He never spoke of it and I finally suggested we go to the movies. And wonder of all wonders he went with me. I can't remember when we last went to the movies together. All ended like that. The week went by, another week—he was a little upset but nothing serious. One evening we discussed our troubles and I felt maybe after all we can understand each other if we talk. But then today all went wrong.

I tried tonight, after I had signed the letter, to plead with him, to laugh, to be angry. I tried everything I could think of in my tired mind. I remember you once saying that sometimes I am not sensitive to a situation. Well, I know I don't know how to put on an act. While he was packing I tried to help. He did not want it. I put the cards out thinking he might want to play. He did not. He went and lay on the bed. I went to him and put my head on his chest and I cried. And cried. And cried. Then I suppose I got my sense of humor back at the whole sad situation and began to laugh. Thank God I never seem to lose my sense of humor even in the most tragic situations. I think that is what has saved me all through these years. I told him to take some Bellargin before he left and not to dramatize things to such an extent, but he would not hear of it.

Earlier I went down to see his new Ferrari. It is a monster that does over three hundred kilometers an hour. I told him it looked like a flying saucer and it does. I sat in it for a moment and I put my fingers on the wheel in the sign of the cross like we do on the forehead of the children when they go to bed. I am sure Roberto does not know the effect it has on me when he roars off in one of these monsters.

I want you to keep this letter and I want you to keep the envelope to show that it was written today and sent today. I don't know what I am afraid of. I think it is of things I don't understand. I am afraid of losing my children again. I am not afraid of being alone, but of having made four children and all taken away from me.

———————— • ————————

As usual things quieted down.

Roberto got an offer to do a play in the Théâtre de Paris and got very excited about it. The play was about Judas and he started studying the period. He'd never directed a play in the theater— *Joan of Arc at the Stake* didn't really come into that category—but he had all kinds of ideas. They started to rehearse, but the leading actor didn't like Roberto's ideas, so all the complications started. And one day Roberto came home with a bleak face, and said, "They have asked me to leave; they want another director." I felt so sorry for him because this had seemed a possibility for him to get back and really do something substantial again. And the idea of living in Paris was so exciting to me; I loved the city. There were so many more things going on than in Rome.

Roberto was absolutely destroyed by this experience. I just had to take him in my arms and say, "Something else is round the corner, I'm sure there'll be something else."

The Théâtre de Paris felt very sad about having to fire Roberto, so they asked whether he could direct *Tea and Sympathy*: they had an option on it. Then they said, "Wouldn't your wife like to play in it?" I said, "With my French? That's impossible." But Madame Popesco, who owned the theater, said, "Listen, I come from Rumania; if I can make it, you can make it." She had this very heavy accent, and she'd never tried to lose it, and everybody loved her.

I went home and read the play in English and liked it.

Of course, there were doubts in my mind. Roberto had still never directed a stage play before. And I suppose I was thinking—an Italian directing a Swedish actress in an American play in French for a Paris audience? Oh well, we'd face that when the time came.

But first came *Anastasia.*

My old friend Kay Brown had been determined to pick me up off the ground and get me back into American pictures. She had brought me the play of *Anastasia* some time before. Twentieth Century-Fox had bought the rights for an enormous sum and Anatole Litvak was going to direct it. I didn't know it at the time, but Anatole had declared his condition: he would not direct unless he could get me to play in it.

We'd met several times in Hollywood, and he'd wanted me for a picture called *The Snake Pit,* but I didn't want to do it. Then Olivia de Havilland took the part and she got an Oscar for her performance which was marvelous. And Anatole kept saying, "Look what you turned down!" And I'd reply, "I know what I turned down. It all takes place in an insane asylum and I couldn't bear that. It was a very good part, but if I had played it, I wouldn't have got an Oscar for it." I also turned down the part of a young Swedish girl with a heavy accent in *The Farmer's Daughter.* I turned it down; Loretta Young played it and got an Oscar. Good luck to her. For me to play my *own* part as a Swedish girl was not what I wanted to do. Ruth Roberts taught Loretta her Swedish accent and she was very good, very funny and fresh, and absolutely right for the character. But I've never regretted refusing either of those parts.

Anyway, in Paris, a friend of mine, a Canadian girl, Elaine Kennedy, called me up and asked whether I could meet Anatole Litvak in the bar of the Plaza Athénée Hotel. It was very very important.

So Anatole and I sat in the corner of the bar, and we discussed *Anastasia.*

He said, "I just want to know if you will do it if I can make the other people agree?" The "other people" in Twentieth Century-Fox thought I was box-office poison; anything they put me in would be destroyed, banned, and thrown out of America. The picture was going to be made in England. Was I interested? Yes, I was interested. It was a marvelous part. Fox discussed this for a long time and finally I got a telegram that they had agreed. Fox would take a chance on me. Then, of course, I had to tell Roberto that not only did I want to do *Anastasia,* but that it was going to be made in England.

Roberto didn't like that. So a big fight started and as usual he threatened to drive the Ferrari into a tree. In the past he had always frightened me with this suicide threat: he was going to commit suicide and it would be on my conscience. And I had enough on my conscience as it was. But I was determined to do *Anastasia*. I just didn't believe his suicide threat any more. I said, "We must think of the children. We must have more money. We must pay our bills. I must get back to the kind of work I can do successfully." But it was very hard.

———— • ————

It was, as Ingrid knew, too marvelous a role to lose. She played Anna Tschaikowsky, a bedraggled confused young woman fished out of a Berlin canal by the police after a suicide attempt in 1920. But who was Anna? Was she only a bewildered Polish peasant girl, or was she really the Grand Duchess Anastasia, youngest daughter of Czar Nicholas II, the only survivor after he was murdered together with the rest of his royal family? Had she been rescued by two Red Army brothers and smuggled into Germany? Was the bayonet wound through her palm a result of that dreadful massacre?

Yul Brynner was the cruel and domineering Colonel Bournine, coaching Anna to impersonate Anastasia and so lay claim to a vast fortune, but slowly beginning to realize that perhaps he really had a royal heiress on his hands. Helen Hayes was the Dowager Empress of All the Russias, from whom Anna must win approval if she was to be accepted as Anastasia.

———— • ————

It was a fine film, and I was working with a great actress, Helen Hayes, and a great director, Anatole Litvak. And Yul Brynner was really at the beginning of his career. He'd had this huge success in *The King and I*, and he was so helpful and understanding, such a wonderful friend.

Roberto only came to see me once while I was making the picture. I think a lot of people sensed that the marriage was cracking.

Anatole and I got on very well, though he was a bit worried occasionally about my slowness in learning the dialogue. I remember him saying, "Ingrid, you are marvelous in this picture, but think how much better you would be if only you knew your dialogue." Then one day he passed me in my little trailer, and there

I was reading the script. "Great! You are actually studying the dialogue," he said. I didn't have the heart to tell him I was studying *Tea and Sympathy.* In French.

When *Anastasia* finished, I went back to Paris knowing that trouble with Roberto was certain to break out. *Tea and Sympathy* is the story of a young boarding-school boy who is afraid he is a homosexual. Roberto was always disturbed by any sort of homosexuality. When I wanted to send Robertino to a Swiss or English boarding school, he blew up. "What!" he screamed, "That's where it all starts, in those boarding schools." So Robertino never got a boarding-school education, though I did manage to send him to a summer camp near Oxford to learn English. When he came back, I said in my best English accent, "How do you do?" And he said, "Eh?" "Didn't you learn any English?" I asked. And he answered, "Not much. The camp was full of Italian boys."

I was working regularly with my French teacher on the dialogue of *Tea and Sympathy* by the time Roberto decided he'd read the play. He sat down and soon I heard him mutter, "It's funny, this dialogue here? And this bit? Do you understand what it means?"

"Yes, I understand what it means. Go on reading it."

The whole theme was too distasteful to him. It wasn't the writing or the writer; he just hated the general theme. He also hated the fact that in the play I was going to prove to this boy that he wasn't a homosexual, lead him into sex. The whole part disturbed Roberto immensely. He finished the play, stood up, and threw the script across the room against the wall where it scattered all over the floor.

"It's the most awful play I've ever read, and you're not going to do it."

I said, "We've both signed."

"What does that signify?"

"It means that I've signed a contract."

"Never in my life have I read such a play. This homosexuality. . . ."

"I'm sorry, I'm not breaking my word. I like my part and I'm working on it, and we're starting rehearsals in a few days. You could have read it before you signed."

"You're not going to do it, and I'm not going to do it."

I suppose that two or three years earlier I might have been a submissive little Italian wife, but I don't think so because I've never been submissive as far as my work is concerned.

"You can walk out on it," I said. "I don't usually walk out on something I've signed my name to, and have promised to do. Besides, I *like* the play."

"Like the play! It is going to be laughed off the boards of Paris, and it will be closed in a week."

"Fine. I'll play one week in Paris. There are many people who've never played in Paris all their acting lives. I'll play one week."

He couldn't make me leave the play. He went and told Elvire Popesco that he wouldn't do the play, that it was terrible. I don't think Elvire even looked disappointed. She simply said, "Okay. Sorry you're not doing it. We'll find another director." And they found another director. Jean Mercure moved in and we began rehearsing. All the time Roberto kept nagging: "This silly play. You're going to act in this stupid play! The audience is certainly going to walk out in the middle of it!"

I answered, "Yes, maybe they will. I'll do my best, that's all I can do," and I went on practicing the French dialogue with my teacher.

On opening night, he was in the dressing room still chattering away in Italian. I said, "Roberto, will you *please* speak French to me. I've got to act in French." He wouldn't. He said, "You won't be on very long. Be prepared when the first intermission comes for half of them to walk out."

I didn't answer that. I made the little cross on his forehead that we always used, meaning *Dieu te bénisse* (God bless you), and I went out to the wings, as usual, petrified with stage fright. But everything went fairly well.

When I came back to change my dress, Roberto was still there. "How many walked out?"

"I don't know who walked out. I was too busy."

"Wait till the intermission."

The intermission came. Still no walkout.

I did the last act and I saw Roberto standing in the wings. I stood there with the cast and the ovation was enormous. I remembered when I did *Joan of Lorraine* in New York, I thought I'd never receive applause like that again. But this was the same. The house went wild. You couldn't stop them. They were standing up and screaming, standing up and applauding, and the "bravos" never stopped. Then I took my solo bow in the center of the stage, and as I bent over I turned my head and looked at Roberto. Our eyes met. We looked straight at each other. I knew then my marriage was over even though we might stay together.

I had to go out to a party with Roberto and all his Italian friends that night. We laughed a lot. Nobody talked about the play. Nobody said anything about its being a success. The following day Roberto packed his suitcases in the Raphael Hotel and I went to the railway station to see him off. I don't know why he took a train. I remember his suitcases were full of spaghetti. As we stood there in the noise and the smoke amid all the people, I had this very strange feeling that this was the end of an episode and that things would never be the same again.

———— • ————

Tea and Sympathy filled the twelve hundred seats at the Théâtre de Paris every night with passionate adherents. "Magic came back to the theater last night," said one of the critics. All the reviews were superb. And even when Ingrid occasionally made a slip in her dialogue, the audience treated it as an integral part of the entertainment:

———— • ————

I am the headmaster's wife, and in one scene the father of a boy comes to talk to me because he is terribly worried that his son is such a weakling and doesn't play any manly sports. And trying to protect the boy, I say, "How can you think that! He is the champion in tennis, the tennis champion of the whole school." I got the line out in my best French, and the entire audience collapsed. The house rocked. I looked around at the other two actors, the headmaster and the father. They were not even looking at the audience. They had their backs to it and their shoulders were shaking; they were helpless with laughter. I sidled up very close to the father and asked, "What did I say?"

"You said, 'champignon—champignon!'" Which, of course, means mushroom. Instead of "champion," I'd called the son the "mushroom" of the whole school. I began to laugh too. I turned to face the audience, and I held my arm high in the air to admit my error as I shouted, *Il est le champion de l'ecole.* The audience stood as one man and shouted, "Bravo, bravo." Then there was great applause and we just stood there laughing for another five minutes before the show could go on.

———— • ————

Anastasia, released during the run of *Tea and Sympathy,* was an immediate and immense worldwide success. It was a "watershed" film both in her career as an actress, and in her personal life, and it confronted her with two of the most important decisions she had ever had to make: one concerned Roberto, the other Pia. The enthusiasm of the New York critics was primarily responsible.

Bosley Crowther in *The New York Times:* "Miss Bergman's performance is nothing short of superb. It is a beautifully molded performance worthy of an Academy Award." Alton Cook in the *New York World Telegram:* "Miss Bergman is the same torrent of passionate and impulsive ardor that she was before leaving American films seven years ago." Kate Cameron in the *Daily News:* "If Hollywood spent more of its time, money and talent on pictures like *Anastasia,* there would be less cause for worry now about the state of the motion picture industry."

Without much argument, in the autumn of 1956 the New York critics gave Ingrid their award as the best actress of the year.

———————— • ————————

Twentieth Century-Fox wanted me to come to New York to receive the New York Critic's Award. They had invested a lot of money in *Anastasia.* They wanted to go on making movies with me. But they also wanted me to go to America as a sort of "try-out," to see if the public would lynch me or love me. They wanted to buy out three "full-house" performances of *Tea and Sympathy,* the Saturday night and the two Sunday shows, fly me across to New York so I could receive the award, and then fly me back on Monday morning to be available for the Théâtre de Paris that night.

———————— • ————————

At the same time, Ed Sullivan, whose Sunday night television show was popular with millions of viewers, was conducting his own poll as to whether the American public wanted to love or lynch Ingrid.

In July 1956, he had informed his audience that he had just returned from London's film studios where *Anastasia* was being made, and had television coverage of Helen Hayes, Yul Brynner, and "that great Swedish star," Ingrid Bergman. He had also heard a rumor that at the completion of the picture Miss Bergman might be visiting the United States once more. As Ed became even more expansive, he went on to say that he thought it was up to his audience to decide whether or not they wanted to see him interview this "controversial figure on our show."

Even more perilously, he continued: "I think a lot of you think that this woman has had seven and a half years of time for penance. Others may not think so, but whatever you think, it would help us clarify because everybody's rung up this morning, wanting to know what the decision has been on the Ingrid Bergman appearance, and I told them what I told you: it's entirely up to the public."

Many of Ed's fellow journalists and television pundits quickly reminded him that it was none of his business to act as a referee in condemnation or approval. One paper published a letter from a priest alleging that Ed was stepping into the terrain of the Almighty: "The public cannot know where Miss Bergman's conscience has led her. Is Sullivan the one to say there have been seven years of penance? How can Sullivan's public react to Miss Bergman's completely private torture if they can't read Miss Bergman's mind."

The same paper revealed that "a source close to Ed Sullivan stated: 'We've got a million or so letters, plus a zillion telephone calls, and the majority are vociferously in favor of keeping Miss Bergman's assets firmly frozen in France.'" The letters were also against her appearance on his show.

Ed Sullivan hastily dispatched a cable to Ingrid saying the whole thing had been a mistake which he regretted. Another cable, a short time later, said that the letters received so far indicated roughly 1500 against her visit and 2500 saying they would love to see her.

Ingrid was not deeply concerned about Ed Sullivan's dilemma. She was certainly not going to appear on his show. But she had Roberto to worry about. She knew his hatred against Ameica at this moment was almost pathological.

———— • ————

Of course I was very doubtful that visiting the United States was the right thing to do, especially as Roberto and his brother Renzo were against it. As Roberto was now in India, Renzo took it upon himself to write me saying it was a kind of breach of promise. But I had never promised I would not go back to America. I had been so hurt, I had taken it for granted that I would stay away from America for the rest of my life. But then came this outstretched hand. I felt that many Americans wanted to see me; I'd always had a big following and a lot of fans in America. And with all the letters that streamed into Italy during the years, I realized that there were an awful lot of people who really wanted me back.

I knew I would have to meet the American press in New York, and the questions would be very nasty. Yul Brynner called me up in Paris when he heard I was going, and said, "Take some tranquilizers with you." And for the first time in my life, I did. I actually took one. But what touched me most was Leonard Lyons, the American columnist. He'd always been a very good friend without even knowing me very well. He called me up too and said, "Ingrid, I'm down here in the bar of your hotel, and I have with me a devoted admirer who wants to punch everyone in the nose who stands in your way: Papa Hemingway. Can we come up?"

They came up and we kissed each other, and Ernest looked at me over the top of his glasses and said, very seriously, "Daughter, I want to come with you to New York and protect you. It's no trouble; I can jump on that plane with you tomorrow morning, I shall be by your side. If any goddamn reporter asks you a nasty question, I shall knock him down. No one's going to get in your way while I'm there."

I said, "That's very sweet of you, Ernest, but I must go completely alone. If I have a secretary, a public relations person, a friend, a husband, or if I have *you*, they'll only say, 'Look at her dragging her defenses around with her. She's afraid.' Yes, I am afraid, but I must be completely alone and unprotected to let them say what they've got to say. That's the only way I feel I can go back. All by myself."

———————— • ————————

At just after eight o'clock on Sunday, January 20, 1957, the big Constellation came out of the leaden skies and onto a runway at Idlewild Airport. Ingrid peered out apprehensively at the waiting crowds, muffled against the biting wind. Then her eyes widened. Could it be true? Could *they* be there? After all these years? But they were! That small bunch of people standing behind the wire fence with their big white placards: "We Love You Ingrid! Welcome Home Ingrid Bergman. The Alvin Gang."

After all these years, the Alvin Gang! Among them—as their leader—a most unusual and devoted young man who had given his whole life over to her. His name was Warren Thomas, and he has told his own story of how the Gang came to be:

"I was twelve years old when I first knew about Ingrid Bergman. As a Christmas present, my sister was taking me to the Radio City Music Hall where she was playing in *The Bells of St. Mary's*. We went by subway from Brooklyn up to Fifth Avenue and the center of New York, and there were lines a mile long, no hope of getting in. I remember being so bitterly disappointed—it was a shock, an immense shock. It had been so important to me.

"My mother died when I was born. My friends say this Ingrid Bergman thing is a sort of mother fixation; maybe they're right. We lived in Brooklyn in a very bad neighborhood. My father and I shared one room in a rooming house that was full of prostitutes. My elder sister was boarded out with an aunt somewhere upstate, and I was shifted off there every so often. Then I came back to this tough neighborhood, full of every sort of ethnic group, and tough, very tough. There was trouble with theft, murder, drugs, prostitution, every sort of crime. Kids got into trouble everywhere in that neighborhood. It was nearly impossible to stay alive and not get into trouble.

"But when I was twelve or thirteen, my chief buddy was Adaire. She was a black girl, same age, and like pepper and salt we were together everywhere. So after just missing *The Bells of St. Mary's,* we heard that Ingrid Bergman was opening in *Joan of Lorraine* at the Alvin Theater. She was already in town, staying at the Hampshire House. So we decided we had to see this. Into the subway, up to Manhattan and there we were, waiting outside the Hampshire House when Ingrid Bergman came out to go for a walk. We followed her for about twelve blocks, and she knew we were behind her. I suppose a white boy and black girl tracking you are pretty easy to spot. So eventually she stopped and said, 'Why are you following me?' I said, very quickly, the first thing that came into my head, 'Because we love you.' 'Well,' she said, 'I don't like being followed. It annoys me. So don't follow me any more.'

"Well, that was terrible—my loved one was annoyed at me on our first meeting. But, of course, it did not stop me at all. I decided I just had to see her every week. The best time was Wednesday afternoon when she had her matinee. I could see her at two o'clock when she went in and at five o'clock when she came out, and that was all I wanted out of life. Every Wednesday and Saturday afternoons, that was what I did. Of course the principal also noticed my absence and sent for me. What did I do which kept me away every Wednesday afternoon? So I told him the truth. I adored Ingrid Bergman. She was playing at the Alvin, and I just had to see her on her matinee on Wednesday. He laughed and said, 'Well, at least we know where you are now.' Then he said, 'All right, we'll do a deal. Your English is good. Your reading is good. You can have Wednesday afternoons off if you take over a backward reading class on Friday afternoons and instruct those kids—right?' Right. So for the rest of the run of *Joan of Lorraine,* I got Wednesday afternoons off and the backward kids got extra instruction on Fridays. Then, of course, I managed to get Friday night into the picture. Friday night was pay night and my father would come home and give me a dollar. Then he went out and wouldn't be back until midnight or one. So off I ran to the subway and there I was, waiting outside when she went in for the evening performance, and waiting outside again at eleven when she came out. Then I raced for the subway to get home before my old man. And I couldn't get into trouble in my neighborhood. Suppose Miss Bergman ever found out that I was in trouble? She'd never be a friend of mine. And that's the way I molded my life.

"Then Adaire and I found a regular group waiting outside the stage door at the Alvin. A dozen or so kids like us, and then a few women in their thirties and forties, and a few older people too: we became the nucleus of the Alvin Gang. On the Saturday afternoon matinee, they'd leave the doors open after the intermission, and allow us kids in to stand at the back, so I saw the second half of *Joan of Lorraine* between thirty and forty times. That was the part we wanted to see because it was all about Joan of Arc, the real thing with Ingrid, not all the political talk. Finally we managed to scrape our pennies together and raise the four dollars to see the whole play, but really it was the second half which gave us our kicks.

"And at the end of the run on that very last performance, Ingrid sent Joe Steele out to see us, and he said Ingrid wanted to say good-bye to us. But, of course, a lot of the real theater-goers were coming out too, and they heard what was going on, so when we poured back inside, half of New York was there. I think Ingrid was a bit surprised to see such a big crowd. She came on stage, and she made a little speech saying how grateful she was to us, and how lovely it was to have such devoted fans. She thanked us for being so loyal, and if she'd been annoyed at us sometimes she hoped we'd understand. We all cheered. This was the greatest thing in the world. We'd been acknowledged.

"We all went out to the airport to see her off, and we met Dr. Petter Lindstrom for the first time. He'd seen us outside the Hampshire House and he hadn't been very pleased. He was even less pleased to see us at the airport. 'Why weren't we at home? What were we doing out here?' I remember, I couldn't understand his attitude and I was very hurt. Didn't he understand she was our life?

"During the six-month run of the play, Ingrid was also doing radio shows for the Theater Guild on Sunday evenings. The tickets were free and we got to know the announcer and he was a sympathetic guy, so we got tickets in the afternoon *and* the evening. Then later, she used to come back from California and do radio for the Ford Theater. She did *Camille* the Friday night before she left for Italy. We were at that show, and at the end she was given a little box of three camelias. We knew she'd be going back to the Hampshire House, so Adaire and I raced to wait for her there. We got to the Hampshire House at eleven o'clock and at two thirty we were still standing there. We managed to shelter out of the wind a bit by standing in the doorway where they take the luggage in. And at two thirty A.M. the cab finally pulled up, and out stepped Ingrid, still with her box of camelias. She saw us and she was furious. 'What are you doing here at this time in the morning! In this cold! You should be home! Why aren't you home?' Then she looked at us again and started to laugh. 'I'm very angry with you,' she said, 'but let me give you something anyway,' and she opened her box and gave one camelia to me, and one to Adaire. I treasured mine. Kept it for years along with all the photographs, cuttings, and programs, until it browned and fell into pieces.

"Of course we followed Ingrid every time she came to New York. But we were cleverer now. She couldn't tell we were following her when she went to see *Paisan.* It was a matinee and the movie was pretty empty and we sat right behind her, quiet as mice. She had no idea we were there.

"So, anyway, she went off to Rome. Then it all started. You know, you live in a fantasy world, you know things are wrong, people are bad, people are good, but you're not part of that because you're here and you don't want anything to touch you. So all of a sudden there was this big explosion. I was sixteen now, and I wondered, How do I scream out: 'Stop, leave her alone'? I was so upset. It was then I realized how rotten people are. She'd done *Joan of Arc,* she'd been *that* person. How rotten can they be? And I suffered for her. Those years, I kept in contact with the Alvin Gang; we rang each other up and commiserated together. If I read a columnist was going overseas, I'd try and catch him: Earl Wilson, for example. 'Mr. Wilson if you go to Rome will you try and speak to Miss Bergman. Just tell her the Alvin Gang misses her, loves her, or simply say, "New York— Alvin Gang." ' I never knew if she ever got those messages. I wrote to the Excelsior Hotel, Rome, but I don't suppose she got those letters either. I even wrote to Pia in California! 'I know she's your mother, but she's also my friend. Even though she's never met me, she's also my friend.' I couldn't believe it was happening to Ingrid. Those headlines. It was awful. I remember one day the *New York Post* changed its headlines four times in one day, and each of them said something nasty about Ingrid.

"I must have aged ten years when I was sixteen. And of course the Alvin Gang pretty well went to pieces; some for, some against. Then I got drafted. There were two commands I might be sent to: Europe or Korea. And I knew I had to go to Europe. I went to the Army: 'I'll enlist,' I said, 'I'll enlist for four years if you'll send me to Europe.' In Europe, I knew I'd be able to see her. I'd find her there. But they didn't buy my thing. I went to Korea. I was there for thirteen months as an engineer, and the twins were born during that period. And when I got the news I was ecstatic. I remember I went up a hill by myself and stood on the top, looking up at that Korean sky and yelling at the top of my voice, 'Congratulations, Ingrid! Well done! Give my love to the twins! And have some more babies. Have more!'

"And then, of course, came the day I was back in the United States and she was coming back. I got to the Alvin Gang in a flash. Adaire was still around but not many of the others; but I drummed up ten of them and got them to come along to the airport. I bought these big white placards, illustration boards, and I sat up all night for two nights painting the messages on them: how much we missed her. And now that she was Italian, we had to have something in Italian, so I got out: *'Viva la Regina!'*

"The plane was due at seven in the morning, so we took the subway out the night before, and we were there at eleven thirty P.M. We waited all night for the plane to arrive; it was two and a half hours late, and we were all panicking. She's not coming! She's chickened out! She's staying in Europe! There was an awful lot of confusion. We'd never seen so many reporters in all our lives. We got out on the field, behind the wire fence, and there was the plane turning in and stopping. We prayed she would see us, and we had to make enough noise so at least she would hear us. I remember my throat was so sore I couldn't speak for two days afterwards. But by this time the press realized who we were, and they took pictures, and Ingrid came out and stood with us, and that was a great morning. Of course, I'd still never met her. It took another seven years for a chance to talk to her and eventually become a friend."

———————— • ————————

At that airport press conference I was asked every question under the sun. "Would I be coming back to live in the United States?" I said, "I'm a European. My husband is a European. I have an Italian passport in my purse. My children are European. Why should I want to uproot them?" And they plugged on about rumors that there was trouble between Roberto and me. "Are you and Rossellini happy?" I said, "Whenever people ask me that I say we are separated." Gave them a second for the startled look, then I added, "He's working on a film in India, and I'm in Paris." Then of course they got on to Pia, and was I going to meet her? And I knew by now it was doubtful. I hedged. "I don't know yet. Probably not on a trip as short as this. I must be back in Paris for the play on Monday night. When Pia and I meet again, I want it to be alone and in peace. To see her for only a few snatched minutes after all these years would be torture." That was true enough, but I think it was one of the greatest mistakes of my life.

I was so moved by the marvelous reception at the airport. I'd expected harsh questions and possibly an angry jeering crowd, and instead all those wonderful supporters in the Alvin Gang.

I left the airport and went to Irene Selznick's apartment in New York. There I read the first American newspaper I'd seen in years. And read in it that Signe Hasso's son was killed in a car accident. My God, I thought, that can't be true. Signe and I were at dramatic school together. In Sweden she worked mostly on the stage. She came to Hollywood with a contract to one of the big studios.

In Hollywood we were together quite a lot. She gave little parties; she came to ours, and Petter and Signe became very good friends. We were always close and kept in touch. Then she moved to New York, and went to live in Harlem because she wanted to get to know the black people better. She was the most warm and generous person.

All that time she had great medical problems with her son: he had to go to many doctors and hospitals, and she spent all her money and all her love trying to get him well. Now, she was in a play in New York, and her son—oh, he was so handsome and twenty-one years old—had been cured of all his illnesses, and he had his first film contract with a studio. And he was driving along a highway with his best friend, and they were in an accident and he was killed. How cruel can life be?

So I ran to Irene and said, "I must get hold of Signe. Do you know where she is?"

"She's right here with her play. I haven't got her phone number but if you call Viveca Lindfors, she'll know where she is."

Viveca is another Swedish actress whom I hardly knew at all. I called her and she said, "Why Signe's right here. Hold on."

So Signe got on the phone and began to chat away. "Ingrid, how good to hear from you. And you're in New York to receive the New York Critic's Award. I'm so glad for you, and how wonderful it is to have you back in America. I know there's a big party at Sardi's tonight. I've been invited and I don't know if I shall be able to make it. But so good to hear from you. . . ." and on and on. . . .

I thought, something had gone wrong with my brain. I said, "Wait a minute. I read in the paper that your son was killed in a car accident."

"Yes, isn't it terrible. He was killed. And I feel so sorry for the boy who was driving the car. It was his best friend. He didn't get killed. I've asked him to come here so that I can take care of him because he must feel awful. . . ."

"But aren't you going to California?"

"For what? My son is dead. What good can I do? The only good I can do is to help the other boy, to take him away from there and bring him here."

"You're going to stay in New York?"

"Yes, I'm going down to the theater in a few hours."

I couldn't believe what I was hearing. "Are you going to be able to play tonight? Are you really going to play?"

And she said very quietly, "Yes, Ingrid, I must play tonight. Otherwise, I'll go insane."

I was the one who began to cry. And that dialogue with Signe stayed with me for years afterwards.

Then I knew I had to call Pia. She knew I was coming. I'd written and told her how wonderful it would be to see her again after all these years. I'd told Irene and Kay Brown to tell her.

Now I knew I couldn't see her. After the airport interrogation, the Alvin Gang, and Signe Hasso, and with the Critic's Award coming and an appearance on Steve Allen's TV show in a special relay from Sardi's restaurant, I just couldn't bear the thought of all those photographers and reporters who would crowd in and wait for me to cry when I met her, and see how overwhelmed and distraught I was. I couldn't face this emotional climax. I knew that at most I could have one hour alone with my daughter. I called Pia and told her this. I tried to tell her that I didn't know how to fit in what was the most important thing in my life on this journey: to see her. I tried to explain that I couldn't handle it because I was afraid I would absolutely go to pieces emotionally, and not be able to do another thing on this trip. And maybe that's what I should have done. But I'd used up all my courage just getting here. And now I hadn't enough courage to face my daughter.

But poor Pia didn't understand that. She thought I didn't want to see her; she thought that my career was more important to me, that all I wanted was to see my friends and then go on television. So she unpacked her suitcase and went back to class. Reporters telephoned her and she told them she had so much work to do that she couldn't leave because she would fall behind. And everyone thought it was very strange. I understood that it *was* very strange.

And that was one of the big wounds that Pia carried for many years. It was only later, when we were at Choisel in France, that she recalled that incident and said she understood then that my career was more important to me than she was. I tried to explain the emotional intensity of that first return to New York—how I couldn't take any more. I couldn't have been any sort of mother to her—just a weeping woman. I had to wait until I could see her alone without the press. But she had a very hard time understanding that, and to this very day, though she can understand it with her brain, I am afraid she does not accept it with her heart.

———— • ————

That long anticipated meeting took place six months later on July 8, 1957. Dr. Petter Lindstrom had remarried and was visiting Stockholm with his wife Agnes and their small son Peter. Pia, now eighteen, a student at the University of Colorado, called Ingrid and arranged to meet her in Paris:

I knew it would be a very emotional meeting. It was the first time we had met for six long years. I knew I would weep. I expected that Pia would cry also. And I didn't really want all this in front of the dozens of cameramen who were bound to be there. So I talked to Scandinavian Airlines. They were very understanding. They said, "We'll keep her aboard until all the passengers have disembarked, and then you can go onto the aircraft and be alone together."

So I was on the plane and there was Pia and we fell into each other's arms, and immediately a flashbulb went off.

Paris Match had sent a photographer all the way from New York so that he could watch Pia and get the first reunion picture. When he had realized that Pia was being kept back, he hid himself on the floor at the back of the plane. Well, they threw him off. Pia looked at me very curiously and said, "How young you look."

———————— • ————————

They were alone for twelve minutes before they reappeared on the aircraft steps to face the milling photographers.

"We are happy to be together after six years; no, we don't know what we'll do together in Paris," was Ingrid's only statement.

Pia remembers it well:

"Meeting in Paris wasn't a trauma. It's a trauma when things happen at age ten. As I look back on it, I found that Paris meeting very exciting; all that attention was very exciting; there were hundreds and hundreds of people at the airport just to see my mother and me. I mean, it was really a combination of being excited and being, I suppose, a little embarrassed and ill at ease because so many people are staring at you, and taking pictures of you. But to say I was afraid would be wrong because I wasn't. I was by then a pretty big person."

They had to slip out of the back door of their hotel to manage to enjoy one night of seeing the town without photographers. For the rest of Pia's stay, they were besieged wherever they went. Pia was in Europe for more than two months. Ingrid wanted to show her all she could. They visited Sicily. And at last Pia's room at Santa Marinella was occupied and all the children could meet.

Ingrid wrote to Irene Selznick:

The young people are dancing on the terrace and I have
to pretend to be old and go to bed. Of course it's not what I
feel like, but I think it is the part to play. Anyway, I am so
happy I'd rather be alone. Everything worked out so much
better than we thought. Pia is happy here, so open-minded,
likes everything, is very sweet to the little children. She told
me the first day she could not come home to Europe next
summer, but the second day she said, "Why in the world
should I stay in America when it is so wonderful here?" Of
course everybody is trying to make each day a feast. Each
day we do different things, but what is nice is that when we
come home alone or stay alone here at Santa Marinella she
thinks that is wonderful too. She is lots of fun, sensible and
intelligent. She is so much more than I ever hoped for. I
can't tell you how happy I am these days. It seems impossible and still I can't really believe it. I behave very casually
—just as if the whole thing was natural—just not to scare
her—I leave her much alone to be with the young ones or to
read a book in a corner. I long for the moments we talk, but
I won't force myself on her.

———————— • ————————

Back in Paris after Pia returned to America it was now quite a
different sort of existence. I had the children with me; Roberto was
going to be away in India for many months; he was away for nine
altogether. I was on my own having to make my own decisions.

I remember getting my first salary check for *Tea and Sympathy*.
I don't think I'd held any money I'd earned since I was given the
ten kronor for being an extra at sixteen! I didn't know what to do
with it. One of the cast told me of a lawyer, and he opened a bank
account for me; the money went in there every week or every month.
Then later, I heard I had to pay taxes on the money I earned in
France. I didn't know anything about taxes. In Italy, Roberto had
done everything: he didn't pay many taxes. Finally I was told that
it was absolutely illegal for me, as a foreigner, to have a bank
account in France in the first place; that every check should be
withheld and so much money taken from it; and that I should have
declared all this. I called back my lawyer and said, "You didn't tell
me all these things. So what do I do now?"

"Well, what have you paid for?" he asked.

"I've paid for the hotel and the three children and the governess's expenses and salary. Now when the tax people come and ask for a lot of money, what do I tell them?"

"Oh, that's easy. You say that you have a lover you have to keep, and that's where all the money has gone."

"I'm keeping a lover and *paying* for him!"

"That's right. He took all your money. That's very normal. They'll understand that, and you'll get by."

"I don't care very much for this idea."

"Now don't worry. Wait till they come after you, and then we'll decide."

So I didn't do anything, and I waited for the tax people to approach me. Nothing happened, so I called the lawyer, and said, "Nothing has happened."

"Oh good, if they don't catch you within ten years, then it's all right."

"I don't very much care. . . ."

"Don't worry, leave it all to me."

In the ninth year, the tax people caught up with me. By this time I was married again and I had this huge amount of money to pay. All because of my lawyer's good advice. I've tried to keep away from lawyers ever since.

But in those days when I was in the Paris theater I was so very naïve. And I still blushed so much. At every intermission the stage manager would come into my dressing room, and the rest of the cast would gather there too, and sit and tell dirty stories. They said the object of the exercise was to teach Ingrid *not* to blush. See how far we can go. Finally, she will get hardened. She won't blush any more. Half the time I didn't understand the jokes, and they had to explain them, and still I couldn't understand. But we laughed and laughed. Then I'd go back on stage and play the schoolmaster's wife. It was so much fun. The theater was so packed with people and enthusiasm, and the newspapers never stopped writing about it. It was very exciting to have this success in Paris.

Kay Brown called me up and told me about Robert Anderson, the playwright who'd written *Tea and Sympathy*. He'd just lost his wife from a terrible form of cancer—a long, desperate illness with him watching her die a little more each day. And Kay said, "It's almost destroyed him. I don't really think he wants to live himself. Do help him. I'm getting him to fly to Paris for the opening night. Maybe he'll start living and working again."

He had an awful flight across the Atlantic—the plane had to turn back—and he arrived just in time to see the opening.

We became great friends. I realized very quickly that he was a man who couldn't cope any longer with anything, and I did all I could to help him survive. He was very close to me in those days. Maybe I was in need too. I knew it was important perhaps to both of us.

It was around this time also that I first met Lars Schmidt, a Swede like me, who had produced a great number of plays. His show, Tennessee Williams's *Cat on a Hot Tin Roof*, was also running in Paris.

———————— • ————————

He had clear memories of how they met:

"In 1956 I had managed to get Peter Brook across from London to direct *Cat on A Hot Tin Roof*. I had a fabulous cast and we were very successful. Then, just before Christmas I heard that Ingrid Bergman, who was playing in Robert Anderson's *Tea and Sympathy*, was coming to see our show. I played the host and went up to her before the performance. 'Miss Bergman, if you and Robert would like a glass of champagne during the intermission? . . .' 'That would be very nice. Thank you very much.' A ravishing smile and off to their seats.

"With me, during the intermission, was an old friend of mine, a big, tall, handsome Swede named Gustav, who had met Ingrid before. And Ingrid was chatting away gaily to Gustav, and I was running around pouring champagne and seeing that everybody was served. That's as close as I got to Miss Bergman. But she was very beautiful and very gracious.

"Then a few weeks later, Kay Brown arrived in Paris. Kay is Ingrid's agent, and she's also my American agent. 'It's ridiculous,' she said, 'Two Swedes living in Paris and you don't know each other! Why you're even living in the same hotel. I'll fix it.'

"So we were introduced and I invited Ingrid out to dinner, and we went to a little restaurant called the Coq d'Or. Ingrid sat there looking at me and said, 'Isn't it strange, us not meeting before.'

" 'But we have met before.'

" 'Have we? Where?'

" 'You came to see my production of *Cat on a Hot Tin Roof.*'

" 'Oh, is that your production? But I didn't meet you.'

" 'Yes you did. You had champagne at the intermission. I poured it for you.'

" '*You* poured it! Oh dear, I thought you were the waiter!'

"That evening at dinner we talked about Sweden, we talked about everything, but then as the weeks passed I rushed all over the world, as usual. We were still staying in the same hotel, but she was busy and I was busy, and we didn't meet again.

"One day I came back and called her up in the morning, and said, 'Would you care to have lunch with me?'

" 'Oh, I am so sorry. I have to take care of my children.'

"I understood that and I went to lunch instead with a friend. We drove out to this pleasant little restaurant in the Bois de Boulogne, and whom did I find sitting at a table very close to the lake there in a very romantic setting—none other than Miss Bergman! So at the end of the meal I wandered over and said in Swedish—for she was with Bob Anderson—'Ah, Miss Bergman, so this is the way you take care of your children.'

"And she looked up at me and she blushed. I'd never seen anyone blush like it. Then she looked at me with this most divine smile. And that night I called her again. And that broke the ice completely."

———————— • ————————

It was in that period I won my second Oscar: for *Anastasia.*

Cary Grant, who was a very good friend, had promised to stand by at the Academy Awards just in case I got lucky, to go up and collect the prize. I did the evening performance of *Tea and Sympathy* and went to bed as usual in the Raphael Hotel. I was awakened at seven in the morning by Twentieth Century-Fox publicity men shouting into the phone, "You've won! You've won!"

I went to take my bath, and have a glass of champagne to celebrate, and there was little Robertino carrying his radio around and saying, "Mama, they're talking about you!" He couldn't understand English very well, but he got my name. It was a repeat over the French radio of the Oscar ceremony in Hollywood, and Robertino had heard the announcement of "Ingrid Bergman" and then the applause. I could still hear the applause as he put the radio on the bathroom floor, and then Cary began his speech: "Dear Ingrid,

wherever you are. . . ." And I was saying, "I'm in the bathtub!"
"Wherever you are in the world, we, your friends, want to congratu-
late you, and I have your Oscar here for your marvelous performance, and may you be as happy as we are for you."

Poor little Robertino didn't understand at all why Mama was
crying into her bath when obviously she'd been so delighted with
what they were saying on the radio.

Then a new drama started with Roberto. There was no thought
in my mind that I would ever divorce Roberto. I would have gone
through hell and still stayed with him, having had such hell to
marry him in the first place.

Besides I could not leave him because I would have felt I had
abandoned somebody that I had been part of ruining. After all,
who took the first step? I did. I was the one who wrote to him
that I wanted to make a movie with him. It had all started with
that. And I felt that when he came back from India we would
pick up the situation and go on in the same way—or try to—
because even that was unlikely now that I had gone back to
American movies.

Then in the middle of one night in the spring of 1956 the phone
rang in my Raphael Hotel bedroom. "Roberto! Where are you
phoning from? . . . India?" It must have cost him a fortune. "How
are things going along?" "Oh, fine, fine, but there are these newspaper stories going around about this woman. If any newspaper
people call you regarding some romance of mine, you will deny it.
Not a word of it is true! Not a word!"

"All right. If you say so."

We went on chatting for a little while longer, and we hung up.

Someone wrote somewhere about my life with Roberto that although I was probably always troubled by my puritanical conscience, with him I had found a world that for me was probably
better than most of us ever attain. And that is true. I did have
marvelous happiness with Roberto as well as deep troubles. But
trouble is part of one's life. If you have never had any trouble, if
you have never cried, if you have never been really miserable and
thought that you could not go on, what kind of understanding
would you have for other people who are in trouble? You wouldn't
have any patience with them. Now you *know* what it feels like. I
think that's what life is all about. You have to have your ups and
downs, you can't be happy all the time.

I would think a person who is always happy would be a big bore. And Roberto was never a bore.

I tried many ways to live with him. I remember saying to him during the difficulties we had with money, "Look, let us go bankrupt. People go bankrupt, don't they? What can happen? We don't go to jail, do we? Let us just live on whatever we have. Let them take the house away. Give it all away, everything, everything. And we start from nothing. We take a small apartment. I shall do the cleaning, the scrubbing, cook the food. We won't have any servants or anything." And Roberto looked at me as if I were mad. *"That* life isn't worth living," he said. That was such a slap in my face, because I thought I offered him everything and he wouldn't even think of it. "That life is not worth living!" Life had to be in the grand style.

As I put the phone down on Roberto and sat on the bed, I was thinking about all these things. And wondering what I would do. Because I knew now that things had changed forever. I knew that when he rang me up to tell me a thing like that, he did have another woman. He had fallen in love again. Certainly she would be in love with him, and now she would look after him and make him happy.

He had left *me*. As I sat on the bed, I could feel the smile spreading right around up to my ears. I was so pleased. For him. And for me. Now we had solved it.

A few nights later, the phone rang again in the middle of the night. Roberto again! The husband of the woman he was not supposed to be having an affair with, who was also a very important producer, was so angry about the whole business that he'd pulled all sorts of strings. Not only had he managed to stop Roberto from filming any more, he had also managed to get the film impounded so that Roberto could not take the film out of India with him. So Roberto said, "Now it's all nothing—it's stupid—this woman I'm supposed to be in love with. I don't understand what they're talking about. . . . But the only man who can help me with the film is the Prime Minister of India, Nehru. He's in London. You know lots of people in London. Can you get to him and see to it that I'm allowed to bring my film out of India?"

"I'll try," I said, "I'll try."

As is the custom in France, *Tea and Sympathy* was being rested for the summer vacation, so the next morning I called up my very good friend, Ann Todd in London, and said, "Ann, you move around in these sorts of circles. How can I get to meet Nehru and ask him to let Roberto's film leave India?" Ann said, "Well, I know Nehru's sister. She's in London, and I will speak to her."

Ann called back and said, "Lunch tomorrow. Fly over from Paris, and meet me at my flat." So there we were at lunch. Ann, Nehru's sister, me, and Prime Minister Nehru himself. He was the most beautiful man. We had lunch, and I thought, He must wonder why I am here. Only when we walked in the garden after lunch did I realize he already knew.

I said, "My husband, Roberto Rossellini, is in trouble over in your country."

"So I have heard," he said very quietly. Then we walked a bit farther and he said, "I'm sure he'll be allowed to leave sooner or later."

"But he can't leave India without his film," I said. "That's the whole reason for his existence." Again we walked a little farther.

"Well, I understand there are many stories and scandals and money troubles connected with that. I hear there are many problems."

I said, "Yes, I'm sure. He always has problems. But he's such a good man. He's a great artist. That sort of man always has problems. I think it would be very generous if you would allow him to take his film out of India."

"Yes, yes. It will happen."

But I couldn't leave it there. I said, "There's a Swedish saying: 'While the grass is growing, the cow is dying.' You can't leave him marooned in India for too long. He's too good to let go down the drain. Whatever he has done, he's made his picture. Let him leave with his film?"

Well, we went on walking and this time Nehru only smiled and nodded. But he didn't say anything.

The very next day Roberto received permission to take his film out of India. And he left immediately.

People thought I acted strangely, for now the newspapers were full of how Roberto had pursued, fallen in love with, and run off with this Indian producer's wife.

But people do a lot of strange things. And you have to weigh their actions. You have to balance them. You say, "This is good, and that is not so good, but what is really important?" That this man come back with the movie he had made; maybe it had something important to say about India. Maybe the film was no good? You took that chance. Maybe he'd had a love affair? So what! That wasn't important. He had great talent, even genius. No one could take that away from him. And talent is important.

When he arrived back at the Paris airport, I went to meet him. That confused all the newspaper reporters who were around me clamoring, "Miss Bergman, I understand your husband has run away with an Indian girl?" "Hasn't he eloped with the wife of an Indian producer, Miss Bergman?" And I said, "Has he? I didn't know that. I'm just here to meet him."

Roberto came into the airport and I threw myself into his arms. He gave me a great big hug and we kissed; this photograph was all over the world's press, with the caption saying how silly all those rumors were. Here was Ingrid Bergman meeting Roberto Rossellini and here was their wonderful embrace.

But it was a good thing the newsmen were not allowed to come back to the Hotel Raphael with us. There we were in my suite. Roberto was sitting in the armchair twisting a lock of his hair. It was a long nine months since we'd seen each other. He said, "You're still in that idiotic play?"

"Yes, I most certainly am. It's still going strong. Not a seat to be had at any performance. But I can get you a seat tonight if you want to come?"

"No. I don't think I'll come."

So I did the show and I went back to the hotel. Maybe Roberto had been out, or had dinner, or done something, but he was still sitting in the armchair, still pulling that lock of hair. And I thought, Well, perhaps now's the time.

I didn't tell him right away that I had already met Sonali, the Indian woman he'd run away with. She had arrived in Paris a few days before Roberto. I hadn't intended to meet her, but a mutual friend called up and said, "She has arrived from India, and *she* wants to meet you." So I had said, "I'll come right over."

I had found her pretty and very nice, and very serious. She had this little baby in her arms, and I thought, Oh, my goodness. It's not possible. It's not possible is it? How long has Roberto been away? Nine months. No, of course it's not possible, this baby is quite a few months old.

Then Sonali and I talked together. The baby was her youngest son by her Indian husband. She had left her other son, the older one, back in India with her husband. "The papers were terrible," she said, "they spread a lot of scandal, and they told a lot of lies."

I said I'd had a lot of experience with the lies papers tell. She said she did not want anything, she just thought she ought to meet me. And my thought was, Poor woman. Isn't it strange? She has left a child behind exactly as I did.

Now I was in the Raphael Hotel suite with Roberto, and I said very gently, "Look Roberto, would you like a divorce?" I remember he leaned back in the chair, still twiddling with that lock of hair, and looked at the ceiling light and didn't answer. Perhaps he hadn't heard me. I said again, very quietly, "Roberto, do you think it a good idea if we get a divorce?"

Not a word came out, just the looking at the light. And I thought, I'm not going to repeat myself three times. I'll just wait. I waited and waited. It seemed like eternity. He just went on twiddling with that lock of hair, and his face was very sad. Then finally he said, very slowly, "Yes, I'm tired of being Mr. Bergman."

I felt that was a strange thing to say because he was always a big name, always himself, always Roberto Rossellini, never but *never* Mr. Bergman.

"Yes, that's what I feel like, and I'm tired of it."

And I said, "All right. I understand. We'll get a divorce."

We had resolved all those difficult years. We were happy. We kissed each other. Then I told him how I'd met Sonali, and I wished him luck.

He said, "You must have the children. They belong to their mother. But there are two things I must ask you."

"Yes, what are they?"

"The children must never go to America." He hated the United States and Howard Hughes so much that no one was ever to be allowed to fly TWA ever again.

"Never go to America! How can I prevent my children when they grow up from going to America? Let's say we give them a European education—Switzerland, France, Italy, England—but when they're eighteen we've got to give them liberty to go where they please, including America if they want to."

"All right, all right. When they're eighteen."

"So what's the second thing?"

"That you'll never marry again."

"I should never marry again?"

"That's right, not at your age."

"My age! Look, you're almost ten years older than I am. You're going out with a lovely young Indian woman. You've found some- one else who is young and beautiful, but I'm not supposed to go out and find someone who is young and beautiful. I'm *not* to marry again. You have no right to prevent me."

"You are supposed to take care of the children. You have three children, four children with Pia. I mean, what more do you want?"

"I'm not going to promise you that," I said. I began to laugh. It was all very funny, I couldn't help laughing. That was Roberto.

Chapter 21

I remember one Sunday in Paris Lars and I went up to Montmartre. We went into the Sacré-Coeur and each lit a candle. Lars was standing there very solemnly.

I said, "Are you praying?"

"Yes," Lars said. "I'm praying that you will be mine."

I smiled and said, "How dare you! I'm married."

Lars smiled back. "Well, I can always pray can't I?"

In the beginning I was not sure that Lars and I should marry. Maybe Roberto was right? Two marriages? Four children. Maybe that was enough.

The children were now with me most of the time in Paris, and Roberto seemed quite satisfied with this arrangement because he didn't know Lars was very much in the background. Roberto was absolutely sure I just sat faithfully in Paris doing *Tea and Sympathy* and then doing *Indiscreet*. After that I was to do *The Inn of the Sixth Happiness* with Twentieth Century-Fox. He thought I took care of the children, and then sat there alone every night; never for a moment did it occur to him that someone else had entered my life. I asked my Italian lawyer, Ercole Grazadei, when he came to Paris, "How long will a divorce take?" He said, "Can you wait three months?" "Sure I can wait three months," I said.

We started off with the separation. No trouble. A quick visit to the lawyers. My French lawyer, René Floriot, said, "Have you really thought about it and made up your mind?" "Absolutely." "And both of you are convinced this is the right thing to do?" "Absolutely." "Well, there's the custody of the children to consider, but a French court will certainly grant custody to the mother as long as the father is allowed reasonable access."

We were in fact only asking that the Mexican proxy marriage should be annulled. To a court in Rome, that was perfectly possible and legal but would take a little time.

That Christmas the children and Roberto and I all gathered in the Bruno Buozi apartment. We had such a good time. And the press gathered outside saying, "You're separated and you're spending Christmas together?" I said, "Yes we are, because why should we upset the children? We're having a very nice Christmas party and then I'm going to England in January to make a movie."

I remember it so well. Roberto lying with his head in my lap, and I was laughing. "My goodness, all those people down there in the street. They should see us now. It would be the picture of the week."

We were both drinking glögg—a Swedish drink, half-warm red wine and half-schnapps, with nuts and raisins and cinnamon in it. It's very strong. I sent a big bottle of it down to the press.

"I feel terribly sorry for you," I said, "freezing to death down there waiting for something to happen. So you have some too, and go home because we're not coming out." Roberto went back to his apartment when the photographers left.

Of course they couldn't make head or tail of our actions. But until the real trouble started, that was the way Roberto and I behaved.

I went to London to make *Indiscreet* with Cary Grant and the press was waiting at Heathrow for a statement. I'd ruined my career by marrying Roberto Rossellini, they said, and now was I going to ruin it again by leaving Roberto Rossellini? I was taken into the transit lounge for the press conference, and there was Cary Grant sitting up on the table. He shouted across the heads of the journalists, "Ingrid, wait till you hear my problems!"

That broke the ice. Everybody burst into laughter. He held them at bay in such a nice way. "Come on, fellas, you can't ask a lady that! Ask me the same question and I'll give you an answer. So, you're not interested in my life? It's twice as colorful as Ingrid's."

Finally we escaped. Sydney Bernstein was waiting outside in his car, and we drove to the Connaught Hotel. We were all laughing.

I was telling stories about Roberto and my problems, and Cary was talking about his problems, and Sydney suddenly said quietly, "Isn't anybody interested in my problems?"

He was right. That's film stars for you. Always talking about themselves and their problems.

Indiscreet was a light comedy. I played a famous, wealthy actress; Cary Grant was an American diplomat protecting his bachelor status by pretending he was already married. I found out and asked how dare he make love to me when he wasn't even a married man! It ended happily ever after. And that's what I wanted to be. I was in love with Lars, and we wanted to get married.

———————— • ————————

Lars Schmidt was born in Gothenburg of a wealthy family with military traditions, but Lars's chief interest all his life was theater. In his teens he was sent by his family to Swansea in Wales to increase his knowledge of the shipping business. Encouraged by the miners he met in the local pubs who said, "If you are going to learn about loading Welsh coal into Swedish ships, come down the mine with us and see where it all starts," Lars worked at the coalface for a few months before the pull of London and its bright theatrical lights grew too strong.

His theatrical ventures were going along nicely when the war broke out, and London's theater was blacked out.

With Sweden neutral, his target was now New York where theater was booming. But in the early forties there were no commercial aircraft flying the Atlantic, and ship travel was hazardous, thanks to Nazi submarines. Lars managed to sail on a small Finnish vessel, but near the Faeroe Islands, German bombers came out of low cloud cover and began to attack. When Lars dashed below for his money and passport, a bomb crashed right through the ship taking the cabin next to his to the bottom of the ocean. At that time of year in the North Atlantic there was not much daylight, but the flames and smoke from the burning vessel guided a Swedish ship to their rescue. It took half the crew and passengers—and was never heard of again. A British ship which arrived a little later took Lars and the other passengers and deposited them on the Faeroe Islands. There Lars spent eight miserable weeks before he eventually got passage to New York, arriving in the clothes on his back, a penniless survivor. In New York, still determined to learn the trade, he took jobs as stagehand, scene-shifter, errand boy, assistant to the assistant. And he bought the foreign rights to his very first American play, *Arsenic and Old Lace.*

He went on promoting and producing plays, opened offices in New York, London, Paris, all over Europe.

———————— • ————————

Lars's career was much like mine in that he too was born in Sweden, had a Swedish upbringing, and then spent his life as a foreigner, always speaking foreign languages. That brought us very close; we understood each other. We didn't even have to talk. I knew when Lars disliked something that was done or said; we could just look at each other and know. Lars knew me very well; indeed he knew all my reactions, all the things that irritated me, all the things I wanted, and what was wrong with me. And I knew him too. Silly things make you fall in love; even things that sometimes irritate you.

There was one thing that was very important to Lars: Danholmen, his island. If I wanted to spend summers in St. Tropez, Capri, or Monte Carlo, then the marriage was off. If I liked his island, we would get married. So in the middle of a Swedish winter we set off to see the island, which is a few miles off the western coast of Sweden hidden among a huge scattering of other rocky islands. He'd fallen in love with Danholmen many years before when he'd gone there with a friend of his, Göran von Essen.

Lars wrote in a guest book, "The next time I see this island, I hope it's mine." And he told the astonished owners, "When you want to sell it, just tell me." Ten years later, and just as he met me, he bought the island.

It took quite a big fishing boat to smash through the ice so that we could reach the island. I loved every minute of the journey and the island itself. So lonely. Huge skies, immense seas. An island full of enormous rounded boulders and little coves—the sea everywhere. In the summer, everything so bright and shining—sea and rocks, and sky. And such a feeling of isolation.

It was so close to nature. In those early days no electricity or telephone. You had to pump up the fresh water. We had to find the wood to make our fires, and catch our fish ourselves with our nets. It was so far from the world. I could understand why Lars loved it.

That first visit we sat on the big round rocks near the house and

I said, "I love your island." And Lars said, "Right, let's get married." It all sounded very simple, but it wasn't as simple as all that.

Meanwhile, I had to learn to be a missionary.

———————— • ————————

Alan Burgess's part in this biography of Ingrid Bergman dates back to 1958 when his book *The Small Woman* was purchased by Twentieth Century-Fox for a film they retitled *The Inn of the Sixth Happiness.*

Mark Robson, the Canadian-born director who made the picture, informed executive producer Buddy Adler that Ingrid Bergman was the only adequate candidate for the role of Gladys Aylward—the London parlormaid who in 1930 went to remotest China to become a missionary and who, during the Chinese-Japanese war, led a hundred Chinese children to safety across the Shansi mountains.

When Buddy Adler said he didn't think Mark would ever get Ingrid, Mark caught a plane to Paris and headed straight for Ingrid's suite in the Hotel Raphael. As soon as he walked in, he saw the copy of *The Small Woman* which he had had Twentieth Century's London office send her. Yes, she liked the part, and she would do it.

At the start of filming, Ingrid wrote a letter to Formosa where Gladys Aylward was living on her half-share of the book and film proceeds and planning to open another orphanage for Chinese infants.

> Dear Miss Aylward,
> It is so strange to realize that you actually exist. You are not a figure of fantasy that I make-believe to say your words and feel your feelings. But I have not met you, therefore this is difficult. How I regret that we did not go to Formosa so I could have had your help. (You know they thought of making the picture in Formosa first.) But I want you to know, although you will find many occasions to wonder why we did this or that, that we are always trying to be throughout honest, and that the picture is made with great affection and respect for you. But after all it is a movie, and to become entertainment certain liberties must be taken. My personal admiration for you and your work is enormous and I only hope the picture will be worthy of you. Warmest regards.

Gladys Aylward received the letter but did not answer it. From her point of view for a very good reason.

In the early spring of 1958, Mark Robson and his Twentieth Century-Fox film technicians had gone to the island of Formosa, the natural setting for the story, and enlisted Gladys Aylward's help. One of the more enthusiastic assistant producers had told her to collect her friends and induce them to make hats and costumes for use in the film; they would also be employed as extras.

Then, the Nationalist Chinese Government in exile in Formosa had demanded to see a script of *The Inn of the Sixth Happiness.* Having read it, they pointed out indignantly that poverty, backwardness, deprivation, and inequality had been unknown in Nationalist China. All had been light, charm, and benevolence before the Communists arrived. Unless the script was amended, the picture was going to meet many difficulties.

Mark Robson made a quick decision: Twentieth Century-Fox pulled out of Formosa practically overnight—and everybody had forgotten to tell Gladys! She was left with dozens of angry Formosans demanding payment for their services or their half-finished goods. On one occasion, she was almost dragged bodily from a rickshaw. It is understandable, therefore, that she looked with strong disfavor upon the film and never made any attempt to see it screened.

The mountainous region of Snowdonia in Wales was chosen to represent Shansi, and the walled town of Yangcheng where Gladys Aylward had lived was built on a Welsh mountain top. Chinese laundries and restaurants in Cardiff, London, and Liverpool were denuded as Chinese children—speaking with outrageous Cockney or London accents—together with their parents and others of Chinese extraction were recruited for the film.

At the end of March 1958, Ingrid wrote to Ruth Roberts:

I have found such a grand person in Lars, Ruthie. I am so happy, and I think this time I found the *right* one. All good things are three. We stay in Sweden. It's strange he should be Swedish, but he's like me, he likes to visit it and certain things are awfully nice in Sweden, but then away to France! We are so alike in *everything.*

So let's hope. If I can get my divorce in May, I'll soon be a bride again! I think my little children will take it quite calmly, but Pia will be more upset and surprised. . . .

A letter from Pia warned that Ingrid might be jumping from the frying pay into the fire and reminded her mother that "you are *not good* at choosing your husbands." She told her mother to take her time before making up her mind, said that it seemed too soon for the two of them to know each other well, and asked whether Lars had been married before and, if so, what happened to that marriage. She reminded Ingrid of her responsibilities to her children, said that people watched what she did and judged her children accordingly. But she ended by saying, "I'm behind you whatever you decide."

————————— • —————————

Pia came across to see us in Paris not long after that. Lars and she got on famously. I was sent out of the room to see to the dinner while they went on laughing and chatting away and making fun of me. And late that night when Pia and I were alone, she said to me, "Mother, if you don't marry that man, I shall marry him. We must keep him in the family."

So Pia was happy, but I thought I'd better find out what the twins thought about the idea.

I was doing *The Inn of the Sixth Happiness* in Wales and I had the two little girls with me. One evening we had all washed our hair and were blowing it dry while sitting on the floor in our bathrobes. And I said to the six-year-olds, Ingrid and Isabella, "What do you think? How would you like it if Mama got married again?" They brightened up at once. "That would be great." And then they thought again, "Have you found somebody?" I said, "Yes, you remember that nice person, Lars, who came to visit us here in Wales?" "Oh, yes, we liked him; when can you marry him?"

At this time Robertino was in Paris with Renzo, Roberto's thirteen-year-old son by his first wife. I couldn't visit Robertino because of the picture.

I said to the girls, "Don't you tell Robertino because I want to tell him about it."

But Roberto now knew about it and he had told Renzo, and Renzo immediately told Robertino. When I finally got to Paris with the girls and walked into the bedroom, the two boys had obviously heard me coming and there they were, the two of them, on cue, weeping and wailing. "What is going on," I said *"what* is going on?"

"Oh . . . boo-hoo, you're going to get married again. Boo-hoo, boo-hoo."

"Well, I'm sorry. I was going to tell you, but now you've got it from somebody else."

Young Ingrid and Isabella became worried. Maybe their older brother was right and something disastrous was about to happen.

I had to go out in the park with the two girls and Robertino—a newspaper wanted photographs of us—and by now all three of them had long faces. It was absolutely horrible having photos taken with those three upset children.

Afterwards, I said to Robertino, "But you've met Lars. You've been to the zoo with Lars. . . ."

"Yes, I don't mind Lars, I like Lars, but that doesn't mean you have to *marry* him. I don't mind him living with us, but why must you marry him?"

So now I had Papa and the three kids all aligned against me. But the girls still had romantic ideas. They'd whispered together, and they weren't sure that their brother was right.

Lars picked us up at the entrance to the park. We were all going to look at the country house we were interested in buying, in the village of Choisel, nearly forty kilometers outside Paris. Robertino was sitting in the front with Lars. Ingrid, Isabella, and I sat in the back. And Robertino wouldn't look at Lars; he just glared through the window and never said a word.

Little Ingrid whispered, "Mama? Does Lars know that you want to marry him?"

"Well, I think so."

"But you haven't asked him?"

"No, I haven't asked him."

She was very worried. "But you must ask him." And to make sure, she learned forward, and said, "Lars, would you like to marry my mother?"

Lars was so surprised he took one quick glance at me in the back, and then drove on without saying anything because he was quite moved.

And Ingrid turned back to me and said, anxiously, "What did he say?"

"He didn't say anything."

"Oh!" She was so shocked that maybe Lars wouldn't marry me. She leaned forward again and said, "Lars, my mother is still young."

I almost cried, because I thought it was the sweetest proposal that any little girl of six could make on behalf of her mama.

Lars smiled and said, "Well, if you want me to marry your mother, maybe I will."

Isabella now joined the conversation. "Yes," she said, "We would like very much if you would marry our mother. And don't worry about Robertino because we will talk to him and make him understand."

———— • ————

They reached the huge green painted door set in the long, gray stone wall, and stepped through to find themselves staring across a wide green lawn to a group of the most beautiful and unusual cedar trees Ingrid had ever seen. Like enormous Walt Disney creations with pale green feathery branches they swept down to touch the lawn. She took a few steps forward and saw the small, gray stone farmhouse and the old walls.

Immediately, as with Lars's island, she knew that this was exactly the right house for them.

On July 7, 1958, she wrote to Liana Ferri in Rome:

> To get rid of all the provocation, suspicion, and rumors—especially since some newspapers discovered we bought a house—I announced, *of course,* I intended to marry Mr. L. S. when I was free. Well, since then the press got worse. We are hunted like rabbits. When and where are we to marry? Now I wish I'd never said anything. It's impossible to plan where to marry as the annulment seems further and further away. The twins know I want to marry and take it very well. Robertino was unfortunately informed by Renzo and got a shock, but I think by now he is happy too, if only the family doesn't start crying and showing their disapproval. I have told Roberto that all he has to say to the children is that he is *not* unhappy and all will be okay. But does he say it? He has promised to do all he can, but I think he is worried the children will like Lars too much.
>
> For your peace of mind, I am confident and serene. I am sure this is the best thing that ever happened to me. This man is the only one who has ever understood me with both

the good and the bad in me. I have never in my life felt such complete understanding with any human being.
. . .

On July 15, 1958, Ingrid wrote to Liana Ferri:

Roberto still has the children. Just as I was getting really angry with him little Isa came down with appendicitis. Now she is well again but he won't let me have the children until two more weeks. I do hope Roberto soon sells his TV documentaries, because this can't go on forever. He can't understand why he is so unlucky. I try to explain that very much is of his own doing, but of course he'll never believe that.

Ten days later in a second letter she added:

I am leaving tonight for Paris, and I will have the children back with me. The children said over the phone: "Poor Papa, he has been crying all night." It makes me mad that instead of making it natural and easy for them, Roberto must play it out in true Italian dramatic style. I have promised that they'll go back to Santa Marinella to stay with him in the summer.

September 5, 1958, and Ingrid wrote Liana:

Pia loved the house in France, but best of all she loved this little island. Of course it's unique but I'm so glad she was so happy. The best part was she liked Lars and couldn't be happier for me. The two of them had so much fun together. So now all my three little girls are happy for me. . . .
I am not so worried about the children as you are. Would Roberto try to keep the children in Italy? But he is not there himself. He has not—at least not yet—the money to keep them nor a house to put them in. Thank God I am out of it—looking back it seems a nightmare, such was my life: changes, promises, confusion, misunderstandings, lies . . . help! Dear dear friend, I thank God for such friends as you. May you soon get a chance to come

to France, so I can show you the man I love. And our wonderful home.

And again to Liana from Choisel, October 5, 1958:

> It makes me scared the way you feel things—either you *dream* or you *feel*! Of course I have had troubles with Roberto all along in regard to the children. He is trying in every way with any excuse to get custody of them. I have refused and finally said if we could make it 50/50 I would go along. He finds all kinds of excuses to make it difficult for me, such as the house in Choisel is not in my name but in Lars's. This was done purely because the press would not discover the house right away.
>
> I have given Roberto the right to see the children during the week whenever he wants, and every other weekend completely, two months in Italy, as I take only one month, to make him happy. Still he wants legal custody and their home to be with him in Paris, when all he owns is one bedroom at the Raphael Hotel. If now that is paid for! His basis for all this is that I intend to get married. He knows in his heart I would never separate him from the children, nor them from Italy. I really don't know what more I can do for him. It seems he just likes to fight and wants to get to court. . . .
>
> Too many years I never knew what was happening around me—now I see from the outside what a game he is playing. Any word, any angle he'll attack . . . If it wasn't that my children are concerned in this game, it is quite an interesting study in man's egocentricities. Now of course it worries me terribly.

A few weeks before Ingrid completed *The Inn of the Sixth Happiness,* Robert Donat, the brilliant British actor who had come out of retirement in order to play the part of the Mandarin, was taken ill. All other production was stopped while he struggled to complete the voice dubbing of his part. A few days later he died. Many of his friends thought of the film as his final requiem. The film itself was well received, and the scenes between Donat and Ingrid were praised all over the world.

Dilys Powell in *The Sunday Times* wrote: "Miss Bergman with her candid look, her natural grace, has the gift of being able to imply invincible goodness . . . it is the best, the most moving thing she has done."

London's *Daily Sketch* called it "a picture touching greatness at a dozen moments, in which Miss Bergman gives the finest performance of her life—the most beautiful, indeed, since Garbo's peak."

Time magazine, after lamenting its five-million-dollar budget, its running time of 157 minutes, its "worst chinoiserie ever seen on the screen, a success story that is invincibly feminist and relentlessly cheery, and more sheer treacle than anybody has seen since the Great Boston Molasses Flood (1919)" added: "The pity is that in itself the story is strongly moving . . . Something of the woman's flame-simple, stone-actual spirit is unquestionably preserved."

On a tour to Japan some ten years later, Ingrid made a special side trip to Formosa to try to meet Gladys Aylward. She arrived too late. Gladys had died ten days earlier. Ingrid sent a sad little letter back to England, to Alan Burgess:

> I am here, finally after all these years, and Gladys Aylward is gone. It is so sad. This afternoon I went with Kathleen Langton-Smith [the young English girl who had come out from England to help Gladys in her orphanage and took over the orphanage after Gladys's death] to see Gladys's home; her room was just as she left it. I was terribly moved by the humble surroundings. I met many of her children. It is so strange and it breaks my heart that I should have missed her, by so little. She worked until her very last day. What a magnificent woman.

Kathleen Langton-Smith showed Ingrid a scrapbook she had found in the back of one of Gladys's cupboards. In it Gladys had pasted a thick mass of cuttings and photos concerning Ingrid and the film. The oddest thing of all perhaps was that the tall woman from Sweden and the small woman from London had been alike in so many ways: both emotional, determined, and dedicated. Since that meeting with Kathleen Langton-Smith in Formosa, Ingrid has devoted much time to insure that the Gladys Aylward orphanage receives contributions and help; it was through her intervention that the Variety Club of America became one of its most generous benefactors.

Chapter 22

Avoiding the photographers and reporters during those months when Lars and I were planning to get married was nearly impossible. Lars wanted me to meet his parents who lived just outside Gothenburg. I flew to Copenhagen to fool the press into thinking I was on a visit to my Aunt Mutti who now lived in retirement there. I stayed overnight at a hotel in Copenhagen and the next morning I slipped out of the back exit and into the back seat of a car driven by one of Lars's friends, Frede Skaarup, where I hid under a blanket. Lars got into another car quite openly and drove off, so all the photographers followed him. Now I could sit up normally and that's what I was doing when we got to Aunt Mutti's. But there were photographers all over the place. They spotted me at once. I shouted, "Drive on, drive on!" The photographers dashed for their cars to follow us. I told Frede, "Make a quick turn left. Slow down, I'll roll out and hide. Let them chase you." He swung left into a narrow road. I opened the door, rolled out across the snow and into the ditch and crouched there until the photographers went past.

Then I walked back to Aunt Mutti's and got into Lars's car and we headed for the Swedish border. But there were more photographers there, and again I had to hide under the blanket. Of course, the photographers recognized Lars and they knew where he was heading. When he stopped on the road to telephone his parents, they told him, "The whole garden is full of people. They have spotlights fixed on the roofs of their cars which turn backwards and forwards to find out if you're coming, and which way you might come in."

Lars decided to drive on to Dageborg where his parents lived; he knew a back road behind the house. In the darkness we stopped at a graveyard and made our way through the gravestones. We climbed over a wall into a field which was full of snow and mud. Then we crawled over a gate where I ripped my stockings to pieces, over another high wall where the family butler had left a ladder to help us, and then we were in the grounds. It was like a concentration camp scene with these spotlights playing backwards and forwards over the snow and through the trees. We lay flat in the snow till the lights passed over us, then we dashed forward and threw ourselves flat again, and finally we reached the back door.

I've made many entrances in film and on stage but few like that. I was muddy and dirty and my stockings were torn and that was the way I met my prospective parents-in-law. The first thing I said to Lars's mother was, "Can I please borrow a pair of stockings to wear for dinner?"

Then, of course, the telephone began to ring and never stopped ringing. Lars told his parents to say we were not there, but his father was so gentlemanly and polite he could not tell that sort of lie, so to the first inquirer he replied politely: "Just a minute I shall ask them if they are here or not."

The journalists and photographers finally left, and very early in the morning we left and found refuge with our friends Göran and Marianne.

What with the legal complications in Mexico, California, and Sweden, I did not know for a long time whether I was legally divorced or not, but at last the annulment came through. Now we started to try to get married. In France we got nowhere at all.

But Lars found a nice lawyer in England who looked into our case, examined all the documents, and said, "Certainly you can get married here." So we arranged it, just before Christmas 1958, at Caxton Hall. Lars wanted it to be secret as he wants everything else to be secret: everyone is entitled to a private life so why should it be on the front page, he says. So again all the planning: Göran and Marianne von Essen, Lars's oldest friends from Sweden, and Sydney Bernstein and his wife acting as our witnesses. I crept out of the back door of the Connaught Hotel, and everyone arrived by different routes. The ceremony was conducted by the registrar in whispers, and then he asked to be allowed to take a photograph just for his private collection. We believed him, until the picture appeared in the papers a day later.

We went back to the Connaught Hotel for lunch, and we all toasted each other in champagne and said, "Happy birthday" to confuse the waiters. Then Sydney asked, "Can I be the first to break the news on Granada Television at six o'clock?" Sydney owns Granada as well as being a film producer. He explained, "You'll be on the plane back to France by then and almost in Choisel." So we said, "Of course," which turned out to be a slight mistake.

We were back in Choisel with Marianne and Göran when the French press heard the Granada Television flash from London and piled into their cars. Suddenly the quiet and country calm of Choisel ended and all hell broke loose. French cameramen and photographers are about the same as Italians. They were climbing over the walls, breaking through the hedges, and trying to pry shutters open, while their flashbulbs went off like fireworks. "No," we protested, "we're not going to have photographs taken at this time of night. We'll give you photos tomorrow." But that didn't stop them. The invasion continued. Marianne was in her bedroom when suddenly the shutters burst open and someone was popping a flashbulb. As Marianne laughed, "All they got was my big behind bending over my suitcase!"

Lars called the police. They arrived with flashing lights and the photographers all ran away. The police said to us, "What is the matter with you? Why don't you let them take a photograph and then we'll all get some sleep?"

We were stubborn. "No," we said, "we'll decide when the photographs are taken." We were under siege, and we weren't giving way.

The police stayed till four in the morning drinking champagne with us and celebrating the wedding, and the next day all the photographs were taken and everybody was happy.

Except Roberto, that is.

For now the trouble with Roberto truly began.

He started a lawsuit for custody of the children and brought in every weapon he could find. I was a Protestant; I had no family—no grandmother, no aunts, no uncles—and I was married to a

Swede, so who was I to look after his children? He played that up very big. He also brought up the fact that my name was not on Robertino's birth certificate at all; so who was I to claim custody of *his* son? Besides, was I legally married or had I committed bigamy? I was never quite certain that Roberto wouldn't try to have me thrown into prison every time I visited Italy.

Then he brought his mother and his sister, Marcella, both of whom I loved dearly—and they me—to sign a declaration that they would live in his house in Rome and look after the children. So many times afterwards his mother cried to me and said, "Ingrid, I didn't want to sign that paper and neither did Marcella." I said, "I know exactly what Roberto is like. He forces people to do what he wants them to do; he is the most stubborn human being I have ever met; but when he gets what he wants he becomes very nice."

———————— • ————————

At the end of January 1959, in an almost empty courtroom in Paris, Judge René Drouillat gave Ingrid temporary custody of the three children. He also decreed that the children must attend an Italian school in Paris, and that Mr. Rossellini should have visiting rights on weekends.

Roberto had already started to try to block the action of the French court by claiming that they did not have proper jurisdiction. "I am an Italian citizen," he said, "and so are the three children. I consider an Italian court decision on custody of the children more important than any ruling made in France."

It was, as Ingrid knew it would be, open war. Now she had to fight also in the Italian courts.

It was during this time that Liana Ferri said to Ingrid, "You are an actress. You can go in front of the Italian judge and you can weep and you will get the children. I know Italians." Ingrid replied, "I am an actress when I am on the stage, but I cannot do those things in life." She could not deceive in so important a matter.

After the enormous success of *Anastasia, Indiscreet,* and *The Inn of the Sixth Happiness,* Ingrid was back in her position as one of the great film stars of the decade and receiving film offers in abundance. As usual, she favored the people she liked, and she liked Twentieth Century-Fox because Spyros Skouras was head of that organization.

———————— • ————————

I first met Spyros before we started *Anastasia.* I found him very charming and gentle. "I am your Greek uncle," he used to say. Mind you, his accent was very Greek, and very heavy.

I was at a big lunch in London with Spyros and Twentieth Century representatives who'd come in from all over Europe—I was the only woman there. They knew that before I had signed *their* contract, I had had to break the only contract I had ever broken in my life: a contract to tour South America with *Joan of Arc at the Stake.* At the luncheon table they were all going on about how lucky I was to get out of that contract.

"Yes, I was lucky," I said, "but it cost me a lot of money."

"Cost *you?*" said Spyros.

"Yes, I paid thirty seven thousand dollars to get out of the contract."

"*You* paid that? And we didn't?"

"No."

"We asked you to do *Anastasia* and we didn't pay for the cancelled tour of South America?"

"No."

So Spyros raised his eyebrows.

The meal was over by now, and the waiter came in with the bill and for some reason placed it on a plate next to me.

I picked it up to look at it, and Spyros said, "Now look at Ingrid. You see! She's even going to pay the bill!"

But eventually came a check from Spyros for thirty seven thousand dollars.

And, more than that, he seemed to sense back then the drama that was growing between Roberto and me. He said, "I am going to do something for Roberto. It's very difficult to help Roberto because you are going to go from one success to another and you will need no help. But there is a movie we are going to start in Jamaica with Richard Burton and Joan Collins. We will engage Roberto to direct it."

And he did. And Roberto accepted. But there were all sorts of troubles. He realized if he was going to work in Jamaica he had to fly there. And he was terribly superstitious about flying. Years before, when Robertino was born, he'd taken him from the cradle and carried him to the window to show his son the stars, and there he'd had this overwhelming premonition that if he ever flew, harm would come to Robertino. So he had an awful migraine, and postponed going for several days, and by the time he got there they had started with another director. Roberto walked about absolutely useless. He phoned me, and I said "Come back to London." Very dispirited, he passed through London on his way back to Rome. It was while he was in London that the story of his doing a documentary film in India came up. If he had made a success of that film in Jamaica, things between Roberto and I might have been very different.

———————— • ————————

It was in 1959, with all her successful recent films that her "Greek uncle" wrote to her at the Connaught Hotel:

Dear Ingrid,

We were delighted to have lunch with you and Lars today, and it was very kind of you to stay over and give us the opportunity to discuss the proposal of your making four pictures for our company. To elaborate a little, and put it down in a short memo so that you can study it, the following is as discussed with you, and if it is acceptable to you, I will be very happy to recommend it to our Board for approval.

1. We would like to make four pictures with you at the rate of one picture a year. However, it is possible that these four pictures will take a period of five years. Of course, as I mentioned to you before, in any year in which you had not yet made our picture, we would have the usual preemptive right on any outside picture until ours is made.

2. The payment of each of the four pictures will be $250,000 each plus 25 percent of the profits of each picture. As I have emphasized to you, it is my sincere belief and recommendation that you spread the payment for these four pictures, totaling one million dollars, over a period of twenty years. As I had the opportunity to tell you before, and at lunch again today, it is in your interest, as a safeguard and protection—not only for you and your children and your estate—that you follow this recommendation. If, however, it is your desire to have payment made for each picture as it is made, I will be only

too happy to comply with your wishes. As for the 25 percent profits mentioned above, these will be paid as the profits accrue.

We would have a list of directors approved by you, subject to the addition of approved names from time to time to keep the list up to date. We explained that you and we should mutually agree on story material which would be most suitable, but if one of the approved directors should be satisfied with our selection then you would naturally approve too. Directors we have in mind would include: David Lean, Alfred Hitchcock, Elia Kazan, Sir Carol Reed, William Wyler, Mark Robson, Anatole Litvak, George Stevens, Henry King, Fred Zinnemann, William Wilder, Joe Mankiewicz, Edward Dmytryk, Nunnally Johnson.

Affectionately and sincerely as always.
Spyros P. Skouras.

What more could she possibly want? A million dollars! Twenty five per cent of the profits! The choice from fourteen of the greatest directors in the history of movies?

Ingrid sighed. Without any agent's advice she recognized the two sentences which provided Catch One and Catch Two. Catch One: Essentially they contracted her for five years. Catch Two: Whether she liked it or not, if the film company found a story *they* liked and one of their "approved directors" agreed to do it, she was obliged to take that part.

Ingrid had taken a long time to emerge from the contractual small print of Hollywood documents. Certainly if they found her a script as good as *Anastasia, Indiscreet,* or *The Inn of the Sixth Happiness,* she would do it for practically nothing. But she was certainly not interested in all that well-intentioned "Greek-uncle" advice about "spreading her money" and "protecting her estate, and her children." She was in acting, not insurance. The kids would have to grow up and go hunting themselves. She wanted a part, not a fortune. Give her a fine part and she would fly barefoot through the streets to your front door.

She did not sign the contract. She was willing to do a separate deal and make a film for Twentieth Century any day, but she had to have a good script.

Over the next few years they did not give her a script she liked,

Ingrid and Pia shop in the local French village. (UNITED PRESS INTERNATIONAL PHOTO)

Pia with her mother, brother, and sisters at Santa Marinella. (KING FEATURES SYNDICATE, INC.)

With Cary Grant in *Indiscreet*. (WARNER BROS.)

With Lars on their island off the coast of Sweden. (H.T. BILD)

Lars and Ingrid arriving at the first night of *My Fair Lady* in Stockholm. (ARNE SCHWERTZ FOR PHOTO EXPRESSEN)

Ingrid with Alan Burgess on the set of *The Inn of the Sixth Happiness*. (20TH CENTURY-FOX)

As Gladys Aylward in *The Inn of the Sixth Happiness*. (20TH CENTURY-FOX)

Goodbye Again. Ingrid, Anthony Perkins, author Françoise Sagan, director Anatole Litvak, and Yves Montand. (UNITED ARTISTS)

As Hedda Gabler in the French production produced by Lars Schmidt. (ROGER PIC–PARIS)

The trial scene in *The Visit*. (20TH CENTURY-FOX)

With Gustav Mollander, the Swedish director who came out of retirement to work with her in *The Necklace*. (SWEDISH FILM INDUSTRY)

In *The Yellow Rolls-Royce*. (NORMAN HARGOOD)

With Michael Redgrave in *A Month in the Country*. (ZOË DOMINIC)

With Colleen Dewhurst in *More Stately Mansions*. (BILL RAY, LIFE MAGAZINE ©1967 TIME, INC.)

With Goldie Hawn
in *Cactus Flower.*
(COLUMBIA)

With Fritz Weaver
and Anthony
Quinn in *A Walk
in the Spring Rain.*
(JOHN MONTE
FOR COLUMBIA)

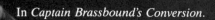
In *Captain Brassbound's Conversion.*

With Kay Brown. (PRISCILLA MC CULLOUGH)

With Sally Prager and Johnny Doran in *From the Mixed-Up Files of Mrs. Basil E. Frankweiler.* (RANDY MUNKACSI)

Madame la Présidente and her son, Robertino,
at the Cannes Film Festival, 1973.

Company manager Griffith James pushes the wheelchair in which Ingrid, her foot broken, played *The Constant Wife.*

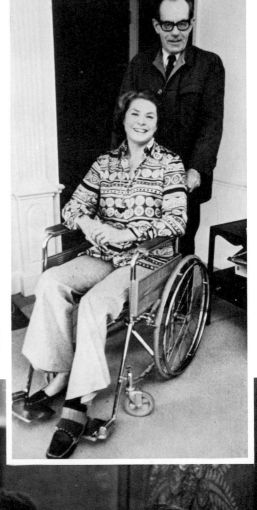

With Lauren Bacall in *Murder on the Orient Express,* for which Ingrid won her third Oscar.

A Matter of Time. Ingrid as the old Contessa and Isabella
in her first film role as a nursing sister. (ZOË DOMINIC)

Brigitte Kahn, Wendy Hiller, Ingrid, and Doris Hare
in *Waters of the Moon*. (ZOË DOMINIC)

Ingmar Bergman, Liv Ullmann, and Ingrid in *Autumn Sonata*.

Dubbing *Autumn Sonata* in New York. Liv Ullmann, Ingmar Bergman, and Ingrid.

Ingrid with her children at Choisel:
the twins, Isabella and Ingrid, Ingrid, Robertino, Pia, and Fiorella.

and they pleaded for her to find one herself. One day she rummaged through a great heap piled up in Lars's office and came up with Friedrich Duerrenmatt's play *The Visit*. Spyros agreed to do it, but he died not long afterwards. Ingrid was very sad. She had liked her "Greek uncle" very much indeed.

Darryl Zanuck took over at Twentieth Century-Fox and he didn't like *The Visit*. Nevertheless the company had bought the rights to a very successful play and for the next three years the writers were preparing scripts for Ingrid's approval.

She, however, was mainly concerned with getting her children settled.

———————— • ————————

Now the children were living with Lars and me in Choisel, and every day driving into Paris to the Italian school. Roberto had the right to see them any time he wanted to; that's the agreement I made. He complained to the judge in Rome that I was going to kill the children with these long trips back and forth between Choisel and the Italian school in Paris even though they had a chauffeur to drive them. Roberto said it was too dangerous to have that long drive every day. We argued about that for a long time. Eventually I had to give in.

The children had to live in Paris. I rented an apartment in a small hotel. Elena di Montis, our housekeeper, was there permanently and I was there practically every day, and at night I drove home to Choisel to Lars.

Then Roberto decided he would come to Paris every weekend so he could spend two days in his Raphael Hotel room with them. I wanted them out in Choisel where there was fresh air and they could play with the dogs and run in the woods. But when Roberto wanted it *his* way it was difficult to stop him. I remember once, the children had been with him in Italy and I was meeting them at the station. When I got there, I found Roberto waiting at the station: he had flown up to beat the train. I said, "What are you doing here?"

"I'm going to take the children to my hotel."

"But I'm here with the car. I haven't had them for so long. I want to take them out to the country. . . ."

"No. I want them and they are going to come to my hotel and be with me."

The children arrived and threw themselves into my arms and of course everyone wanted to get into my car. Roberto said, "No, you can have the girls and I'll take Robertino, and you follow me."

I was supposed to follow him to the Hotel Raphael and discuss the situation. Instead of that, I drove to Choisel with the two girls and called him up and said, "Now I'm coming in to pick up Robertino."

By the time I got back to Paris, Robertino had disappeared. Roberto had hidden him. For three days I didn't know where he was.

Finally I had permission to pick up my son. The poor little eight-year-old was crying. "Papa said you stole Ingrid and Isabella, you stole them . . ."

And I said, "Well, let him call it stealing but it was my period to have you."

"Yes," he said, "But, Mama, why didn't you steal me?"

June 8, 1959.

Dearest Liana,

Can you imagine Roberto arranged to ruin my summer with the children? I asked for July and said he could have August-September. I explained the Swedish summer is only July. September is winter and I should be working anyway (American TV show). Despite that, Roberto got July and August.

Our lawyer has offered no other explanation than that Roberto went to the judge and cried on his shoulder how much he loves his children. I am really furious and I want to appeal despite the short time. The lawyer says I have no chance to change the verdict, but I don't care. I will come to Rome myself and tell the judge what I have on my mind. No one can stop me. I would not like to live in a hotel because of the press. Is it possible you could put me up for one night? A chair would do. Or do you have any idea where I could hide? This is my secret. Only the lawyer and Lars know I intend to go to Rome. You know you are one of my best friends in Rome, that's why I come to you with this discomfort. Lots of love,

Ingrid.

That next summer in June 1960, I took the children out to Lars's island. If Roberto had his way he wouldn't allow it. Sleep in a wooden house? Far too dangerous! Wooden houses burn down. Then someone told him that all Swedes lived in wooden houses.

Elena came too. It rained all the time but the children didn't care. They explored the island and played with the boats, and swam in the coves. In Italy, if it rains you stay indoors, but the Swedes can't do that because then they might be indoors all year round. So we bought the children rubber hats and jackets and trousers, and they never had had so much fun. But Elena was very ill-tempered because her idea of a summer was long and hot and lying on the beach.

"Poor children" she cried. "And this water so freezing cold!"

I introduced them to Lars's sauna bath: a short time in the dry heat, and then splash into the cold water. They screamed with delight, and Elena thought it was absolutely diabolical. How could I let children risk their lives in such water? I thought as they were half-Swedish they'd better learn.

Of course we always swam without bathing suits; there wasn't a soul within miles. That horrified Elena. She screamed, "Wait until Mr. Rossellini will hear that Mr. Schmidt is *naked* when he swims!"

I said, "Elena, if *you* don't tell Mr. Rossellini he will never know."

She loved us all with fierce Italian devotion. Even Mr. Schmidt. But gamboling around naked in a cold Swedish sea just went against her better nature. She didn't realize that all Sweden bathes naked. All she knew was that in Italy even a year-old baby is put into a bathing costume.

The difficulties with the children got worse and worse. When they came to us from Italy, they were filled with the idea that *we* were Protestants and *they* were *Catholics.* They had been told that it was a deadly sin for them to pray with their Protestant mother. I used to say a little Swedish prayer, and one day they refused to say the prayer with me. I asked, "Why don't you pray with me?"

They said, "Father says you're a heathen."

I said, "No, I'm not a heathen. Really, it's the same God. It's just a different way of praying to him. But you don't have to pray with me unless you want to. I'll pray alone." I began and first one little voice and then another little voice began to join in.

Religion has always presented problems to me. On live television shows, the interviewer sometimes asks before the show begins, "Is there anything you don't want me to ask you?" And I reply immediately, "Don't talk to me about religion."

You see I was once caught by David Frost right out of a clear blue sky. He was asking me about Gladys Aylward, and I told him how I'd arrived in Formosa to see her, but she had already died ten days previously; how her friends said, "She is not yet buried, would you like to see her?" And I answered, "Oh no, not ten days after her death!" "Oh, but she looks lovely," they said. But having missed Gladys Aylward in life I certainly had no wish to see her in death. I said, "No thank you, I don't want to meet her now." And David Frost said very quietly, "You're very religious, aren't you, Miss Bergman?"

I sat there, stunned, and thought, Now what do I say? *What* do I say?

Lars and Pia were sitting in the producer's cubicle watching the monitor screen, and Pia began to laugh and said, "Now watch Mother. She is going to say, 'Yes and no.'"

So I came back with my answer after a big hesitation, "More or less," I said. And Pia roared with laughter.

When I was young I prayed. I got on my knees every night and said my prayers. And very often, as I've said, I went to the graveyard where my mother and father were buried, and sat under the beautiful birch trees which surrounded them and I prayed.

I went to church very often. The night before an opening in the theater, I go to a Catholic church because they are always open. Lutheran churches are closed: Catholic churches sit there, and I sit too and light a candle for the play . . . pray that the show will go well.

As the arguments with Roberto increased, I began to realize what we were doing to the children. They jumped when the telephone rang, "The lawyer! Is it the lawyer?" And I decided that we were going too far: the children were frightened because their parents were fighting.

I tried to resolve their fears. "Now tell me whether you would like to stay here in Choisel or would like to go back to Italy and stay with your father? Look I've made up papers with 'No's,' and 'Yes's,' here. If you want to stay, put an X by the 'Yes'—I won't look. You each take a paper and put it in this hat and I will never know which way you voted. We'll take the vote and then we'll do what the majority wants."

But they refused.

Of course Lars suffered. Here he was helping to provide a beautiful home in Choisel, and I'd hear the children whispering among themselves, "You're not going to kiss him, are you?" "You're not going to play with him, are you?"

Roberto and I wrote letters to each other but nothing really cleared the air:

Roberto wrote:

> Both of us want the happiness of the children and as you know the children are not happy in the place where they are with a stranger. Try not to make mistakes; you have to be very careful. You are always making mistakes. Last year the children had to make a long trip to go to school in Paris, and it was cold and they were sick so many times, and here when they are in Rome with me they don't see this stranger [Lars] and they are happier and they are always more comfortable with me. In the beginning of our lawsuit I could have arranged that you see the children as often as you wished, but now you are making things very difficult. . . .

Roberto wanted to take the children to Sicily with him while he made a film there. And I objected:

> To take them to Sicily to see the swordfish is just a new try to keep them in Italy and away from me and my taking them to Sweden. Besides, as I have told you already, the children do too much, they live too much as adults. It isn't the trip to Sicily, then to Sweden, and then back to Rome in their holiday months that will tire them. It is all the new impressions and people they constantly come into contact with. That you let them stay up late at night, that they are exhausted, that they are with you in restaurants, in movies (even forbidden for children under sixteen). Our children are eight and ten and should live quietly and organized

and play the games eight- and ten-year-olds play. And they should not be upset by stories you tell them like the details of Chessman's death in the United States, or how the Germans threw babies in the air and fired at them. Can't you understand that these things stay in their minds and hurt them? Their brains can't take all you put in them of horrors and hatred.

I ask you to bring the girls' passports to Paris next time, and after school the children will stay here in the country for a while—as I have hardly had them here this winter —and then we will go to Sweden, and you can have them in Santa Marinella from around the 20th of July.

I had to go down to Italy to court once again. Roberto had taken the children to Sicily and had had them for three months, and I tried to get them back. The judge said to me, "Of course you can take the children back to France."

When we left the court, Roberto was looking very black. And I said, "You cannot have it all your own way. You haven't got complete custody of the children yet. I still have custody. Until you win custody I insist they come back with me. They've been so long with you."

"All right," he said. "Take the children, take the children, have them."

So I packed everything and I said, "Where are the passports?"

"Ah," said Roberto, "the judge never said anything about the passports!"

"You mean to say you're not going to give me the passports?"

"No. There's not a word in this judgment about passports. You read it for yourself."

Fortunately I had a friend in the Swedish ambassador.

He said, "I can issue Swedish passports for the children because they have a Swedish mother, and they are allowed two passports, one Swedish, one Italian."

So he opened his office though it was late, and we had photographs taken; and I got three Swedish passports by the next morning. Off we went to the airport, and of course dear Roberto had his friends and spies everywhere. One spotted me going through immigration. He telephoned Roberto saying, "Ingrid is at the airport and she's got the children and passports!"

"No," said Roberto. "She has no passports. I have the passports right on me."

"Roberto, she must have three new Swedish passports. They are leaving."

Roberto went mad. He rang the police. Police cars came screaming out to the tarmac toward the plane, sirens going, lights flashing. Just give the Italians a chance for drama and they take it with both hands. I came down the steps of the plane and I said, "There is no way you can take me off this plane with these children. Our passports are in order. Here they are. I am their mother. I have legal custody of these children. They have spent three months in Italy here with their father . . . We are going. Good-bye."

And the police said, "We are very sorry. We were only trying to do our duty."

"Well now you've done your duty. Good-bye!"

Roberto always said that caused his first heart attack.

I mean, this wasn't an ordinary legal fight. These were his children, blood of his blood, taken away from his beloved country and placed under the care of this Swedish "what's-his-name" whom I had married. Lars met us at the airport just in case Roberto had telephoned his contacts in Paris to try to take the children away as they got off the plane. You never could tell what Roberto might be up to.

That Christmas I decided to do a little stealing on my own. Lars was opening his production of *My Fair Lady* in Norway and Roberto was out of the country.

Elena was in Paris with the children, and I knew she would have a fit if she learned that Lars and I were going to take the children to Scandinavia without anybody's permission. I knew there was no point in asking Roberto. I went to the apartment in Paris and when Elena was not looking, I took a sweater and put it in my bag, and the next time another sweater and a pair of boots. Little by little I built up a small wardrobe for the three children. Then I gave Elena a letter to open after I took a car to the children's school to whisk them away. In the letter I explained what I was doing, and gave her a ticket to Rome, and thirty thousand francs to spend on her holiday.

The children were delighted they were going to Norway. What an adventure! So it was all a great success, until it all suddenly went wrong on New Year's Eve.

It started when I read about Eduardo de Filippo, an Italian actor and author we knew. He had a child whom he adored, who was absolutely normal, absolutely well. The child was on vacation and suddenly contracted a disease and was dead within twenty four hours. Poor Eduardo was simply destroyed.

I began to think: suppose that happened to one of our three? Roberto had already lost his first son with peritonitis when the boy was staying with his grandmother in Spain.

It was New Year's Eve, and on New Year's Eve I'm always very sentimental; it's always meant a lot to me. I think, another year gone and what have I done? To whom have I brought happiness? What have I done wrong? Next year, can I be kinder and nicer? And all the time the bells are caroling peace and goodwill across the countryside. And here I was fighting over the three children as I'd fought over Pia!

I had already telephoned Roberto to tell him we were all right. He was dreadfully angry. We were like the two mothers claiming the child before Solomon.

I began to wonder how much of this was my fault. I could never abandon my children, but between us we were tearing them to pieces. Someone had to give way if we were to preserve their happiness.

I called Roberto again. "All right, you can have the children. I give up. You can have the children in Italy and bring them up there. I'm bringing them down to you right away." And I did.

I went to the judge and said, "Thank you very much, I'm not waiting for your verdict."

And my lawyer said, "But you're going to *win*. We have information about Roberto Rossellini. It isn't enough that he's the father, and he's Italian and says he has a big family to look after the children. This Italian court will not reverse the French court's decision. You are going to win this case and be granted custody."

"I'm terribly sorry," I answered, "I'm not going on. No one's going to win this case, least of all the children. I'm not going to go on, I'm not coming here any more to go to the law courts. I'm giving Roberto the children."

Of course, once Roberto had got what he wanted he couldn't have been nicer.

When I brought the children down and gave them to Roberto, he was the kindest human being you could ever imagine: gifts, the apartment was ready for them. I was told I was welcome any time.

From that time, Roberto and I never had a serious disagreement ever again and we were always in touch with each other.

Commuting back and forth between Rome and Paris became a natural part of my life for the next twelve years. I'd be in Paris for three or four weeks, then down to Rome for ten days or so. Then back to Paris to Lars for perhaps two weeks and back to Rome again. I did everything I could to stay as close as I possibly could to the children under these conditions. And they were very difficult. But I was saved by one marvelous Italian woman, Argenide Pascolini, the housekeeper who took over when Elena left. She stayed with us fourteen years. She watched out for the children and became a second mother to them. If something went wrong concerning a governess—and there were many during these years— and the children were worried or unhappy, Argenide would be on the phone immediately saying, "You'd better come back and sort it out." And back to Rome I'd fly.

She was the rock in the storm, and I don't know what I would have done without her. The children have adored her ever since: she was one of the witnesses at Isabella's wedding; the first person Ingrid runs to is Argenide; and Robin never visits Rome without seeing her.

Chapter 23

"In many ways those years of the late fifties and early sixties were tough years for Ingrid," said Lars. "With her honesty she would talk to Roberto about absolutely everything, and she was so determined that her children's upbringing should be right. On the other hand, she didn't want to disturb the new-found happiness we had discovered.

"Naturally the children, even when their home was in Italy, were up with us for a lot of the time, and stayed on the island during their summer holidays. We were completely happy. It was a complete marriage, mentally and physically. If there was a cloud in the sky it was the children—not the children as such, they were marvelous— but the traumas Roberto was always likely to start. But we always had those wonderful summers together. Our summers on the island were sacred. Work stopped. We all went to the island. We got there by the end of June, and stayed right through July."

———— • ————

From the very beginning, as I have said, Lars and I had a lot of things in common. Our lives were so alike. We both wanted to leave Sweden; we both wanted a career that was bigger than Sweden could give us. We had to move out. We shared a sense of humor together. Yes, we understood each other very well.

The first thing Lars and I did together was television. In 1959, I did *The Turn of the Screw* for NBC in New York, the Henry James ghost story about two young children influenced by the evil spirits of two servants who had died. I was the governess who attempts to protect the children from the supernatural forces which are trying to overwhelm them, and which eventually cause the little boy to die in my arms. It was powerful stuff. All very frightening. I got my first television award, an "Emmy," for that.

———————— • ————————

For several months now Anatole Litvak, with whom she had worked so successfully in *Anastasia,* had been in touch with her about playing the part of Paula in a film version of Françoise Sagan's book *Aimez-vous Brahms?*

August 16, 1960, she wrote to Liana:

> At last I have the script. It is not as good as I had hoped. I wrote three pages typewritten to Tola Litvak with complaints. Sagan after all is an artist. Of course not much happens in the book, and it's hard therefore to get any action in the picture. But I hope that Tola himself and his cast will put back the atmosphere that I feel is lost. Yves Montand can't start until September 15 so I am forced to prolong my contract. . . .
>
> Thanks for the letters and clippings. So they caught me in a bathing suit at last. I have refused that kind of photo all my life, but a telephoto lens at Santa Marinella, and there I stand a half-naked 45! I never knew they could get such a close picture from *the road.* My God, pretty soon they'll be shooting us inside the house.
>
> We had a wonderful time in Sweden. . . . We had a long session with Ingmar Bergman who has made up his mind to make a picture with me. Recently I saw a showing of his *Virgin Spring.* It was so beautiful in the beginning but at the end it was heavy and brutal. But as always his films stay in your mind for days, while others are gone the minute the picture ends. . . .
>
> He is *somebody,* and an extraordinary, sensitive person.

You know his father is a priest who confirmed me, and who baptized Pia twenty-one years ago.

On October 7, 1960, again to Liana:

> Today on the set of *Aimez-vous Brahms?* there is confusion without end. I sit and look out from my corner here on sixty newspaper men drinking from a bar. TV cameras are going and Françoise Sagan is here. We are doing scenes in a nightclub for the film: they have copied exactly the most popular nightclub in Paris at the present time—Epic Club—and we have "famous people" sitting around like Marcel Archard. Yul Brynner is playing an extra, and Sagan is playing herself sitting at a table too. As they are not getting paid, they get drinks! It's a very amusing scene from the film when Anthony Perkins comes to the table where Yves Montand and I are sitting, and he's very drunk. These two actors are wonderful for their parts. It's a long time since I worked with *two* actors I enjoyed so much. They are both charming, both great personalities and very different, and you understand why I—in my part as Paula—love them both. . . .

Her old friend Bosley Crowther found *Goodbye Again*, as it was called in the United States, not only a very predictable story, but soggy around the edges. As for Ingrid's part: ". . . she is neither that interesting nor is she sufficiently well played by Miss Bergman to cause an old reviewer of regenerate heroines to care. Neither passion nor wildness seems to seize her. She is just a nice, comfortable, unhappy woman."

"Report from Hollywood" placed its finger on the picture's fundamental flaw: "Bergman cast as a middle-aged woman torn between an unfaithful lover [Yves Montand] and an unstable, love-starved boy [Tony Perkins] is as beautiful as ever—a fact which paradoxically is the film's greatest weakness. At 46, she is still too radiant, too dynamic, too poised to be convincing in the role of an aging woman."

———— • ————

I remember, I made a special trip to San Francisco to see Pia who was in college there and I hadn't even gone through customs when the press who were waiting for me started calling, "Why did you do that horrible movie?"

I went out to the press conference, and said, "What horrible movie?" "This *Goodbye Again*—what's it called in France, *Aimez-vous Brahms?*"

I said, "It's adapted from a book by Françoise Sagan, and it's a big success in Paris."

"Oh, terrible movie—*dreadful* movie."

"What's dreadful about it?"

"You live with a man you're not married to, and then you take a lover who's young enough to be your son. It's shameful. And then you go back to this man you're living with who's been unfaithful to you all these years and is going to go on being unfaithful. What sort of film is that?"

This from the hard-boiled, cynical San Francisco press! But they certainly reflected American opinion. The movie had no success whatsoever in the United States, even though it was a huge success in Europe.

———— • ————

Lars comments on those early years of their marriage:

"In the beginning with Ingrid I suppose I was a bit scared. The price of loving a woman in Ingrid's circumstances, of marrying, was to give up private life—at least a part of it. And I've always been a very private man. Maybe it's a Swedish characteristic. And suddenly to become a public person. . . . I can't remember clearly how it worked; it's not a daily problem, but a daily and inevitable factor in life. There was, I suppose, far more publicity in Ingrid's life before she married me, because when we married we did make a stand against publicity, we did close up. We were very happy together and we didn't want the edge taken away because of publicity.

"And during those years we were both working very hard—in my time I've put on more than seventy plays in Paris—both shooting off in all directions. There were sometimes weeks, even months when we didn't see each other while we went through our own respective work traumas.

"And certainly my main work trauma at that time was *My Fair Lady.* I'd got the European rights to that musical. Both Ingrid and I attended the opening night in Copenhagen—Ingrid came to practically all the opening nights all over Europe—but that night in December 1960 in Copenhagen, I think we both aged a hundred years. At least I did. We staged it in an enormous theater, 2200 seats, and not only the city itself but the whole of Denmark was on its toes waiting to see this record-breaking musical. And we were sold out for the opening night and a month ahead—that's unbelievable. So we rehearsed right up to Christmas. We were opening on Boxing Day. And you know, at that last rehearsal, I felt there was something a little strange about the actress who was playing the lead, Eliza Doolittle. Nothing I could put my finger on, but she was just a little shaky.

"So Ingrid and I flew to Gothenburg for Christmas Eve and Christmas Day with my parents. On Christmas morning my lawyer called me and said, 'You must return to Copenhagen at once. No, I cannot tell you over the phone. Just get back here at once.'

"I called the airport. Christmas Day, there were no planes. We got into a car and rushed down from Sweden to Copenhagen. Eliza Doolittle was very ill. The doctor said, 'Yes, we will save her life, but there is no way she is going to perform.'

"The only thing to save the show was to get her understudy into the theater and rehearse her until she was blue in the face—see if she could catch up in time for the opening. We got her in and we rehearsed her until three in the morning. And of course if this had been a Hollywood movie she would have staggered on, sung like an angel, and brought the curtain down to enormous cheers. But Copenhagen wasn't Hollywood. At three in the afternoon of the opening night, she collapsed. Gone! No hope of performing. So the opening was off. Two thousand two hundred seats sold and no performance. We announced it on television, radio, and in the press. I tossed a coin with my co-producer to see who would stand outside the front door with a sad smile and tell the customers as they arrived that there was no show. I lost.

"Now our great difficulty was to get another Eliza Doolittle. Denmark is not New York, Paris, or London. There are not many Danish singer-actresses who can play that part. Well we got one at last—a very good opera singer, and she had six clear days before the next opening. So she started to work, and after three days she had a fall and twisted her knee. She had three days to go. She was in great pain and should have been home in bed. We carried her from position to position. We said, 'Here you sing so-and-so, here you do this.' She was so tired she fell asleep and even the prompter couldn't wake her up. So finally came the first night and we carried her on to the stage. The curtain rose, she limped around and she got to her first song, 'Wouldn't It Be Loverly?' At the end of it the entire house stood up —they had read in the press all about our troubles—and they cheered her. They cheered and cheered. Applause that I've never heard in my whole life. Oh, what the theater can do to you! And I was standing in the back crying like a little child.

"The entire performance went through absolutely heavenly. But the next day she had sung so hard she had lost her voice. She could hardly croak—and she could hardly walk, but she kept on. Then after ten days she stumbled again and fell and broke four of her ribs. But she went on. We bound her up and she went on. Now she only croaked, limped, and could hardly move, but she went on. Then Professor Higgins fell ill and his understudy took over for three full weeks; then the understudy fell down and broke his leg. I called the original Higgins. Was he well enough to go back into the part? Yes, he was.

"I tell you, there was never one performance when we didn't wonder who was going to break a leg, try to commit suicide, have a heart attack. And then the day we closed I called my lawyer—the one who rang me on Christmas morning—and I said, 'Thank God it's all over.' He said, 'What do you mean, all over! This morning, I fell down and now *I've* got a broken leg!' "

On August 16, 1961, Ingrid wrote to Ruth Roberts:

As far as work is concerned it's not all perfect. I *can't* find anything good. Now all the scripts are old woman–young man! I can't do that again.

The Visit has too many script problems. They're still trying to get the story right. I don't think it will come off. I can do *The Lady from the Sea* by Ibsen in my French theater, but I hesitate—it seems so old fashioned to me. Women's "free will" is no problem today. So in the meantime, Lars is busy with many productions of *My Fair Lady* in many countries. But you know me, I am a little unhappy, too, when I have nothing to do and nothing even to look forward to. I was asked to do *Mourning Becomes*

Electra on Broadway. It was difficult to turn down. I would have loved it.

As you say, let's not talk about Gary's and Hemingway's going. It hurts so. It's strange how they went together. I think they had planned it. I heard from a mutual friend that the two used to telephone each other all the time through their sickness and laugh, "I'll race you to the grave."

In November 1961, again in New York, this time for CBS Television, Ingrid made *Twenty-four Hours in a Woman's Life,* adapted from a story by Stefan Zweig, playing the part of an old grandmother who realizes her young granddaughter is about to ruin her life by an affair with a young playboy. To prevent it, she tells the girl about the love affair she had—going back into the past in a flashback—and showing the bitterness which resulted. Lars was the executive producer on that show.

———— • ————

After *Twenty-four Hours in a Woman's Life,* Lars fixed up a continuing contract to do various plays with me as the star with the Columbia Broadcasting System, a co-production with British television, Lars and David Susskind acting as co-producers. The first was an adaptation of Henrik Ibsen's play, *Hedda Gabler,* a co-production between BBC and CBS. We had a wonderful cast: Michael Redgrave, Ralph Richardson, and Trevor Howard. Lars was immensely helpful about every show in which I appeared. "At that point you have to be more forceful, give it a lot more voice. Now you're moving too much, being too theatrical, don't move your hands as if you're talking in Italian, this is an English play. Ah, now that's *very* good, when you turn your head and pause: that establishes a completely new situation. . . ."

I'd always been intrigued by the role of Hedda. Such an interesting part, and Hedda is such a strange woman. The play is a classic, and I wanted to try a classic for a change. And I liked TV even though at this time I was rationing myself to one TV performance a year.

———— • ————

On the whole, the British critics approved of the exercise. Eric Shorter in the *Daily Telegraph* summarized: "Well, if old Ibsen must be bolted through in 75 minutes flat, who better to do it than Ingrid Bergman, Ralph Richardson, Michael Redgrave and Trevor Howard. . . ."

In the United States, the TV release produced much the same story. Jack Gould of *The New York Times* welcomed the production as an "opportunity to witness a major star's approach to a classic portrait in the history of the theater," even though he found, "Hedda was too much the suffering heroine of the cinema, and not enough the Ibsen animal of cold cunning and temperament who savors her evil acts."

Across the continent, in the *Los Angeles Times,* Cecil Smith's opinion was warmer: "It was Ingrid's night. Cold, mocking, arrogant, cowardly, vengeful, poisonous, charming, exalted, her Hedda was a portrayal that seared the brain."

When we completed the television version, I said to Lars, "My God, just as I'm beginning to understand what Hedda is all about, it's finished. We shot it in three days and it's over. You know this is very sad, because I think this play is great, and there is so much more I have to learn about this woman; I haven't got her yet. I would like to do the part in the theater."

Lars said, "All right. Study it in French, and we'll put it on in Paris."

So we started all over again with a French cast and Raymond Rouleau directing, and there I was playing in the Paris theater again. And the cities were very kind to us.

I used to drive home after the performance in my little car every night to Choisel. It was usually after eleven when I left and there was very little traffic. I never had a drink before I left because I didn't care for the night drive at all. And this night, perfectly sober, and naturally tired, I set off. Maybe I was in the middle of the road, maybe I took a corner too fast, but there was very little traffic about, when suddenly this big black police van overtook me, waved me down, and stopped in front of me. It was full of police. They came across and one of them said I had been driving on the wrong side of the road. I said, "That's nonsense. I was not on the wrong side of the road; it could be I was in the middle following the white line, but how long have you been following me?" They didn't take that very well, and they didn't like it either when I added, "I drive this way home every night, and I'm coming from the theater and I'm tired, and please don't bother me." Of course you shouldn't say that to the police. They got all offended and I had to explain who I was. They said, "You know the way you answer, we can take you to the police station and you will spend the night in prison."

That struck me as an absolutely wonderful idea. One night in prison! I didn't want to spend more than one night in prison, but one night would be wonderful. Roberto always said there was no chance of ever being famous unless you'd been to prison, so here was my big opportunity. So I said, "Please do take me to prison. You go ahead and I'll follow you, and if you don't trust me, one of your police can sit with me in my car so I can't escape. I can't think of anything more wonderful. I will call my husband as soon as we arrive at the police station tonight and tell him I'm in prison. We can get it on the front pages of all the newspapers tomorrow and it's going to be marvelous publicity for the theater and our show."

They didn't like that at all. They all went into a huddle. I could see now I had a group of very worried policemen trying to work out why this woman was so anxious to go to prison. They let me go. They said, "Just drive on home, madam."

I think they were trying to play some sort of joke. There were so many of them in that van, and they saw a lonely woman, and maybe they recognized me and decided to have some fun with me and frighten me. But as it turned out, I was the one who frightened them.

Often Lars and I used to drive home together. I remember one night when we had both been to a party and it was very late, and this was long before the days of breath analyzers and drink laws. So after a couple of miles Lars stopped the car and said, "Move over, you can drive now." We changed places and started off, and then I thought, What am I doing! I've had just as much to drink as he has. By this time he was snoring in the front seat so I couldn't really do anything about it. But it was very late, and there was absolutely nothing on the road. I drove very slowly and carefully until a police car stopped me.

Two gendarmes. Very polite. "Ah, good evening, madam," one said, "may I see your driver's license?"

"Driver's license!" I said. "Good heavens, no. I never carry my driver's license with me. I might lose it."

"But it is the law, madam, that you carry your driver's license."

"Well listen, we've just been to a party, and my husband was driving first, but he was so tired I drove. And I can't carry my driver's license with me. My purse is too small. I mean, it won't go in."

At this moment Lars decided to wake up and said something original like, "Wasmarra—" I thought, if this was Sweden we'd both be under lock and key by now. But as I've said, this was long before all the drink laws came in, and the French after all are very French, especially to women.

"Very well, madam," said the gendarme, "Please continue. But remember, you must get yourself a bigger purse. We wish you a good journey home." And with that they both saluted and off we went.

———————— • ————————

Ingrid arrived in Rome in the autumn of 1963 to costar with Anthony Quinn in *The Visit*. Duerrenmatt's play had been a great success on Broadway in 1958 as performed by Alfred Lunt and Lynn Fontanne.

"The world made me a whore. Now I will turn the world into a brothel," declaimed Ingrid in the role of Countess Karia Zachanassian, wealthiest woman in the world, returning to the tiny, mid-European town of Guellen to revenge herself upon Serge Miller (Anthony Quinn). When she was seventeen he had seduced her, renounced their child, hired perjurers to testify to her depravity, and finally forced her into prostitution and to flee the town.

The town of Guellen was poor. Karia offered to make its citizens rich. But only if they would find Serge Miller guilty now and legally execute him. Slowly the citizens weakened. They needed the money. They convinced themselves that in bringing Serge to justice they were acting as good citizens righting a great wrong.

Upon the New York stage, Duerrenmatt's theme that both men and their justice can be bought, and that every human being has a price, had been reviewed as "a stunning chiller" and "a grisly horror story of greed and betrayal." Now, watered down for the wider distribution of a commercial film, it was still highly dramatic.

In the Broadway production, Serge is executed. Such retribution in a film was thought to be too dramatic. So for the movie version, Karia has a change of character and the terrified Serge is allowed to go free.

———————— • ————————

Nunnally Johnson did one script which turned the story into a Western; *I* came riding into the small town and *I* was shot because I was such a mean person. I refused to do that script. I stuck to Duerrenmatt. I'm always faithful to authors. I said, that's the play I picked and that's what I want to do. Even so, they took out a lot of things, softened it.

They would have nothing to do with black comedy in the movie. It became just a straight picture, and they refused to kill Anthony Quinn at the end. When Tony arrived, I told him, "In the play you are killed," and Tony replied, "I expect they were hoping to get Cary Grant to play this part. If they'd known that I was going to play it, they would have killed *me* without hesitation."

As Duerrenmatt is Swiss, we had the big opening night in Geneva, but he refused to come, and gave an interview in a newspaper saying that we had destroyed his play.

He hadn't wanted me in the part; he'd wanted Bette Davis. So that didn't help our opening night. And the critics were not very helpful either.

American critics found it somber and stolid, a trivial story of a woman's vengeance. Kate Cameron said: "The new Bergman is less assured than she has been in other films. She seems to have lost some of her former confidence."

It was a year later, 1964, when the phone rang in our house in Choisel and a voice told me that the Swedish Film Industry was making a movie and they wanted me in it. It was thirty years since I'd worked in a Swedish film!

The film was to be made up of seven different episodes, each done by a different, famous director. Ingmar Bergman was going to direct one episode, and they had approached Gustav Molander to do another.

"What?" Gustav had said. "Me! I'm seventy-seven years old. I haven't made a film for ten years, and I certainly don't intend to go back to work." But they pleaded with him, saying he was far too famous to be left out, so eventually he relented and said, "All right, but I'll only do it on one condition: that you get Ingrid to work with me again." As soon as they told me that, I said, "I'm coming, I'm on my way." They asked, "Don't you want to know anything about the story?" I said, "No, just tell Gustav I'm coming."

It was so wonderful to be directed by him again. He was doing de Maupassant's *The Necklace* with Gunnar Björnstrand, my old friend from the Royal Dramatic School, playing opposite me. Gustav had a little trouble hearing, and kept saying to the sound man, "Do they speak up? Can *you* hear them?" But he was reassured when the sound man said everything was fine.

We had a party afterwards and the reporters asked Gunnar and me what our plans were; we told them about movies and plays we each wanted to do. Then they turned to Gustav, saying, "And what are your plans for the future, Mr. Molander?" He smiled and said simply, "The graveyard."

It was during 1964 that Pia decided she would like to go to Rome and live with the children. She had always been an only child and she had borne the brunt of the troubles between Petter and me. Now she'd been around a bit—she was in her middle twenties—and she decided she'd like a change, and to settle down somewhere for a while. I encouraged her. Robertino—or Robin as we called him now that he had grown so tall—was fourteen and the twins were twelve.

———————— • ————————

As Pia tells it:
"My father and I lived in Pittsburgh for three years where I went to a girls' school, and then we went to Salt Lake City where my father and Agnes got married. I lived with them for one year, then I went away to college: the University of Colorado. I was there for about a year and a half, then I transferred to Mills College outside San Francisco and I graduated from there. And I got married for a year —a combination of love and escape and going on my own. Then, too, he pushed me a lot. He was about eight years older; he'd been married before. I thought eight years was a great difference. I suppose I had the same reaction as my mother: eight years when you're twenty and he is twenty-eight seems like a lot. You know, he has a car and he can order wine. . . . So this was very different from the other twenty-year-old boys I knew. He seemed very mature. I was about to graduate: he was there; he was very good looking; he had

lots of money; and he wanted to marry me. So it seemed like fate. ... Well, it wasn't. We traveled. The first six months of our marriage we traveled. And traveling together, we grew to dislike each other. So we didn't stay married very long. A year.

"Then I moved to Paris, by myself. I was about twenty-one. And I was lonely. I'd read all these books about expatriates living in Paris, Hemingway and all that, cafés and gay nights. And it wasn't like that when I got there. I worked for a time for UNESCO. I went to school and studied French; I really couldn't find a job I liked.

"I lived with mother and Lars; I was going to make up for the time I hadn't lived with them. I lived in Choisel for about six months, then I got myself an apartment in Paris, and I lived there for another six or eight months or so. Of course I got to know mother in an entirely different way, and I loved her. For a young person, she was such an extraordinary mother to have. She was so gay and funny and she always wanted to go out and do things—see this, and go to the movies and the theater, go to dinners and run around, and get up early and shop. She was so full of energy. It was just wonderful. And I wanted to be around and I wanted to be like she was. I thought she was just—beautiful.

"I went to London and I couldn't get a job. Here I had a degree in history and government, I'd worked for UNESCO, and people kept asking me, 'Aren't you going to become an actress?' I wasn't planning on it, but I started thinking that maybe I should try to see if I could do it. And I did try, and I got a job, but I don't think I was any good; I know I wasn't any good. I probably should have been looking for a job in some other area but I didn't know what area that was to be. I really couldn't figure out where I should put myself.

"I couldn't just go on living there, spending money and never making any, so I went to Italy. The children's grandmother had died: Ingrid, Isabella, and Robin were now living alone with a cook and a nurse. They lived in an apartment and Mother suggested that if I went to live in Rome I could look after the management of their house.

"So I did. It seemed like something to do, it seemed to have importance to somebody. I stayed there for about three years with them. Mother sent me the money. I paid the salaries, and I took them to the dentist, and horseback riding, and for lessons; I took Robin skiing and organized the family.

"Roberto was a big talker, a big conversationalist. And I learned Italian; I speak very good Italian.

"When I arrived there, nobody spoke one word of English. Not the cook, not the governess nor any of the children. I sat for the first six months at the dinner table, night after night—gabble, gabble. I was going insane. I couldn't understand one word. I went to an Italian school. I had just finished French, and now I was getting Italian lessons. It was funny, I was sitting there at the table and they were talking and talking and all of a sudden I thought, God, I can understand what they're saying! So in two years I learned to speak very well, particularly since I didn't speak any English to anyone, and I didn't have any American friends. I didn't know anybody in Italy.

"It was a very good experience because in a sense I needed it. I really didn't have a place; I wasn't married; I was at loose ends. I couldn't figure out a profession that I was capable of doing; so I really needed roots and a place to live, a feeling that I was functioning, helping somebody, and doing something that was necessary.

"And I felt that I was. Sometimes, I'd say, 'This is ridiculous! What am I doing here? What would my father think?' I'm sure my father did not think well of it: he must have thought it was a terrible thing for me to go to Italy and live with those three children. Anyway I did it and it did strike me sometimes as very peculiar. The three children were fourteen and twelve—Robin fourteen and the girls twelve—and when I left, Robin was seventeen and the girls over fourteen.

"Roberto used to come for lunch. We would always set a place for him. Sometimes he would show up and sometimes he wouldn't, but he always had a place. As soon as he walked in the door, he would go to the telephone, and he would have a long conversation. Then he would sit down at the table and the phone would ring, and he'd go to the telephone and have another long conversation. Money discussions usually. By then it was dessert time and he would come back to the table for a few more minutes and regale everybody and then he would kiss everybody good-bye—kisses, kisses, kisses—and then the phone would ring and Roberto would run out. That was Roberto's visit with the children.

"That was the way we lived. And I loved Italy. I loved being there. I was glad I got to know them, glad I got to know Roberto because I saw him for myself, and didn't just have other people's opinions or other people's ideas of what he was. I'm glad I know Sonali and everybody, because it was very good for me to see and know everything that went on so that I could have some sense of how all this occurred.

"Roberto wasn't handsome, but he was very charming. He could talk so well: the history of the world, the food crisis of the world. He had these enormous subjects and he seemed so authoritative about them. He could talk about them for a long time and you'd be mesmerized; he was fascinating. I didn't know him in the period when he was driving racing cars around, when he was a night person, with Anna Magnani and all that. I knew him when that movie period was failing. He had difficulty making money; he had not made a movie that was any good and he was starting in with those television things that nobody wanted to see and he couldn't sell. So I was seeing him when he was at a low point in his life, and he was very depressed. One of his main problems was that he had all these children to support, and all these houses. He had a first wife and a first son to support, and our three, and now Sonali and two children. Of course, everybody needed money, and the only way he could support these people was to make movies.

"I liked my Italian period because I had been alone and had a kind of isolated upbringing, and this whole atmosphere, this chaotic thing was fascinating to me, and very appealing. There was something fascinating about all those children being together even though their parents were off doing something else. I mean, it was sort of wonderful that here were also Sonali's children, Raffaella and Gil, and cousins, and there were other people I could relate to like Roberto's sister, Marcella, and her daughter Fiorella. I felt very happy with them.

"Roberto was an egocentric person; children were extensions of his ego. That's my own interpretation. As many creative people do, he took himself and his life as being the most important, and his own needs as the ones that should be satisfied first. I think he felt himself to be unique, and he was. So he just went ahead doing what he wanted to do, and I don't think there was much thought of consequences to other people. I mean, he never wanted to be bothered with middle-class ideas of duty or responsibility; all that was for the bourgeois—caring what other people think—and those kinds of values would be put down, considered as unworthy of a great person.

"I was planning to stay in Italy. However, I met a man from New York who owned a public relations firm, who offered me a three months' job in America doing a promotion stunt for Fiat Motor Company. I agreed because it was a job, and they would pay me three hundred dollars a week, which sounded like an enormous amount at that time.

"For three months I was to drive a car all the way around America and promote the car and talk on television and radio about it. And I did. When I got to San Francisco, where my father was living, I thought I might spend some time with him. So I went to the television station in San Francisco and asked, 'Is there any job in this building, any job I could do for a few weeks?' And they said there was a morning television show and the woman on it was pregnant; they were looking for a replacement. They would hire me for two weeks until they found one. But at the end of two weeks, nobody said anything, so I came back for the third and fourth and fifth. That was ten years ago and I've never stopped working in television since."

———————— • ————————

John O'Gorman was my make-up man for over ten years, even going to America with me. I was very fond of John because he had such humor, and when you have to get up early in the morning and sit in a make-up chair it's good to have someone who is funny and can make you laugh. The day is easier.

I was on the set of *The Yellow Rolls-Royce* and John O'Gorman was making me up, when along came this very shabby little man in frayed blue overalls and an old shirt, carrying a bunch of flowers which he handed to me saying, "Welcome. I'm so pleased to see you."

"Thank you, how kind of you," I said.

He went away. I turned to John. "I suppose I must have met him on an earlier picture; he must have been a stagehand or one of the electricians."

"Ingrid!" said John patiently, "That was your director." It was Anthony Asquith.

We started to film and I learned that Anthony Asquith has been given new overalls by practically every actor he's ever worked with. But Anthony wouldn't wear them. His old overalls were lucky. He wore them through the whole picture to keep the luck with us. He was the kindest and most polite director I have ever known. He was so polite that if he stumbled over a cable he would turn back and say, "Oh, please forgive me." When he needed the extras he would say, "Ladies and gentlemen I don't want to disturb you—please finish your tea by all means—but when you have a few moments would you please come up and stand in the background, because I need a few people there. Don't rush."

The picture consisted of three sequences, and the yellow Rolls-Royce had the star part in each. I was a wealthy American widow who on her travels through Europe bumps into Omar Sharif who played a Yugoslav partisan. In the Rolls-Royce we rescue the wounded, get involved in the war, and have a very quick love affair. Then I go on my way with a lovely memory of "Better to have loved and lost than never to have loved at all"—the theme in so many films in those days, with the poor woman left tearfully facing her future, a little smile at the corner of her mouth which tells you it's all been worthwhile.

The next thing I knew Michael Redgrave was ringing from London. A new theater was opening in Guildford and he wanted the first production to be Ivan Turgenev's *A Month in the Country*. Would I play Natalya Petrovna with him as Mikhail Rakitin? I said "no" immediately.

"I'm so sorry, Michael, but Lars and I always leave the summers free—we promised each other that—and we go to our island. We work in the winter if anything comes up, but never in the middle of the summer. . . ."

Then Lars came into the room and overheard what I was saying. He took the phone out of my hand and said, "Michael, send her the play because it fits her like a glove. It's a marvelous part for her."

I looked at him and said, "But we promised each other we'd have these three months in the summer without work. Now you want me to go to England and work in this play?"

"Yes, I don't want to be accused of having been an obstacle in your life. This is a marvelous play and after Guildford you might well go to London. How shall I feel later in life if you say, 'But for you I would have appeared in the West End'?"

I hadn't read the play; but Lars knew it as an old Russian classic about the torment of a beautiful, middle-aged, well-married woman who falls in love for the first time in her life with a young man of twenty-one. And he knew I would like the play. He didn't want to be in my way, and that was generous of him. But I had a feeling in my bones that maybe it was all going to take too long. A movie only takes two or three months, but if a play's a success you can be sure it's going to be seven months: one month rehearsing at least, and then a contract lasting six months. Lars himself had said he would never accept any actor who asked for a contract for less than six months.

Still, I read the play and I adored it. So off I went to Guildford, and there, through Michael Redgrave, I met Dirk Bogarde. He thought it was terrible for me to live in a Guildford hotel because then I should meet my audience every time I went in or out. He insisted I come and be a guest in his house in the country where he and his manager and friend Tony Forwood were living.

The entire stay in Guildford was one of the happiest times of my life.

———————— • ————————

The critics helped to make it so:

"Just before the curtain went up on Guildford's island theatre last night," wrote Felix Barker in London's *Evening News,* "a swan rose from the River Wey and flew past in the evening sunshine. This was as always a beautiful sight; and it was to be repeated on the stage toward the end of the first act. As graceful and almost as long-necked as a swan, Ingrid Bergman dressed in pure white threw back her head and as Turgenev's heroine Natalya Petrovna cried to herself, 'What is happening? Poor unhappy woman. For the first time you are in love.' At that moment the play, carried on her wings, also rose and took off."

"Visually," said *The New Yorker,* "Ingrid Bergman was perfection, beautiful and ageless in a series of superb dresses designed by Alix Stone—pale, wild silks cut to show off her splendid shoulders and torment poor Rakitin."

———————— • ————————

But they weren't all like that. Pia and Lars had come to Guildford for the opening, and were staying with me at Dirk's house. The morning after the opening, in came Pia and Lars with my breakfast tray and all the papers. They piled them on the bed and we all started to read. Then I saw a little foot that took a paper and pushed it under the bed. And I said, "I wonder what happened to *The Times?* Is that *The Times* you have kicked under the bed?"

"No, no, no, look at what Mr. R. B. Marriot says here—'Miss Bergman gives a performance of rare understanding, one that moves and fascinates as it explores the heartbreak, fear, joy and humiliation. . . .' What about that—eh?"

"Very nice." Then another paper fell on the floor and under the bed it went, and I said, "It's no use kicking them under the bed. I know how many papers we ordered and I intend to read them all."

"No, no, no, if you must read the bad ones, save them till the end of the week. But I can't see any bad ones. They're all marvelous."

"I'm still going to read them all."

The kicked-under-the-bed *Times* said: "In appearance she is the picture of the part, but her performance hardly goes beyond the pictorial." The *Guardian* which shared the floor with *The Times* said, "There was very little in this uneasy play uneasily presented and acted, very little except Ingrid Bergman, and even she, splendid, handsome, and grave, was not enough to save it."

Then, of course, up came the question: did we take the play to London? Lars said I should go, absolutely.

I discussed it with Dirk and Tony. They said, "You should *not* go. It's very good for Guildford, but it's not good enough for London." Then I talked to Michael Redgrave, and his opinion was, "Yes, I think we should take it in." And finally, my desire to go to London and appear in a play in the West End for the first time in my life—*Joan of Arc at the Stake* had been an oratorio—won and I said, "Yes."

I went back to Dirk's house. He was asleep, so I left him a little note which said, "I've been a very naughty girl. I've gone against your advice. I'm going to the West End with the play."

We filled the Cambridge Theatre for eight months, and forever afterwards Dirk and Tony said, "Never ask for our advice again. We told you not to go to London and you could have run forever."

Our London success had something to do with the fact that people had seen me in quite a few movies. Some of them must have said to themselves, "I remember her in *Intermezzo* and *Casablanca*. But is she still acting? She must be one hundred and five by now." So they came out of curiosity. The first time an autograph hunter told me, "You are my mother's favorite actress," I aged twenty years.

It was during the London run that we had a surprising happening. One night there were a couple of empty seats left at the end of a row, and just as the lights went down a couple walked in and occupied them. Immediately the ushers began to whisper: "Isn't that the Queen? Yes, it must be."

Of course the buzz reached us backstage very quickly. But there had been no phone call to the theater, no announcement; there were no police or guards. The Queen doesn't just walk in and sit in an aisle seat—or does she?

The manager rang up Emile Littler who owned the theater and he rang up Buckingham Palace and spoke to a private secretary or an equerry or somebody who said, "It's the Queen's night off. She has one night off a month when she can go to bed early, or have her friends in, or do what she likes."

Of course Emile Littler summoned the photographers, just in case. In the intermission he went down and escorted the Queen and her Lady-in-Waiting to a small private room. The Queen said very graciously, "Tell the cast that I'm not coming backstage because I'm not working. It's my night off. But also tell them I enjoyed the play very much."

She stayed to the final curtain, and we all felt so very pleased that she'd spent her one night off with us.

Those were memorable days in so many ways. On one occasion Pia—who was in Rome with Robertino, Isabella, and Ingrid—had brought the children to England for a few days; I was taking them all to see the play that evening. We were in the apartment and Pia went into the bedroom to lie down for a few minutes. But the door was open and she could hear me talking to the children as I tried to explain something about the play so they could understand it. We came to the word "rapier" which I used every night on the stage. And they said, "What is a rapier?"

I said, "It's a great big scaly animal with a big long tongue, and he throws out his tongue—zut—just like that, and takes a fly out of the air or an ant off the ground so quickly you can hardly see it."

Their eyes opened. They were very impressed by that animal. Then I heard Pia's voice from the bedroom, growling away, "Mother, it's not *true*. Don't give them all those *ideas*. I'm listening to your translations and you've gone too far! A rapier is not an *animal*. It's a *sword* !"

"Good heavens. I've been using it all these weeks at the theater thinking it was an animal with a big long tongue!"

I guess my English still had its flaws.

What I did think was rather disturbing about the London theater in those days was the trend toward brutality. All those angry young men. They frightened me. I suppose that sadism and perversion are a part of life, but it seemed to me they took very rare cases; they went out of their way to be sensational. I think most people are very ordinary; maybe not so kind-hearted, but not cruel to that extent. Perhaps that was one of the reasons I turned back to Turgenev where nobody was brutally hurt; at any rate only mentally.

But it was still a golden age for young actors, writers, and directors in England.

When I look back *now* at what I was doing then, I can recognize all the danger signs. The theater took me away from Choisel and Lars for months on end and that wasn't good for any marriage. My first instincts were right when I told Lars, "We promised each other that we'd always go to the island." Still, I pushed such thoughts into the background.

Chapter 24

I went to Rome to visit the children and was suddenly faced with one of the most worrying periods of my life. I was asked to see Isabella and Ingrid's school doctor. He had examined the girls to see whether they were fit for gymnastics.

"Yes, I can see her spine is not straight, it has a slight S-shape," I said to him as he asked Isa to lean forward. "But surely that isn't anything serious?"

"It's a condition we call scoliosis," he answered. "You have to take her to a specialist. She needs the sort of treatment we can't give her. You have to watch that the curvature doesn't get worse."

I looked at my thirteen-year-old daughter. She looked healthy and happy. Surely nothing could be wrong with her? But my heart seemed to stay strangely still.

I talked to Roberto about it. We started to inquire among friends and got advice about doctors. I took her to one doctor who advised us to put something in her shoe to make one hip higher than the other, and to have her put a pillow under one side of her behind whenever she sat down. We tried that, but I felt it would do little to change the curve in her spine. I went to another doctor who suggested a leather corset. It was made for her, but it was so painful we took it off. More advice, more doctors. I took her to Sweden to see the best doctor for scoliosis. He suggested exercises. I called doctors in the United States. Should I bring her over? Did they have some special treatment, some special doctors?

Of course they had. Come over? I hesitated. I waited for some miracle. Treatments in the United States meant we would have to remain there.

I spoke to Peter Viertel whose daughter had had the same illness. "But it stopped," he said, "it doesn't always go any further." But if it didn't? . . .

Back to the Italian doctor. "Your daughter's scoliosis is galloping," he said. "She's much worse than the last time I saw her."

I panicked. Where was the solution? It came through Isabella herself. "I was at a party last night and there was a girl who'd had the same thing and been operated on at the Scaglietti Hospital in Florence."

We took Isabella there. The three of us, Isa, Roberto, and I, looked at the beautiful city of Florence and saw no beauty at all. Only fear. Isa went through the examinations and X rays. Roberto and I sat outside without saying a word. Dr. Scaglietti beckoned us into his office. Isa's X rays were hanging on a rack.

"You see this curve here and here and here . . ." I couldn't understand what he was saying, but suddenly I heard quite clearly, "It could be the beginning of hunchback."

Roberto and I reached for a hand. We held on to each other.

"What can be done about it?"

"I am sorry to tell you, I think an operation is necessary."

We stood there. I had my arm around Isa. The three of us stood as if hit by lightning.

"Let's go home and think it over," said Roberto.

"Don't wait too long," were the last words I heard as we closed the door.

"There must be another way," I said. "I haven't tried hard enough to find it. I'll call New York tomorrow again."

Yes, I found there was the Milwaukee Corset but she would have to wear it for years.

"I don't want to wear a corset," Isa said. "I couldn't stand the one you bought me before."

Finally it was she who made up our minds. "I want the operation," she said. "Call the doctor and say I want it."

Oh, dear God, find me another solution, I thought. "There must be something simpler than an operation on the spine."

"I want it, Mama," Isa repeated.

The day was set for our departure to the clinic. We had no idea what we were in for. But Pia, who was in Rome, had met a lady whose daughter had gone through the same operation. Pia asked her to call on me to reassure me all was going to be well. This woman sat down in the living room and started to tell me what it was going to be like. "It will be all right in the end," she said with a sad smile, "but it is a cross. It is a cross." As we drove closer to the beautiful clinic in the hills outside Florence I remembered her, "It will be a cross."

They told us the operation couldn't take place for six months because Isa's curved spine had to be pulled as straight as possible first. The pulling couldn't be completed in one session. The spine had to be stretched gradually. How long it would take would depend on how flexible the spine was.

My child was put on what looked like a medieval torture rack. She was smiling at me as they tied her to it.

"Out!" I heard a voice say, "We don't want any squeamish mothers around."

So out I went. Through the door I could hear my child's screams. The doctor had explained that they couldn't give her an anaesthetic because they had to know how much it hurt in order to know when to stop. So there was my child on the rack screaming, and it seemed to me to last forever. Finally somebody said, "She's fine, you can come in now." She was covered in plaster from her neck to her hips. She looked as if she had fainted. They brought her to her room.

"Mama, Mama, it hurts so much."

Immediately I called the nurse. "Can't you do something? She can't stand it. We have to take her out of the cast."

I suppose the nurses were used to hysterical mothers.

"Now Signora, be calm. When the plaster has dried you can help her by gently pulling her head. It's a small relief for them."

It was hours before the plaster dried. I sat there helplessly holding my little girl's hand.

Finally I could begin to pull her head to stretch the spine. It wasn't easy. I tried to be brave but I couldn't help myself. She was in pain and I was in pain. I fought my tears but they streamed down my face. She fell asleep, and so did I sitting in a chair next to her.

It was remarkable how quickly she recovered. Soon she was eating, laughing, looking at television. Other girls in plaster casts were brought in on beds on wheels. They cheered each other up and they played cards. She was soon walking around in her plaster prison and we were allowed to go home.

There was a big to-do about clothes. How to cover all that plaster? I bought material and had a seamstress come.

One day, one of Isa's friends from the hospital called. "Isabella, we are invited to a dance. Come on, it will be fun."

Isa looked horrified: "How can you go to a dance in plaster?"

"Sure you can. It's not often the boys have a chance to dance with girls in plaster."

She was very hesitant. I could understand her fears. The cast made her so misshapen and it weighed a ton. But I was determined she should go. "Come on now, Isa, we'll get you a dress."

She finally gave in. She went and she danced, and sure enough there was a young man who fell in love with her.

"Mama stopped work," said Isabella remembering, "and I was very touched by that because I know how she loves her work and I love her working. I was very touched that she didn't work for that whole eighteen months except for one two-week period when she was contracted to do a television film of Jean Cocteau's *The Human Voice.*"

It was a lonely time for Lars also, because I saw so little of him during this long period in Rome and Florence. It was Lars who had come up with the idea of *The Human Voice* in the first place, and the contract had been signed long before we dreamt that Isa would have to have this operation.

Jean Cocteau's monologue of a lonely woman in her apartment talking on the telephone to her lover who is about to leave her for another woman is a magnificent piece of drama. I'd done it before as a recording.

I rehearsed for twelve days, mainly alone with Ted Kotcheff, the director, and a couple of assistants, and worked out all the moves. When you're playing fifty minutes all by yourself there have to be a great many changes of position and camera angle. We had two more days to record the fifty minutes, and no hope of any extension because television studios in London are very heavily booked.

The first day was disastrous. I felt hemmed in. The four cameras were very close to me the whole time and I was never certain which was "on" at any particular second. The four production assistants mumbled into their microphones continually as they received instructions on their head-sets, and that threw me also. I was so off balance I constantly forgot my lines, and the result was that at the end of that first day we had filmed only *three* minutes out of the fifty we needed. I didn't have to be a mind reader to know from their faces that Lars and his associate producer, David Susskind, were very worried men. And that first day had been one long agony for me.

However, after a good night's sleep, I returned ready for all the mumbling and the camera shifting, and everything went smoothly. We finished on schedule.

———————— • ————————

The New York Times said of *The Human Voice:* "Miss Bergman's delicate playing was a tour-de-force, a brilliant portrait of the woman whose life is wrenched out of joint by the fates of the heart." *The Times* of London reported: "She imparted great dramatic power to this harrowing monologue on the telephone, reflecting the depths of despair."

———————— • ————————

We had to go back to the clinic in Florence for the next pulling. Now we knew what we were in for and that made it altogether worse for both of us. Roberto drove us to Florence and Isabella's face was like a statue, determination in her eyes.

She had to kneel on the seat the whole way; she couldn't sit in a normal position because of her cast. When she had gone to a performance of one of Lars's plays, she had stood all the way through it.

The old plaster was taken off. The spine had accepted its new position. Now for another pulling. I can't bear to think or write about it. But she made the same quick recovery. At that age, such things are possible. I lagged behind.

We went back to the apartment in Rome. She went back to school. Of course the teachers were good to her; they felt so sorry for her. I really don't think she did any school work at all. What was necessary was done by young Ingrid. She worked very hard for both of them.

There were three pullings altogether, but finally the day of the operation was set. We had to collect blood because the hospital could not supply all that was needed for the necessary transfusions. Everybody in the family—parents, cousins, friends—even the kids at school volunteered to give blood for Isabella.

Fiorella helped me to carry the big wooden box full of bottles packed in ice to the car. I held my arm around the box to keep it steady as we drove to Florence, all the time thinking, There must be another way. This is a bad dream. Why didn't I take her to America?

The three of us sat in the car without a word. But our thoughts were the same. The calmest one was Isabella.

We arrived. Isabella was brought down to the operating theater. We were assured all would be well: Isabella was a strong healthy girl except for this spinal trouble. I followed her to the elevator, kissed her forehead and she pressed my hand. No words were necessary. I watched the elevator descend.

It was not until after the operation that Dr. Scaglietti showed me a documentary film of the whole process. He said he could not have shown it to me earlier because I would have been too frightened.

The operation begins with a cut from the knee to the foot to take out one third of the shin-bone; the bone will grow back, but Isa's leg will be in a cast and she will not be able to stand on it for six months. The shin-bone is shaved into small sticks the size of matches. They must use the patient's own shin bone; otherwise the body might reject it. Then the back is opened down the length of the spine and the bone "matches" inserted between the discs to prevent the spine from curving back to its original position. The spine will be kept completely rigid. So she will be put into a new plaster cast.

We had been told the operation would take between five and seven hours. So we waited. Roberto did crosswords, endless crosswords. I couldn't read, couldn't write letters, and I hadn't brought my knitting. I just walked up and down and suddenly I disappeared into the bathroom. "What are you doing that takes so long?" called Roberto.

"I am washing my hair."

"You are washing your hair! Now? At this moment when they are operating on our daughter?" He sounded quite angry.

"I must have something to do, otherwise I'll go crazy."

It's a strange thing. Ever since that occasion, whenever I'm distressed or depressed, I wash my hair. It seems to take my mind off what's troubling me; it lessens the agony. It needs no concentration. It's mechanical. It's something to *do*.

We got word from the operating room. All was going well. Her heart was strong. I dried my hair in the Florentine sunshine out on the balcony. Roberto didn't even look up; he just went on with his crossword puzzles. We did not dare to touch each other for fear of a complete breakdown.

I went out into the corridor to ask if they had a chapel. Yes they did and indicated the way. I sat in the semi-darkness and prayed. I am uneasy praying to a God I need only when things go wrong. Why don't I pray when thing go well? But that is the way it is. I sat and argued inside myself over this. When I am happy I am grateful. I say, "Thank you, God, and I feel profoundly grateful for all the good things that I have had in my life." I remember my son Robertino when he was small asking, "Who is God?" That was difficult. I finally said, "Well, one day you might have a sick child and you will fall on your knees and pray to God."

Robertino looked at me and said, "I think I'd rather fall on my knees and pray to the doctor."

I went back to Roberto who reported that everything was going according to schedule.

The hours passed. Isabella was doing fine. It started to get dark.

Finally Dr. Ponti, who performed the operation, was standing at the door. "It's over. You can come and see your daughter now." We had waited six-and-a-half hours.

I rushed out, leaving Roberto and the doctor far behind. I knew exactly on which floor and in what direction the operating rooms lay. I couldn't wait for the elevator. I flew down the stairs racing toward my child. Behind me I heard Dr. Ponti shouting, "Take it easy. Everything is all right."

I dashed into the operating area. I saw an open door. I raced through and there lay a child on a stretcher. I screamed, "What have you done to my child? She's so short! You've shortened her! Good heavens, what have you done!"

I felt the comforting arm of Dr. Ponti around my shoulder, "Signora, you are in the wrong room. This is not your child."

Gently, he led me into the right room. There she lay, our darling daughter, asleep and so pale. And full of tubes. Both Roberto and I started to sob.

Finally the tubes were removed and she was taken back to her room, with Roberto and I walking alongside staring at the pale white face that pressed up through the enormous plaster cast. She was still unconscious when the nurse came in and began to slap her face, "Come on now, Isabella. You all right? Wake up, everything is fine."

I flew at the nurse, "How can you do that! Stop slapping her face . . . Everything is not fine. She feels awful, don't you realize that?"

Roberto pulled me away. "Ingrid, please don't get angry with the nurse. This is routine. Don't you understand, Isabella must wake up. Please calm down."

I stared at him and then I just fell forward into his arms as I fainted.

I woke up in the dark, and didn't know where I was. Then I realized that somebody was at the door. It was Roberto. I'd been carried into the room next door. Was I all right? "Yes," I managed to answer. "But I'm useless. I just can't take any more."

"Don't worry. Go back to sleep. I'll stay with her through the night. I'll wake you if anything happens."

Poor Roberto. That night he had a hard time with me and Isabella. She woke up and began to mumble, and he couldn't make out what she was trying to say. She went on and on. He put his ear close to her mouth to try and catch what she was saying. At last he heard. "Belfagor—Belfagor." What on earth did she mean? Then at last he got it. "Belfagor—television." It was a television mystery series my children were crazy about. It was shown on Thursdays—the day of her operation. She couldn't bear to miss a single installment. She didn't realize it was four A.M.. Roberto comforted her. If she went to sleep now she could see it in the morning. And quite content, she fell asleep.

The days that followed were full of pain for Isa but she was full of courage. We helped her a little by pulling her head, but she was also in pain now from her leg. The days were long. I read her stories and tried to lessen the irritation of the plaster cast by putting cream on little sticks and pushing them under it. I rearranged her pillows, and tried to get her to eat. And I remember how I blessed six o'clock when Italian television came on.

It was hard going and sometimes I just had to go out into the corridor so that she shouldn't see my tears. Always there was someone there, offering comfort, a cigarette, another mother saying very little, but understanding—understanding—and murmuring, "It will be all right. It will be all right." Once, when I went back to Isabella she said, "Mother, don't cry so much. I'm not sorry this has happened to me. In the future when people talk about pain, I will know what it means. It might help me to help others who suffer."

Those words from my fourteen-year-old daughter sent me back into the corridor again in tears.

The days passed. Roberto had to go back to Rome. Fiorella came for a visit. Other girls visited our room, and they chatted, comparing operations and pain. And they played cards. One day, in the middle of a game, a nurse came in to tell one girl they were ready for her pulling. I shall never ever forget that look of anguish on her face as she called out, "This time I won't make it. This time I'll die!"

The girls looked at each other and there was a long silence. Then they went on with their game. There was nothing else to do, except go on.

Another time a boy came to the door of Isa's room and asked if he could see her. He said he had driven from Rome to Florence with a friend. He was the boy who had met her at the dance when she was in her plaster cast. Could I ask Isabella if she would see him?

I turned to Isa and asked if she wanted the boy to come in. Is there any medicine stronger than love? Her whole face lit up. I didn't need to wait for an answer. I said, "Come in boy. She'll be happy to see you." Her happiness was boundless. So was his. I left them alone.

When she was well enough we went back to Rome, this time by ambulance as she had to maintain this prone position—her little body in one plaster cast, her right leg in another up to her knee —for six months. I had arranged her bed with pretty sheets so that it wouldn't remind her of the hospital. She had a low table by the side of her bed so she could roll over on her stomach and write on it. We washed her hair in that position pouring a can of hot water over it into a bucket beneath, with a heavy towel to protect the cast.

Isabella figured out that if she rolled she could move. Before long she was a master roller. She became very clever at grabbing the headboard and twisting herself over.

Friends arrived every day to bring gifts. From the boy who loved her came a Beatles record and that was played every day. Every day too, I heard her laughter as her little dachshund Ferdinando played games with her on the bed or hid behind her cast. He never left her.

In the summer we took Isabella to Fiorella's house in the hills at Circeo. We managed to get hold of a bed on wheels so Isa could be pulled around the garden. We had picnics under the trees.

Thank God, Fiorella was there to help me pull that bed through sand and stones and weeds.

The six months were finally over and we went back to Florence so that Isabella could be given a new cast. Her leg had healed and she could stand up and move around. She could go back to school, she could go dancing again, but the spine was held in its prison for still another six months.

When, at long last, the day came when she was going to be cut out of her plaster, we were frightened. After eighteen months it seemed unbelievable that at last she might be able to move around normally again. We knew there would be a long scar on her back and another on her leg; that she would be stiff, unable to bend over. But she would be out of that terrible armor of plaster.

I watched the male nurse start to cut through the plaster with his electric saw. It was very noisy and for a few seconds I was afraid he might cut into her body, but he smiled at me and said, "I've done this for years."

Slowly her thin body appeared out of all that plaster; she looked so frail. On a stretcher she was carried to her first bath in eighteen months. "How divine," she said, lying back in the warm water.

In her nightgown she was carried back to her bed, and Dr. Ponti arrived, smiling at us both.

"Well, it's all over. You can get up, Isabella."

"No, no," she whispered, "I can't stand up alone. I don't dare."

"Yes, you can. Get out of bed and stand up."

Again I had a very hard time to keep my tears back. To see her face of hope, of disbelief, of fear; I have never seen anything so beautiful. She hung on to his eyes as if she were hypnotized, and slowly she stood up.

Doctor and patient looked at each other.

"You see, you can do it," said Dr. Ponti. "Would you like to go swimming in the pool?"

And how she wanted to swim! Into a bathing suit and into the water she went. Pia had taught the other children to swim very well when she was in Rome and Isabella was very good at it. She went across the pool, as if she expected to win the Olympics. Alongside the pool ran a male nurse shouting, "You are not supposed to swim like that. Stop it. You'll hurt yourself."

She didn't hear him. At the other end of the pool her head came up and she looked at him.

"Did I do something wrong?" she asked, but her face was radiant.

"Just stop going so fast. You're supposed to do the breaststroke."

She swam around the pool doing the breaststroke.

It was wonderful to take her home and Isabella seemed strong and healthy. We were all celebrating and laughter echoed through the apartment. Cousins, aunts, friends, everybody came to see the new Isa. There was a telephone call from the boy in love. Could he come and see her too? Of course. Isa was terribly shy; she was really worried about what he would think of her, now that she was just herself.

When I opened the door I realized he was as scared as she was. They stood there and stared at each other. I had to rush away so they wouldn't see that once again I was in tears.

Chapter 25

It was no more than a few weeks after Isabella's recovery: I
almost had the pen in my hand to sign for a play in Paris based
on Tolstoy's *Anna Karenina,* when José Quintero came to Paris
with Eugene O'Neill's *More Stately Mansions.* I dropped the pen.
Anna would have been fine. What every actress loves. David Selznick always wanted me to do it and I was attracted to the part, but
I thought, Anna's been done by Garbo and she impressed me so
much.

Yet José Quintero coming with this offer was so strange. It was
as if O'Neill's ghost had come forward saying, "You refused to work
with me twenty-five years ago. Now is your chance. Do it!"

I had met Eugene O'Neill when I was playing *Anna Christie* in
the early forties. We'd opened in Selznick's summer theater in
Santa Barbara and then moved on for a short run in San Francisco.
After the show one night, they told me O'Neill's wife Carlotta was
waiting to talk to me.

She was a very beautiful, dark-haired woman and she told me
that her husband was pleased that his play was being performed.
He could not come to the theater himself because he was ill, but
he would like to meet me. Could I have lunch with them the
following Sunday? She sent a car to pick me up.

The house was near San Francisco on the coast, a strange place.
The whole episode was mysterious. I arrived and waited and waited
in the great hall. Then Carlotta came and said, "I'll give you a sign
when you have to go because he gets very tired. I'll go and get him."

The staircase was very broad, and suddenly he was standing there. So handsome you couldn't believe it. He had burning eyes, dark black eyes, a beautiful face, and he was very thin and very tall. He came down and said he had heard how good I was in *Anna Christie,* and would I come up to his studio and see how he was working on nine plays. They concerned a hundred and fifty years of American history dealing with generations of an Irish family who emigrated to America.

His handwriting was so tiny that even my young eyes couldn't read it. Carlotta told me she typed all his manuscripts using a magnifying glass. O'Neill said he wanted to gather together a repertory company to perform the entire cycle of plays; each actor and actress would play different members of the great family through the centuries. It was a very challenging idea. He said he would like me to join that company. I asked immediately, "How long would this repertory company work together?" He said, "Four years." I exclaimed, "Four years! That is impossible. I am under contract to David Selznick."

So I left and I never saw him again, but long afterwards Carlotta told me that his Parkinson's disease had made his hands tremble so terribly that he could hardly write. He tried to dictate but that wouldn't work. They'd moved by then to the East Coast, near Boston University, and O'Neill had decided that as there was no hope of his finishing his plays before he died he would destroy them. He didn't want people altering or rewriting them. "It was like burning children," Carlotta said.

But O'Neill had forgotten that one typed copy of *More Stately Mansions* had been deposited with the Yale University Library, together with all his corrections and notes and suggestions for future work on it. It was found there in 1958, five years after his death, by a Swedish theatrical producer, and despite the fact that it was labeled "Unfinished work—to be destroyed in the event of my death," they felt it was far too valuable to burn. Carlotta gave permission for it to be translated into Swedish and it was performed in Sweden in 1962.

So into my life came José Quintero.

———————— • ————————

José Quintero was fascinated by the work of Eugene O'Neill. He had obtained Carlotta's permission to produce *The Iceman Cometh* in New York, and after seeing it, she had given him permission to produce other O'Neill plays including *Long Day's Journey Into Night.*

To prepare *More Stately Mansions* for the theater, José Quintero worked at Yale University, burrowing through O'Neill's notes and suggestions, editing and cutting the play to an acceptable length while preserving the essence of O'Neill's purpose. The occasion was not just another theatrical venture. It would be the first production of the first season of the vast new two-thousand seat Ahmanson Theater in Los Angeles. And José Quintero wanted Ingrid Bergman for the part of the elegant Deborah Harford, with Colleen Dewhurst as Sara, her Irish daughter-in-law.

———————— • ————————

José told me what he'd done, and the cuts he'd made.

I read it.

Then Kay Brown called me from New York and said, "I've called you one day before the deadline, dear, but I'm sorry I can't wait any longer. I'm just going to pieces. Have you decided?"

"Yes, I have, and the answer is Yes."

"You mean to say you will come and do it?"

"That's what I said."

"Oh, thank God," said Kay, "because it's so damn dignified."

I always loved that. "So damn dignified!"

José was still with us, so we sat in the living room in Choisel cutting it, and trying to shape it, and working out my ideas against his.

Now it meant going to America and working both in Los Angeles and the New York theater, for about six months. And I wanted to take young Ingrid with me. She had had rather a tough time while Isabella was ill. Everybody was concentrating on Isabella. Always pouring past her asking, "How is Isabella?" No one asked, "How is Ingrid?" Yet she was so marvelous to Isabella, helping her with her schoolwork, doing it for her often.

And she worked so hard in school. She was so frightened of exams that she worked for hours into the night. Then she'd come home with the highest marks saying, "Of course Isabella will get through, she has no problems with school."

But I noticed that a bitter line was growing round young Ingrid's mouth. We had neglected her shamefully for her twin sister. She was healthy and running around and no one gave her a second thought, so now more and more I tried to concentrate on her.

What could I do to help? A holiday in America while I was doing *More Stately Mansions* would be a good start.

"America!" said Roberto. "Out of the question. No discussion."

Of course, young Ingrid was so disappointed, but I said, "Now, I've got to leave Rome, but I shall be back to reopen the subject. Don't despair." A few weeks later I was back in Rome and young Ingrid and Roberto and I were together. And I started to say, "Well you know I'm going to America. Now what about Ingrid?"

"Ingrid?" said Roberto. "Isn't she going to America with you?"

I was speechless.

"I'm going over to America and I'll bring our Ingrid with me, and then I have to go to Houston on business and I'll leave her with you in Los Angeles."

Dear Roberto. He'd just gone from one extreme to the other. Now he was on good terms with America. I hope they were pleased.

Through the years that followed, Ingrid was mostly with me. She was in America all through the run of *More Stately Mansions*. Every summer she was on Lars's island in Sweden. She was with me on holidays in France, in England, wherever I went. Her schooling in the United States was by a private teacher, and she managed her exams in Italy very well. There were, of course, many emotional moments. I remember toward the end of *More Stately Mansions* she had to go back to Rome for her exams. I had to go to the theater. I took one look at Ruth Roberts who was with us, a "help me" look as I kissed Ingrid good-bye. But she clung to me crying. She wouldn't let go and I had to take her arms away from my neck and push her away. I felt so brutal, but what could I do? I had to be in the theater for the performance. I ran down the hallway, feeling awful.

After I had put on my make-up there was time to call Ruth to ask if Ingrid had calmed down. Ingrid answered the phone, and her agonized, "Mama, Mama, Mama," broke my heart. Her tears seemed to flood down the telephone wires. I was completely destroyed. They had to hold the curtain ten minutes before I could go out and perform.

The Ahmanson Theater was so cavernous that the joke was "You shout in Act One and the echo comes back to you in Act Three!" I was very excited to be there: it was my first trip back to Los Angeles in sixteen years!

José Quintero and I had agreed on all the changes and the cuts. We got on, and I liked him very much, though there were arguments during the rehearsals. In my very first entrance I have a meeting in the forest with my son. José said, "You come running in and you stop—dead still—and stand there transfixed."

I insisted, "But I'm a mother who hasn't seen her son for four long years. She's going to meet him at this little deserted cottage in the forest. Surely she'll creep in hesitating and worried, frightened to see him, fearful that she's aged."

José said, "I see her flying in. . . ."

So I said, "Well I don't want to stop rehearsals, but perhaps we can discuss it later. . . . Now, what's next?"

"Next you come right down stage to the footlights. Right down to the steps there, and you sit on the steps there."

I looked at the front of the stage in horror. "You mean I dash in, stand transfixed, then walk right down to the audience and sit in their laps?"

It was one of those new theaters with no footlights and two steps leading down into the audience.

"Yes, do that."

"But they'll hear my heart going bang-bang-bang. I can't do that. I just can't. I start off by running in—all right, we'll discuss that later—and then I go down front and sit almost on top of the front row. In those very first moments I'm *frightened* of the audience. . . . I'm terrified of the audience. You're close enough to say hello to them. You can hear them talking about you. 'She still looks pretty good for her age. How old do you think she is?' "

From then on, José Quintero was a bit terse, and didn't say anything much to me except, "Well, what do you suggest?" So I said, "Well if I could sit back there where the cottage is, get my breath, and let my heart calm down, and then begin the monologue —when I've found my voice then I'll come down front and sit with the audience."

———— • ————

She wrote to Lars:

> My darling,
> We've had a big revolution in the theater but I didn't want to tell you until it was all over, because I knew somehow it would turn out well.

I drove poor José crazy. I confess that. He blew his top and bawled me out and told me off. I thought at first he was talking to somebody else. You know how sure I am of myself. He said he couldn't work any more with me. This happened in the morning but by the afternoon he came and asked for my forgiveness, and he absolutely went to pieces when I thanked him for having bawled me out, and he said he must go home now, he couldn't take any more. So we all went home. Thank God the air is now clear and everything is well. I accept José's direction and he said when we met yesterday the first time after the storm, "Now, I can take anything from you."

Now I must run to rehearsals. Oh, it is so interesting—what a play. Thank you for your letter which came yesterday. I can imagine that you have had a difficult time with your monsters in your theater and I'm sure they don't like you because you bawl them out. You're better off with me, I think. I kiss you, my little old man, and I love you very much. You can be sure of that. Everybody thinks I'm so docile, and I'm only just realizing it myself. I fight like mad about everything.

———— • ————

José was very funny afterwards about my behavior. "I didn't dare to open my mouth," he said. "Everything I said, Ingrid said, 'Oh, you're wrong!' So I didn't say anything. Just 'Well, how do you feel about this scene?' and 'Where do you want to be now?'—that sort of thing, just have it the way she wanted it. And then after a couple of days of rehearsal, I was rehearsing Arthur Hill and Colleen Dewhurst who played the son and daughter-in-law, and I heard Ingrid say, 'Ah, that's good. That's very good.' And do you know, instead of hitting her I felt like falling on my knees and saying, 'Thank you Ingrid, thank you!' I got so mad at myself. After all, I am the director, and there she stands saying, 'That's good' ... or ... 'Hmm! That's not so good' ... 'No, I can't do it that way ...' And when at last she said something's good—*I* am the one who is thanking her!"

We became such good friends. José is a marvelous director. We worked very well; we both compromised. I did his run onto the stage, and then he let me sit down to catch my breath; then I came and sat down next to the audience. And, of course, on opening night I found myself staring straight into the eyes of Sam Goldwyn who was in the front row. That helped my performance no end! Opening night, as usual, I was absolutely petrified. Absolute mind-boggling fear. This occasion was even more difficult because I knew the play wasn't easy, and O'Neill was a hard playwright. And after all, it wasn't one of O'Neill's best plays, and it had never been played before. I knew I had all Hollywood in front of me for the first time after sixteen years. All the people who had *not* been very kind to me were there.

It was hard even to put a foot on the stage. I stood in the wings and José was right with me. He held my hand and said, "Do it for *him!*"—which meant, of course, Eugene O'Neill. Then he gave me a little push, and I ran out—the way he wanted me to—right into the middle of the stage. And at that moment I knew he was absolutely right and I had been absolutely wrong. Coming out like a flash on this enormous stage and just stopping motionless, in profile, was good theater and got entirely the effect he intended. The audience just applauded and applauded and applauded. I stood there. Listening. To me it seemed the applause would never end. All the years came back to me . . . all the tears of Stromboli, all the agony, all the despair, everything. I kept saying to myself, "You mustn't cry, you mustn't cry, you'll lose your eyelashes and the mascara will run, you mustn't cry. . . ." And I could feel the tears coming down as I stood there, under that enormous applause, and then it died down . . . and I couldn't remember one word—not one word.

Ruth was in the wings whispering in her nice little voice . . . sheesph . . . sheesph . . . sheesph. I could hear that she was whispering but I couldn't get it. I walked closer to that wing and leaned toward her, but I still couldn't get it. Finally the stage manager, who had a stronger voice, threw me the line. I know the audience heard it, but they understood that I was completely speechless, that everything had left my brain. I started and then it rolled and rolled—thank God!

———————— • ————————

The play arrived at the Broadhurst Theater in New York on October 31, 1967, and critical opinion was fairly unanimous: "O'Neill's mansion is still a shambles without form." "The play is born a ruin: a great architectural emptiness." "Creaking melodrama complete with soliloquies, brow-clutching, incest, hatred . . . starchy with rhetoric and exposition." "A drama of power without form."

Time magazine summed up: "A remnant of O'Neill's melancholy conviction that hell hath no fury like a human family."

Clive Barnes in *The New York Times:* "Ingrid Bergman returning to the Broadway stage is a woman so beautiful that she is herself a work of art."

Ingrid was not overly concerned. The entire O'Neill experience was so personal and unique that reviews did not seem to matter very much.

———— • ————

I saw Carlotta when we brought the play to New York. I said she must come and see it. "No," she said, "I never go out any more. I have nothing to wear, and I can't see." And this was true. She had worn her eyes out peering at that tiny writing of O'Neill's, and she wore glasses with very thick pebble lenses. I tried to cheer her up with flowers and little presents; I bought her two dresses, and I often had tea with her. She said, "You know, I don't like women. I just don't like them. And I don't know why I do love you." She gave me a photograph of herself taken when she was a young woman—she was very very lovely. She showed me a book—it had been published—containing all the cards O'Neill had sent her. In most of them he was begging her forgiveness: "Forgive me, I was terrible," and "I don't understand how you can bear to stay with me." He was obviously very difficult to live with.

Finally one day she said she would try and come to the theater, to a matinee. I arranged a car and Ruth went with it to help her. We alerted the company manager to make things as easy as possible: not to recognize her or make a fuss, just to let her sit quietly. Afterwards Ruth brought her backstage and the tears were pouring down her cheeks. She said, "I couldn't see you much. But I could hear you. Oh, how I wish that he could have heard you."

She was so very sweet. That was the last time I ever saw her. She went back to her apartment and not long after that into an insane asylum where she died.

———— • ————

Chapter 26

From the time we were married, both Lars and I will admit it, we were certainly not a normal married couple. He was running all over the world with his theatrical productions, and I was in London doing *A Month in the Country,* and the next year in Rome taking care of Isabella, and then that autumn off for another six months to do *More Stately Mansions.* Yes, we were in touch all that time by telephone—and we wrote letters and Lars flew across to London or New York or Hollywood—but it wasn't really a married existence. I think we both accepted that, but I don't think we took into account the dangers.

It was Liana Ferri who first directly and bluntly said, "Ingrid, you're putting a terrible strain on your marriage. Are you sure that you want to work that much?"

I said, "I've got to work. It's my life!"

But as I've said, down in my subconscious I was already aware of the dangers; aware that it had started with *A Month in the Country.* Of course I still saw a lot of Lars then: he came to Guildford for the opening; he came to London to visit. And I sometimes flew over to Choisel for a weekend. I would fly Sunday morning and come back Monday afternoon. But it was very nerve-racking, the French and English weather being so treacherous, and there was always the danger that fog would ground all the planes. And I wasn't really allowed to go, according to the terms of my contract, which said how many miles I was permitted to go outside London over the weekend. So I could have been sued for breaking my contract, especially if I hadn't been back in the theater in time for the evening performance Monday night. (When years later, in 1971, I did *Captain Brassbound's Conversion,* Binkie Beaumont knew all about my weekend flights. He'd call me up on Monday afternoon at four and I'd say, "Hello?" And all I'd hear was, "Thank God," and the phone being put down.)

I thought it out very carefully. I knew I had to decide what I really wanted in my life. Was it really to sit in Choisel and wait for Lars to come home from his work, or was it to go to the theater and perform? Well, I am one of those performing dogs. So I decided that for the next job I would go again.

But I knew, and I was warned—Lars told me in all his letters that broke my heart because he kept saying, "I'm so lonely." "You are always away from me and it's no fun to sit here alone and I can't wait for you to come back." "Please stay with me." But he understood me enough to realize that I wanted to work. And, of course, he also went on trips a lot: he had companies running in Germany and in Sweden and in Denmark. I don't think he ever stayed home more than a week before he was off again on a trip.

I stayed out there in the country and it was very beautiful but very lonely.

When I was in New York finishing the run of *More Stately Mansions,* Kay Brown sent me a novel by Rachel Maddux called *A Walk in the Spring Rain* and I liked it very much. I thought it was wonderful finally to get a story where the woman is fifty, and the husband is fifty-two, and she falls in love with a man who might be older still.

Kay told me that Stirling Silliphant, who'd won an Oscar for his script of *In the Heat of the Night,* was very interested. He came to see me to discuss it, and we both got excited about the story. He said, "I'm so crazy about the book I'd like to produce it myself. I've never produced before but I don't want anyone else to get his hands on it."

I'd now finished *More Stately Mansions* and I was going back to France, and then with Lars up to the island. So I invited Stirling and his wife to the island.

Stirling enjoyed the boats and the fishing, but as the days went by he never got around to the script. Finally I said, "Look, we have to talk about it. Have you got any of it with you?"

"Yes," he said, "but it's not on marble you know. We can change anything we don't like."

He hadn't written the whole script. I said, "You have written up to where it gets difficult and then you stopped!" But by that time I liked him so much and I had confidence that he could write a good script. Columbia was willing to back it, and we found the location.

That was *one* film set up for 1969.

Then we were back in Choisel and the phone rang and it was Mike Frankovich from Beverly Hills.

"Ingrid, I've got the film rights to the play *Cactus Flower*, and I would very much like you to do it."

There was a long pause from me.

"I've got Walter Matthau for the dentist, and Goldie Hawn as his girlfriend."

"Yes."

"I can feel you hesitating."

Of course he could. I'd read the play because Binkie Beaumont had asked me to do it in a London theater, but I'd refused because I didn't want to be away from Lars for another long period.

"Yes, I'm hesitating."

"Why?"

"The part of the dentist's assistant calls for a thirty-five-year-old woman."

"So?"

"I'm fifty-four."

"So what the hell?"

I laughed and said, "Mike, I think you'd better come to Paris and take a look at me before you make up your mind. And I shall be very understanding."

Mike and his director, Gene Saks, arrived in Paris and came to see me. When they arrived, I stood under a very bright light, and Mike walked around me grinning broadly, examining me from every angle like you do if you're looking over a head of cattle for sale. Then he announced his verdict:

"Ingrid. You're fine! And you'll also be pleased to know that we have a very good cameraman!"

And indeed he was a good cameraman. He was so good I insisted on having Charles Lang for *A Walk in the Spring Rain* afterwards. *Spring Rain* would come second because Anthony Quinn, the leading man, was busy with another picture.

So there were *two* pictures I was going to do in Hollywood in 1969, with hardly any break at all between them.

———————— • ————————

In March, from a Beverly Hills Hotel bungalow, she was in great good humor and tongue-in-cheek writing to Lars:

> I think Gene Saks, the director, is very thankful for all the good advice I'm giving him as—as usual—I interfere with his direction. The only real sourpuss is the poor author, I.A.L. Diamond, because I try to make them cut all his jokes which I don't find all that funny. So far I haven't succeeded, and don't think I will, because as we sat round the table at the read-through everybody was falling over laughing. I knew then that I was lost. . . .

Mike Frankovich said, "Walter Matthau is notoriously unimpressionable. But just before Ingrid arrived, he looked very worried and kept nagging me, 'How do you think we will get on? Will she like me?' Ingrid loved him. The three of them, Ingrid, Goldie, and Walter got on like a house on fire. And at the end of the film Goldie said, 'Oh, but she's a woman's woman. I mean, she's everything a woman should be. She's the kind of woman men aren't afraid of because she's so warm. I thought I'd be awfully intimidated by her, so intimidated I wouldn't be able to function. It wasn't that way at all. I didn't feel I had to compete. I just felt privileged to be in the same picture with her. She has a regal quality. It's too bad she isn't the queen of some country.' "

Time magazine said: "*Cactus Flower* answers one of the less pressing but more engaging questions facing America today: Can *Laugh-In*'s Goldie Hawn really act? Yes she can and so can Walter Matthau and Ingrid Bergman. . . . *Cactus Flower* succeeds on the screen thanks to two old masters—and a shiny new one—who have learned that actors get known by the comedy they keep."

It was a resounding universal success.

———————— • ————————

Of course I did get into a little trouble with Lauren Bacall over *Cactus Flower*. Lauren had created the part on Broadway. She had a tremendous success. Then they sold the movie rights to Mike Frankovich, and Lauren said to her agent, "Well, you'd better go after it, but I don't think you will have an awful lot of trouble unless of course they want a woman who is *younger* than me."

When Lauren found out that I had been given the part she was furious. She said in an interview that she didn't mind losing out to a woman who was *younger* than herself, but they had chosen Ingrid Bergman who was *ten years* older than she.

She had been led to believe that the part was hers and then she'd heard that I'd been chosen instead. I could understand her feelings.

The trouble was I didn't feel very guilty. I too thought it a marvelous part. And after all, I had turned down the chance to do it on the stage in London for Lars's sake. I felt I deserved it now.

Years before, I was offered Anne Bancroft's part in *The Miracle Worker* after Anne had made such a tremendous success out of the play in New York. I had loved the role. I wanted to do it in France. Lars talked to people about it but nobody liked it. They wouldn't believe that the story of a deaf and dumb child and her teacher could work, so I never could get anybody to produce it in the French theater. Then came the call from Hollywood asking me to do it on the screen. That time I said, "No, absolutely no, I will not do it." "Why not?" "Because you're out of your mind if you don't put Anne Bancroft in it." "But she's not a star." I said, "No, but put her in the part and she will be a star." They did, and she won the Oscar.

Anyway, Lauren Bacall was so angry that when Pia, who was now working in New York in television, was given the assignment of interviewing her, the first thing she said was, "Don't talk to me about your mother! Don't even mention your mother's name!" So Pia said, "No, I don't intend to mention my mother's name. I've come to do an interview with you." Which she did.

Months later I was back in New York and Lauren had another tremendous success on Broadway in *Applause.* I told Pia I was going to see it with Kay Brown, and I said, "I think I'll go backstage and meet Lauren." Pia nearly dropped. "Oh no, don't! She really hates you."

I said, "Well I don't think she can hate me all that much anymore, now that she has this enormous success. That always helps the pain."

Kay and I saw *Applause,* and Lauren was marvelous in it, so I said, "I'm going backstage to meet her."

Kay was trembling, visibly trembling, "Do you think that's wise, Ingrid?"

"Of course it's wise."

So Kay said, "I'll wait for you out here."

I found Lauren's dressing room, and knocked on the door, and the dresser answered and said, "Whom can I announce?" And I said, "Tell her the woman she hates more than anyone else in the world wants to see her."

I could see through the crack in the door Lauren's face reflected in her mirror, and suddenly I saw this huge smile. She came bounding toward me and we embraced, and we've been great friends ever since.

———————— • ————————

The Smoky Mountains of Tennessee lie in a comparatively remote part of the United States, a region of high green mountains, silver lakes, vast stretches of silver birch trees and, in the spring, a blaze of dogwood and azalea blossoms. It was against this setting that Rachel Maddux set her short novel, and it was to Knoxville, Tennessee, that Ingrid Bergman, Anthony Quinn, and Fritz Weaver went to make *A Walk in the Spring Rain*.

———————— • ————————

We shot on location up in the Smokies, and it was wonderful. The story was really very simple. I'm just the ordinary wife of a college professor, played by Fritz Weaver. He decides to take a year's vacation, a sabbatical, to write the book he's always wanted to write. We go down to Tennessee to live in an old cottage. I meet the local handyman, a man steeped in the countryside, uneducated but very male: Anthony Quinn. We fall in love. His teenage son hears about it. In a fight with his father, the boy is accidentally killed. Anthony Quinn and I realize it's all over. We say good-bye. My husband decides he's a failure as a novelist. We go back to New York.

But the plot doesn't give you any idea of the atmosphere and the real beauty of Rachel Maddux's book.

As a result of *The Visit*, Tony Quinn and I were very good friends. But that doesn't mean we didn't argue heatedly about various scenes as I always had great difficulty in being diplomatic and didn't think about what I was going to say before I said it. I remember in one scene, the sun was just right, everything was ready to shoot. We did a rehearsal and I turned to Tony and said, "You are not going to play it *that* way, are you?" Well, he was furious. "Who is directing this movie, anyway, you or Guy?" He went over to Guy Green and said he wanted to get out of the picture. Burt Lancaster was free and he was sure Burt would be happy to do the part with me. He'd had enough of my interfering.

I sat with Ruth behind a wagon and said, "What am I going to do?" We could see the two of them sitting on the grass, Tony arguing with Guy Green and pointing at me. But then nothing happened and I thought Guy Green would come up and say, "Come on, don't be silly. It's foolish, we'll start from the beginning."

But no, it didn't work. I was in the wrong. Therefore it was up to me to take the first step. I said to Ruth, "I'm going over there." Ruth said, "Wait, it's up to them."

"I can't. The sun is going down. God, we might lose a whole day's shooting!"

I went across to Tony, and said, "I'm sorry, I am so terribly sorry. I shall never ever open my mouth again about how you should play a scene. Let's just go on shooting, because we want this picture in the can." So we made up.

———————— • ————————

On May 13, 1969, she was writing from Knoxville:

Dear Lars,

We are working on the scene from the fair, four hundred and fifty people, all the people from Gatlinburg, and all the time we have to talk and be introduced and write autographs. This is the second day and I hope the last. You must write me more about your dinner at Choisel with Malraux, the Minister of Culture. What fine guests you have when I'm not at home. But it's good for you because I would have become completely hysterical if the service hadn't been as if it was at the royal court.

I have calmed down a bit. I can understand now that I can be very tiresome. When *you* say it, I think it is because you are tired and irritated and you've been alone so long and have got used to making the decisions yourself. But now both Tony Quinn and Guy Green say it and have helped me understand what was wrong. I never listen and I talk about something else right in the middle of somebody else's conversation; you know that well. *That* Tony Quinn has taken out of me. He looks at me without saying a word until I've asked his forgiveness.

My little old man, I'm much kinder now, you wait and see.

———————— • ————————

They had a lot of previews of the film, showing it to invited audiences, and selected audiences, that sort of thing. I think they used the old method of sending cards out into the audience for people to write what they think about it: "I disliked the story" . . . "The whole thing is stupid" . . . "I don't understand it" . . . "I thought so-and-so was awful . . ." They decide if the audience didn't laugh in the right places or didn't get *this* point, and they often shoot new sequences or re-edit.

I've always thought it was silly. I think it should be one person who makes the story, stands for his story, presents it the way he wants it presented, and then accepts the responsibility for a success or failure. But, of course, Hollywood catered all the time to what the audience wanted. And using these methods they fiddled around and altered our film. I saw it first at the première in Knoxville.

———————— • ————————

The first showing of *A Walk in the Spring Rain* was treated as a gala occasion in the town. Ingrid planted a flowering dogwood tree in the main avenue, and was presented with the silver-plated spade. She also left her handprint and signature engraved in a block of wet concrete outside the theater.

The critics came from miles around, for a world première was a comparatively rare event in Knoxville. Among them was Dudley Sanders, critic of the *Louisiana Times:* "It has some good things. Good moments. The right idea. Occasionally the right feel. But the picture simply doesn't work. You know it. You suspect that just everybody around you knows it."

I sat next to Rachel Maddux, and all through the film she was saying to me, "What is this? . . . What happened to the scene when she? . . . This isn't meant to be here . . . this is later. . . . Haven't they understood that? . . ."

I said, "Yes, I understand, and they understand. But this is what they do. They alter, they change, they cut, they edit. This happens very often in the movies."

I didn't know what I could do to help her. The book had been so well written, full of the country and the true feelings of a woman in this situation . . . and now poor Rachel Maddux had seen her book go down the drain. So she went to the ladies room and cried. I went after her and tried to comfort her, and I said, "You know, I'm very sorry. . . ."

The film had been a good try. We'd started off with such high hopes. I thought maybe we could do a film with that elusive feeling which *Brief Encounter* had. We'd worked hard. We'd done our best and at the end of it we'd made Rachel Maddux cry.

———————— • ————————

The outside critics were practically unanimous. *Variety* for April 15, 1970, headed the column: "Dreary sudser for older femmes." Howard Thompson in *The New York Times* hammered in another nail: "A dreary, tedious, unconvincing drama of middle-aged love. . . ."

Middle-aged love might be dreary, tedious, and unconvincing on the screen, but in those intervals known as *real life* it can be surprising, dramatic, and heartbreaking.

It was a glorious summer day when the aircraft landed at Paris's Orly airport and Ingrid found Lars waiting for her.

Driving back to Choisel, Ingrid did most of the talking. She had lots of news to tell him about her last six months in Hollywood. After all, she had seen him only once in that time.

It was not until later that evening that Lars told her he had found someone else—Kristina. Lars and Ingrid had been married for twelve years at the time.

At first I didn't take it calmly or peacefully. I realized I had given myself this blow. It was my own fault and Liana had warned me long ago. I knew I couldn't blame Lars, but at first I didn't accept it with much patience. I was angry with him. We discussed divorce, but it was only discussion. I thought I would leave. I would go away. Then I thought, maybe this other relationship will end. There was so much that Lars and I had between us. Perhaps we could make up and go on as we had before—which of course is not possible. You make up, but it's not the same as it was before.

Then, I faced the old dilemma. Was it more important to keep my marriage going or—and I know it sounds selfish—to keep my acting going? Was it better to make films, entertain people in the theater, or sit at home and be a good, but bored, wife? So far we had managed to live with that problem—but suddenly it was all different.

We did nothing. Lars's young woman was still in the background. We made each other fairly unhappy, I guess, but went on mainly as we'd done before. My antidote, as always, was work and more work. That was when Binkie Beaumont came on the scene again. I'd known Binkie even before I'd played *A Month in the Country.* He was one of the most successful producers in London and an old friend of ours.

I was sitting at Choisel, reading, watching television news, looking at the time, and figuring out when Lars would get home. Then the telephone rang and it was Lars saying, "I am rehearsing tonight. Don't wait up for me because I shall be very late."

What was I going to do all evening? I tried reading. Then the phone rang again, and a voice said, "Are you bored?" It was Binkie.

"Why do you ask?"

"Because I have a play for you."

"What is it?"

"It is *Captain Brassbound's Conversion* by George Bernard Shaw."

"I've never heard of it."

"Well, I'm going to send it to you. Do you have any plans for the future?"

"No, nothing."

"Okay. Read it and we'll discuss it."

I read it. I didn't think it was a very good play. But it had an extraordinary part for a woman. She's very original, quick-witted, intelligent, and funny, and set against twenty-four not-so-clever men. I mean, how lucky can you get?

I called Binkie back and said, "I have a marvelous part, but the play is kind of boring and it's unbelievable. You know the theater. Do you think it will work? Do you think people will come and see it?"

"With you in it," he said, "they will."

Every time I get a good part I think that's the last I shall ever get, so I play it and milk it to the last drop. And although the New York theater is wonderful—and so is the French—there's something about the London theater which is very special.

I was very tempted. I discussed it with Lars and he thought it was a good idea. I rang Binkie and said I was coming.

Even getting the costumes right was such fun. In a book I saw photographs of Jenny Churchill, Winston Churchill's mother, when she was on safari in Africa long ago, and I said, "That is exactly the right period for Lady Cecily Waynflete when she's in Morocco. That's what I want to wear."

Binkie said, "Too mannish!"

"All right," I said. "We'll make a deal. I'll be very feminine in the first act, and very mannish in the second." That's how we compromised.

We opened in Brighton, my twenty-four men and I. Joss Ackland was Captain Brassbound, and Kenneth Williams was Drinkwater. Sir Laurence Olivier came to the opening night—I found that very exciting. A dinner was arranged a few nights later. And before I went, my twenty-four men said, "Do be careful. You're going to get such a lot of advice from Sir Laurence you won't know where you are." I said, "I shall be very happy to get all the advice I can. I am dying to hear what he is going to say."

We had our dinner and through most of it Sir Laurence was going on to Joss about this and that. All very good stuff. And I was thinking, Now when is he going to get round to me? When's my turn coming?

It was after coffee, just as we were about to leave—he just took one look at me and said, "Once you really know the dialogue, you'll be fine."

In London we opened at the Cambridge Theatre and received mixed notices. Not only was I stumbling around I suppose—as is usual with my dialogue—but I was also criticized because I was not

British. They said, why in the world bring over a foreigner to play Lady Cecily.

———————— • ————————

The British public was oblivious to such trivialities. They packed the theater every night. London's *Daily Express* theater critic, Herman Kretzmer, announced that when he approached the box office to return one of his two allocated tickets, he was practically assaulted by a queue of middle-aged hopefuls waiting for cancellations. They had all come to see INGRID BERGMAN.

Griffith James, the company manager, recalls what it was like when he met her:

"It was the first rehearsal. Everybody assembled and I went up to the stage door to await the arrival of Ingrid Bergman, the great star. She arrived on time, looking marvelous, came down the stairs and walked onto the stage where we had saved a chair in the center. That was important. You arrange the semicircle of chairs for the actors in order of superiority. It's quite a thing; the cast sets great store by it; they must have the right place. And there in the center was the chair for her, and she walked in and said hello to everybody, and then she said, 'Oh no, I don't think I would like to sit in that chair. I think I would rather sit down here.' So she just sat down in one at the end. Typically Bergman.

"The thing I remember about Ingrid during that show was we could never keep her cool enough. It was rather a warm time and the theater wasn't air-conditioned. We opened every window we could, but of course it used to get very hot on stage. Whenever she came off-stage, we would rush her to the huge scenery door which opened into the fresh air, and push her out. I remember passersby being rather amazed when the door opened, and there was Ingrid Bergman in this Victorian dress being shoved out and being told to take ten deep breaths before she went back on stage! Taxis used to pass by and practically stop in amazement."

After such boisterous beginnings, it is hardly surprising that Ingrid and Griff became very good friends.

Griff spent several years being an actor. One night he decided he didn't like imitating other people. He liked being himself. He has been himself ever since.

Griff is tall, lean as a lamppost. The eyes behind the horn-rimmed spectacles are alert; the personality, contemplative; the grin, sudden and unexpected; the theatrical knowledge, wide; the criticism, expert; the humor, impious.

Ingrid and a newly assembled American cast were in Washington to present *Captain Brassbound* at the Kennedy Center. The play had opened in Wilmington, and would eventually move to Toronto and end on Broadway. Its success had been spectacular. Ingrid had been praised wherever she performed. The critics had reacted in the same way as their British counterparts: they found a lot to criticize in Shaw's rarely performed play, but as a block they voted that Ingrid was marvelous and that it was good to see her back. Every seat for every performance was sold out. (It was noted later that of fifty-six new productions on Broadway that year, only *Captain Brassbound* had recouped its investment.)

In Washington she was delighted when the National Press Association invited her to hold a press conference. This was an opportunity she had craved for twenty-two years. She had never managed to erase from her mind the vitriolic speech Senator Johnson delivered in the United States Senate and entered into the *Congressional Record* of March 1950, especially its ending: "If out of the degradation associated with *Stromboli,* decency and common sense can be established in Hollywood, Ingrid Bergman will not have destroyed her career for naught. Out of her ashes may come a better Hollywood."

That hurt. That hurt very deeply. She had been raised to observe the decencies of life, to be honest and truthful, to do unto others *better* than they did unto you, and she had done her best to live up to her upbringing. She did not think that by falling in love with Roberto Rossellini and having his child, she deserved to be held up to continued shame. To be attacked by the newspapers was one thing; reporters had to earn a living and newspapers to be sold. But to be held in contempt in the Senate of the United States of America, in the capital city, where marble porticos proclaimed dedication to those virtues—truth, justice, freedom, and the rights of men and women—in which she implicitly believed; that was very unfair. That was a very big hammer crashing down on a small sin.

By April 1972, it was also apparent that if anything lay in ashes, it was not Ingrid Bergman but the Hollywood movie business. It had been overtaken and laid waste by television, while Ingrid had risen phoenix-like from the smoke and flames to a pinnacle of success rarely attained by any actress. Now, with the normal instinct of any red-blooded female, she wished to register this fact. And imbued with a positive sense of timing, like every good actress, she knew the iron was hot. This was the moment of truth in America. All she needed was the right question to lead her into a reply which would stand Senator Johnson's prophecy on its head.

The National Press Association had never held a comparable conference of critics, journalists, writers, television and radio reporters. The assembled members far outnumbered those who collected to interview such luminaries as Khruschev or the first men on the moon. It is possible that in the minds of some of the gentlemen of the press was the knowledge that the media had hounded this lady —who all through *her* life had sought only to bring pleasure into *their* lives—beyond both the call of duty and of common decency. At any rate, they greeted Ingrid's appearance as positively as if they were a warm and expectant theater audience. Their questions were reasonable and fair. Many she had answered dozens of times before: "Do you find comedy harder to play than drama?" "What do you think about the Kennedy Center compared to other theaters you've played in?" "How come you look so young?" and "Can an actor be interested in more than the theater, politics for instance?"

Answering that one, Ingrid said that she had never learned to be politically inspired or motivated: "I have been an entertainer. It's nothing that I have—except a certain talent that I have been given and the rest is just pure luck and hard work. I try to live in a way that I am of help to other people, but that's not politics. I am interested in humanity and children and prisoners of war, and orphans of war, and that's the only thing my politics are concerned with."

They asked her, How did she study? How did she approach a role?

"I haven't read many of those books about acting. Stanislavsky I tried to plow through. I think, instinctively, even the first time I read a script I know exactly how the woman is. That is why I turn down many things I don't understand. I must understand the person and the character completely; I mean, there must be something inside me that is that person, and then immediately I feel it. It is more a feeling than a technique. I set out to get a person. And then I look around. Always, if I'm walking in the streets or sitting on a bus, there are people to look at. And I say, I must remember how she sits and that gesture. I must remember how she is dressed. If ever a part comes up, I must have a hat like that. You take it from life more than from your brain."

The flow of questions continued, and then suddenly the one which rang the warning bell: "We are told that the golden age of Hollywood has gone forever. Is this a great loss or a good thing?"

She began her answer: "I think it is in a sense a loss. It was wonderful when they had the star system that they now try to tear down. You had the right studios, you worked with the same technicians. But time marches on. I suppose everything has to change. Everything became very glossy and unrealistic, and that was one reason why I left. . . ."

Suddenly she realized that this was the question which gave her the lead she needed.

". . . I felt that Hollywood was wonderful, and I couldn't in any way complain because I had a wonderful time, and people seemed to like me, and I hope we made some good pictures. . . . But I just wanted to do something more realistic, and when I saw *Open City* I realized that somewhere in the world they did a different kind of picture, and I left. . . ."

Now she could deliver the punch line! Twenty-two years she had waited for the chance for vengeance. "I have to say that when I left for Italy there was a Senator in Washington who made a speech against me, and he ended by saying that out of Hollywood's ashes will grow a better Hollywood. . . ."

She did not realize she had muffed it. She had said, *"Hollywood's ashes,"* instead of *"Ingrid Bergman's ashes."* She had completely destroyed the irony and her whole point. She paused in some perplexity. Surely they could see what she was trying to imply? They didn't. A few faces looked a little puzzled, but most of them sat there looking pleased and interested. And now who has the next question? . . .

It was not until she returned to France and listened to the tape of the news conference given her by the National Press Association that she understood her mistake. She laughed and laughed. "A line I had been waiting twenty-two years to deliver, and I mess it up!" She still laughs about it today.

Psychiatrists might say her mistake was a Freudian slip; that her need for reprisal had evaporated. And they would be right. All the resentment had been washed away long ago by people like Warren Thomas and the Alvin Gang at the airport; by Burgess Meredith and his little song, "If I can not win you, with so much gin in you"; by the applause of the Hollywood audience for *More Stately Mansions,* applause so warm it blew the opening lines out of her head; and by the warmth and generosity she had received from so many Americans so often in those years since the *Queen Mary* first deposited her in New York, the tall, laughing, golden girl of March 1939. America had helped to make Ingrid Bergman.

Besides, she got the justice she wanted that same April of 1972 when, inspired by her visit to Washington, Senator Charles H. Percy got to his feet in the United States Senate and said: "Mr. President, one of the world's loveliest, most gracious, and most talented women was made the victim of a bitter attack in this Chamber twenty-two years ago. Today I would like to pay long overdue tribute to Ingrid Bergman, a true star in every sense of the word." He complimented her upon her performance in *Captain Brassbound's Conversion*. "Our culture," he said, "would be poorer indeed without her artistry. To the American public she will always hold a place in our hearts as one of the greatest performing artists of our time. I know that across the land millions of Americans would wish to join me in expressing their regrets for the personal and professional persecution that caused Ingrid Bergman to leave this country at the height of her career. And I believe they would also join me in expressing our overwhelming admiration, affection and respect for her today. Miss Bergman is not only welcome in America; we are deeply honored by her visits here."

Senator Johnson had entered into the *Congressional Record* a long list of magazine and newspaper articles detrimental to Ingrid; Senator Percy entered a similar list of articles praising and congratulating her. He sent Ingrid a copy of that *Record*.

Thanking him, Ingrid wrote:

> Dear Senator Percy,
> My war with America was over long ago. The wounds however remained. Now, because of your gallant gesture with your generous and understanding address to the Senate, they are healed forever.

———— • ————

Lars and I were both working very hard in the professions we loved. Lars had his play and copyright organizations. He was in constant association with playwrights and actors; he produced plays by Arthur Miller, Tennessee Williams, Arnold Wesker, and Alan Ayckbourn. But the last production we ever worked on together was *The Human Voice,* in 1967.

In Swedish, jokingly, he used to call me the Golden Goose. I was laying golden eggs because everything I did in the theater was successful. I was married to a producer, so what problems could I possibly have? That's why I resented just a little that Lars never seemed to look for a play for me.

We had our arguments. And finally, when I realized he was never going to find a play for me, Lars said, sweetly, "You must look at this from my point of view, darling. I didn't want to exploit you. I didn't want to take advantage of you. Just putting Ingrid Bergman into something was too easy."

But we got on well in practically everything else, and little by little I didn't feel so hurt anymore. Then we thought we really could get together again and make our marriage what it had once been. We tried, but it didn't work. The marriage was over.

So, as usual, I went back to work. They call it "the creative opiate" I think.

Binkie Beaumont would call me up in Choisel. "What are you doing?" "Well, I'm just sitting here." "Alone?" "Yes, alone." "Then I'll tell you what. Pack a suitcase, get on the plane and come over here. Leave a note for Lars and come."

A car would pick me up at the airport and I'd be driven to Binkie's house, and there'd usually be other actors there, and the conversation was always about the theater. It was such a warm feeling, our closed society: all actors talking about themselves and about this scene and that occasion. And laughter and friendship.

Binkie was so witty, he knew so much about the theater. He was creative and I always felt I was in good hands. If he said it was all right, it *was* all right. I might not agree with him, but if he said it's going to be that way, it was that way, and I went along with him. There are certain people that you have that confidence in. The way he presented his case, you simply had to say, "That's right, that's it."

---·---

In 1973, Ingrid made a short film with the odd title of *From the Mixed-Up Files of Mrs. Basil E. Frankweiler,* adapted from an award-winning children's book, a heartwarming story about a brother and sister who run away from home and use New York's Metropolitan Museum of Art as their hideout. The Metropolitan allowed its premises to be used for filming for the first time in its history.

Exploring the museum the young girl, unhappy in her modern world and longing to be a romantic heroine like Lady Guinevere, stumbles upon the statue of an angel, reputedly the work of Michelangelo, and determines to find out if the sculpture is authentic. Her search leads her to a rich and eccentric old lady, played by Ingrid in a white wig with frosted eyebrows. She is wise as well as old, and understands the ache in the girl's heart. Her advice brings peace and solutions. It was not a major film, but it was well reviewed, and its publicity made much of the fact that it included Ingrid Bergman among the cast.

————— • —————

During the filming of *Mrs. Frankweiler* in New York, I met Arthur Cantor again and he began to play a big role in my theatrical life. I say "again" because Arthur told me he'd worked as a boy in the Alvin Theater when I did *Joan of Lorraine* there. He did all the odd jobs: "Miss Bergman wants a corned beef sandwich! Arthur, run out and get her one!"

He'd climbed in the theatrical world since then, and had collaborated with Binkie Beaumont, raising money for various projects. One day Arthur called me up and said, "I've just read a very funny play by Somerset Maugham, *The Constant Wife*. Binkie likes it. I'm sending it to you to see if you like it."

I did like it but I thought it was a bit old-fashioned. I knew that Ethel Barrymore had played it in America and made an awful hash of her dialogue on opening night—something I could well understand. Somerset Maugham had arrived in her dressing room after the performance, and she had seen by his face how upset he was: all his beautiful dialogue turned upside down. So before he could speak, she said cheerfully, "Don't worry, Mr. Maugham, we'll run for a year." Which they did.

Nevertheless this was 1973, not 1927, and I thought it was a little dated, and I said as much to John Gielgud who was going to direct it.

He replied in that very soft, sweet way of his, "What is old-fashioned about this play, Ingrid, is its *charm.*"

That was what I wanted to hear and we started work.

John and I went to see Binkie about the costumes one day. Binkie wasn't feeling very well; he was in bed. But he said he was going to get up later to go to a party.

We all looked at old magazines from about 1920 to give ourselves ideas about the clothes and discussed where we might open. Binkie said it might be a good idea to open some place unusual, perhaps Amsterdam, somewhere on the Continent, wouldn't that be more fun? I thought it a very good idea.

We left and Binkie got up and went to his party. His friends told me later that he was, as usual, the life and soul of the party; his imitation of Marlene Dietrich brought the house down, and he was very happy. He came home, called Arthur Cantor on the phone and said, "I'm so pleased Ingrid likes the idea of opening on the Continent somewhere, and I'm going to look into it tomorrow." Then he hung up, got into bed and went to sleep, and never woke up.

It was John who said eventually, "You know Ingrid, we have to go on. Binkie would never forgive us if he knew we had quit when he had everything going so well."

So we went ahead. But we never had our special opening on the Continent. Two weeks in Brighton, and we opened in London at the Albery Theatre in September 1973.

Chapter 27

Harold Hobson in the *Sunday Times* was still peeved about Ingrid playing yet another Englishwoman when she actually spoke like "a cultivated foreigner." But the theatrical press called it "the wittiest play in London," the *Daily Telegraph,* "unusually entertaining" and the theater was consistently packed.

A large advertisement was inserted in many newspapers: "H. M. Tennant is proud to announce that John Gielgud's production of *The Constant Wife* starring Ingrid Bergman, John McCallum, Barbara Ferris, Michael Allison and Dorothy Reynolds, weeks September 29th and October 6th, broke the box office record at the Albery Theatre."

And Ingrid reached for the telephone.

———— • ————

When I sat in my dressing room at the Albery I could see mice in the corner sometimes as I was making up. I didn't say a word for the first two weeks or so, but then they put the advertisement in the papers and I called up and said, "Are you selling tickets?"

They said, "It's marvelous. It's wonderful. It's an absolute sell-out." I answered, "Then will you do my dressing room over? It has not been cleaned or painted since the theater was built; the carpet is filthy. I can't sit on the sofa; I fall through the springs. I didn't want to disturb you until I knew we had a hit; but now perhaps you might do something about the interior decorating." Which the management did.

—————— • ——————

Interviewed in her dressing room, Ingrid said, yes, she was fifty-eight: "Sad isn't it. But I'll go on celebrating my birthday for two more years, then I'll stop. It's a very good part with lots of funny dialogue. The play is old-fashioned, but I can't find anything new that I can understand. Before I've played in serious things, but it's nice to hear people laugh."

Parrying rumors that her marriage to Lars was breaking up, she said, "We'll sort it out. I don't want to say more."

They were still "sorting it out" when she had to call Lars in Paris with news of grave importance.

—————— • ——————

I'd just returned from the theater and I was in bed in my apartment in Mount Street reading the paper. There was a letter in it from a woman telling how she'd read in a magazine about breast cancer, and if it hadn't been for the article and doing something about it, she'd probably be dead by now.

There was an awful lot of publicity around about this time on breast cancer: how Betty Ford, the President's wife, had had the operation, and then Mrs. Rockefeller, and how all women should check themselves, because a lump, no matter how small, might be serious. And as I was reading the article I was almost subconsciously examining myself. Then my hand stopped and I thought, Oh God! Oh God! No, it can't happen to *me*! It's funny isn't it—it's like having twins—it will happen to other people.

I called Lars immediately in Paris. He said, "You must go to the doctor. Go tomorrow. At once."

"But I'm in the play, and we've got a long run ahead. I can't do anything for the moment."

For the first few days I didn't do anything or say anything, except that I asked Griff, "Am I insured in case I can't go on with the play?"

Griff gave me that quick, severe stare through his horn-rimmed glasses: "Insured? What's the matter with you? Are you sick? You don't look sick to me!"

I said, "All right, I'm not insured, that's all I was asking."

"No, of course you're not insured. Why should you be? No Ingrid Bergman, no play. If you're not in the play, the play comes off."

So that was that. I just went on. But I did go to see a specialist who was reassuring. He said, "Yes, you must do something about it, but there's not all that much of a hurry."

Then, while *The Constant Wife* was still running, I was approached by Sidney Lumet to play a part in the film adaptation of Agatha Christie's *Murder on the Orient Express.* Albert Finney was playing the famous Belgian detective, Hercule Poirot, and Sidney had got more than a dozen top stars to fill all the other roles. He told me over dinner about this marvelous cast he'd assembled: Lauren Bacall, Vanessa Redgrave, Jacqueline Bisset, Sean Connery, John Gielgud, and Wendy Hiller—lots of other famous names.

"I want you to play this absolutely marvelous old Russian princess."

He sent me the script and I read it and I found a Swedish missionary I liked. I called back Sidney Lumet, "Why in the world should I wear a make-up mask and play the Russian princess when you have a very good Swedish missionary part just made for me. I mean, I can put on a very good Swedish accent. I want to play that dopey missionary."

"Oh no! You don't want to do that. Your part is the wonderful princess, this beautiful old lady sitting there looking extraordinary."

"I want to play the little Swedish missionary who is equally extraordinary."

Sidney said the part wasn't good enough. I replied, "The whole story is Albert Finney playing Hercule Poirot. All the other parts are just about the same size, small vignettes, and I think I can be very funny in that small part. I have lots of ideas how to play it. And I want to look absolutely dreadful in it." At last he fell for it and Wendy Hiller took the part of the Russian princess, and did it beautifully.

We all got on very well. Many of us were working in the theater so we had to scurry off back to our plays every evening.

———— • ————

"One of the first things I learned about Ingrid," said Griff, "is that she will always try something different. There are a lot of actors and actresses who get set in their ways, but not Ingrid. She was in *The Constant Wife* for ages, months, and the Friday before we closed, John Gielgud, who directed it, came and sat in the box and he said to me, 'Ask them all to stay on stage afterwards, as I want to say good-bye to everyone.'

"He came backstage at the end of the performance and said, 'Very good, very good, but there is something I would like to change.' This after eight months, and with only two more performances to go!

"Lots of actors would have said to John, 'Please get stuffed! I've been doing it like this for *eight* months. What's the point?' But not Ingrid. She was immediately interested. Interested to try something different! Even for the *last* matinee and Saturday evening perform-ance, she was ready to change her performance. You see, she never stops learning."

———————— • ————————

We finished the run of *The Constant Wife* and I went back to the specialist and said, "Now the play's over, I want to go over to America and see Pia."

Pia was working in television in New York and had met this nice young real estate broker, Joe Daly, and they'd got married and had their first baby. "At the same time," I said, "if you don't mind, I'd like a second opinion from an American doctor."

The British doctor was still very calm about the whole thing, and I flew to New York to visit Justin, my first grandson, again. Strangely enough, the only two relatives besides the father who had been there when the baby was born were the two stepfathers, Lars and Roberto, who both happened to be in New York at that time. They had never met. To hear Roberto talk, you would think they were the greatest enemies. Roberto was with Isabella, then working in New York, and she reported back to me what happened.

They all found themselves staring down through the glass parti-tion shoulder to shoulder at Pia's baby son. An NBC camera team arrived to take pictures of one of their top personalities Pia, and her new baby, and also took pictures of the watching strangers quite unaware of the scoop they were missing.

"They were so immensely polite to each other you couldn't be-lieve it." Isabella laughed. "Opening doors for each other: 'After you, Mr. Rossellini.' 'No, certainly not, after you, Mr. Schmidt.' Offering each other cigarettes, and: 'You have the first taxi, Mr. Schmidt.' 'No, you must have the first taxi, Mr. Rossellini.' 'Well, if you insist."

As the taxi drove off Roberto looked at Isabella, grinned, and said, "Let him get pneumonia!"

It must have been the funniest encounter in all New York.

But it wasn't funny when I went to see the American specialist. He was curt and abrupt as he gave me the news I dreaded. "You've got to have an operation right away." "Well, I've got Lars's birthday party on June 11," I said rather flippantly, "and I want to see the chalet we've bought in Switzerland. Then there's a party for our great friend Hans Ostelius, the travel writer who's been with us to the Far East: his seventieth birthday, and he's in Portugal. That's the fifteenth of June. After that I can have the operation."

It was a foolish reply, but he had frightened me.

He got very angry. He said, "How in the world can you drag on like this? This is ridiculous. Right into the hospital—tonight!"

I said, "No-ooo. Absolutely not! I'm here in New York and I've lots of plans, and when I'm through with them I'll go into the hospital."

He said, "I am going to talk to your doctor in London. If you don't want to be operated on here tomorrow, then you must immediately return to London. I am talking to your doctor now!"

He called up and I could hear them going on. Then he handed the phone to me, and the English specialist said, "Yes, I must agree with my colleague that you are pushing it very very far. You should come back to London immediately."

"I can't come back now because I'm going bicycling tomorrow in Central Park with Pia and my grandson, and I'm not going to have the operation here. If I have it, it's going to be in London where I'm close to Lars and the other children. And I can't change Lars's birthday party plans either."

I put down the phone and the American doctor was really angry: "What is more important? Your husband's birthday party or your life?"

I answered defiantly: "My husband's birthday party!"

Well after that, he didn't really want to have anything more to do with me, and I left. I had the birthday party for Lars. We did go to the chalet in Switzerland, but only for one day. I did not go to Hans Ostelius's birthday party in Portugal. I went into the hospital in London instead, and as a matter of fact my operation was on his birthday.

Roberto sent all three children across to England to me. Pia came flying from America. Lars came.

I was still groggy from the anaesthesia. I was saying, "Oh, how tiresome this woman is, crying all the time. Please ask her not to cry any more. She is just crying and crying." Someone said to me, "Darling, that is you crying." I had my hands locked across my chest, both arms tight across my chest; and it was impossible to move them. It is some sort of protection which comes from the mind which says, "They are not going to do any more to me!" The doctor came and I could read his face like an open book. I felt sorry for him because it must be an awful job to go around telling women they are mutilated. However, you recover from that too.

I didn't take it as badly as I expected. I had all my children around me.

Of course it is sad. I can't deny that, and I didn't want to look at myself in the mirror, that's for sure. I suppose if I had been a younger woman, I would have suffered much more.

I went back to Choisel for two weeks to recuperate at home before I started radiation. When I left the hospital, all the children came in a taxi to pick me up. I was ready with my suitcase and I had arranged for a wheelchair at the airport because I thought I'd never be able to make it through all those long corridors. We got to the airport to discover that Ingrid's and Isabella's tickets were not right; they were made out straight back to Rome. Pia's ticket wasn't valid for Paris either. She had to buy a new one. She ran in one direction, the others ran in another, and I ran all over the place trying to get the plane delayed. But nothing seemed to work. The suitcases were checked on to the plane, and as I ran around I called to Robin, "Never mind, there's more than one plane that goes to Paris!" Isabella and Ingrid ran back, shouting, "We have our tickets!" I caught up with Pia and shouted, "Get on the next plane. We'll take this one because Lars is waiting with the car at Orly for us and all that luggage. We'll wait for you there." I raced along the corridors and jumped into the bus just before the door closed and there was Robin looking mischievous. He said, "Well, Mama, what about the wheelchair?"

I gasped, "I just didn't have time for it did I?" Then just as the bus doors closed, I saw Pia come running as hard as she could toward it. We all shouted to the driver, "Stop, stop!" He did and we all managed to catch the plane together and continue out to Choisel.

After my two weeks I went back to London for radiation. I was so frightened that I would get sick. They had told me that you can have side effects: you get very tired, you can get sick to your stomach, you get terribly depressed and just don't want to live anymore. I had Ingrid and Isabella take turns to come and stay with me, to help me. In the beginning, after the radiation, I always leaned on one of them, and went home and lay down in bed for a rest.

But little by little I realized that I wasn't really sick or tired. I was just afraid. So I said to whichever one was there, "Let's go out and do some shopping."

That went very well. I'd walk around Regent's Street and Piccadilly, and Ingrid or Isabella would ask anxiously, "Aren't you tired?" "No, let's walk home." So we walked home. And I said, "This is silly, me behaving as if I'm an invalid. Let's go to the theater." We went to the theater. And life became terribly normal. In the morning I had the radiation, and in the afternoon and the evening I lived a normal life.

Then I went back to Choisel again and recuperated some more. At first I couldn't hold a spoon. My arm felt useless and I could hardly lift it. But I did exercises and worked up the muscles in my hand and arm, and slowly I improved. I made pencil marks on my wardrobe door to see how high I could raise my arm every day. I swam in the pool. I swam and swam, and finally the pencil lines on the wardrobe door were pretty high. It didn't take much more than two months before I could lift it almost to its normal position, and I felt pretty good.

I told very few people about my operation.

Chapter
28

In January 1975, Ingrid felt quite fit and went off to tour America
with *The Constant Wife*. She had Griff with her as company
manager. He didn't know anything about her illness. She concealed it without difficulty.

They were opening in Los Angeles, but the new American company was rehearsed in New York.

Marti Stevens was a member of the cast:

"It was some gray rehearsal joint on Ninth Avenue. We all sat in
this room with Sir John Gielgud who was directing and Ingrid
breezed in. No make-up at all, and immediately this wonderful
laugh. 'Well, hallo everybody. I am ten minutes late.'

"She was so warm, and we all got off to a good start. Came the
lunch break and there was a cosy joint next door. We all piled in,
and there was no semblance of a *star* table; we all sat where there
was room. It was like that from the very first day. And remember,
it was going to be a very long tour, starting in Los Angeles, then
moving to Denver, Washington, and Boston. But not New York: that
we *did* go there was entirely due to Ingrid.

"What can you say about her? Whenever she arrived on stage in
that show it was an *occasion*—you can say that about her screen
performances too—and when she enters your life as she entered
mine, that's an *occasion* too. She's almost impossible to catch in
words. She's a natural wonder who can transfer the essence of herself
to a part whether on stage or screen. On first impression, you think

there *must* be something phony here. Maybe that's due to a lifetime's experience in a world of actresses. But there isn't. There's a sort of dazzle about her. In a bar, on a street, she doesn't diminish. There's no place you can put her where she gets less; she gets better.

"You can meet some people—twenty, fifty down the years—and you like them but they remain acquaintances, familiar as railroad stations one passes in a train with no intention of getting out at this particular station. Then there are these certain few—very very few —who remain permanent influences in your life. It's an emotional chemistry; they're suddenly familiar like wallpaper, an instant friend with whom you feel safe, not to analyze but to enjoy. Ingrid is about fun and enjoyment. Any excuse for a celebration. Where shall we find a laugh? And an absolute childlike delight and pleasure in whatever adventure big or small is coming next. 'Now we've finished work, let's have a picnic on the ironing board if nothing's open for supper.' 'Drink up all the booze at the end of a run in this town, so we don't have to carry it to the next town. Why don't we enjoy it *now?*' It meaning everything and anything that can be enjoyed.

"She's like an engine whizzing and whirring which once started can't be turned off until it reaches its destination. And that laugh— oh, that laugh. It starts way down in the deep well of her boundless energy, and it burbles and bubbles its way up until it suddenly bursts in an explosion, a torrent that engulfs you, about as irresistible as Niagara. Oh, yes, it was quite a tour. Ask Griff. . . ."

Griff said: "The marvelous thing about Ingrid is that she never gets uptight. We had an antique sofa on the stage in the Los Angeles production. It was the second act, and she was all dressed for the Ascot races. She was going out to the races with Paul Harding, who was trying to become her lover.

"She was sitting on the sofa and the sofa was terribly rickety. I was worried about it, but they were supposed to have fixed it.

"Suddenly the springs went and she disappeared with her knees above her chin. She just fell over with laughter! And of course the audience fell over with laughter too. To make matters worse, she had to get up—she eventually did—and walk around for a while. I stood there in the wings thinking, She won't sit there again, will she? Even *she* will realize that she can't sit there again! But she was so well rehearsed she forgot that the springs had gone, and she sat there again, and again disappeared. The audience had the best time they had ever had in their whole lives! I could have collected the price of admission for a second time on the way out!

"She thought the whole thing hilarious. Lots of actresses would have had a tantrum and demanded that somebody be fired. She thought it was all a huge joke.

"It was all my fault too. I take the ultimate responsibility for checking the furniture, but I had thought the sofa was fixed. What's so marvelous working with her is that she does not get cross if things go wrong, if accidents like that happen. She realizes there is a margin for human error.

"That was just the beginning of our United States tour, remember. We were playing in the Schubert Theater in Century City and we'd been there two or three weeks. And one day, one of the actors told us about a French restaurant about a ten minutes' walk away. So after the Saturday matinee and before the evening performance we decided to pay it a visit. Ingrid stumbled, twisted her ankle on a stone and we had to half-carry her back.

"It was Saturday night and we couldn't find a doctor; when we finally did, he told us she'd broken a bone in her foot and began to put her leg in a plaster cast. I asked, 'How is she going to go on stage with that great thing?' He said, 'I'm the doctor. It's got to go on.' I called the theater manager and said, 'She'll never be able to play tonight.' He panicked. 'But she must. We're sold out! We haven't got enough money in the box office to refund everybody. It's all gone to the bank!'

"So Ingrid said, 'I'm going on!' I said, 'How can you? We can't even get a wheelchair.' She insisted: 'I'm going on!' Then we got all the cast in and had a long discussion. Now, if so-and-so does this, and so-and-so does that, we can work out this scene and that scene. In the meantime, the manager went out and made the announcement. 'Unfortunately Miss Bergman has broken a bone in her foot and it will be at least an hour before we can start the show. If anybody wants their money back they can have it.'

"They all went into the bar, but not one soul left. And we were *an hour and a half late.* It took that long for the plaster cast to dry. Fortunately we had a butler in the play, so Ingrid sat in one of those swivel office chairs on casters and the butler pushed her on. She sat in the middle of the stage, swiveled around and spoke to each actor in turn. But, of course, this ruined their planned stage moves and they started bumping into each other. Ingrid had a whale of a time laughing at all the collisions. So the audience got a sort of play within a play and adored the whole thing.

"Then for the last act we managed to find a wheelchair, and we put her in that. The finale was just the two of them, the husband and Ingrid on the stage, with Ingrid saying, 'I have to leave now,' and going off. And I was saying to myself, 'Now just stay there like a good girl and we'll bring the curtain down.' But not likely. She spun the chair around, headed for the door, missed the door completely, nearly knocked the whole set down—all the books fell off the shelves —and the audience roared. They'd never had such a good time. Then the actors came on and she propelled herself back, and they roared and cheered some more. It was quite remarkable. We moved across the United States pushing Ingrid in her wheelchair. And she played it like that for five weeks.

"We found a bone specialist—the man who fixed up the bones of the New York Yankee baseball team—and he chiseled off the plaster cast and bandaged her. Then eventually a doctor said, 'I think you'll be able to walk now,' but by now Ingrid so loved being pushed around and playing it in a wheelchair—it was a new theatrical experience for her—that she said, 'Oh now, I think I should play it the way I am.' And it was the second week in Washington before she decided she'd play it on her two feet again.

"Of course it was public knowledge now that she had played in a wheelchair and so, though the show went all right, it was really not as big a success as when she was in her chair. So she took her curtain call in the wheelchair and that brought the house down. Because that is what they'd come to see—Ingrid Bergman in a wheelchair. But she really is a very game girl. I couldn't think of any star I've ever worked with who would have gone on in such a situation."

It was during the long run of *The Constant Wife* that Ingrid made two of her most memorable dialogue mistakes. The first was with the line: "You are a liar, a cheat and a humbug," which came out as: "You are a liar, a cheat, and a *hamburger!*" The second to the husband she is leaving in the last act, and who asks humbly: "What shall I do about food?" "Just give cook her head and you'll be all right," replies Ingrid airily, which on the night in question emerged as: "Just give cook *your* head and you'll be all right."

———————— • ————————

We were playing in Boston when I heard that Jean Renoir was being presented with a special award at the Oscar ceremony in Hollywood. Jean was ill at home in Beverly Hills and he said he wouldn't accept the award unless I collected it for him. Arthur Cantor was in charge of the production and he thought Jean's request was so nice that he cancelled several performances so that he and Lars and I could go to Hollywood. At the Oscar presentation I made a little speech and, as the whole ceremony was on television, Jean could see it in his home. I said he created films with intense individuality, and that his lyric eye, poetic realism, and above all his compassion marked all his work; that he was a lover of mankind in all its nobility and despite its folly. . . . And then I presented him with his Special Award—"In gratitude for all you have taught the tribes of young movie makers, and the audiences all over the world, I stand here to say with them, Thank you, we love you, Jean."

Then everyone applauded and I sat down. It never even entered my head that I might be given an award myself. I knew I'd been nominated for my Swedish missionary in *Murder on the Orient Express.* I'd been nominated five times for various films, and made it with *Gaslight* and *Anastasia.* And that was really enough success for anybody. To be nominated for something so *small:* I really had only one scene—a scene in which I explained my work as a missionary, how I took care of little babies and all that. And Sidney Lumet had kept the camera on me through the whole scene.

But Valentina Cortese was so good in the Truffaut movie, *Day for Night,* that I was sure she would get the award. Then came the announcement: "Best supporting actress: Ingrid Bergman for *Murder on the Orient Express.*"

I rushed up on the stage and said what I thought: "This is unfair. I want this award to go to Valentina Cortese . . . She should have won it." Which I suppose wasn't quite the right thing to say as the movie industry which decides the awards are supposed to be impartial. The spotlights and the cameras all swept across to Valentina. And she stood up and blew kisses at me, and everyone applauded.

Valentina was with me for the rest of the evening and we were photographed together. I was really sad that she hadn't gotten it, because she *did* deserve it. I realized later I had acted—as usual —too impulsively. Three other actresses had also been nominated, and they were also very good; they were kind of mad that I'd only mentioned Valentina. It would have been better if I'd kept my mouth shut altogether.

Lars was with me on this occasion as he was on several others. But we were married in name only. Nothing had really changed. I wanted to move out of our marriage entirely. We had to get a divorce. I had no feeling of bitterness.

We got a divorce. It was very secret; not even my friends knew about it for a long time.

I wanted a divorce because I wanted the position clear. I knew Lars wanted a child, and I didn't want that baby ever to be able to accuse me of not letting his father go. Lars's first son had been killed in a tragic accident, and I was too old when we married to give him a child. He had even suggested that we adopt a baby, but I had felt that with four children already, I had enough on my hands. But that was selfish of me too.

Now my marriage was over, but I still had my work.

———————— • ————————

"Imagine putting a small, intimate, drawing-room-size play into Kennedy Center," said Marti Stevens. "I mean it's so huge that from the back rows you need binoculars even to *see* the stage. Yet, thanks to Ingrid, *The Constant Wife* packed it. Broke all records. It even beat *My Fair Lady*. We went on to Boston, Ingrid took time off to collect her third Oscar, and we still packed houses. Then Ingrid did —to my mind—an extraordinarily generous thing. All across America we were sold out but the notices had never been very good. Okay, but not rave. At the beginning of the tour we were not even booked into New York. So why should Ingrid go? She'd been there before. She'd enough money. All she was going to get were lukewarm, possibly sneering reviews. But she agreed to go in for one month to the Schubert. Why? Because in the cast there were a lot of kids, a lot of actors who'd never played New York, and might never get the chance to play New York, and playing New York to an American actor is what playing in the West End is to a British actor. Tops. 'They'll be seen on Broadway and maybe they'll get other jobs,' said Ingrid. So we went in and had a lovely month at the Schubert."

The critics were lukewarm and condescending. Clive Barnes in *The New York Times* said: "Miss Bergman, while a radiantly handsome woman with an imperiously regal air, does not seem a 36-year-old. As a result all the roles have been, as it were, geriatrically upgraded, with results that detract from the play's impact."

Interviewed for *Variety* on her views about critics, Ingrid said, "I'm like the gypsies. The dogs bark when the caravan goes by. But I can't pay too much attention to that. I've been criticized for my acting in films and the theater and for my private life. Criticism is painful, but if I let it affect me I'd never do anything. It's true I had misgivings about bringing *The Constant Wife* to Broadway. That wasn't because I was afraid of what the critics might say about me. They were right in calling *The Cosntant Wife* antiquated in style. But the theme is not dated a bit. It's just as timely as forty-nine years ago, when it was written. As for the age of the characters, Constance Middleton doesn't have to be thirty-five or thirty-six. The romantic life of women today isn't over at forty. Constance could just as well be fifty or even sixty—I don't know yet but maybe she could be seventy."

Ingrid went to Rome in the fall of 1975 to make a movie, *A Matter of Time.* Taken from the best-selling novel *Film of Memory* by Maurice Druon, it was the story, based on fact, of an old Contessa who in her youth had been a great beauty, a famous courtesan, the inspiration of many artists, and who was now barely managing an existence in a seedy Rome hotel with only her memories to keep her alive.

Metro-Goldwyn-Mayer had bought the rights to the book, but never made the film. Now Vincente Minnelli had acquired them, and his daughter, Liza, Ingrid Bergman, and Charles Boyer were to play the chief roles. Ingrid liked Liza very much, adored meeting Charles Boyer again, and enjoyed having both her daughters working on the film: young Ingrid in make-up, and Isabella in a small part as a nursing nun.

The film took fourteen weeks to make and never got off the ground. Liza was badly miscast as the nineteen-year-old peasant girl who worked as a chambermaid in the hotel and was thrilled by the old lady's stories. The critics thought Minnelli's direction was dated.

Kathleen Carroll, writing in *Movies,* agreed with most other critics that: "Once made it would have been kinder never to have released this hilariously inept, painfully old-fashioned movie."

It had little success in America and was never shown in either Britain or France.

———— • ————

I was in Rome for a whole week in the beginning of May 1976 and Roberto's birthday was May 8. When we came to the seventh, Roberto said sadly, "I understand you are leaving tomorrow?"

"Yes, I'm leaving."

"You know it is my birthday and I'm going to be seventy years old."

"Yes, I know, and isn't it too bad I have to leave, but perhaps we can have a little party tonight: Ingrid and Isabella and you and I. Robin's in Paris working for Lars in the theater, so he can't be here but we'll just celebrate this evening, the four of us."

He looked a little disappointed, and he was obviously quite downcast that everybody had forgotten him. That changed on the eighth, however, when the papers were full of articles about him. They all remembered Roberto Rossellini seventy years old! He was pleased about that.

On his birthday at nine o'clock in the morning I picked up a wreath of flowers I'd had made. It was very difficult to make the florists understand that it was supposed to be a wreath of flowers to put on his head, not on a grave. The girls and I arrived at his apartment. He opened the door in his pajamas, and he said, "Oh, it's you again! I thought you'd gone." So we sang "Happy Birthday," and put the wreath on his head, and he sat on his sofa with a daughter on either side of him. He kept that wreath always, even when it was dried up; he never threw it away.

Then I said, "Well, good-bye, I'm leaving now," lying my head off because I had already prepared a party in his favorite restaurant. It had a private annex and I had arranged a U-shaped table covered with fake dollars and lire—we'd glued them all together to make a tablecloth.

After I left, the girls said, offhandedly, "Papa, as it's your birthday, let's have dinner in your favorite restaurant."

So that evening they wandered in, and it was only when he came to the table that Roberto realized that everyone from his sister, his nieces, his older son, the grandchildren, his first wife, the whole family were there. Me too. He looked at me and said, "Ah, you did this!"

Then we had a speech for him that Ingrid and Isabella had written. It was a little bit naughty because we imitated many of the favorite sayings he made in anger or frustration such as "I take the bread out of my own mouth to give to the children." All those exaggerated phrases he used. The girls were a little afraid that Papa might be offended, but I said, "Don't worry. I know him better than you do. He'll love it."

Isabella read the speech and Roberto loved it so much he cried with laughter. He made her read it again, and took it home with him, had it framed and hung it up in his apartment.

I had also got Robin down from Paris, dressed him as a waiter, so as soon as we had Roberto settled, Robin came up with the menu. Roberto took it, looked at it, and took not the slightest notice of his son. Why should he? It was only a waiter. After about sixty seconds of suspense Robin was absolutely destroyed that his father hadn't recognized him. He cried, "Papa! It's me! Robin." Ruined the whole joke.

Roberto jumped up, caught him in his arms and embraced him, and over his shoulder he looked straight at me. That look he gave me was worth—well, it was worth the whole effort.

It was a marvelous night. We had so many things to remember because in so many ways those Italian days were precious, and the Italians are such a generous and warmhearted people.

In Sweden, when you drive up in a big expensive car, no one's very happy for you. But in Italy: I remember once Roberto had parked his red Ferrari outside a small fish restaurant. We went shopping and when we came back there was this great big beautiful red lobster wrapped up on the front seat. We took the lobster into the restaurant and said this must be a mistake, we didn't buy a lobster, we haven't ordered one. And they said, it is our gift, for the pleasure, for the honor that you parked this beautiful car out in front of our restaurant.

Mind you, the Ferrari got Roberto into trouble a few times when he least expected it. He used to race in that car all over Europe: in Sweden, and in that very long and dangerous two thousand-kilo-meter race all around Italy, the "Mille Miglia." I remember he was in that race once, and it was on the radio. I was listening and walking up and down so nervous for him that I was in tears. Robertino was with me; he was between four and five years old. The race ended. Roberto didn't win but he came home a hero—champagne, and all his friends congratulating him. And Robertino walked up as his father sat down and slapped him right across the face. Roberto was so surprised he just stared. Robertino said, "That's for making my mother cry!"

The next time I saw Roberto after the birthday party was about nine months later in the spring of 1977 and it was purely accidental. I'd been across to Choisel to collect a few things. Except for the two servants, the house was empty and everything got to me. Memories. Mistakes. Arguments. Joys. All the years.

I couldn't stand it any longer. I moved to Paris and into the Raphael Hotel. Who was staying there? Roberto.

He took me out to dinner. He knew when I was upset, and he bought me a hot-water bottle and some aspirin. He sensed, without my saying a word to him, that I was disturbed about the divorce, and that I was looking backwards in some despair.

He took me out to lunch the next day and said, "Ingrid, don't ever look back. You're a nervous wreck trying to figure out what to do with the past. To hell with the past. Look ahead—go forward." He kissed me on the cheek and went away to catch his plane. I didn't know I would never see him alive again.

Roberto rang me two months later in May when I was playing in N. C. Hunter's *Waters of the Moon* in Chichester Theatre's summer season. Keith Michel asked me to do it; John Clements was directing.

Wendy Hiller costarred with me. I remember so well her coming into my dressing room one day when I was making up and saying, "I really should hate you—I should hate you." "But why Wendy, what have I done?" "Every time I go shopping in Chichester," she said, "people stop me in the street and say, "Miss Hill*ier*—they always call me that—I saw the play last night and isn't Miss Bergman wonderful!" She smiled.

Roberto had been invited to attend the Cannes Film Festival as President. "Can you imagine I have to see *all* these movies," he said. I laughed. "Of course you do. You're President of the Jury. When I was President of the Jury in 1973 I thought that seeing all the movies was the only pleasant thing about the entire festival."

He felt very tired he said. He would be very glad when he got back to his apartment in Rome. We chatted and laughed and he rang off.

Chichester is a pretty old English town in Hampshire. Ruth and I had rented a cottage about half an hour's drive away, and I had hired a small car. The performance started at seven in the evening so I drove in quite early because I always needed an hour and a half to relax, not telephone, not talk to people, and to make myself look forty-five, the age of Helen Lancaster, the part I was playing.

We had a maid come into the cottage once a week to clean up. The place was so small there was not enough room for the three of us in there at the same time, so Ruth and I went to a country pub for lunch on the maid's day.

It was the third of June 1977 and when we came back to the cottage, the maid had gone but there was a phone message from

Fiorella in Rome: "Please call Rome urgently. Children are okay."
I thought that was very sweet of her because, you know, your heart
stops and the first thought is: the children—something's happened
to one of the children?

I called Fiorella immediately and she gave me the news. Roberto
had died of a heart attack. He had called his first wife who lived
in an apartment just across the street; she'd run to him, but it was
too late; he died almost immediately. I sat with Ruth and I started
to telephone. I called my children. I called Pia and Lars and all the
people I thought should know. And of course I was dreadfully
upset. Roberto had filled, and still filled, a big part of my life. His
seventieth birthday seemed like only yesterday. Then Ruth said,
"Ingrid, it's five o'clock, we'd better get into the car."

"Get in the car! I can't. I just can't. I can't go down and play this
gay, amusing, lighthearted Helen Lancaster and listen to all the
laughs, and do all the things . . ."

"It's time we got into the car," said Ruth.

So we went to the theater and nobody said anything, but everybody had heard the news on the radio. Then somebody came up and
just pressed my hand. Then, of course, everybody wanted to help:
"We're with you. We'll help you out. Don't worry, darling, we'll
manage."

And then into my mind came Signe Hasso and that night when
she knew her son was dead, and she went on and played. Now I knew
what she meant. I'd always known it really. I was Helen Lancaster.
I wasn't Ingrid Bergman. I was that gay, wealthy, happy woman,
who stayed happy by pushing most of reality out of sight.

It worked. I got through the play. Then I went back to the cottage
and the telephone; people were ringing me or I was ringing them
all night, or so it seemed. I remember, it was four o'clock in the
morning when Robin called. He said, "I know it's late but I've been
trying to give other people encouragement and keep them going all
this time. I've tried so hard all day, but now I want to cry with you."
And he burst into tears. So did I.

I said as soon as the funeral was over, all three children must
come and stay with me.

I cried for Roberto and I thought how ironic it was that many
of his movies which were attacked when he made them were now
considered masterpieces. Then I remembered what he had said
about my crying. It was when I told him I saw on television the

film he made in India. In it was a sequence about an old beggar man and the little monkey he had attached to a chain on his wrist. The monkey jumped around and chattered and made the children laugh and then held out a little tin cup for money. The old man fell sick and wandered into the jungle, staggered and fell, and it was plain he was going to die. And overhead came the vultures swooping in the sky. The poor little monkey grew so agitated. He tried to pull the old man to wake him up, to say, look there's danger! Then he tried to cover him up as if to shelter him. He chattered away heartbreakingly, all the time his eyes on those terrible vultures. But he was chained so he couldn't leave, and finally he nestled down with his little head crouched as if he were going to defend the old man. It was so moving. I just wept.

When I told Roberto, he smiled: "You know why? That was you and me. You were the monkey. Always trying to protect me from the vultures. That's why you cried."

So there was death, and there was life. The day after Roberto died, Lars rang me from New York and told me Kristina Belfrage had given birth to his son. That was what Lars had been missing all those years. I was happy for him.

My relationship with Lars, which began so long ago, continues to be the most important of my life.

I finished with the Chichester season in the middle of June. Rehearsals for the Brighton pre-London run and the Haymarket performance of *Waters of the Moon* didn't start until the late autumn. Before that time I had contracted to go to Stockholm and Norway where Ingmar Bergman was going to shoot *Autumn Sonata.*

In the summer I went to New York and while I was there I returned to the doctor I'd seen before for a check-up, because you're supposed to do that every six months. He said that I had a gland that was swollen, and I had to watch it. Nothing to be frightened of, but when I returned to England I should go back to my own doctor and let him take a look.

Chapter
29

I ngmar Bergman had had the same bad experience with Sweden that Ingrid had. The Swedish habit of apparently wishing to convey to their world-famous artists that they are nothing special was certainly a force when, in January 1976, Ingmar Bergman, undoubtedly their greatest film writer and director, was arrested by the police while actually at work on a stage in the Royal Dramatic Theater and marched off to prison for alleged tax fraud.

Detained at the police station for five hours, his house and papers were searched. The only charge the prosecution ever brought against him was thrown swiftly out of court, but like Ingrid, he found such peremptory and ungracious treatment hard to forgive or forget. He looked all over Europe and on the west coast of America and New York for a new place to live and finally settled in Munich. He retained only his island home off the coast of Sweden which he didn't consider a part of the country anyway.

And he would make all of his movies outside of Sweden.

———— • ————

I met Ingmar Bergman for the first time about fifteen years ago. He had known Lars for longer than either of them could remember; they both started in the theater in Malmö in the south of Sweden. Copenhagen and Denmark is just a ferryboat ride away, and on one occasion Lars and Ingmar journeyed across to see a Danish play.

The play ended. It was night, and Ingmar announced he wanted to sleep in Sweden.

"But you can see Sweden over there!" Lars protested. "You are no distance away."

No use. Ingmar did not intend to sleep in a _foreign_ country. Lars had never heard of anyone with such _roots._

When I met Ingmar in Paris at the Swedish Embassy, he was showing his stage production of _The Saga_ written by yet another Swedish Bergman—the late Hjalmar Bergman. Out of his own country, Ingmar was not feeling well at all and I thought, He's like good wine, he can't travel. I remember we all went to the old Sarah Bernhardt Theater to see Bibi Andersson, and then Ingmar flew back to Sweden and we never really exchanged a word with each other.

A few years later I had lunch with Lars and Ingmar in Stockholm and this time it was instant sympathy between us. Lars had to go back to his office and Ingmar and I went on chatting for another hour or so. We had to do a picture together, he declared. I was so pleased he said that. I would never have dared to bring up the subject because I knew how he worked with almost a repertory team of actors and his own camera team and technicians. He discussed a book, _The Boss Ingeborg_, by our namesake Hjalmar Bergman and said, wouldn't it be fun to have the _three_ Bergmans, none of them related, all involved in the same picture.

We exchanged a few letters on the subject. Then he decided he would write an original story for our picture. The next thing I knew was that he became Director of our Royal Dramatic Theater which, of course, put a stop to our plans.

I wrote to him sending my congratulations and my regrets that now he would not have time to do our movie. His answer came back: "It's written on my forehead in fire. The picture with Ingrid shall be done."

I heard no more from him.

Several years later I was invited to the Cannes Film Festival as President of the Jury. Just before I left for Cannes, I was clearing out a few drawers, throwing away a lot of stored letters, for I have an incorrigible squirrel-habit of saving everything. I found Ingmar's letter. It was ten years old.

Now I knew he was attending Cannes, making a guest appearance, and showing his film, _Cries and Whispers,_ out of the competition. I made a copy of his letter, and underneath I wrote, "It is not with anger or bitterness I give you back your letter, but just to show you how time marches on.''

In Cannes I saw him in the middle of a mass of photographers and journalists. I got through to him and said, "I'm putting a letter in your pocket."

He laughed, "Can't I read it now?"

"No, read it when you get home." Then he was swept away in the pushing crowd of people.

Two more years passed. I was on the island with Lars, and Ingmar was on the telephone.

"Now I have a story for you. It's about a mother and a daughter."

"Fine, Ingmar, you didn't get hurt because I put that letter in your pocket?"

"No, you did very well, because it reminded me and I've been working and thinking about it ever since I read that little piece of paper. I have this idea. The only thing is, do you want to play the mother of Liv Ullmann?"

"Of course I do."

"Because my friends tell me that you wouldn't want to do that since Liv Ullmann is too old to be your daughter."

"She's not. I have a daughter exactly her age."

"And then I want to do it in Swedish."

"That's fine with me."

"My friends don't believe it. They think you want to do it in English so that the picture can be sold on the international market."

I was getting a bit fed up with Ingmar's friends.

"They're wrong," I answered. "Your friends are completely wrong. I want to do it in Swedish." After all these years of struggling with English, French, and Italian, I was delighted at the thought of working in my own language.

When I received the script I had a shock. It was so big it seemed to me to be a six-hour movie. I liked the idea of his story—there never was any hesitation about that—but it was just *too much*. I phoned him, and he said, "I write everything down that comes into my head. Of course we will cut. Why don't you come to my island this summer and we'll discuss the whole thing."

I agreed, although you always feel nervous about invading people's privacy in Sweden. A perfect holiday for a Swede is to spend it far far away from anyone and come home saying, "It was marvel-

ous. I never saw another house or another person the whole time."
My children never could understand this Swedish mania for being
alone; in Italy it's always the more the merrier.

Ingmar's island, Fårö, is very much bigger than Lars's island,
Danholmen. It is a flat island with trees and sheep and a church,
and country stores, and you drive by car from one house to the
other. And right next to where Ingmar lives is the naval base. At
the airport, Ingmar was waiting for me in his car.

———————— • ————————

"I had gone out to the airport to pick up Ingrid. She got into the
car, and I had barely driven off and changed gear when she said,
'Ingmar, I don't like this-and-that, and that-and-this in the script.
Why does this mother have to talk like she does in her conversation.
She's so brutal in the way she expresses herself.'

"I replied: 'It's a long story. It's *her* way of expressing herself.'

"We drove in silence for a few moments, and I must admit I was
a bit shocked that she should start off like this. Then Ingrid said,
'Ingmar, I have to say one thing to you before we start working
together. I always *talk* first and *think* afterwards.'

"I thought that was a remarkable and wonderful revelation. It
became the key to our relationship, because her absolutely spontane-
ous reaction—even when it's not tactful—is the key to her whole
character. You have to listen when Ingrid says things. Sometimes,
at first you might even find them nonsensical and silly, but it turns
out differently. You have to listen because that immediate reaction
of hers is very important.

"I saw all the pictures that Ingrid made in America. The only one
I didn't see was the remake of *Intermezzo* with Leslie Howard. I was
a young director in those days and we were all absorbed and fascinated by the American film and its techniques. We liked also the
dark style of the French films, but we knew we had an immense
amount to learn from the American way of making pictures. Of
course, some of Ingrid's pictures in those early American years were
not masterpieces, but I remember very clearly that whatever she did
I was always fascinated by her face. In her face—the skin, the eyes,
the mouth—especially the mouth—there was this very strange radiance and an enormous erotic attraction.

"It had nothing to do with her body, but in the relationship
between her mouth, her skin, and her eyes. So I was always very

attracted by her as an actress. One of the very first times I saw her in person she was already married to Lars Schmidt. She had been shopping in Stockholm, and we were sitting in the hotel suite when she came back—it was in the winter—and she came in loaded with packages and with a high coloring, and I had exactly the same feeling from the first moment: a very strong erotic attraction and she was very beautiful.

"I always thought that when she appeared in Sweden in *Joan of Arc at the Stake,* the reception was very unfair. I didn't think the director helped her much; it seemed to me she created herself. I thought it was a great scandal when all the critics together tried to kill her. I felt it was not only completely unfair, it was also some sort of revenge. Ingrid had had her great successes, and sometimes in Sweden that makes people very unhappy, for Ingrid didn't hide her success. In Sweden the common man hides his success; he does not like people who enjoy theirs. And about Ingrid I felt this was the typical Swedish reaction; she had to be cut off. Secondly, of course, the truth is the oratorio was not perfect. Sometimes it was—I had the feeling as I sat there, that it was close to catastrophe, but in *my* truth—because I don't believe *objective* truth exists—fifty percent of Ingrid's performance was absolutely stunning, absolutely marvelous; twenty percent was acceptable, and thirty percent was absolutely catastrophic. And it was very unfair of the critics to take that thirty percent to kill her with. I wasn't present at the famous occasion at our concert hall when she hurled her speech at the Swedish critics. I'm sorry I wasn't there, because I think she's fantastic; I admired so much the way she had of transforming this terrible experience into something of a triumph. It's very strange. If you live outside Sweden, even if you have success through the whole world, and they write mean things about you in Sweden, you don't care about what they write about you in the whole world; the only thing that hurts is that they write mean things about you in Sweden. I know it myself from experience."

———— • ————

Driving from the airport in Ingmar's car I told him about Roberto, how he'd never let me work with other directors except Jean Renoir, and how, the last time I saw Roberto, I had plucked up my courage to tell him I was about to do a movie with Ingmar.

I explained that I had almost put my hands to my ears to shield myself from Roberto's blast when I saw his eyes fill up with tears. To my amazement he said, "How perfect, how right—and you must make it in Swedish." I told him we were doing that and he was delighted.

As I was telling Ingmar this story, I glanced across at him and he was stopping the car because *his* eyes were now full of tears. There were so many things about the two men which were alike; if they'd ever met I'm sure they would have got on so well.

We arrived at Ingmar's house and I met his wife, also named Ingrid, so we had two Ingrid Bergmans for dinner. We arranged our next morning's meeting for ten thirty. I was up early, took a swim in his pool, walked in the woods, admired the country-side, arrived in Ingmar's study at ten thirty sharp, opened the script and said, "How can a mother stay away from her children seven years?"

Ingmar burst out laughing. "I'm so glad you don't start on page one," he said.

———————— • ————————

Autumn Sonata is the story of a world-famous pianist who goes home to Norway to see her two daughters. Liv is married to a country clergyman. The other daughter, inarticulate and suffering from a degenerative disease, is living with them. It is after midnight that Liv and Ingrid meet down in the living room in one of the most searing emotional confrontations ever seen on the screen.

———————— • ————————

Ingmar was certain it was all about love. The presence and absence of love; the longing for love—love's lies, love's distortions, and love as our sole chance of survival. And I suppose he was right. Well, almost right. Nevertheless, I said, "Look, the script is terribly depressing. In life I have three real daughters, and we do have our little *discussions* from time to time—but this! Can't we have a little joke here and there?"

"No," said Ingmar, "No jokes. We're not doing *your* story. Her name is Charlotte, the world-famous pianist."

"But seven years without seeing her daughters? I mean! And one of them is paralyzed and almost dying. It's unbelievable."

So Liv and I, both mothers, teased him. I said, "Ingmar, the people you know must be *monsters.*" But no, we couldn't budge him.

————————— • —————————

Liv Ullmann said: "I'd worked in twelve films with Ingmar Bergman and when he rang me up and said, 'I'm hoping this time I can get Ingrid Bergman with us,' I was very pleased. He thought the combination of me and Ingrid would be good, with many similarities between us. He also looks for similarities between himself and his artists since we have to project so much of him. I was looking forward to meeting Ingrid as a person and working with her as an actress, for like the rest of the world I almost felt I knew her. I'd read all about her and at a certain time in my life I was compared to her because of the scandal of having a child of Ingmar's out of wedlock. Norway, where I was born, was at that time very conservative and priests on television reproved me for what I'd done; I could not even find a priest to christen my child until she was three years old.

"Meeting Ingrid was a great experience because I thought a woman who had been through so many things might be full of regrets and also, as a Hollywood film star, perhaps full of sentimentality. Instead, here was the most straightforward woman I've ever met in my life, and I truly mean that.

"In the beginning, of course, there were lots of 'discussions' between Ingmar and her because Ingmar is so used to me and other people of his repertory company. We have a sort of dialogue without words; we understand him without questioning. But Ingrid, in her very direct way, started to question the script at the first reading: 'Listen, we can't talk so much. We have to take away a lot of this talking. Do you really mean that this woman is going to say all this? I'm not going to say all this.' And by the end of the reading, you know, the whole crew who knew Ingmar, all of us, were nearly under the table. We thought this was the first and last day of the entire movie. I remember I went into another room and I cried because I was sure it wouldn't work. Ingmar was not used to it, and Ingrid, if she is this direct and wants this response, won't be happy either. I was disturbed for both of them, but of course at that time mostly for Ingmar because I know how vulnerable he is about what he has written, and how often he thinks, Oh this is perhaps silly? And if somebody says it *is* silly, then he's shattered. I was just standing there crying and Ingmar came in; he looked like a dog who had been through storm and rain. He said, 'I don't know what to do. Is the script bad?' I said, 'No, it's not bad. And I'm sure Ingrid doesn't feel it is bad either. She's not used to your language, and you're not used to hers. But maybe you will get used to each other.' "

———————— • ————————

We certainly had our troubles to start with.

We began filming in the autumn of 1977. There were only fifteen in the whole company making *Autumn Sonata* in the Oslo studio, and two-thirds of them were women. Ingmar told me he found them so much more efficient and less hysterical than men. With Ingmar there is so much concentration, so much intimacy—that's how he creates the intensity that he is after, and that's what makes him the artist he is. He hardly seems to eat at all; he lives on yoghurt, very little sleep, and a lot of worry all the time he is making a film.

Whatever I play—even if I play a woman who is not like me at all—I must understand her. In *The Visit* for example, I played a woman obsessed by a great vendetta: her desire for the death of the man who had ruined her. It's not in my character to be compelled like that, but I can understand her feelings. It's perfectly possible that it could happen; I can *understand* that feeling and *that* I can play. But I cannot play things I cannot feel, and there were many things in *Autumn Sonata* that I could not feel, and that did not feel right. Ingmar kept saying, "But other people are different from you. You are playing a different kind of mother, so just get in there and do it."

———————— • ————————

Ingmar said: "I told Ingrid, 'This mother, Charlotte, is not going to be easy for you. You have to discover the functions and realities of this woman. I am here to help you and perhaps we can do it together.' But I found it a little strange that the things Ingrid protested against were characteristics which were very close to herself. Ingrid occasionally can be very brutal in her own opinions, and Charlotte had that quality also."

———————— • ————————

I went on arguing with him. "Seven years! Staying away from her children for seven years! Impossible!"

So to keep me quiet, he cut it to five—even though I noticed seven came back in the finished picture—and he still insisted: "There are women who stay away from their children like that; they don't want to be bothered with them; they don't want to hear their problems. They have their own careers, their own lives; they just block everything else out; that's what this movie is about. About *them.*"

He didn't care that all my friends went around saying, "I hear you're playing yourself at last!"

————— • —————

Ingmar said: "There was a scene in *Autumn Sonata*—the midnight confrontation—the mother is absolutely defeated. She is in pieces and she just pleads with her revenged daughter and says, 'I can't take any more. Help me. Touch me. Can't you love me? Can't you try to understand?' She says this without any expression, just naked in every way. And we rehearsed it in Stockholm before we started the shooting in Oslo. Ingrid and I had the feeling, both of us, that she was not at ease with this scene.

"Then we came to the shooting, and we had set the camera position and the lighting. We had a break for coffee, and I was sitting with Sven Nykvist, and suddenly Ingrid arrived. She stood in front of me and said with such a fury, 'Now Ingmar you have to explain this scene to me! You can't let me down like this. You must explain it to me.' Very angry. Very very angry.

"I don't know what I said. I don't think I said anything of importance, but the fact that Ingrid got furious was her way to discover the expressions and motivations of the scene. Of that I am absolutely convinced."

————— • —————

I remember that flare-up very well. I came out and shouted at Ingmar, "I can't do this scene. You have not given me a reason." Liv was sitting next to him, and she got up and left very quickly, and then just as quickly came back again with a little smile on her face. She was going to observe how far I could get with him.

He jumped out of his seat and marched right at me. He was

furious but instinctively I knew he recognized my predicament. And he said the right words: "If you had been in a concentration camp, you'd say *anything* for help!"

At once I understood him, the hopelessness and depths of my defeat and despair. Yes, in a concentration camp—it must have been like that. I could play the scene now.

Ingmar loves actors and actresses. He's lived all his life in the theater, and he treats them like his little children. He's so concerned that they be happy. And as a director you know he's suffering for you and with you. When you are struggling through a difficult scene, he's helping you with the struggle. You just look at his eyes and you can read, "That wasn't any good! But *this*—now *this*"—and there are tears in his eyes.

Maybe he'll direct you with a few words, but he's not like some directors who do the whole scene for you and speak all the dialogue, so you wonder maybe he should be playing the part instead of you. He'll give you a little picture; give you the image in your head which opens up what he wants. He doesn't waste your energy. He immediately sees your discomfort and stops to see what's wrong. Or he'll say, "We're not going to rehearse any more, it's fine." Sometimes he says, "What are you *thinking* about?" You tell him and he says, "That's all wrong," and he gives you the thought that gives you the idea. And he never raises his voice. At least he didn't in this picture.

Ingmar's wonderful craft is that he gets so close, so deep into the characters he creates: the camera is always in close-up, picking up every nuance on your face, every suggestion made by the brow or the eye, the lips, or the chin. To a certain extent this was new to me. I'd been so long in the theater where you have to play out to people up in the third balcony that I'd always been very big in my gestures and my voice. They've paid for the tickets so they've got to get something. They may not be able to see you very well, but at least they can hear you. On the other hand, I knew the things a close-up can do, sometimes invent things that aren't there at all. In *Casablanca* there was often nothing in my face, nothing at all. But the audience put into my face what they thought I was giving. They were inventing my thoughts the way they wanted them: they were doing the acting for me.

———————— • ————————

Ingmar said: "Slowly I began to understand that Ingrid's need for security, tenderness, and contact is enormous. And she didn't feel at home with me; she didn't trust me one hundred percent, so I just had to demonstrate how I really felt toward her. That was fantastic because I had the feeling I had not to be polite any more, or strategic, or diplomatic, or search for the right words. So I revealed myself. I got furious when I felt furious. I was occasionally brutal; sometimes I was very tough with her, but at the same time I showed her how much I loved her.

"Our misunderstandings were in those opening days—in the rehearsals which lasted about two weeks. After that time we had no difficulties, no complications; we had opened between us a common blood circulation, and emotions ebbed and flowed through our work together, and there were no problems.

"Then I believe, during that time, she experienced something she had not experienced before. In the film there were many women operating in different jobs, and I think—possibly for the first time during the making of a film—she had this sister relationship with those girls, particularly with Liv, and that also added, I think, to her emotional security.

"Myself, in reality, I have only known Ingrid for about three years, yet I have the feeling that I have known her for a lifetime. We talk about each other like brother and sister; and that is not only a joke but a reality because sometimes I have the feeling that she is my sister; sometimes a little sister that I have to take care of, and sometimes my older sister who has a lot of common sense and talks to her younger brother who doesn't behave very well.

"In her privacy she is absolutely without any masks at all, and that is so beautiful; but sometimes in her profession she puts on masks which do not fit her very well, for she likes so much to play. She enjoys it so much that you can see she enjoys it, and that, in part, is not good. She knows she does it because she knows everything, but if a director lets her get away with it, it makes her furious.

"The results of playing in a foreign language which she has been doing all her life are also difficult to analyze. I always have a suspicion that an actor cannot play one hundred percent in another language. Ingrid—when she's good—has a fantastic way of saying things: everything comes out of her as if it were newborn, as if it were said for the first time on earth. Nevertheless, even if you are perfect in that language and speak it without any accent, there is always a glass—a film—between you and the language which makes you—not hesitate—but still leave hundreds of tiny notes which are not quite in tune—interruptions in the rhythm of the language. That only proves, of course, what an enormous charisma Ingrid carries on film to have made almost her entire career in another language.

"Somebody said about Ingrid: 'Ingrid is married to the camera, and the camera loves Ingrid.' It is true. The camera loves real movie actresses: the camera is hungry for their faces, their emotions, the way they move their heads and bodies. The camera has favorites. It is very cruel to people it doesn't like. You can't explain it. It's inexplicable. An actor can be wonderful, peerless in a scene on stage, but you put him in front of a camera playing the same scene, and the camera does not care. It yawns. It almost seeks revenge. He is revealed as absolutely dead.

"Ingrid has so much joy in her performance; she has a real lust and desire to perform; she is the real actress, and she has an enormous baggage of experience, technical know-how, imagination, emotion, fantasy, even black humor.

"I regret very much that we have not worked together many times before, because there is something very exciting about her which stimulates me to write parts for her. In *Autumn Sonata* there is, to me, one of the most beautiful moments of the picture—the scene where she sits down and tells about the death of her friend in the hospital, and their last night. Whenever I looked at that scene I found it wonderful, quite perfect in the way she balanced and rounded it. To me it was one of the most beautiful film scenes in my whole life as a director."

———————— • ————————

Two years later, in the summer of 1979, I went back to see Ingmar again on his island and he showed me the long documentary he'd shot about the making of *Autumn Sonata.* I was completely unaware most of the time that they were shooting it, because cameramen and lighting people are always around you doing things, and often they were shooting from a position behind me and the camera was hidden.

I saw myself as I've never seen myself before. It was a most revealing experience. I said to Ingmar, "I wish I'd seen this film before we started to work. Then maybe I would have been a little less difficult."

Because I couldn't believe I was so difficult. I talk all the time.

I argue all the time. I was very embarrassing. Maybe it's good to see yourself as you really are. I hope I was nicer when I was younger. I doubt it.

The documentary starts with Ingmar sitting there on the table with his feet on a chair, saying "Hallo" to everybody. "How nice to work with you again." Then we start reading through the script, and right away I start to argue. "This piece is the dullest thing I've ever read. This is much too long. And this piece, I just don't understand what it means at all."

Now the hidden camera is focused on the face of one of the women who does the film administration, and she's glaring at me with a look that's trying to kill me, a look which says, With her in it, this film is never going to end! I don't blame her. If I can do this in the first five minutes, how are they going to stand six weeks of it? (She told me later she hadn't hated me at all. She was just flabbergasted that anyone had the nerve to start off with Ingmar like this.)

Ingmar is very reassuring. "All right, all right, Ingrid. When we get to that piece we'll rehearse it and see how it goes. Now, can we move on and come back to that later?"

Then we're on the floor itself with all the positions marked out, and I'm still complaining: "What! Lie on the floor? Whatever for? Are you crazy? That will just make the audience laugh!" Finally we get to the actual shooting itself and now I'm a bit better.

You know, even though I was in the film, looking at that documentary was a wonderful experience, almost like a thriller. Would it all work? Would it all come together? It was exciting. It really is the best documentary on the making of a movie I've ever seen, even though my part in it is a bit—er—abrasive. Ingmar will give it to the Swedish National Film Institute eventually.

———— • ————

"Another thing which was very unusual about Ingrid," said Liv Ullmann, "is that even though she had these *enormous* monologues, there wasn't a day when she didn't know her lines. She had the same kind of night life that we had: she watched movies, had parties, shared the whole family thing we have in Ingmar's movies. She didn't lock herself in her room and study, but there was never one take we ever had to do again because Ingrid didn't know her lines. And naturally her Swedish was flawless.

"I love and admire her so much. I just feel that this is what women's liberation is striving for; here's somebody who's lived it and is living it every day. I think this is a thing that the liberation of women has given me: to look at other women with pride. I look at her with the pride of my own sex and with such love. I wouldn't say I wish she had been my mother, or sister; I just wish I could have had a friend like her from when I was very young, and that I could have been affected by her. That's the way I feel about Ingrid."

———————— • ————————

I was enjoying working with Ingmar and Liv and their team—they were so original and they all cared so much for what they were doing. But we had about two weeks to go before we finished and I started to get this tiny feeling under my other arm. I began to think something is growing, and I became terribly nervous and upset, and of course my anxiety began to show.

One day Ingmar came and sat with me and said:

"What is it? Why are you so worried?"

I told him. "It means I shall have to go back into the hospital."

Ingmar was so understanding: "I'll shorten the film immediately. You don't have to do the location shots; I'll do them with an understudy wearing your clothes. We won't shoot the scene we're working on outdoors; we'll shoot it indoors, right away, so that you can go back to London immediately."

I finished all the scenes he needed for me and I flew back to London. Saw the doctor.

"We should take it out," he said.

They took it out. And it was the same story. It was malignant. It was really a small, simple operation. I stayed only three days in the hospital. They sewed me together again and it didn't disturb the movements of my arm or anything. But, of course, it was very worrying. I realized now that this was something that had moved from one side to the other.

I had to have radiation again. I went in the morning to the hospital, and then straight on to rehearsals of *Waters of the Moon*. We were opening in Brighton for two weeks in January 1978, and then coming in to the Haymarket for a London season.

I remember a taxi driver who picked me up outside the hotel one morning and recognizing me, said, "I thought all you film stars stayed in bed until twelve?"

"Some of us have to start rehearsals pretty early," I said. I expect he was a bit puzzled as to what rehearsal I was up to when he dropped me off at the Middlesex Hospital.

Opening night at Brighton was chaotic. So much went wrong. N. C. Hunter's play is set in a country-house hotel in Devonshire. It's full of paying guests who live there permanently and are not very happy with their lives. I play Helen Lancaster, the wealthy, spoiled woman who, along with her husband and pretty young daughter are marooned with them when their Rolls gets stuck in a snowdrift. On New Year's Eve I arrange a party.

It is a key scene with everything depending upon Wendy Hiller playing the piano and all of us dancing. That opening night Wendy's hands fell upon the piano keys. No sound. She tried three times. Still no sound. We stood there transfixed and I could hear them running around backstage. I could also hear the audience beginning to murmur about someone forgetting lines, so I knew it was time to do something. I stepped forward and said, "I'm terribly sorry, but the piano does not seem to work. Please forgive us, but we have to bring the curtain down for a moment. We'll bring it up again when the piano is ready." The silliest thing about the whole business was that Wendy plays the piano very well, and had played the dance music for the tape. But with the piano now mute, she wasn't able to play at all.

So they fixed the tape, and we moved on until we got to the scene where it is midnight. The windows are thrown open and I rush forward, "Listen the bells—the bells are ringing!" Not a bell. Not a single bell! The people in the audience were tilting their heads in case the bells were faint and far away, but no . . . no bells! Of course there was a great roar of laughter, and we all joined in.

Our next mishap that night came when I said, "I hope the New Year will bring you all closer to your hearts' desires," and I stepped down a little step and almost missed it, and fell on my husband, Paul Hardwick, spilling my full glass of champagne all over him. So I improvised a quick line, "I don't mean that close."

As I've said, I learned long ago that when the public comes to the theater they don't want to heckle you. They come because they want to see you and they hope it's going to be wonderful and they will remember it all their lives. They are on your side. And that night, leaving the theater, I was told they were saying, "Nothing like live theater. That would never happen on TV."

We moved to London and the Haymarket Theatre. I'd always wanted to play there because it is the most beautiful and historic theater that I've ever seen. Plays and players there since 1720. The opening night I stood in the wings, my hands clasped. The music started. I said to myself, "Dear God, I'm at the Haymarket." Griff rushed by: "Nothing can stop us now!"

We had a marvelous success and I felt absolutely fine. Then, only one week before we ended our season—it's as if you have to pay for every success, and this was perhaps my biggest, well certainly a success to rival *Joan of Lorraine* and *Tea and Sympathy*—just as I was putting on a dress, I felt something and I knew: it had started again. I sat down in a chair, and I said to little Louie, my dresser, "Isn't it funny. I have just one more week to go, and then I have to go back into the hospital."

Then it was Louie who burst into tears and I had to comfort her.

Epilogue

T here is something so dramatic, nostalgic, and almost heart-breaking about the end of a run of a play. We'd been a wonderfully friendly and tightly knit company and we'd had our great success in this beautiful old theater.

Then of course it comes to an end. You have to move out of your dressing room and that in itself is awful. You take down your telegrams, the cards, the good-luck pieces, the little animals that people send you. Actresses are so superstitious; they say it's all right to take the charms down after the hundredth performance, but then the room always looks so empty, so I keep them up. You have a party at the end of the last show on Saturday evening. You have it in the theater bar or you go from dressing room to dressing room and everybody's kissing everybody else, and everybody's in tears. It's such a desperation when you leave; it's divorce from the people you've learned to love, and you say, Shall we ever meet again? And I suppose it was doubly wrenching for me this time because I thought, Is this the last?

The car which should have taken me home didn't arrive, and I said to Griff, "Don't worry about it. I'm going to sit in the theater and see how beautiful it is." I had this feeling as I sat in the empty theater on a plush seat in the fifth row, with the chandeliers overhead and the huge curtains and the gilt figures, that this might be my swan song. All right I was dramatizing. As Griff once said about me: "When she goes into the hospital she always thinks she's going to die. She'll be very disappointed if she doesn't!"

Griff kept calling, "It's very late. Why don't you go home. I'll get you a taxi." But I didn't want to leave. When I left, a chapter would be over. So I watched the stagehands knock down the scenery and cart it away. Then they came back and scrubbed and polished, and I was very impressed with the way *they* worked. The manager of the theater came and chatted for a few minutes and said, "I don't suppose this will ever happen again in the history of the Haymarket, every seat sold for every performance. We could have run for years and years."

He told me about the group of Japanese who'd come who didn't speak a word of English. They'd only had Ingrid Bergman dubbed in Japanese, so they wanted to hear my voice. And they sat through the whole performance to hear it!

I watched until the very end. On Sunday the new scenery is put up; on Monday the new show opens and it's as if you'd never existed. But I felt that my life had been rounded out with *Autumn Sonata* and *Waters of the Moon.* Yes, I might make more movies and more plays, but if I didn't I was satisfied with this finale.

I went to the doctor and they found I had a tumor in the other breast. He said, "Now! Into the hospital. Let's not waste a minute."

"No," I said. "I've been working for six days a week giving eight exhausting performances for six months. I'm going to France for a two-week holiday. Then I'll come back."

So I went and laid in the sun and swam in the pool and laughed with Griff and Alan Burgess. Being that sort of orderly person, I wanted to give Alan all the cuttings, scrapbooks, diaries, and letters so that he could go on with the book. Then I went back to London for the operation and afterwards for the radiation treatment.

One of the things I regretted was having to cancel the tour of *Waters of the Moon* in America. One of my friends said I should simply say I was too tired. But I couldn't let my producer, Louis Michaels, who'd done all the arranging, just get a message I was tired. I wrote him a letter and told him the whole story. Then I decided I would see him first so that he would believe me. I called him up and said, "You can come over to the hospital."

He came across, and said, "I knew you wouldn't just give up a tour because you had something better to do, or changed your mind, or were tired. I knew you were ill but nobody wanted to tell me what it was." He put the letter in his pocket, and he said, "I won't read it, I'll put it in my safe."

Then he got in touch with Roger Stevens, who is head of the Kennedy Center in Washington, and he announced, "She's ill, that's all I can tell you." That's how I suppose all the talk about my cancer started.

———————— • ————————

Guided by her sense of symmetry and order, believing that her career and indeed her life might be close to ending, Ingrid wanted her last curtain calls to be—if not epic—then at least honorable. So she was especially pleased with the overwhelming critical acclaim she received for *Autumn Sonata.* For once the critics in all countries agreed that the film and the performances of Ingrid and Liv were superlative. Even the usually disparaging Swedes were unanimous in their praise.

In the United States, Stanley Kaufman in *The New Republic* wrote: "The astonishment is Ingrid Bergman's performance. We've all adored her for decades but not many of us have thought her a superb actress . . . She's exalted in the hands of a master." From *Playboy*'s "perfect eloquence," to *The Christian Science Monitor*'s "mighty performance," from *Newsweek*'s "an expressive force we can't even remember seeing since Hollywood grabbed her" through *Newsday*'s "compulsive perfectionism," to *Time*'s "superb," all were agreed that the midnight drama between Liv and Ingrid would survive as one of the classic scenes in movie history.

The Times of London concurred with: "A tour de force such as the cinema rarely sees"; the *Observer,* "she has never done anything remotely comparable"; and the Sunday *Telegraph,* "the power to take the breath away."

Ingrid and Liv won the New York Film Critic's Award and Italy's most prestigious film prize, the Donatello, for the picture.

———————— • ————————

In the spring of 1979, I was invited to Hollywood for the television show—*A Tribute to Hitchcock*—and found they'd scheduled me as Mistress of Ceremonies. That went all right because I loved Hitch.

That year my daughter Ingrid and her husband, Alberto Acciatrito, had a baby son, Tomasso; Isabella got married to film director Martin Scorsese; Pia happily married to Joe Daly, with her two young sons, Justin and Nicholas, growing up, went on working in television; and Robin was busy with real estate in Monte Carlo.

In November 1979, I was invited back to Hollywood to be the Variety Club of America's guest of honor at a television show to raise funds to build an Ingrid Bergman wing for underprivileged and handicapped children. They held it at Warner Bros. studios, on Stage 9 where we made *Casablanca* all those years ago, and they still had the sets of Rick's Café Américain.

There's a big orchestra, a great crowd of guests including Helen Hayes, Signe Hasso, and Joseph Cotten, and I'm waiting nervously in a dressing room with Cary Grant who is looking brown, lean, handsome, and healthy. I'm wearing a long white dress, and I'm pleased the skirt is fairly wide so that they can't see my knees knocking together.

My husband in *Casablanca,* Paul Henreid, opens the doors of the famous set and says, "Ingrid, come in. Welcome back to Rick's and let's have a glass of champagne." The champagne is served by the same waiter who poured it thirty-seven years before. Paul raises his glass and says: "To Bogie." I drink to that, and add, "And to Mike Curtiz and all the others."

Teddy Wilson is sitting at the piano in Dooley Wilson's place— Dooley died some time ago—and he smiles and asks me to hum "As Time Goes By." I start to hum and I hear a voice behind me take up the song. It's Frank Sinatra. When he finishes I give him a kiss, and I learn afterwards that despite the fact that Frank and I have never worked together and hardly know each other, out of the blue he rang Mike Frankovich, who with Paul Keyes put the whole show together, and said, "I want to be part of Ingrid's tribute because I've always wanted to sing 'As Time Goes By' to her." Although Frank is opening in Atlantic City with his own show the next night, he's flown three thousand miles to attend our show, sing one song, and fly straight back again. I was very touched by his generous gesture.

I have always thought that I will go on acting and acting and acting because I belong to these people of the theater and the movies and the make-believe world we create. I know the opening nights are agony, but even that binds us together like a family. Every evening we go out there on the stage and share our beautiful world. And you need never give up. After all, they always need an old witch in some production or other, espically around Christmas time. So at the end of my life, I'll be ready and there.

Chronology of the Films, Plays, and Television Appearances of Ingrid Bergman

MUNKBROGREVEN *The Count of the Monk's Bridge*
Released in 1934.
Svenskfilmindustri. Produced by AB Fribergs Filmbyra.
Directed by Edvin Adolphson and Sigurd Wallen.
Screenplay by Gösta Stevens from the play *Greven fran Gamla Sta'n* by Arthur and Siegfried Fischer.
Cast: Valdemar Dahlquist, Sigurd Wallen, Eric Abrahamson, Weyler Hildebrand, Edvin Adolphson, Tollie Zellman, Julia Caesar, Arthur Fischer, Emil Fjellstrom, Victor Andersson.

BRANNINGAR *Ocean Breakers*
Released in 1935.
Svenskfilmindustri. Produced by Film AB Skandinavien.
Directed by Ivar Johansson. Screenplay by Ivar Johansson from an idea by Henning Ohlsson.
Cast: Tore Svennberg, Sten Lindgren, Carl Strom, Brof Ohlsson, Knut Frankman, Karin Swenson, Weyler Hildebrand, Henning Ohlsson, Georg Skarstedt, Vera Lindby.

SWEDENHIELMS *The Family Swedenhielms*
Released in 1935.
Svenskfilmindustri. Produced by AB Svenskfilmindustri.
Directed by Gustav Molander. Screenplay by Stina Bergman from the play by Hjalmar Bergman.
Cast: Gösta Ekman, Bjorn Berglund, Karin Swanstrom, Hakan Westergren, Tutta Rolf, Sigurd Wallen, Nils Ericsson, Adele Soderblom, Mona Geijer-Falkner, Hjalmar Peters.

VALBORGSMASSOAFTON *Walpurgis Night*
Released in 1935.
Svenskfilmindustri. Produced by AB Svenskfilmindustri.

Directed by Gustav Edgren. Screenplay by Oscar Rydquist and Gustav Edgren from their original story.
Cast: Lars Hanson, Karin Carlsson, Victor Seastrom, Erik Berglund, Sture Lagerwall, Georg Rydeberg, Georg Blickingberg, Rickard Lund, Stig Jarrel, Marie-Louise Sorbon.

PA SOLSIDAN *On the Sunny Side*
Released in 1936.
Svenskfilmindustri. Produced by Aktiebolaget Wivefilm.
Directed by Gustav Molander. Screenplay by Oscar Hemberg and Gösta Stevens from the play by Helge Krog.
Cast: Lars Hanson, Karin Swanstrom, Edvin Adolphson, Einar Axelson, Marianne Lofgren, Carl Browallius, Bullen Berglund, Eddie Figge, Olga Andersson, Viktor Andersson, Eric Gustafsson.

INTERMEZZO Swedish Version
Released in 1936.
Svenskfilmindustri. Produced by AB Svenskfilmindustri.
Directed by Gustav Molander. Screenplay by Gustav Molander and Gösta Stevens from an original story by Mr. Molander.
Cast: Gösta Ekman, Inga Tidblad, Hans Ekman, Britt Hagman, Erik Berglund, Hugo Bjorne, Emma Meissner, Anders Henrikson. Millan Bolander, George Fant.

DOLLAR
Released in 1938.
Svenskfilmindustri. Produced by AB Svenskfilmindustri.
Directed by Gustav Molander. Screenplay by Stina Bergman and Gustav Molander from the comedy by Hjalmar Bergman.
Cast: Georg Rydeberg, Kotti Chave, Tutta Rolf, Hakan Westergren, Birgit Tengroth, Elsa Burnett, Edvin Adolphson, Gösta Cederlund, Eric Rosen, Carl Strom.

EN KVINNAS ANSIKTE *A Woman's Face*
Released in 1938.
Svenskfilmindustri. Produced by AB Svenskfilmindustri.
Directed by Gustav Molander. Screenplay by Gösta Stevens from the play *Il Etait Une Fois* by François de Croisset.
Cast: Anders Henrikson, Erik Berglund, Magnus Kesster, Gösta Cederlund, Georg Rydeberg, Tore Svennberg, Goran Bernhard, Gunnar Sjöberg, Hilda Borgstrom, John Ericsson.

DIE VIER GESELLEN *The Four Companions*
Released in 1938.
UFA. Produced by UFA in Germany. Directed by Karl Frölich.
Screenplay by Jochen Huth from his play.
Cast: Sabine Peters, Ursula Herking, Carsta Lock, Hans Sohnker, Leo Slezak, Heinz Weizel, Willi Rose, Erich Ponto, Karl Haubenreiber, Wilhelm P. Kruger.

EN ENDA NATT *Only One Night*
Released in 1939.
Svenskfilmindustri. Produced by AB Svenskfilmindustri.
Directed by Gustav Molander. Screenplay by Gösta Stevens from the story "En Eneste Natt" by Harald Tandrup.
Assistant director, Hugo Bolander.

Cast: Edvin Adolphson, Aino Taube, Olof Sandborg, Erik "Bullen" Berglund, Marianne Lofgren, Magnus Kesster, Sophus Dahl, Ragna Breda, John Eklof, Tor Borong.

INTERMEZZO *A Love Story*
Released in 1939.
Selznick International-United Artists. Produced by David O. Selznick. Associate producer, Leslie Howard. Directed by Gregory Ratoff. Screenplay by George O'Neil based on the original Swedish screen scenario, *Intermezzo,* by Gösta Stevens and Gustav Molander.
Cast: Leslie Howard, Edna Best, John Halliday, Cecil Kellaway, Enid Bennett, Ann Todd.

JUNINATTEN *A Night in June*
Released in 1940.
Svenskfilmindustri. Produced by AB Svenskfilmindustri.
Directed by Per Lindberg. Screenplay by Ragnar Hylten-Cavallius from a story by Tora Nordstrom-Bonnier.
Cast: Marianne Lofgren, Lill-Tollie Zellman, Marianne Aminoff, Olof Widgren, Gunnar Sjöberg, Gabriel Alw, Olof Winnerstrand, Sigurd Wallen, Hasse Ekman.

LILIOM
A play by Ferenc Molnár. Adapted by Benjamin Glazer.
Produced and directed by Vinton Freedley.
Forty-Fourth Street Theater, New York, 1940.
Cast: Burgess Meredith, Margaret Wycherly, John Emery, Ann Mason, Elia Kazan, Beatrice Pearson, Elaine Perry.

ADAM HAD FOUR SONS
Released in 1941.
Columbia. Produced by Robert Sherwood. Directed by Gregory Ratoff. Screenplay by William Hurlbutt and Michael Blankfort. From the novel *Legacy* by Charles Bonner.
Cast: Warner Baxter, Susan Hayward, Fay Wray, Richard Denning, Johnny Downs, Robert Shaw, Charles Lind, Helen Westley, June Lockhart.

RAGE IN HEAVEN
Released in 1941.
Metro-Goldwyn-Mayer. Produced by Gottfried Reinhardt.
Directed by W.S. Van Dyke II. Screenplay by Christopher Isherwood and Robert Thoeren. Based on the novel by James Hilton.
Cast: Robert Montgomery, George Sanders, Lucile Watson, Oscar Homolka, Philip Merivale.

DR. JEKYLL AND MR. HYDE
Released in 1941.
Metro-Goldwyn-Mayer. Produced and directed by Victor Fleming. Screenplay by John Lee Mahin, based on the story by Robert Louis Stevenson.
Cast: Spencer Tracy, Lana Turner, Ian Hunter, Donald Crisp, Barton MacLane, C. Aubrey Smith, Sara Allgood.

ANNA CHRISTIE
A play by Eugene O'Neill. Produced by The Selznick Company.

Directed by John Houseman and Alfred de Qiagre, Jr.
Lobero Theater, Santa Barbara, 1941.
Cast: Damian O'Flynn, Jessie Bosley, J. Edward Bromberg.

CASABLANCA
Released in 1942.
Warner Bros. Produced by Hal B. Wallis. Directed by Michael Curtiz. Screenplay by Julius J. and Philip G. Epstein and Howard Koch from the play *Everybody Comes to Rick's* by Murray Burnett and Joan Alison.
Cast: Humphrey Bogart, Paul Henreid, Claude Rains, Conrad Veidt, Sydney Greenstreet, Peter Lorre, S. Z. Sakall, Madeleine Le Beau, Dooley Wilson, Joy Page, John Qualen, Leonid Kinsky, Helmut Dantine.

FOR WHOM THE BELL TOLLS
Released in 1943.
Paramount. Produced and directed by Sam Wood. Screenplay by Dudley Nichols from the novel by Ernest Hemingway. Executive producer, B. G. DeSylva.
Cast: Gary Cooper, Akim Tamiroff, Katina Paxinou, Joseph Calleia, Vladimir Sokoloff, Arturo de Cordova, Mikhail Rasumny, Eduardo Ciannelli, Fortunio Bonanova, Duncan Renaldo, George Coulouris.

SWEDES IN AMERICA
Released in 1943.
Office of War Information. Produced by The Office of War Information's Overseas Bureau. Directed by Irving Lerner.
Cast: the Charles Swensons and their family of Chisago County, Minnesota, and assorted neighbors.

GASLIGHT
Released in 1944.
Metro-Goldwyn-Mayer. Produced by Arthur Hornblow, Jr.
Directed by George Cukor. Screenplay by John Van Druten, Walter Reisch, and John L. Balderston. Based on the play *Angel Street* by Patrick Hamilton.
Cast: Charles Boyer, Joseph Cotten, Dame May Whitty, Angela Lansbury, Ralph Dunn.

SARATOGA TRUNK
Released in 1945.
Warner Bros. Produced by Hal B. Wallis. Directed by Sam Wood. Screenplay by Casey Robinson. Based on the novel by Edna Ferber.
Cast: Gary Cooper, Flora Robson, Jerry Austin, Florence Bates, John Warburton, John Abbott, Curt Bois, Ethel Griffies, Minor Watson.

SPELLBOUND
Released in 1945.
Selznick-United Artists. Produced by David O. Selznick.
Directed by Alfred Hitchcock. Screenplay by Ben Hecht.
Adaptation by Angus MacPhail from the novel *The House of Doctor Edwards* by Francis Beeding.
Cast: Gregory Peck, Michael Chekhov, Jean Acker, Donald Curtis, Rhonda Fleming, Leo G. Carroll, Norman Lloyd, John Emery, Paul Harvey, Steven Geray.

THE BELLS OF ST. MARY'S
Released in 1945.
RKO Radio. Produced and directed by Leo McCarey.
Screenplay by Dudley Nichols from a story by Leo McCarey.
Cast: Bing Crosby, Henry Travers, William Gargan, Ruth Donnelly, Joan Carroll, Martha Sleeper, Rhys Williams, Dickie Tyler, Una O'Connor.

NOTORIOUS
Released in 1946.
RKO Radio. Produced and directed by Alfred Hitchcock.
Written by Ben Hecht.
Cast: Cary Grant, Claude Rains, Louis Calhern.

JOAN OF LORRAINE
A play by Maxwell Anderson. Presented by The Playwright's Company.
Directed by Margo Jones.
Alvin Theater, New York, 1946.
Cast: Sam Wanamaker, Kenneth Tobey, Gilmore Brush, Romney Brent, Roger De Koven, Kevin McCarthy, Joseph Wiseman.

ARCH OF TRIUMPH
Released in 1948.
Enterprise-United Artists. A David Lewis Production.
Directed by Lewis Milestone.
Screenplay by Lewis Milestone and Harry Brown, based on the novel by Erich Maria Remarque.
Cast: Charles Boyer, Charles Laughton, Louis Calhern, Roman Bohner, Stephen Bekassy.

JOAN OF ARC
Released in 1948.
Sierra Pictures-RKO Radio.
Produced by Walter Wanger. Directed by Victor Fleming.
Adapted from the play *Joan of Lorraine* by Maxwell Anderson.
Screenplay by Maxwell Anderson and Andrew Solt.
Cast: José Ferrer, George Coulouris, Richard Derr, Selena Royle, Jimmy Lydon, Francis L. Sullivan, Irene Rich, Gene Lockhart, Nicholas Joy, Richard Ney, Colin Keith-Johnston, Leif Erickson, John Emery, John Ireland, Ward Bond, J. Carrol Naish, Hurd Hatfield, Cecil Kellaway, Philip Bourneuf, Sheppard Strudwick, Taylor Holmes.

UNDER CAPRICORN
Released in 1949.
Warner Bros. A Transatlantic pictures production. Directed by Alfred Hitchcock.
Screenplay by James Bridie from Hume Cronyn's adaptation of the play by John Colton and Margaret Linden and the novel by Helen Simpson.
Cast: Joseph Cotten, Michael Wilding, Margaret Leighton, Cecil Parker.

STROMBOLI
Released in 1950.
RKO Radio. Produced and directed by Roberto Rossellini.

Story by Signor Rossellini in collaboration with Art Cohn, Renzo Cesana, Sergio Amidei, and G.P. Callegari.
Cast: Mario Vitale, Renzo Cesana, Mario Sponza.

EUROPA '51 *The Greatest Love*
Released in 1951, 1954 (U.S. release).
I.F.E. Releasing Corp. Produced and directed by Roberto Rossellini. A Ponti-DeLaurentiis Production.
Screenplay by Signor Rossellini, Sandro de Leo, Mario Pannunzio, Ivo Perilli, and Brunello Rondi, from Signor Rossellini's original story.
Cast: Alexander Knox, Ettore Giannini, Giulietta Masina.

JOAN OF ARC AT THE STAKE
Oratorio by Arthur Honegger. Written by Paul Claudel. Produced and directed by Roberto Rossellini.
San Carlo Opera House, Naples, 1953.
Cast: Tullio Carminati, Marcella Pobbe, Florence Quartarar, Miriam Pirazzini, Giacinto Prantelli.

SIAMO DONNE *We, the Women*
Released in 1953.
Titanus. "The Chicken," third of five segments. Directed by Roberto Rossellini. Stories and screenplays by Cesare Zavattini. Luigi Chiarini collaborated on the screenplay of "The Chicken."
Cast: Anna Magnani, Isa Miranda, Alida Valli, Emma Danieli, Anna Amendola.

GIOVANNA D'ARCO AL ROGO *Joan at the Stake*
Released in 1954.
ENIC. Directed by Roberto Rossellini. Screenplay by Roberto Rossellini, based on the story and dialogue of Paul Claudel and on the oratorio of Paul Claudel and Arthur Honegger.
Cast: Tullio Carminati, Giacinto Prantelli, Augusto Romani, Plinio Clabassi, Saturno Meletti.
Voices of: Pina Esca, Marcella Pillo, Giovanni Acolati, Miriam Pirazzini.

VIAGGIO IN ITALIA *Journey to Italy*
Released in 1954.
Titanus. A Roberto Rossellini Production in association with Sveva-Junior Films.
Directed by Roberto Rossellini. Story and screenplay by Signor Rossellini and Vitaliano Brancati.
Cast: George Sanders, Paul Muller, Anna Proclemer.

FEAR *Angst*
Released in 1955.
Minerva Films. A Minerva Films Production. Directed by Roberto Rossellini in Germany. Screenplay by Roberto Rossellini, Sergio Amidei, and Franz Graf Treuberg.
Based on the novel *Der Angst* by Stefan Zweig.
Cast: Mathias Wiemann, Renate Mannhardt, Kurt Kreuger, Elise Aulinger.

ANASTASIA
Released in 1956.

20th Century-Fox. Produced by Buddy Adler. Directed by Anatole Litvak. Screenplay by Arthur Laurents from a play by Marcel Maurette as adapted by Guy Bolton.
Cast: Yul Brynner, Helen Hayes, Akim Tamiroff, Martita Hunt, Felix Aylmer, Sacha Piteoff, Ivan Desny, Natalie Schafer.

TEA AND SYMPATHY
A play by Robert Anderson. Presented by Elvire Popesco and Hubert de Malet. Director: Jean Mecure. French adaptation by Roger-Ferdinand. Théâtre de Paris, Paris, 1956.
Cast: Jean-Loup Philippe, Yves Vincent, Georges Berger.

PARIS DOES STRANGE THINGS *Elena et les Hommes*
Released in 1957.
Warner Bros. Produced and directed by Jean Renoir.
Screenplay by Jean Renoir, based on his original story.
Cast: Mel Ferrer, Jean Marais, Juliette Greco.

INDISCREET
Released in 1958.
Warner Bros. Produced and directed by Stanley Donen. Screenplay by Norman Krasna, based on his play *Kind Sir.*
Cast: Cary Grant, Cecil Parker, Phyllis Calvert.

THE INN OF THE SIXTH HAPPINESS
Released in 1958.
20th Century-Fox. Produced by Buddy Adler. Directed by Mark Robson. Screenplay by Isobel Lennart, based on the novel *The Small Woman* by Alan Burgess.
Cast: Curt Jurgens, Robert Donat, Michael David.

THE TURN OF THE SCREW
NBC-TV, 1959. Executive producer, Hubbell Robinson, Jr.. Directed by John Frankenheimer. Associate producer-director, Gordon Rigby. Adapted for television by James Costigan from the 1898 novella by Henry James.
Cast: Hayward Morse, Alexandra Wager, Isobel Elsom, Laurinda Barrett, Paul Stevens.

AIMEZ-VOUS BRAHMS? *Goodbye Again*
Released in 1961.
United Artists. An Anatole Litvak production released through United Artists. Directed by Anatole Litvak. Screenplay by Samuel Taylor, based on the novel *Aimez-vous Brahms?* by Françoise Sagan.
Cast: Yves Montand, Anthony Perkins, Jessie Royce Landis.

24 HOURS IN A WOMAN'S LIFE
CBS-TV, 1961. Executive producer, Lars Schmidt. Directed by Silvio Narizzano. A television drama by John Mortimer based on a story by Stefan Zweig.
Cast: Rip Torn, John Williams, Lili Darvas, Helena de Crespo, Jerry Orbach.

HEDDA GABLER
A play by Henrik Ibsen. Produced by Lars Schmidt. Translation by Gilbert Sigaux. Directed by Raymond Rouleau.
Théâtre Montparnasse Geston Baty, Paris, 1962.
Cast: Claude Dauphin, Jean Serbais, Jacques Dacomine.

HEDDA GABLER
CBS-TV, 1963. Produced by David Susskind, Lars Schmidt, and Norman Tutherford. Directed by Alex Segal. A television adaptation by Phil Reisman, Jr., of an Eva LeGallienne translation of a play by Henrik Ibsen.
Cast: Michael Redgrave, Ralph Richardson, Trevor Howard, Dilys Hamlett, Ursula Jeans, Beatrice Varley.

THE VISIT
Released in 1964.
20th Century-Fox. Produced by Julian Derode. Directed by Bernhard Wicki. From the screenplay by Ben Barzman based on the play by Friedrich Duerrenmatt.
Cast: Anthony Quinn, Irina Demick, Valentina Cortese.

THE YELLOW ROLLS-ROYCE
Released in 1965.
Metro-Goldwyn-Mayer. Produced by Anatole de Grunwald. Directed by Anthony Asquith. Screenplay by Terence Rattigan. (Third of three episodes of a film.)
Cast: Omar Sharif, Joyce Grenfell, Wally Cox.

A MONTH IN THE COUNTRY
Produced and directed by Michael Redgrave. Adapted from the play by Ivan Turgenev.
Yvonne Arnaud Memorial Theatre, Guildford, England, 1965.
Cast: Michael Redgrave, Fay Compton, Daniel Massey, Max Adrian, Jennifer Hilary, Geoffrey Chater, Peter Pratt.

STIMULANTIA
Released in 1967.
Omnia Film. An eight-part Swedish film featuring episodes, each with a different director. Miss Bergman appeared in the episode *Smycket (The Necklace)* written and directed by Gustav Molander from the tale by Guy de Maupassant.
Cast: Gunnar Björnstrand, Gunnel Brostrom.

MORE STATELY MANSIONS
A play by Eugene O'Neill. Directed by José Quintero. Production: William Weaver. Presented by Elliot Martin in association with Center Theater Group by arrangement with Quinto Productions, Inc.
Broadhurst Theater, New York, 1967.
Cast: Colleen Dewhurst, Arthur Hill, Fred Stewart.

THE HUMAN VOICE
ABC-TV, 1967. Produced by David Susskind and Lars Schmidt.
A Stage 67 Presentation. Directed by Ted Kotcheff.
Adapted for TV by Clive Exton from an idiomatic translation by Carl Wildman of a story by Jean Cocteau.
Cast: Ingrid Bergman.

CACTUS FLOWER
Released in 1969.
Columbia. Produced by M.J. Frankovich. Directed by Gene Saks.
Screenplay by I.A.L. Diamond from the stage play by Abe Burrows.
Cast: Walter Matthau, Goldie Hawn, Jack Weston.

A WALK IN THE SPRING RAIN
Released in 1970.
Columbia. A Stirling Silliphant-Guy Green Production.
Directed by Guy Green. Written for the screen and produced by Stirling Silliphant.
Based on the novel by Rachel Maddux.
Cast: Anthony Quinn, Fritz Weaver, Katherine Crawford.

CAPTAIN BRASSBOUND'S CONVERSION
A play by George Bernard Shaw. Produced by Roger Stevens and Arthur Cantor.
Staged by Stephen Porter.
Opera House, Kennedy Center, Washington, 1972.
Cast: Leo Leyden, Geoff Garland, Yusef Bulos, Eric Berry, Zito Kozan.

FROM THE MIXED-UP FILES OF MRS. BASIL E. FRANKWEILER
Released in 1973.
Cinema 5. A Westfall Production. Produced by Charles G. Mortimer, Jr. Directed
by Fielder Cook, Screenplay by Blanche Hanalis, based on the novel by E.L.
Konigsburg.
Cast: Sally Prager, Johnny Doran, George Rose, Georgann Johnson, Richard Mulligan, Madeline Kahn.

MURDER ON THE ORIENT EXPRESS
Released in 1974. Paramount Pictures.
Produced by John Brabourne and Richard Goodwin. Directed by Sidney Lumet.
Screenplay by Paul Dehn based on the novel by Agatha Christie.
Cast: Albert Finney, Lauren Bacall, Martin Balsam, Jacqueline Bisset, Jean-Pierre
Cassel, Sean Connery, John Gielgud, Wendy Hiller, Anthony Perkins, Vanessa
Redgrave, Rachel Roberts, Richard Widmark, Michael York, Colin Blakely,
George Coulouris, Denis Quilley.

THE CONSTANT WIFE
A play by Somerset Maugham. Produced by Arthur Cantor. Directed by John
Gielgud.
Shubert Theater, New York, 1975.
Cast: Jack Gwillim, Brenda Forbes, Carolyn Lagerfelt, Marti Stevens.

A MATTER OF TIME
Released in 1976.
American International Pictures. Produced by Jack H. Skirball, J. Edmund
Grainger. Directed by Vincente Minelli. Screenplay by John Gay based on the novel,
The Film of the Memory of Maurice Druon.
Cast: Liza Minnelli, Charles Boyer, Spiros Andros, Tina Aumont, Fernando Rey,
Isabella Rossellini.

AUTUMN SONATA
Released in 1978.
New World Pictures. Production Company: Personafilm GMBH, Munich. Producer—writer—director: Ingmar Bergman
Cast: Liv Ullmann, Lena Nyman, Halvar Bjork, Georg Lokkeberg, Gunnar
Björnstrand.

WATERS OF THE MOON
A play by N. C. Hunter. Produced by Duncan C. Weldon and Louis Michaels.

Directed by Patrick Garland.
Haymarket Theatre, London, 1979.
Cast: Wendy Hiller, Doris Hare, Frances Cuka, Derek Godfrey, Charles Lloyd
Pack, Paul Hardwick, Brigitte Kahn, Carmen Silvera, Paul Geoffrey.

Index

Index

Wassermann, Lew, 243, 254
Waters of the Moon, 461, 463, 477–79, 493–94
Wayne, John, 325
Weaver, Fritz, 431
Webb, Mary, 114
Wegner, Peter, 284–85
Wesker, Arnold, 441
We, The Women. See Siamo Donne
Whitney, Jock, 59, 62, 86, 104
Wiemann, Mathias, 326
Wilder, Billy, 200, 325, 376
Wilding, Michael, 192
Williams, Kenneth, 436
Williams, Tennessee, 350, 441
Wilson, Dooley, 483
Wilson, Earl, 343
Wilson, Teddy, 483
Winchell, Walter, 88
Woman's Face, A, 44–46, 486

Wood, Sam, 110, 111, 117, 118, 121, 123ff.
World War II, 81ff., 84, 99–101, 116, 118, 120, 127–32, 149–55, 360
Wyler, William, 66, 73–74, 376

Yale University Library, 419, 420
Yellow Rolls-Royce, The, 401–2, 492
Young, Loretta, 332

Zanuck, Darryl, 377
Zeffirelli, Franco, 326
Zellman, Tollie, 38
Zetterling, Mai, 30
Zinnemann, Fred, 376
Zorina, Vera, 110, 117
Zweig, Stephan, 392

— 504 —